THE SAMOA READER

Anthropologists Take Stock

Edited by
Hiram Caton

UNIVERSITY
PRESS OF
AMERICA

Lanham • New York • London

Copyright © 1990 by
University Press of America®, Inc.
4720 Boston Way
Lanham, Maryland 20706

3 Henrietta Street
London WC2E 8LU England

Library of Congress Cataloging-in-Publication Data

The Samoa reader : anthropologists take stock /
edited by Hiram Caton.
p.   cm.
Includes bibliographical references.
1. Ethnology—Samoan Islands.   2. Samoan Islands—
Social life and customs.   3. Ethnology—Philosophy.
4. Nature and nurture.   I. Caton, Hiram.
GN671.S2S25   1990   306'.09961'3—dc20   89–70423 CIP

ISBN 0–8191–7720–2 (alk. paper)
ISBN 0–8191–7721–0 (pbk. : alk. paper)

For Angela

Acknowledgements

Preparation of *The Samoa Reader* has been generously assisted by numerous colleagues.

Thanks to George N. Appell and Benson Saler for information and encouragement, and to the Brandeis University anthropology department for the opportunity to present some of my findings.

My understanding of the meaning of the controversy to American anthropologists was appreciably assisted by Roy A. Rappaport.

Richard Basham, Geoff Samuel, Les Hiatt, Frank Heimans, Lola Romanucci-Ross, Richard Goodman, Lowell D. Holmes, Bradd Shore, Ivan Brady, Mary Catherine Bateson, Vernon Reynolds, Edwin McDowell, E. O. Wilson, Jeannette Mageo, and Tim O'Meara have helped in various says. Special thanks to Robin Fox.

The cheerful cooperation of the permissions staff of the *American Anthropologist* is greatly appreciated.

Derek Freeman permitted me entrance his workshop for the duration of the project while respecting the independence of my judgment. It is an unusual establishment, consisting of more than 50,000 pages of notes, 2000 pages of diary entries, and uncounted correspondence accumulated over nearly fifty years. This large record has scarcely been touched; its scrutiny by some future historian or biographer is likely to cast new light on those aspects of the controversy that relate to motive and personal achievement.

The Division of Humanities, Griffith University, funded the research and stenographic costs, while the Utah Foundation provided a subvention for publication. My thanks to both.

Contents

vii

Contents viii

Chapter III
History of Anthropology

Contents   x

Chapter IV
The Controversy

Chapter V
Professional Ethics

Contents xii

The Editor

Hiram Caton, D.Litt., is professor of politics and history at Griffith University, Brisbane, Australia. He is well qualified for his task. He holds the M.A. in Arabic and Islamic Civilization from the Oriental Institute of the University of Chicago and the doctorate in Philosophy from Yale University. He is familiar with the project to unite the social and biological sciences, having contributed to that effort as a historian, political psychologist, human ethologist, and bibliographer. As a political scientist he is at home with cultural politics that lent passion to the controversy. His philosophical training and policy studies on applications of biomedical technology have equipped him to deal with the challenging problems of knowledge evaluation raised by the clash between the two images of Samoa. Among his current publications are *The Politics of Progress: The Origins and Development of the Commercial Republic 1600-1835,* University of Florida Press, and *Trends in Biomedical Regulation* (editor), Butterworths, in press.

Introduction

This collection of essays is offered in the belief that the Samoa controversy, touched off by the publication of Derek Freeman's *Margaret Mead and Samoa: The Making and Unmaking of an Anthropological Myth,* prompted a stock-taking that is of immediate importance and probably of lasting significance as well. The theory and methods of a key social science were examined from many sides, and evaluated in the light of the field's history. It is hoped that by bringing the chief contributions together with other related essays and unpublished writings, the energy unleashed in this uncommon review will more effectively work out its result.

The controversy ranged over many topics, and perceptions of the central issues varied. Some dismissed it as a prestige struggle of no particular theoretical relevance, even if it furnished sociologists of knowledge rare grist for their mill. At the other end of the spectrum were those who believed that it marked a watershed in the history of anthropology.

The selection of readings presented here is meant to preserve that range of opinion. Nevertheless my own interest in the debate is nourished by the belief that one of its themes is deeply significant for anthropologists and social scientists generally. I mean the broad question on what terms the methods and findings of the biological sciences, behavioral biology especially, can be integrated with anthropology and the social sciences. It is fitting that this question should have arisen forcefully in anthropology, since it is the social science most conscious of its proximity to evolutionary science. For this reason the Samoa controversy is likely to hold lessons that may apply more broadly.

What sort of lessons? It is easy to say what they are not. No discussion of the application of specific biological methods in anthropology took place. One cannot learn from the exchanges how actually to conduct the nature/nurture "interactionist" anthropological research that various protagonists in the debate espouse.

1

We do learn that anthropologists differ markedly about the reality, possibility, and desirability of the interactionist option. The terms of these disagreements, I suggest, mark out the broad lines of the problematic of any project to unite cultural anthropology with behavioral biology, or, for that matter, to maintain its separate existence. The debate here is essentially *how* anthropology interfaces and should interface with biology; and about what a robust integrated anthropology would look like. A few patterns that recur in the selections may be indicated.

Surprisingly, there is disagreement as to whether a body of interactionist anthropological research exists. Freeman, a tireless student of this subject since 1962, has spoken as if the integration of biology into anthropology is a project for the future. What is needful now, he thinks, is an unclouded view of basic issues to provide orientation for existing methodologies.

His view is supported in this volume by Robin Fox, who is often named as a leading contributor to "bio-anthropology." In his essay, "The Disunity of Anthropology and the Unity of Mankind," Fox reconnoiters the conceptual terrain obstructing passage into the new continent, and proposes some simple yet basic renovations meant to cut a conceptual path into virgin forest. Another voice in the same key is the pioneer of human ethology and author of the first textbook on that subject, Irenäus Eibl-Eibesfeldt. In his forward to the German translation of *Margaret Mead and Samoa,* Eibl identified Freeman's critique of environmentalist or cultural determinist theory as his fundamental contribution to the anthropology of the future.[1] A similar view has been expressed by sociobiologist E. O. Wilson.

Mead's protagonists tended to dismiss Freeman's dramatic proposal for interactionist anthropology as old hat. They rejected as tendentious his foray into anthropological history, which was meant to show how the environmentalist or cultural determinist presuppositions of American cultural anthropology were created from the anti-evolutionary anxieties of Franz Boas and his students. Boas, they retorted, included biology in the discipline as physical anthropology and proved his seriousness by conducting such research himself. As for the contemporary scene, they

---

[1]Derek Freeman, *Liebe ohne Aggression: Margaret Meads Legende von der Friedfertigkeit der Naturvölker* (Munich: Kindler Verlag, 1983), pp. 11, 13. Similarly, Vernon Reynolds: "Your own book marks, for social anthropology, the dawning awareness of the modern period [of gene-environment interaction]." Letter to Derek Freeman, March 6, 1987.

pointed out that biological variables were incorporated into numerous anthropological sub-fields.

Those making these criticisms were not speaking from a distance. Roy Rappaport integrated ecology, demography, and adaptation in his study of ritual and religion among the Maring of New Guinea. Marvin Harris, a critic of conventional cultural anthropology, made ecological opportunities and constraints integral to his effort to establish a materialist macro-anthropology. Melvin Ember's kinship study adopted the sociobiological calculus of inclusive fitness without apology.

Such examples, which could easily be multiplied, would seem to be conclusive against the alleged neglect of biology by cultural anthropologists but for one thing: the three mentioned practitioners of integrated anthropology firmly rejected the integration proposed by Freeman. Harris identified Freeman's agenda with sociobiology and cast it into the void. Ember found Freeman's ethnographic refutation to be unscientific, and implied that his interactionism was misguided. Rappaport maintained that cultural anthropology, understood as the study of symbol and meaning, could not appreciably assimilate biology because the biological dimension of meaning is negligible.

Thus we have the following paradox. We see interactionists who seem to practice what they preach but who say that the new era is only just dawning. Opposing them we see those who deny that there was ever a rejection of biology by cultural anthropology—as witnessed by their own research—but who yet reject *Freeman's* proposed assimilation of biology into cultural anthropology as unviable.

If confusions perplex this debate—and the protagonists are sure that the other is confused—hopefully the confusions are of the fruitful variety. In any event, the participants have felt impelled to go to the roots of anthropological thinking and in that way have shown that the controversy is not a curiosity of circumstance but rather that it foreshadows patterns of future development.

The Struggle for Samoa

It is rare that a scholarly book captures public attention in the way that *Margaret Mead and Samoa* did. Edwin McDowell's front page article in the *New York Times* touched off a "seismic event" that was world news and remained national news in the United States for several months. The news was that Margaret Mead's most famous work, read by many millions around the world, had been wrong about Samoa. Her idyll of trysts under the palms and no thought for the morrow, relaxed social relations and an absence of disruptive anger and jealousy, chartered the liberalization of sexual attitudes in the Thirties and subsequently became a model for the "flower children" of the Sixties. By 1983, when Freeman's book appeared, public attitudes toward sexual experimentation had changed. An epidemic of venereal disease, abortions running at 1.5 million per year, drug addiction, broken marriages and the economic decline of divorced women, on-going revelations about the health risks of contraceptive interventions, confusion of gender among the youth, and finally AIDS, were inconveniences associated with the charter of the self-fulfillment life-style for which Margaret Mead had been an unswerving advocate. The refutation of her Samoa ethnography thus confirmed what many had already learned from personal experience: Samoa, once a emblem of aspiration, was now the hair shirt of disillusion.

The ensuing debate about Samoa was influenced by motives and hidden agendas that are not always easy to discern. This is true of the motivations that the protagonists ascribed to one another. Mead's defenders said that Derek Freeman's refutation was a "vendetta" against a woman whose immense authority kept his own research in obscurity for so long. The revenge was sweet because he capitalized on her celebrity to tarnish her name and catapult himself to celebrity. But he had waited until Mead could no longer defend herself to execute this craven deed. Mead's defenders felt that they were confronted with a great iniquity.

Freeman for his part maintained that his opponents condemned themselves to the "indignity of persisting in an error" because *Coming of Age in Samoa* was and remained the primary validation of the ideology of cultural anthropology, cultural determinism.

These two motive ascriptions are pertinent markers of the complexity of this dimension of the debate. Let us examine them briefly.

How can one tell whether Freeman was on a vendetta, and what difference would it make anyway? In Italian as well as English there is a close etymological relation between "avenge," "vindicate," "revenge," and "vindictive." As Freeman tells the story, his Samoa researches have been a quest to vindicate the truth from Margaret Mead's errors. He resolved on this course in 1943 when, after admission to the *fono* or council, cases of rape and assault came to his attention that directly contradicted Mead's testimony about Samoan life. As a result he experienced "an awakening":

> I had grave difficulties because I would say even to the Samoans, 'But how can this be? This is not what Margaret Mead says.' I was still in a frame of mind where I was prepared to accept the doctrine rather than the facts that were before my eyes day in, day out. And from that stage I realized that ultimately there was a kind of scientific obligation for me to continue investigation of this problem. Because by that time Margaret Mead's conclusions had become very widely published and were almost universally accepted.[1]

Freeman's discovery of a goal sanctioned by high duty is the very stuff of heroic endeavor. Girded with such authority, his quest was forearmed against thoughts of revenge, whether low or sublime—a fact which stands out in his personal relations with Mead.[2] Nevertheless, the motivational elements of revenge were present. He went to Samoa a "fervent believer" in the ethnography of *Coming of Age* as well as in the ideology of cultural anthropology. His awakening was recognition that he had been deceived; "setting the record straight," as he has also styled his quest, is thus not far removed from pay-back.[3]

Yet there is another spring board for Freeman's endeavor: Samoan resentment. As a Samoan chief Freeman bears distinct duties, including the general duty to defend and foster his people. Some Samoans detest Mead's celebrated book because it portrays them as "animals" (the alleged absence sexual restraint is meant) and, they say, grotesquely misrepresents their customs. On his return to Samoa in 1965 "many Samoans," including the then Prime Minister, pleaded with him to "do something" about

---

[1] Derek Freeman, *et al.*, *Transcript of Interviews by Frank Heimans for the Documentary Film Margaret Mead and Samoa*, Tape 1, p. 13. The same account is given, but less fully, in *Margaret Mead and Samoa*, xiii-xiv.

[2] See below, pp. 201-204.

[3] The Freeman Papers contain abundant documentation of Freeman's motives over the years. A key statement is contained in his letter to Lowell D. Holmes of October 10, 1967 (see Chapter VI for the text), in which he wrote: "What I want to do is to get the record straight both for the sake of Samoa and the science of anthropology. And this I shall do." It may be noted that the manuscript Freeman submitted for publication bore the title: *On Coming of Age in Samoa: The Nemesis of an Anthropological Myth*. Its published title was suggested by the Princeton University Press.

Mead's falsification. Thus Freeman was enjoined to share a Samoan grievance similar to his own. "And so," he continues, "I began to turn to that interest."[1] Significantly, it was on this field trip that Samoan chiefs assembled witnesses who in a solemn *fono* revealed Mead's unseemly behavior in her village, Ta'ū. That event furnished the basis of the opinion current among Samoans that in describing lax Samoan sexual attitudes Margaret Mead "was talking about her own self."[2] It is significant as well that Freeman described these findings in a letter to Lowell D. Holmes (see Chapter VI), who formed the impression then that Freeman was on a vendetta.[3]

The bond between Freeman and a circle of Samoans meant that his heroic endeavor had the support of scholars who read his manuscript to purge it of error; and the support of the Iuniversite o Samoa,[4] which at the height of the acrimonious debate named him professor of Samoan studies and academic pro-vice-chancellor for life. These events went unnoticed in the debate although they are critical to understanding the tangled question of motivation. The imprimatur of the Iuniversite o Samoa marks the closing of ranks behind the war canoe of a venerable Samoan chief locked in mortal combat with the *palagi* (Caucasians).[5] He was out to recover the Holy Grail—the Samoan way (*fa'aSamoa*) that a colonial power had expropriated for its own purposes.

We see then that the perception of a vendetta correctly alerts to retaliation but misreads the source of the animus. The punitive intent so apparent in Freeman's vibrant righteousness is not the effect of a merely private resentment. Nor does it follow only from devotion to scientific truth. Instead it probably expresses the Samoan grievance that vouchsafed to him the duty to vindi-

---

[1]Derek Freeman, *et al., op. cit.*, Tape 2, p. 23. Theodore Schwartz has noted Freeman's "direct personal identification with the Samoans, whose dignity, worth, and morality he sees as impugned by Mead's portrayal." Schwartz, "Anthropology: A Quaint Science," *American Anthropologist* 85 (1983):921.

[2]Derek Freeman, *et al., op. cit.*, Tape 37, p. 69 (interview with Aiono Dr. Fanaafi Le Tagaloa, professor of Samoan studies, Iuniversite o Samoa).

[3]Lowell D. Holmes, personal communication, January 2, 1986.

[4]Not to be confounded with the University of Samoa, in American Samoa.

[5]The occasion is memorialized in Freeman's address, A University for Samoa, August 24, 1983, unpublished manuscript. Two Samoanists, in personal communications, have cast doubt on the significance of this honor and even on the existence of the Iuniversite. Such scruples do not affect the point being made about Freeman's perceived solidarity with the Samoans.

cate Samoan honor.[1] Freeman's fortitude in the face of massed
battalions in the first year of the debate no doubt owes something
to his solidarity with the Samoans.
   Once it is realized that Freeman's scientific persona speaks in
a Samoan accent, the vehemence of the controversy is more readily appreciated. The correction of Mead's Samoan ethnography
was not *initially* the main issue. Indeed, had Freeman confined
himself to this he might have reaped kudos from those in a profession who for many years had chafed at what was regarded as
Mead's slap-dash field methods and theoretical arbitrariness.
Samoanist Bradd Shore voiced this sentiment in the opening
round of the publicity when he stated that "people who work on
Samoa know Margaret Mead was wrong, and Freeman's book
shows that beyond doubt."
   However, it soon became apparent that Freeman had shaped
his refutation of Mead's Samoan ethnography into a missile to
destroy the credibility of cultural anthropology and its ideology of
cultural determinism. This was serious business indeed. It
deeply shocked American anthropologists and galvanized the profession to self-defense, framed in terms of a defense of Margaret
Mead as the patron saint of the ideology.
   Many were at a loss to comprehend the vehemence of Freeman's assault on cultural determinism, particularly since they
could not identify the ideology intended as its replacement.
Freeman's flag of interactionism was unhelpful, for it was not
clear what that meant in terms of the on-going contest of values.
In the history of the discipline, all protagonists were agreed, the
flag of cultural determinism had been raised by the Boas school
in opposition to the racist eugenic biologism stemming from
Darwinian anthropologists. There were sporadic attempts to sit-
uate Freeman on this turf; but the better informed knew that his
strong condemnation of racism corresponded to a life-long
commitment. What then was the burr under the saddle?
   Again Samoan origins are the key; for seen through Samoan
eyes, cultural determinism is the ideology of a global empire that

---

[1]The Samoan writer Felix S. Wendt reported it as a local opinion that "Freeman's
'love' for Samoa and Samoans motivated him to 'champion' their cause, and he
set out to undo the damage Mead had done." Felix S. Wendt, book review, *Pacific
Studies* 7 (1984):95. Freeman has stated that "I indeed do have love and admiration for the people of Samoa . . . it is my belief that if only we Westerners can understand the Samoans in all their human complexity, then we shall also be able to
understand ourselves." Derek Freeman, "Response to Reviews," *Pacific Studies*
7 (1984):142.

prepared the absorption of local custom into the imperial melting pot. This will be news to many, so let me explain.

The ideology of cultural determinism arose toward the end of the last century from the main streams of European social and political thought. The essential idea is that individual human behavior is the aggregate effect of environmental influence, where environment embraces up-bringing, custom, and social milieu. Custom and social milieu, for their part, are not fixed by nature or history but are effects of themselves: a *sui generis* self-causing agency. This doctrine was propagated by Emile Durkheim, L. T. Hobhouse, Franz Boas, John Dewey and others in a conscious effort to contrive a theory of social development to displace the then dominant theory of progress authored by Herbert Spencer.

Spencer's sociology enjoyed immense prestige because it justified the bewildering experience of rapid social change by inscribing progressive change into the very fabric of nature. The demise of venerable traditions was not to be regretted because the future would bring ever brighter vistas of enlightened practice and uncoerced cooperation. Spencer's mechanism of social evolution, the competitive struggle for existence, tapped a pervasive experience of the first century of industrial capitalism and justified it in the name of Evolution. He was a vigorous critic of big government on economic, moral, and scientific grounds. Finally, Spencer's cosmogony identified European civilization as the engine of progress and assigned each of the world's civilizations and peoples a distinct rung on the evolutionary ladder.

But there were misgivings about Spencer's theory. The doctrine of competition was perceived to be divisive in domestic and international politics, setting class against class and nation against nation. The alternative was to conceive the state as resolving domestic conflict through expanded instrumentalities of the welfare state; competitive national economies were to be steered into a global community of nations. Spencer's mechanism of social change, competition, was based upon a motivational model of the self-interested individual. The new school of thought retained the dynamism inherent in the individualist model, but superimposed upon it models of sociability that stressed conformity and social esteem as a significant dimension of motivation. Finally, Spencer's evolutionary ranking of peoples made Europeans the cultural impresarios of the world, with nothing to learn from others. This was far too narrow and arrogant for a globally integrative doctrine. Although they did not doubt the superiority of European civilization, the new school of cultural determinists introduced the doctrine of the relativity of cultures. The doctrine conferred legitimacy on all cultures by admitting them to the pantheon of the family of man. The doctrine opened the imperial West to diversification by the inflow of enormous cultural variety; but at the same time it legitimated the outflow of the imperial culture into all peoples of the world.

Logically, cultural relativism is impartial between cultures. But in practice it is an arrangement tending to promote and enhance colonial hegemony. This is readily seen by examining at random actual contacts between imperial nations and their clients. There is no parity between their powers. The imperial nation sets up military bases and commercial establishments. The host-client is obliged to accept not only this practical proof of superiority, but also the disruption of their own culture by a variety of interventions instigated by the imperial nation. Not the least of these interventions is the education and ideology generously given to the host-client. The education provided by anthropologists will tend to moderate local resentment by lifting the sights beyond the narrow confines of the colony to the imperial pantheon of peoples—all equally valuable and worthy in the new world order over which the empire presides. This of course is the view from the seat of power, where there can be no question of the absolute validity of the quaint customs of the natives. But the native who accepts this cosmopolitanism has by that very fact forsaken the old ways.

Margaret Mead was not consciously an agent of imperialism; the very suggestion would have staggered her.[1] Nevertheless, no private person since Benjamin Franklin has remotely approached her ability to convey the American vision of peace, tolerance, and human welfare to literally millions of colonial and semi-colonial people throughout the world. Her genuine human appeal and many goods works are unquestionable. There can also be no doubt that her prodigious traffic in peoples and cultures greatly assisted America's acquisition of cosmopolitan sophistication required to manage the domestic melting pot as well as the empire. But her concern with these practical matters substantially affected what she was prepared to see or report from the field. Thus her collaborator Theodore Schwartz wrote:

What makes Freeman's claim that Mead's preconceptions may have had a strong effect on her Samoan obser-

---

[1]Americans tend to deny the existence of the empire because the imperial concept offends the concept of national self-determination. A new word, "superpower," was invented to get around this awkwardness.

vations plausible is my experience in 1953 of her resistance to the idea that the Manus people of Pere village were full participants in cargo cults. They were supposed to be too pragmatic and rational for their participation to have been other than a temporary aberration. Much of what we eventually learned about the cults did not emerge fully until after her departure after six months of fieldwork.

. . . Further I found in *New Lives for Old* (1956), the same reliable and extraordinarily vivid descriptions of everyday life and events in the middle chapters, and the same dramatic extrapolations inspired by her sense of what the world needs to learn about itself from the Manus. Before we left for the field Mead told me that if Manus turned out to be another cultural shambles—a slum culture, undermined and demoralized as a result of the drastic culture contact and change they had experienced—she would not write about it. What the world needed was a success story: people could undergo rapid culture change without disintegration. . . . I felt uncomfortable with characterizations about the Manus leap from the stone age to the jet age. No one would have been more surprised than the Manus. . . . Margaret Mead was like no other anthropologist. Her fieldwork had to serve many purposes, including providing the license for prescription and prophesy.[1]

These words succinctly describe the mission of the anthropologist as facilitator of the imperial dispensation. The Manus were chosen to be yet another emblem of hope in a world battered and demoralized by rapid change fuelled in part by superpower rivalry. The Manus had successfully exchanged the old native customs for the new life of self-improvement and urban development. The evidence to the contrary—cargo cults are the salvation religion of colonial peoples suffering cultural depression resulting from European contact—was set down as a temporary aberration.

The Manus, having almost no intelligentsia to contemplate the expropriation of their culture to prove the benignity of the new dispensation, have only just begun to engage the anthropologist in dialogue. The Samoans, being a few steps ahead, have elo-

---

[1]Theodore Schwartz, "Anthropology: A Quaint Science," *American Anthropologist*, 85 (1983):927-28.

quently registered the humiliations suffered from Mead's first book. For the men it meant that their sisters and mothers are exposed to the world as sluts.[1] Samoan women who travelled abroad were embarrassed by overtures from *palagi* who believed Mead's report.[2] Young Samoans entering the universities were distressed by lecturers who, accepting Mead's descriptions, disfigured Samoan custom.[3] These indignities had to be suffered in silence because a mere Samoan was no match for the high authority of the *palagi* who as a youth had once spent nine months among them.[4] Felix S. Wendt, a leading Samoan writer, summarized these feelings in a review of Freeman's book:

While our outrage in the early years against our portrayal as a joyously promiscuous society mattered little to the intellectual world, the damage Margaret Mead did has, with time, healed. We learned to live with it. As advances in communication made the world smaller, Samoa opened up to the world at large. Through actual experience many people found out for themselves that

---

[1] Derek Freeman, *et al., op. cit.,* Tape 35, p. 56 (interview with High Chief Galea'i Poumele, then Secretary of Samoan Affairs, American Samoa); Tape 37, pp. 66, 68.

[2] Ibid, Tape 37, p. 66.

[3] Ibid, Tape 35, pp. 45-46 (interview with A. P. Lutali, Governor of American Samoa); Tape 37, p. 67 (interview with Fanaafi Le Tagaloa).

[4] The accents of contemporary Samoan resentment of colonialism might be usefully quoted: "The fact that our nations were colonized is not a new concept. We were victims of Western 'dare sport' of exploration and domination of the then called 'dark and uncivilized lands'. . . . They came with their education and we got educated. Their way. We learnt their language, but they did not learn ours. If we did have a history, we were told to forget it because it is a history of savages. Their manners and ways of living became a model . . . suddenly, we open our eyes and see . . . and ironically enough, we realize that we have actually learnt of how our countries were exploited, our ancestors murdered and enslaved, our values discarded, our cultures vanishing . . . ." Lafi A. Sanerivi, General Secretary of the YMCA of Western Samoa. Quoted by Eleanor Leacock in her Postscript, in Lowell D. Holmes, *The Quest for the Real Samoa,* pp. 180-181. For another such protest, see the letters of Aiono Dr. Fanaafi Le Tagaloa and Afafili La'au Tuitolova'a in *Oceania* 65 (1984):145-147. Both letters purport to identify major errors in Bradd Shore's opus *Sala'ilua: A Samoan Mystery.* One of these errors concerns Shore's supposed mistranslation of two words, *aga* and *amio,* that form the core of his interpretation, while the other concerns Shore's supposed misdescription of the motive for the murder whose "mystery" Shore undertakes to unravel. The confessed murdered, Agafili, wrote: "In my heart, I don't want to abuse Bradd Shore although he stands on my neck and kicks me hard on the face . . . Shore is creating a very big lie that ruins his work as a scientist."

Margaret Mead's Samoa was, for the most part, a myth.[1]

Samoans explain Mead's demeaning picture of themselves in two ways. They say that her teenage informants told her yarns about their sexual activity, as a tease. And they say that she accepted this information because her own amours while in Samoa corroborated the yarns. However, these two explanations leave something out of account, namely, why did anthropologists, those specialists in human custom, allow her romantic tale of the South Seas to stand unchallenged?

The sense of this question is brought out by Mead's most recent biographer, Phyllis Grosskurth, who said of the success of *Coming of Age*:

> America was at a stage where it was becoming sex obsessed and she catered to that. Listen to this passage: 'Familiarity with sex and the recognition of a need of a technique to deal with sex as an art have produced a scheme of personal relations in which there are no neurotic pictures, no frigidity, no impotence except as a temporary result of severe illness. And the capacity for intercourse only once in a night is counted as senility.' Who could possibly have fallen for that stuff?[2]

Freeman's historical derivation of cultural determinism answers that question: anthropologists could fall for Mead's Samoa because of their belief in the virtually unlimited plasticity of humankind. Whoever believes this lacks a robust sense of what is possible for human cultures and therefore lacks a theoretical apparatus for examining ethnography critically.[3]

This seems to be why Freeman carried the struggle to vindicate Samoan custom beyond Mead's ethnography to the foundations of Boasian anthropology. His critique of those foundations is in service to a science of anthropology founded on knowledge of the natural constraints limiting human behavior. Once such knowledge is assimilated, ethnographic extravaganzas will cease, and the injury done to Samoa will have been rectified.

---

[1] Felix S. Wendt, book review, *Pacific Studies* 7 (1984):94.
[2] Derek Freeman, *et al., op. cit.*, Tape 9, p. 27.
[3] Freeman makes this point in *Margaret Mead and Samoa*, pp. 95-109.

Not all Samoans agree, however. Felix Wendt acknowledged with thanks Freeman's correction of Mead, but blamed him in turn for foisting yet another odious stereotype on the Samoans—the picture of them as temperamental and violent. He ventured that Freeman's description of Samoan aggression catered to "the intense emotions of some of his principal collaborators and informants, staunch advocates of Samoan puritanism as adhered to and preached by many of the Protestant congregational denominations in Samoa."[1] Wendt complained of Freeman's "patronizing and paternalistic" manner and styled him a "pseudo-Samoan in that he did not and could not feel as a Samoan does." Although these remarks purport to express no more than a personal opinion, they do highlight the ambiguity, for Samoans, of anthropologists' use of their culture as a battleground for disputes about high theoretical questions.

Note on Editing

Since the *Reader* is meant to be a source book on the Samoa controversy and the issues it raised for anthropology, I have sought to document opinion and to provide information useful for further study.

About seventy percent of the selections were produced in response to the publication of Freeman's book. Usually the texts have been edited to excerpts. This procedure was adopted to eliminate redundancy, which is considerable in the controversy. The *oeuvre* quality of some carefully crafted essays has thereby been lost or impaired, but then the *Reader* is not meant to replace the original publication. Footnotes and references have also frequently been eliminated or greatly reduced in number.

The selections written prior to the controversy are chosen for their particular relevance to contested issues. The field from which they are selected is very populous; arbitrariness in selection was unavoidable. It is sufficient if each of the selections adds a distinctive insight into the issues.

---

[1]Wendt, *op. cit.*, p 95. Freeman's response to Wendt is in *Pacific Studies* 7 (1984):142.

Chapter I

Theory:
For and Against Cultural
Determinism

Mead's View about
Natural and Cultural Influences on Sex Roles

Peggy Reeves Sanday

Editor's Note

Mead had no single theory of the relation between natural and cultural influence on human behavior. Instead she left many statements, of which *Coming of Age in Samoa* is one, often written as an attempt to explain to herself and the world the complexities of sex roles.

Peggy Sanday's essay collates Mead's changing views as they unfolded over the decades through a series of books. Her study shows that Mead's "configurationalist," "psychological," or "temperament" anthropology (see Marvin Harris' essay in Chapter II) developed in close connection with the study of sex roles. Sanday also shows the ease with which Mead shifted between cultural and natural explanations, so that in her writings are found expressions of traditional as well as progressive views on the psychology and social function of sex roles. Sanday's synopsis exposes this complexity while emphasizing the influence of Mead's life circumstances on her effort to understand sexuality and gender.

It will be noted that however much Mead may have contributed to certifying cultural determinism, she herself was less a determinist than an interactionist. Or as Sanday's study shows that she was both determinist and interactionist because she believed that she could "have it both ways."

Sanday's essay appeared in the Mead memorial issue of the *American Anthropologist,* under the title "Margaret Mead's View of Sex Roles in Her Own and Other Societies." The date of the memorial issue, 1980, means that the author wrote free of the influences of the Samoa debate.

In *Sex and Temperament,* published in 1935, Mead demonstrated the enormous variability in cultural definitions of maleness and femaleness. In *Male and Female,* published in 1949, she argued that cultural variability in sex roles was founded on "primary sex differences" conditioned by the reproductive functions and anatomical differences between the sexes. The tension between cultural and biological explanations for sex-role differences is evident in both books, with the weight on the cultural explanation in *Sex and Temperament,* and on the biological and psychological point of view in *Male and Female.* The manner in which she treated the interaction between biology and culture in *Sex and Temperament* was unparalleled for someone writing on a subject historically fraught with so much waffling in Western thought. The complexity of her approach greatly confused reviewers, who wanted her to decide once and for all whether it was either-or. Commenting on this issue in the preface to the 1950 edition to *Sex and Temperament,* she said:

> In our present day culture, bedeviled by a series of *either-or* problems, there is a tendency to say 'She can't have it both ways; if she shows that different cultures can mold men and women in ways which are opposite to our ideas of innate sex differences, then she can't also claim that there *are* sex differences' [emphasis in original].

Far from yielding to her critics, Mead went on to claim that "we not only have it both ways, but many more than both ways."

She felt that there were other possibilities not yet imagined. She said, for example: "The biological basis of development as human beings, although providing limitations which must be honestly reckoned with, can be seen as potentialities by no means fully tapped by our human imagination" (from Preface to 1950 edition of *Sex and Temperament*).

When discussing such subjects as the relations between biology and culture, Mead commands our attention. She demonstrated an uncanny ability to penetrate complex subjects without reducing the issues to simple formulae. More than most anthropologists, male and female, she was not afraid to grapple with contemporary issues of relevance to her own and others' personal development. Nowhere was this ability more evident than in her studies of sex roles in various societies . . . .

When Mead went into the field with Reo Fortune in December of 1931 she had a specific goal in mind. As she put it in *Blackberry Winter* (1972:196) her task was "to study the different ways in which cultures patterned the expected behavior of males and females." Her ultimate intention in phrasing the problem that way was to develop, she wrote, "a new approach to the basic question of biological differences that are sex-linked." She decided to begin by studying the cultural patterning of sex differences because, as she said, "it seemed to be futile to raise questions about biologically-given sex differences" until the problem of the effects of cultural stylization on feminine and masculine personalities was resolved. Thus, to pave the way for examining biologically governed differences, she began with the question of the way in which culture stylizes the roles of men and women.

The fieldwork with Fortune, which lasted until the spring of 1933, was filled with intense personal pressures for Mead. Sitting alone on the Arapesh mountainside, reduced to hobbling about on a bad ankle and unable to keep up with her restless, temperamental, volatile husband, Mead concluded that the disappointments of her marriage were due to differences in their temperaments. She was struck by the way in which she and Fortune responded to the Arapesh and, later, to the Mundugumor . . . . While Mead identified with the nurturing and cherishing attitude of Arapesh men and women and shared their disapproval of aggressive behavior, Fortune, it seems, was thoroughly infuriated by both the Arapesh and his wife's attitude toward them (Mead 1972:197-199).

Later, when Mead and Fortune were conducting fieldwork among the Mundugumor, their reactions differed in ways that, again, exposed to Mead their basic incompatibility. Mead "loathes the Mundugumor culture," as she wrote later, "with its endless aggressive rivalries, exploitation, and rejection of children." She reacted so strongly to their cavalier attitude toward childbearing that it was there that she decided, she said, to "have a child no matter how many miscarriages it meant." It seemed clear to her that "a culture that so repudiated children could not be," as she put it, "a good culture." Equally distasteful to her was the fact that Fortune was fascinated as well as repelled by the Mundugumor. "They struck some note in him," she said, "that was thoroughly alien to me, and working with them emphasized aspects of his personality with which I could not empathize . . . " (1972:205-206).

Ruth Benedict played an important role in these discussions. Both Mead and Fortune had read a first draft of *Patterns of Culture,* which they had received in the field. Both were in sympathy with Benedict's conceptualization of culture as "personality writ large" and with her idea that every culture is a product of a process by which certain human traits are selectively emphasized and others disallowed. Years earlier, Benedict had made the point that individuals whose innate characteristics are too far removed form the cultural norm find their culture deeply uncongenial. Benedict thought of herself in these terms. Her sense of profound personal anguish and unhappiness led her to wish she had been born in a different time or place—perhaps ancient Egypt. Benedict and Mead adopted the word "deviant" for the individual who was such a "cultural misfit" (Mead 1972:195-196). Interestingly, Mead, also felt that she was a deviant, not so much in the American culture as in the academic culture. "My own interest in children," she wrote, "did not fit the stereotype of the American career woman or, for that matter, the stereotype of the possessive, managing American wife and mother." According to Mead, Bateson also was aware of himself as a "misfit." (p. 219).

The concepts of deviancy, cultural selection, "personality writ large," and innate characteristics were melded in the final formulation of the relationship between sex and temperament that emerged from those intense discussions in that tiny mosquito room in New Guinea. In *Blackberry Winter*, Mead (p. 26) wrote:

As we talked, week after week, about Gregory's material and ours, a new formulation of the relationship between sex and temperament began to emerge. We asked ourselves: What if there were other kinds of innate differences—differences as important as those between the sexes, but that cut across sex lines? What if human beings, innately different at birth, could be shown to fit into systematically defined temperamental types, and what if there were male and female versions of each of these temperamental types? And what if a society—by the way in which children were reared, by the kinds of behavior that were rewarded or punished, and by its traditional depiction of heroes, heroines, and villains, witches, sorcerers, and supernaturals—could place its major emphasis on one type of temperament, as among the Arapesh and the Mundugumor, or could, instead, emphasize a special complementarity between the sexes, as the Iatmul and the Tchambuli did? And what if the expectations about male-female differences, so characteristic of Euro-American cultures, could be reversed, as they seemed to be in Tchambuli, where women were brisk and cooperative, whereas men were responsive, subject to the choices of women, and characterized by the kinds of cattiness, jealousy, and moodiness that feminists have claimed were the outcome of women's subservient and dependent role?

The formulation that appeared in *Sex and Temperament* did not differ significantly from the above statement, written so much later. In *Sex and Temperament* she said:

... because this same relative distribution of individual differences does appear in culture after culture, in spite of the divergence between the cultures, it seems pertinent to offer a hypothesis to explain upon what basis the personalities of men and women have been differently standardized so often in the history of the human race. This hypothesis is an extension of that advanced by Ruth Benedict in her *Patterns of Culture*. Let us assume that there are definite temperamental differences between human beings which if not entirely hereditary at least are established on a hereditary base very soon after birth. (Further than this we cannot at present narrow the matter.) These differences finally embodied in the character structure of adults, then, are the clues from which culture works, selecting one temperament, or a combination of related and congruent types, as desirable, and embodying this choice in every thread of the social fabric—in the care of the young child, the games the children play, the songs the people sing, the structure of political organization, the religious observance, the art and the philosophy [Mead 1935 (1963 ed.:284)].

Thus, Mead recognized the interaction between biology and culture in the standardization of temperamental types. Although she emphasized individual differences based on biological proclivities, she said nothing about sex differences. In fact, she underplayed such differences when she contended that "all of the energies" of the Arapesh and Mundugumor "have gone toward the creation of a single human type, regardless of class, age, or sex." (Mead 1935 [1963 ed.:287]).

Male and Female: A Study of Sex Differences
Published fourteen years after *Sex and Temperament, Male and Female* was both a study of cultural variability in sex roles and of "primary sex differences." The style in which the book was written, with its liberal embellishments on the nature of man and woman placed it more properly on drugstore racks than on the scholar's shelf. Men are described as having a "natural springing potency" and women as exhibiting a "spontaneous slower-flowering responsiveness." Such stylistic flourishes are accompanied by generalizations that touched the heart of middle America and antagonized modern feminists. With something of a shock, we learn: "Each known human society has tried to come to grips with . . . the incompatibility between man's spontaneity and the monotony of the domestic hearth, with the over-compatibility between women's docility and the perpetuation of some outworn tradition" (Mead 1949 [1968 ed.:37]).
Unafraid to advise the American masses, Mead went on to point out the implications of such differences for modern American life. "In this age," she warned, "when millions of women are unmated and childless, or left alone to bring up their children, when so many men, restless and unsettled, wander again over the

face of the earth, this old problem is as pressing as it ever has been, and as inescapable." Pressing home the gravity of the problem, she added: "No people who fail to meet it survive, as whole human beings" (p. 37).

Mead feared that American society did not provide emotionally rewarding roles for men. In the introduction to the 1962 edition of *Male and Female*, she (Mead 1949 [1968 ed.:31-32]) expressed concern that, because the necessary virtues of the time were "essentially domestic"—that is, virtues more appropriate for women, such as patience, endurance, and steadfastness—young men were placed "in a particularly difficult spot . . . without new means to exercise their biologically given aggressive protectiveness or desire for individual bravery." She advised her society to structure male tasks so that "taking risks for that which is loved may still be possible." She thought athletics provided a partial answer, but that "the exploration of space, the depths of the sea, and the center of the earth" offered a more complete answer . . . .

Fortunately, there is much more to *Male and Female* than these overly enthusiastic appeals to the Coca-Cola generation. If one can survive the syrup, one can detect many interesting propositions. A key set of ideas rested on the assumption that, to be fully whole, males and females must accept and experience "full sex membership." This assumption clearly had a personal basis. In the acknowledgments section of the book, Mead expressed gratitude to her grandmother and to her parents for giving her "that sense of membership in my own sex which has directed my research work to the study of children." Carrying the idea of sex membership into the body of the book, Mead (p. 348) claimed that, once a woman "has borne a child, her full sex membership, her ability to conceive and carry and bear another human being, is assured and can never be taken away from her."

Mead had borne a child 10 years before *Male and Female* was published. After numerous miscarriages, this was understandably a very great event in her life. About the birth of her daughter, Catherine Bateson, Mead wrote in her autobiography: "We called her Cathy. She was fair-haired, her head was unmarred by a hard birth or the use of instruments, and her expression was already her own. I was completely happy" (Mead 1972:259). Mead's close friend and colleague Ruth Benedict also felt the need for having a child. In her biography of Benedict, Mead (1974:13) described the younger Benedict as being a woman gripped by an intense inner turmoil who "longed for the child that did not come" but also "realized that having a child would not wholly meet her urgent need."

. . . Mead felt that the male role and asymmetric relations between the sexes were based on the fact that the sex membership of women was more easily assured than that of men. Because paternity remains "to the end inferential," she proposed, a man's full sex membership is achieved through cultural and not biological means. The man's need for achievement both parallels and results from a woman's ability to bear a child. In one of the most memorable passages in *Male and Female,* Mead (1949 [1968 ed.: 168-169]) wrote:

> The recurrent problem of civilization is to define the male role satisfactorily enough . . . so that the male may in the course of his life reach a solid sense of irreversible achievement, of which his childhood knowledge of the satisfactions of child-bearing have given him a glimpse. In the case of women, it is only necessary that they be permitted by the given social arrangements to fulfil their biological role, to attain this sense of irreversible achievement. If women are to be restless and questing, even in the face of child-bearing, they must be made so through education. If men are ever to be at peace, ever certain that their lives have been lived as they were meant to be, they must have, in addition to paternity, culturally elaborated forms of expression that are lasting and sure. Each culture—in its own way—has developed forms that will make men satisfied in their constructive activities without distorting their sure sense of their masculinity. Fewer cultures have yet found ways in which to give women a divine discontent that will demand other satisfactions than those of child-bearing.

Thus, men become but women have only the need to be. Because men are denied the fruits of the womb, envy propels them to monopolize the fruits of civilization. Women do not seek these fruits unless they experience a "divine discontent" that propels them to achieve also. Because of the male need for achievement, Mead conjectured that male activities would be regarded as more important than female activities even when these activities were the same.

   This suggestion of universal sexual asymmetry in the valuation of male and female activities is not consistent with the ethnographic facts as Mead presented them. Referring to the way in which seven societies patterned the relative roles of the sexes in ritual and in ceremony, Mead described some as balanced and symmetrical, and others as conforming to an asymmetric pattern. In Samoa and Bali, for example, she said the young child grows up in a two-sex world in which both men and women are treated in an "even-handed" manner. In Samoa, she reported (1949 [1968 ed.:107-108]), each sex is sure of its sex membership, and both sexes "have satisfactory roles." The Samoan boy is not over-pressured into displays of manhood, and the girl who is ambitious and managing has plenty of outlets in the bustling, organized life of the women's groups. Samoan culture, she said, makes it possible "to develop into easy, balanced human beings, with a balance so sure that even years away from Samoa does [not] disturb its essential symmetry."

References

Mead, Margaret. 1935. *Sex and Temperament in Three Primitive Societies*. New York: William Morrow. [Page numbers in the text refer to the 1965 paperback edition.]
Mead, Margaret. 1949. *Male and Female*. New York: William Morrow [Page numbers in the text refer to the 1968 Laurel edition.]
Mead, Margaret. 1972. *Blackberry Winter: My Earlier Years*. New York: Morrow.

Nature, Nurture, and Behavior

Daniel E. Koshland, Jr.

Editor's Note

This editorial in *Science* was prompted by the discovery of genetic markers for the depressive illness (see Janice A. Egeland, *et al.*, "Bipolar affective disorders linked to DNA markers on chromosome 11," *Nature* 325 [1987]:783-787). Freeman hailed Koshland's editorial as indicative that informed opinion now endorsed the interactionist perspective. "Nature, Nurture, and Behavior" appeared in *Science* 235 (March 20, 1987):1445. Reprinted with permission. Copyright 1987 by the AAAS.

The recent reports of the chromosomal localization of genes related to Alzheimer's disease and manic depression are major discoveries that bring promise of help to those suffering from these dread mental illnesses. These advances also contribute important information to the continuing argument about the roles of nature and nurture in behavior.

Many of the news stories that accompanied the description of the manic depressive gene mentioned this new discovery as a watershed in this traditional debate. Although the recent finding in manic depression is a major advance, it was not a surprise to those who have followed developments in neurobiology. Seymour Kety's classical study following parents and their adopted and biological children in Scandinavian countries provided evidence that schizophrenia has a hereditary component; he also provided a methodology that has been used to study other behavioral disorders. These studies, however, met with major resistance, not only from a large segment of the public but also from many scientists and doctors who maintained that such behavioral disorders must be due to stress.

In retrospect it is easy to ask how anyone could have doubted the mounting evidence. The brain is, after all, an organ, like the kidney, the heart, or the liver, and organs are known to fail because of hereditary factors as well as environmental ones. The answer is probably that to many people the brain is much more than an organ: it is the center of the poetry, the sophistication, the special qualities that make human beings an order of magnitude more complex than the closest related species. To believe that the brain is merely a series of chemical reactions is to denigrate free will, to remove humans from the responsibility for their actions, to eliminate the relation between sin and guilt. Moreover, the recent findings are just the beginning; many other behavioral characteristics have been analyzed by studies of adopted children and identical twins and by biochemical approaches. Those who dread complexity will try to reduce the new evidence to the old confrontation of extremes: chemistry versus free will, heredity versus environment, fate versus responsibility. In fact, the neurobiological evidence indicates that part of the brain is "hardwired" in advance of birth and part is designed to be plastic and learn from experience.

The relation of nature and nurture in manic depression is probably typical of what we can expect to discover about other behavioral disorders. Some individuals who have normal genes become overwhelmed by adversity in their environment, sink into depression, and attempt suicide. At the other extreme, some who have loving parents, ideal schooling, and a stress-free life are overwhelmed by their internal chemistry and also succumb to depression and suicidal intentions. Still others are pushed into depression by stresses that are easily surmounted by individuals with different genetic components. Some of these people will be helped by drug therapy (in the manic depressive case, lithium is a highly effective drug with minimal side effects). Some will be helped by counseling, and some by a combination of the two.

This picture may seem obvious to a scientist, but our judges, journalists, legislators, and philosophers have been slow to learn this lesson. When children do not behave, parents or schools must be at fault. If prisoners are not rehabilitated, prison programs must be inadequate. If suicides are not prevented, stress must be excessive. Equally simplistic is the contention that there is no crime, only disease; no guilt, only a bad combination of genes. The truth is that we are dealing with a very complex problem in which the structure of society and chemical therapy will play roles. Better schools, a better environment, better counseling, and better rehabilitation will help some individuals, but not all. Better drugs and genetic engineering will help others, but not all. It is not going to be easy for those without scientific training to cope with these complicated relationships even when all the factors are well understood. It will be even harder while the scientific research is still unfolding. However, the debate on nature and nurture in regard to behavior is basically over. Both are involved, and we are going to have to live with that complexity to make our society more humane for the individual and more civilized for the body politic.

Anthropology's Mythology

George Peter Murdock

Editor's Note

Murdock used the occasion of the T. H. Huxley Memorial Lecture of 1971 to declare, at the end of a long and productive career, that anthropology has no theory properly so called. The reason is that it has not isolated real units of analysis and causation. "Culture" in particular is not a real causal agent but a "reified abstraction" whose reference is vague. He suggests that the real unit is the individual, and he proposes collaboration between behavioral psychology and anthropology to the end that valid theory is to be found. This excerpt is reprinted with permission of the Royal Anthropological Institute of Great Britain and Ireland. It appeared in _Proceedings of the Royal Anthropological Institute of Great Britain and Ireland_ (1971):17-24.

The late Bronislaw Malinowski used to maintain that good fieldwork depends upon sound theory—by which he implied, of course, his own institutional approach. I would take issue with him in this respect. The quality of ethnographic description naturally improves with innovations in field techniques, especially when these involve prolonged immersion in the life of the people studied and the acquisition of their language. But it seems to me, on the basis of my exposure to the literature, to depend remarkably little on the specific theoretical orientation of the observer. Ethnographic accounts of outstanding quality have been produced by anthropologists with the most diverse theoretical preoccupations, as well as by missionaries such as Junod and Sahangun, by colonial administrators like Rattray and F. E. Williams, and even by political exiles like Bogoras and housewives like Lorna Marshall. What counts is not so much the theoretical orientation of the fieldworker, for this can probably produce as many blind spots as genuine insights, but rather . . . on such qualities as intellectual curiosity, a real interest in the people studied, sensitivity, industry, and objectivity. When two or more ethnographers with such qualities have studied the same people, their independent accounts usually corroborate each other to a highly gratifying extent, or at least provide a basis for a reinterpretation of their findings. In short, my respect for the ethnographic record and for those who have produced it is unqualifiedly high, and grows apace with each year.

I feel far less happy about the body of theory we have produced to account for the diversity of social behavior which we have observed and recorded. Indeed, the more I have sought to expand my own intellectual perceptions by assessing and attempting to incorporate the views of others, the more frustrated and dissatisfied I have become. Very slowly, and very reluctantly, I have come to the conclusion that most of the principles we have advanced to order our data bear little resemblance in kind to the systems of theory that have been developed in the older physical and biological sciences. They have far more in common with the equally complex, but unverified and often unverifiable, systems outside the realm of science which we know as mythology, or perhaps as philosophy or even theology. It is for this reason that I have chosen to designate them in this paper as "anthropology's mythology."

I realize that Evans-Pritchard has anticipated me in this pessimistic conclusion, and I fully share his sense of disillusionment. I nevertheless do not agree with him that anthropology can never become a genuine science and must reconcile itself in perpetuity to the status of a purely humanistic discipline. I merely feel that our predecessors, for all their merits, made a grievous and fateful error in formulating their approach to the explanation of man's collective behavior, and thereby committed us to a mass of derivative errors from which we have never as yet been able to extricate ourselves. My purpose in this paper is to indicate how we were led astray and also hopefully, how we can correct our errors and redirect our course into channels which give promise of immensely more fruitful results in the future.

A number of serious criticisms can be levelled at the theoretical systems of both cultural and social anthropology, and I will shortly allude to some of them. But the most basic objection applies equally to both of them and goes back to a common fundamental error perpetrated at the time when anthropology and sociology were first emerging as an independent discipline (or, if you wish, disciplines). Herbert Spencer, for example, faced squarely the problem of defining the appropriate unit of scientific investigation for the new science. Was it the human individual or some supra-individual phenomenon? While he recognized that the individual is unmistakably the isolable unit of human perception, thought, feeling, and action, he nevertheless—for reasons which need not concern us here—opted for the social aggregate as the preferable unit for study and was thus led to his conception of the superorganic. Durkheim and most subsequent sociologists and social anthropologists have followed in his footsteps without ever seriously questioning whether he had made the correct choice. Tylor likewise rejected the individual as the appropriate unit of investigation in favour of another supra-individual concept, that of culture, and has been unquestioningly followed by subsequent cultural anthropologists. Kroeber even adopted Spencer's term "super-organic" to designate the alleged cultural level of behavior.

It now seems to me distressingly obvious that culture, social system, and all comparable supra-individual concepts, such as collective representations, group mind, and social organism, are illusory conceptual abstractions inferred from observations of the very real phenomena of individuals interacting with one another and with their natural environments. The circumstances of their interaction often lead to similarities in the behavior of different individuals which we tend to reify under the name of culture, and they cause individuals to relate themselves to others in repetitive ways which we tend to reify as structures or systems. But culture and social structure are actually mere epiphenomena—derivative products of the social interaction of pluralities of individuals. More precisely, they resemble the illusory constructs so prevalent in the early days of the natural sciences, such as those of phlogiston and the luminiferous ether in physics, and systems of theory based upon them have no greater validity or unity.

When I characterize the concepts of culture and social system as "myths," I do not imply that they bear no relation to reality, for they are obviously derived from observations in the real world. I mean merely that, as reified abstractions, they cannot legitimately be used to explain human behavior. Culture and social aggregates are explainable as derivatives of behavior, but not vice versa. All systems of theory which are based on the alleged or inferred characteristics of aggregates are consequently inherently fallacious. They are, in short, mythology, not science, and are to be rejected in their entirety—not revised or modified.

This conclusion is supported by a variety of evidence. In any established science, for example, there is substantial agreement among its leading practitioners on the essential core of its body of theory, whereas in anthropology there is virtually no such consensus. In analyzing the recent volume by Fortes I discovered—to my astonishment in view of my great respect for his work—that it contained scarcely a single theoretical assumption, postulate, generalization, or conclusion which I could accept as valid without serious qualification. I had had a similar reaction once before—in reading the theoretical work of Leslie White. And I have since experienced it a third time when, stimulated by Fortes, I reviewed the theoretical writings of Alfred Kroeber. Having known all three men fairly intimately, I am aware that none of them has found my own views any more acceptable than I have found theirs, and that each of them has felt an equally profound skepticism regarding the views of the others. It is inconceivable that four men of comparable standing in any established field of science, such as astronomy, nuclear physics, or genetics, could differ so radically from one another on basic theoretical issues. One can only conclude from this that what Fortes, White, Kroeber, and I have been producing is not scientific theory in any real sense but something much closer to the unverifiable dogmas of differing religious sects.

In some instances this is almost embarrassingly apparent. Thus Kroeber entitles his most succinct expression of his theoretical views "Eighteen Professions," thereby almost explicitly likening his own profession of faith to that of Martin Luther. White is notoriously accepted as a prophet by many of his students—and acts the part. Fortes freely acknowledges his discipleship to Radcliffe-Brown, expounding and explicating the dogmas of the latter but seldom deviating from them. This hidebound adherence to "revealed truth" contrasts strikingly with the fluidity and rapid advances in theory that have characterized such unquestioned sciences as genetics.

Moreover, what passes as theory in anthropology includes remarkably few propositions which meet the basic requirements of science, that is to say, which explicitly state relationships between phenomena, specify precisely how these change as relevant variables are altered, and support such statements with adequate validating evidence. It consists in the main of what

George Homans calls "nonoperating definitions" and "orienting statements." Prominent among the former are the concepts of culture and social system.

I therefore feel no hesitation in rejecting the validity and utility of the entire body of anthropological theory, including the bulk of my own work, which derives from the reified concepts of either culture or social system, and in consigning it to the realm of mythology rather than science. Some of the fragments of existing theory which escape such stigmatization will engage our attention toward the end of this paper.

We may now inquire what led our founding fathers to impose upon us this hydra-headed incubus of false science. The answer seems clear; it was a misconception of the role of the emerging sister discipline of psychology. Spencer, Tylor, and Durkheim understood psychology as the science which had undertaken the study of the behavior of the human individual. With the individual pre-empted as an object of investigation, they felt compelled to search elsewhere for an appropriate subject matter for the new discipline. Sensing that this must be different, but not quite realizing in what respects, they not unreasonably assumed that it must be some supra-individual realm of phenomena. Culture and society presented themselves as the two most logical candidates, and practically everyone plumped for one or the other, or sometimes both, as the primary basis for explaining social behavior. Thus sociology and anthropology alike committed themselves from the outset to an egregious error from which neither has yet recovered.

On the other hand, psychologists have been notably successful in avoiding the pitfalls of anthropology's "mythology." With near unanimity they find the locus of the mechanisms of behavior in the individual human being rather than in such reified supra-individual abstractions as culture or a social system. The same mechanisms are operative in even the most complex forms of behavior. The sociologist Homans, in surveying the scientific propositions advanced by economists, historians, sociologists, and anthropologists, has discovered no valid ones which are not clearly identical with or derivable from the basic principles of behavioral psychology. It seems to me obvious that the psychologists, with their sophisticated experimental techniques, enjoy an enormous advantage in the effort to discover and understand the mechanisms of human behavior, and that the social scientists would be well advised to pay far closer heed to their findings than has been the case in the past.

It is therefore my personal conviction that the future development of a valid and productive science of man will depend largely on an increasingly intimate collaboration between the disciplines of psychology and anthropology. From the former will come an ever fuller understanding of the underlying mechanisms of behavior, from the latter an ever-expanding comprehension of the varying conditions under which the mechanisms operate to produce differing forms of behavior. Neither by itself offers much of intrinsic scientific value. Psychology, generalizing from mechanisms alone without a precise understanding of conditions, can generate only a sort of reductionistic mythology. Anthropology, despite its potential command of the conditions of behavior, produces only cultural and social mythology when it ignores the findings of psychology on the mechanisms of behavior in favour of its own illusory substitutes. Only if the two disciplines collaborate to the full, with anthropology trusting psychology to reveal the basic mechanisms of behavior and with psychology trusting anthropology to ascertain the relevant configurations of conditions, will a genuine and full-fledged science of man emerge.

Vindication of Anthropology

Robert I. Levy

Editor's Note
Levy's essay, entitled "The Attack on Mead," appeared in *Science*, May 1983, when the Samoa controversy was in full trot. The essay describes Mead's place in contemporary anthropology and vindicates the discipline from Freeman's allegation that it is hostile to the integration of behavioral biology into its concepts and fieldwork. Levy's essay prompted a rejoinder from Colleen D. Clements, of the Rochester University School of Medicine, in which she supported Freeman's contention. *Science* did not print her letter. It is printed here for the first time. Levy's article appeared in *Science* 220 (May 20, 1983):829-832. Reprinted by permission. Copyright 1983 by the American Association for the Advancement of Science.

Mead was a model of commitment to fieldwork and to the
people of the anthropological laboratory. A model for the essential humanistic component of anthropology. But whatever her
importance to a many-headed, vigorously developing present-day
anthropology may prove to have been in some future retrospect,
neither her theory nor her method nor her data are at the center of
current discussion—which is not to belittle her enormous contribution to the organization, vitality, and morale of the profession
during her lifetime.

. . . Freeman himself quotes (for different purposes) Boas'
statement that "culture is not an expression of innate mental qualities [but] . . . a result of varied external conditions acting upon
general human characteristics." Boas is clearly rejecting the idea
of specific racial characteristics, but not "biology," which is what
"general human characteristics" meant to him. For Boas worked,
like Freeman, within a model in which all that was not "cultural"
or "exogenetic" (in Freeman's use of Boas' term "exogene") was
"biological" or "genetic." Alfred Kroeber, who argued for the
study of culture as something that (like the subject matter of biology, chemistry, sociology, mathematics, or linguistics) should be
treated at its own level of phenomenology, in its own terms, with
the hope of clarifying regularities and discerning laws, is Freeman's example of the paradigm at its most benighted and dangerous. Kroeber was in such statements proposing the search for a
science. Freeman confuses this (and this is an important part of
the muddle) with the different question of the nature of the proper
explanation of human behavior, of concrete events. For
Kroeber, in regard to such explanation, the emphasis on culture
was a method of investigation. As he wrote later . . . "insofar as
. . . social or acquired traits can be determined and discounted,
the innate and truly racial ones will be isolated, and can then be
examined, weighed, and compared."

Mead, Boas, and Kroeber knew that the "exogenetic" factors
they chose to define as "culture" were, *pace* Freeman, only a
component in human behavior and events. Which is not to say
that they were not emphasizing culture, plasticity, possibility, and
the hope for social and pedagogic rather than "biological" amelio-
rative programs and what seemed to them a biologically based
conservatism and pessimism. Which is to say that they had a
position on the source and necessity of evil.

. . . Both affability and choler among the Samoans are problems of biology and of culture, among other things (the assumption that "biology" and "culture" are analytically exhaustive is itself suspect, but that is another problem), and neither is necessarily more "external" than the other. (Think of the socially produced murderousness of the sometimes internally gentle soldier). In non-ideological ways some anthropologists are, in fact, concerned with biocultural transactions—problems of relations to the ecosystem, or nutrition, of individual development, of stress, of emotion, of biological constraints on cognition, among others. Some, intrigued by such problems, are interested in problems of universals and of the nature of the structures underlying and limiting variation. Others, however, follow Kroeber's method in the search for the possibilities of creative and adaptive innovation revealed in various historical and ecologically varied communities as the contribution to the understanding of the nature and components of humankind that they are best trained to undertake. And some will continue to feel free to try to make of culture and society an autonomous discipline and to pursue the implications of that strategy.

. . . [*Margaret Mead and Samoa*] seems to me to be a prisoner of the same ideological conflicts about the moral relation of man to society that generated the nature-nurture opposition in the first place. Its rhetoric, as well as much of its subject matter, is of battle, of confrontation, of the enlightened against the benighted. This rhetoric has been responsible for the small tumult of its reception in the popular media.

Critique of Levy's Vindication

Colleen D. Clements

Levy maintains Boas, Kroeber, Mead *et al.* did not react against biology but against a "nasty racism" that proposed behavior differences in different groups were the function of genes, and they adequately assumed biology when speaking of "general human characteristics." If we relabel all genetic explanations of some behavior as "nasty racism," we are left with an empty and meaningless "biology" which can be safely embraced because the word means nothing and requires no alterations to our theories. Unless biological explanations do entail that some behavior differences in different groups are the function of genes, or some evolved behaviors in all groups are the function of commonly shared genes, such explanations would be empty of biological content in any but a simplistic or phenomenological sense. This same insensitivity to the fullness of the life sciences (and evolutionary theory) is illustrated by the throw-away phrase "general human characteristics." To consider this vague phrase as paradigmatic of biological science is to betray an armchair humanities perspective. Certainly artists and poets also build on a base of general human characteristics, but this is scarcely what we should define as biology if we are honest about it.

Levy asserts that in "nonideological ways some anthropologists are, in fact, concerned with biocultural transactions—problems of relations to the ecosystem, of nutrition, of individual development, of stress, of emotion, of biological constraints on cognition . . . of universals and of the nature of the structures underlying and limiting variation." I'm afraid this pseudo-argument begins with a significant *ad hominem*: "I am engaged in critical analysis, you are assuming a particular perspective, he is ideological." I doubt Freeman is more ideological than his reviewers, who seem to have achieved this marvelous Archimedian Point in anthropology.

As to the substance of the criticism, again, what is being called "biology" which is supposed to satisfy ethologists, sociobiologists, geneticists and other assorted biological scientists? "Relations to the ecosystem" has man interacting with environment, with the option of being part of or different than the ecosystem, but certainly not necessarily defined or explained within a biological model. It is not a thumbnail sketch of ethology. "Nutrition" is also not an important, fundamental biological explanation of human behavior. "Individual development" covers a conceptual waterfront, but I doubt Levy has in mind a human analog to Lorenz's geese studies. "Stress" can be a valid psychoimmunological study which, in Systems Theory terms, might nicely incorporate all levels of explanation into a more complete life science model, but if we view reaction to stress as descriptive correlations instead of linking the behavior to a reductive explanation, we haven't successfully connected anthropology to biology. "Emotion" can be studied in a psychological context, in a psychology/biology dualism frame, or in a biopsychosocial model. It is hardly proof of a biological framework in anthropology. "Biological constraints on cognition" is an odd way of expressing a biological learning theory, since it could imply a cognition rising from *a priori* categories and limited only slightly by biological considerations, rather than a biological explanation of the development of cognition. The former leaves cognition importantly nonbiological and hence non-evolutionary, maintaining the separateness of the human species in a special way. Finally, Levy talks in the same breath about "universals" and underlying structure (form), a very Platonic language. This ignores the basic characteristic of biological sciences, individual variation, and also the fact of process and change. Biology is not Platonic; to talk in the same breath of biocultural transactions and universals is to betray the reviewer's hidden allegiance to the paradigm he denies exists and Freeman contends is still a stumbling block to the integration of biology and anthropology. It effectively demonstrates Freeman's thesis and additionally underscores the reviewer's lack of understanding of the biological sciences.

Levy goes on to offer two other approaches to anthropology. One concentrates on creative and adaptive innovation in varied communities, without the reviewer paying attention to the critical need for supplying a scientific sense for "adaptive" and biology's significant role in supplying such a sense . . . . The second approach is even less tenable: making culture and society an autonomous discipline. A careful reading of Hierarchy Theory would indicate this is an undesirable impossibility. Each level of organization has its own terms and relationships endogenous to that level. But if we wish to do science, we need to check our theories and terms by either a workable reduction to the next lower level, or an accurate prediction to the next highest level. Otherwise, we insulate our musings and protect our errors. The end result is wild speculation, spurious correlations, and meaningless words. The task of scientific reduction is not to create an 'x is only a, b, c . . .' mentality, but to serve as a powerful tool and corrective in a full Systems explanation. The critics of Freeman miss his legitimate complaint that the tool is not being employed sufficiently in anthropology, and the *Science* review is a beautiful example of how right he is.

For the Autonomy of Culture

Eighteen Professions

A. L. Kroeber

Editor's Note

Alfred Kroeber's "Eighteen Professions" was identified by Freeman as a key statement of cultural determinism. It appeared in the formative period of theory construction in anthropology. George F. Stocking, Jr. has called it "a kind of manifesto of Boasian anthropology." It was also in accord with Emil Durkheim's divorce of sociology from psychology and the evolutionary sciences. Indeed the formulations of the essay may owe more to Durkheim than to Boas. In any case, Kroeber states that anthropology is independent of the methods and findings of the biological sciences. The essay is introduced here rather than in History in order better to enable the reader to judge its contemporaneity.

Kroeber's use of the term "civilization" rather than "culture" is probably due to war conditions. "Culture" had strong Germanic connotations stemming not only from writers in favor, but also from writers such as Hegel and Nietzsche, who were decidedly out of favor because liberals believed that their teachings supported German imperialism—see the selection from Alexander Lesser in Chapter IV. Yet Hegel and Nietzsche were no less concerned than Durkheim to defend the distinction between the natural sciences and *Geisteswissenschaften* (the "moral sciences," as J. S. Mill translated the term), lest the study of man be lost to the mechanical materialism of the natural sciences, including evolutionary theory—see Robin Fox's contribution below.

Toward the end of his career, Kroeber expressed a dissatisfaction with anthropological theory not dissimilar to George Murdoch's complaint in "The Mythology of Anthropology." In an essay significantly titled, "On Human Nature," he called for an effort to synthesize ethnography by extracting cultural universals from the mass of data. His suggested list of universals included knowledge of death, care of the future, incest prohibition, art,

and humor. He proposed a study of the phylogeny of universals based on ethology.
Kroeber's essay was read at the annual meeting of the American Anthropological Association in 1914, and was published in the *American Anthropologist* [N.S.] 17 (1915):283-288.

Anthropology today includes two studies which fundamental differences of aim and method render irreconcilable.
One of these branches is biological and psychological; the other, social or historical.
There is a third field, the special province of anthropology, concerned with the relation of biological and social factors. This is no-man's-land, and therefore used as a picnic-ground by whosoever prefers pleasure excursions to the world of cultivating a patch of understanding. Some day this tract will also be surveyed, fenced, and improved. Biological science already claims it; but the title remains to be established. For the present, the labor in hand is the delimitation of the scope of history from that of science.
In what follows, historical anthropology, history, and sociology are referred to as history. Physical anthropology and psychology are included in biology.
1. *The aim of history is to know the relations of social facts to the whole of civilization.*
Civilization means civilization itself, not its impulses. Relation is actual connection, not cause.
2. *The material studied by history is not man, but his works.*
It is not men, but the results of their deeds, the manifestations of their activities, that are the subject of historical inquiry.
3. *Civilization, though carried by men and existing through them, is an entity in itself, and of another order from life.*
History is not concerned with the agencies producing civilization, but with civilization as such. The causes are the business of the psychologist. The entity civilization has intrinsically nothing to do with individual men nor with the aggregates of men on whom it rests. It springs from the organic, but is independent of it. The mental processes of groups of men are, after all, only the collected processes of individuals reacting under certain special stimuli. Collective psychology is therefore ultimately resolvable into individual human psychology, just as this in turn is resolvable into organic psychology and physiology. But history deals with material which is essentially non-individual and integrally

social. History is not concerned with the relations of civilization to men or organisms, but with the interrelations of civilization. The psychic organization of man in the abstract does not exist for it, save as something given directly and more or less completely to the student's consciousness. The uncivilized man does not exist; if he did, he would mean nothing to the historian. Even civilized man is none of history's business; its sphere is the civilization of which man is the necessary basis but which is inevitable once this basis exists.

4. *A certain mental constitution of man must be assumed by the historian, but may not be used by him as a resolution of a social phenomena.*

The historian can and should obtain for himself the needed interpretation of man's mind from familiarity with social facts and the direct application to them of his own psychic activities. This interpretation is likely to be of service in proportion as it emanates immediately from himself and not from the formulated laws of the biological psychologist. Whether an understanding of civilization will or will not help the psychologist is for the latter to determine.

5. *True instincts lie at the bottom and origin of social phenomena, but cannot be considered or dealt with by history.*

History begins where instincts commence to be expressed in social facts.

6. *The personal or individual has no historical value save as illustration.*

Ethnological genealogies are valuable material. So are the actions of conspicuous historical personages. But their dramatic, anecdotic, or biographic recital is biographic or fictional art, or possibly psychology, not history.

7. *Geography, or physical environment, is material made use of by civilization, not a factor shaping or explaining civilization.*

Civilization reacts to civilization, not to geography. For the historian, geography does not act on civilization, but civilization incorporates geographical circumstances. Agriculture presupposes a climate able to sustain agriculture, and modifies itself according to climatic conditions. It is not caused by climate. The understanding of agricultural activity is to be sought in the other phenomena of civilization affecting it.

8. *The absolute equality and identity of all human races and strains as carriers of civilization must be assumed by the historian.*

The identity has not been proved nor has it been disproved. It remains to be established, or to be limited, by observations directed to this end, perhaps only by experiments. The historical and social influences affecting every race and every large group of persons are closely intertwined with the alleged biological and hereditary ones, and have never yet been sufficiently separated to allow demonstration of the actual efficiency of either. All opinions on this point are only convictions falsely fortified by subjective interpreted evidence. The biologist dealing with man must assume at least some hereditary differences, and often does assume biological factors as the only ones existent. The historian, until such differences are established and exactly defined, must assume their non-existence. If he does not base his studies on this assumption, his work becomes a vitiated mixture of history and biology.

9. *Heredity cannot be allowed to have acted any part in history.*

Individual hereditary differences undoubtedly exist, but are not historical material because they are individual. Hereditary differences between human groups may ultimately be established, but like geography must in that event be converted into material acted upon by the force of civilization, not treated as causes of civilization.

10. *Heredity by acquirement is equally a biological and historical monstrosity.*

This naive explanation may be eliminated on the findings of biology; but should biology ever determine that such heredity operates through a mechanism as yet undiscovered, this heredity must nevertheless be disregarded by history together with congenital heredity. In the present stage of understanding, heredity by acquirement is only too often the cherished inclination of those who confuse their biological thinking by the introduction of social aspects, and of those who confound history by deceiving themselves that they are turning it into biology.

11. *Selection and other factors of organic evolution cannot be admitted as affecting civilization.*

It is actually unproved that the processes of organic evolution are materially influencing civilization or that they have influenced it. Civilization obviously introduces an important factor which is practically or entirely lacking in the existence of animals and plants, and which must at least largely neutralize the operation of any kind of selection. Prehistoric archeology shows with certainty that civilization has changed profoundly without accompanying material alterations in the human organism. Even so far as biological evolution may ultimately be proved in greater or less degree for man, a correspondence between organic types and civilizational forms will have to be definitely established before history can concern itself with these organic types or their changes.

12. *The so-called savage is no transition between the animal and the scientifically educated man.*

All men are totally civilized. All animals are totally uncivilized because they are almost totally uncivilizable. The connecting condition which it is universally believed must have existed, is entirely unknown. If ever it becomes known, it can furnish to the historian only an introduction to history. There is no higher and lower in civilization in any sequence, save the actual one of time, place, and connection, is normally misleading and always valueless. The estimation of the adult savage as similar to the modern European child is superficial and prevents his proper appreciation either biologically or historically.

13. *There are no social species or standard cultural types or stages.*

A social species in history rests on false analogy with organic species. A stage in civilization is merely a preconception made plausible by arbitrarily selected facts.

14. *There is no ethnic mind, but only civilization.*

There are only individual minds. When these react on each other cumulatively, the process is merely physiological. The single ethnic or social existence is civilization, which biologically is resolvable purely into a product of physiological forces, and historically is the only and untranscendable entity.

15. *There are no laws in history similar to the laws of physico-chemical science.*

All asserted civilizational laws are at most tendencies, which, however determinable, are not permanent quantitative expressions. Nor are such tendencies the substitute which history has for the laws of science. History need not deny them and may have to recognize them, but their formulation is not its end.

16. *History deals with conditions sine qua non, not with causes.*

The relations between civilizational phenomena are relations of sequence, not of effect. The principles of mechanical causality, emanating from the underlying biological sciences, are to individual and collective psychology. Applied to history, they convert it into psychology. An insistence that all treatment of civilizational data should be by the methods of mechanical causality is equivalent to a denial of the valid existence of history as a subject of study. The only antecedents of historical phenomena are historical phenomena.

17. *The causality of history is teleological.*

Psychological causes are mechanical. For history, psychology is assumable, not demonstrable. To make the object of historical study the proving of the fundamental identity of the human mind by endless examples is as tedious as barren. If the process of civilization seems the worth-while end of knowledge of civilization, it must be sought as a process distinct from that of mechanical causality, or the result will be a reintegration that is not history. Teleology of course does not suggest theology to those free from the influence of theology. The teleology of history involves the absolute conditioning of historical events by other historical events. This causality of history is as completely unknown and unused as chemical causality was a thousand and physical causality three thousand years ago.

18. *In fine, the determinations and methods of biological, psychological, or natural science do not exist for history, just as the results and the manner of operation of history are disregarded by consistent biological practice.*

Most biologists have implicitly followed their aspect of this doctrine, but their consequent success has tempted many historians, especially sociologists, anthropologists, and theorists, to imitate them instead of pursuing their proper complementary method.

Speaking in the Name of the Real

Ivan Brady

Editor's Note

As book review editor of the *American Anthropologist,* Ivan Brady assembled a Special Section on the Samoa controversy, which was published in the December 1983 issue. All but one of the contributions were selected from a mass of writings that had poured into Brady's office. Brady's Introduction to the Section undertakes to summarize the consensus of American anthropologists as he viewed it from the editor's desk. In correspondence with me, Brady made additional comments which have been incorporated as an addendum and a footnote. Reproduced by permission of the American Anthropological Association from *American Anthropologist* 85:4 (1983):908-910. Not for further reproduction.

The publication of Derek Freeman's book . . . has generated unprecedented controversy over Margaret Mead's fieldwork on Samoa. The book has been reviewed all over the world and has raised questions of authenticity and viability in ethnographic research. Most importantly, it has subjected the work of anthropology's best-known public representative to critical reappraisal in learned journals and in the popular press . . . . [The essays that follow do] not pretend to exhaust the controversy. But many of the issues have had time to lose their "smoke," meta-issues have had time to surface, and for those so inclined, a counting of hands in and out of favor with Freeman has been (or can be) made.[1] The distinguished scholars who address the book and its issues in this special section thus do so with the slight historical advantage of some time on their side. They also have the advantage of several interested perspectives as Samoan field workers (Shore, Holmes, to a lesser degree, Weiner), as field workers in adjacent areas of the Pacific (Schwartz, Silverman, Weiner), and as anthropologist-citizens of the wider world.

One broad but underdetermined topic of enduring value that emerges from these essays, it seems to me, is the problem of how anthropologists get to know what they know and write in the first place—how they authorize themselves, to borrow Michel de Certeau's clever phrase, "to speak in the name of the 'real'." This is obviously a problem of great philosophical vintage and intellectual weight. It is interdisciplinary in scope, and like the issue of biological determinism, which also surfaces in the debate

---

[1] The author's comment, communicated in a letter dated October 22, 1988, is: "This statement is too neutral and has been misconstrued by a few people since it first appeared in print. It seems that messengers are nowhere safe: I intended a simple act of reporting, not advocacy. I also wasn't present when some members of the American Anthropological Association (in the heat of the moment) called for and got a visual vote on the value of Freeman's book. I was then and remain now in favor of expressing criticism in more conventional ways."

over Freeman's book (however inappropriately), it is aporetic in the sense of promising no absolute closure in the short or the long run. The value of pursuing such issues lies less in the certainty of obtaining privileged views and final answers than in the prospect that critical self-reflection offers for intellectual growth in the discipline as a whole. The challenge in this posture is one of cracking both self-delusory and scientific fictions precisely where their merits are exaggerated most, where they are most brittle in claims to privilege, and where claims to secure territory are widest. The trail of broken promises that can result from such orientations in research makes some practitioners uncomfortable. They would rather avoid ragged truths altogether. There is security in neat, local, and highly laundered analytic agreements—in acting *as if* all the paradigms were in place. Others find progress in transcending the fictions of the past, in creating new ways to meet old goals, in developing new goals for old disciplines, and in recognizing that all claims to privileged thought and forms of discourse are only one set among several possibilities, irrespective of discipline or research history. Speaking in the name of the "real" is in any case a difficult language to learn.

Freeman's arguments would appear to be avant-garde in this arena. They are not. His claims to privilege over Mead in "scientific" methods enter into the broad field of reality puzzles and self-conscious science as proverbial grist for the mill. So do the exaggerations, misconstruals, rootless postures, and sometimes muddle-headed pronouncements that have made headlines in the wake of the book's publication. Taken seriously, these arguments add momentum to the wheels of revitalized "thought about thought" and to the related practical problems of "truth" in anthropological expression—not because they are tailored to the flow or instruct the mechanism but rather because they go against these things and make the mill work harder for resolution. There is some intrinsic value in that. But the image of Freeman feeding an intellectual granary still leaves the story short.

Freeman's approach to criticizing Mead has been less domestic than military. His call to battle has forced a fight over thought about Samoa and fieldwork, comparative ethnography, historical continuity and cultural change, proper analytic language in ethnographic reports, anthropology's public image, and much more. Through it all one cannot help but notice that he has made his call from a higher horizon by climbing on the back of a popular giant.

In fact, it might be fair to say that Margaret Mead has once again had a hand in giving anthropology public direction, both as prop for Freeman's high view and through her continued presence as scholar, writer, friend, and mentor in the debates over her work . . . .

Addendum

The content of Freeman's response to criticism on the details of Samoan ethnography was never much an issue with me. In fact I thought much of what he had to say was justified. I was only put off by his great pontifications on "Truth" in scientific method. His timing for those claims could not have been worse: the self-conscious and deconstructive criticisms of ethnographic authority that we now lump under the heading of "post-modernism"—the transition from emphasizing what we know to the development of questions about how we know it—were at the time of the Freeman/Mead controversy just beginning to take root in anthropology. I am convinced that much of the indifference shown to Freeman was based exactly on that emerging uncertainty. There was a common perception (but very little said in print) that even if Mead was wrong, Freeman didn't have (contrary to his persistent claims) the answer to what was right in terms of current demands for research methods and standards of interpretation. The "meta-issues," in other words, seem to have carried the day against Freeman, against closure on multiple interpretations of Samoan ethnography, in favor of continuing uncertainty in the dialogue on how to interpret ethnography in the first place. *Added by the author in a communication of October 22, 1988.*—Ed.

The Impact of the Concept of Culture
on the Concept of Man

Clifford Geertz

Editor's Note
This essay explicates the central conception of cultural anthropology. Geertz employs speculations concerning the evolution of
the cultural capacity in *Homo sapiens* to advocate cultural determinism. Man, he claims, "literally created himself." This includes the biological component of our natures; for "the nervous
system itself" is a product of culture. The particularity of culture,
Geertz argues, is incompatible with a general descriptive and explanatory science of culture. Yet it menaces the concept of the
unity of mankind, which the author recognizes to be foundational
for anthropology. Robin Fox's assertion of the unity of
mankind, in his contribution to this volume, may be usefully
compared with Geertz's notions. This essay originally appeared
in *New Views of the Nature of Man*, edited by John R. Platt
(1965). A condensation was printed in the *Bulletin of the Atomic
Scientists* 22 (1966):2-8. This excerpt has been taken from the
Bulletin. Reprinted with permission of the University of Chicago
Press.

The rise of a scientific concept of culture was connected with
the overthrow of the view of human nature dominant in the Enlightenment which . . . was both clear and simple, and its replacement by a view, not only more complicated but enormously
less clear. The attempt to clarify it, to reconstruct an intelligible
account of what man is, has underlain scientific thinking about
culture ever since. Having sought complexity and, on a scale
grander than they ever imagined, found it, anthropologists became entangled in a tortuous effort to order it. And the end is not
yet in sight.
    The Enlightenment view of man was, of course, that he was
wholly of a piece with nature and shared in the general uniformity
of composition which natural science, under Bacon's urging and
Newton's guidance, had discovered there. There is a human nature as regularly organized, as thoroughly invariant, and as mar-
velously simple as Newton's universe. Perhaps some of its laws

are different, but there *are* laws; perhaps some of its immutability is obscured by the trappings of local fashion, but it *is* immutable.

The notion of a constant human nature independent of time, place, and circumstance may, however, be an illusion; what man is may be so entangled with where he is, who he is, and what he believes as to be inseparable from them. It is precisely this hypothesis that has given rise to the concept of culture and the decline of the uniformitarian view of man. Modern anthropology is firm in the conviction that men unmodified by the customs of particular places do not in fact exist, have never existed, and most important, could not, in the very nature of the case, exist.

By the same token, it is extremely difficult to draw a line between what is natural, universal, and constant in man and what is conventional, local, and variable. In fact, to draw such a line is to falsify the human situation.

Consider the Balinese trance. The Balinese fall into extreme dissociated states in which they perform all sorts of spectacular activities—biting off the heads of living chickens, stabbing themselves, performing miraculous feats of equilibration, mimicking sexual intercourse, eating feces—rather more easily and much more suddenly than most of us fall asleep. Trance states are a crucial part of every ceremony. In some, 50 or 60 people may fall, one after the other, "like a string of firecrackers going off," coming to from five minutes to several hours later, totally unaware of what they have been doing, and convinced, despite the amnesia, that they have had a most extraordinary and satisfying experience.

What does one learn about human nature from this and from the thousand equally peculiar things anthropologists discover, investigate, and describe? That the Balinese are peculiar sorts of beings, South Sea Martians? That they are exactly like us, except for some peculiar, but really incidental, customs we do not happen to have? That they are more innately gifted or even more instinctively driven in some directions than others? That human nature does not exist and that men are simply what their cultures make them?

It is among such interpretations, all unsatisfactory, that anthropology has attempted to find a more viable concept of man, one in which culture and its variability would be taken into account without reducing the governing principle of the field, "the basic unity of mankind," to an empty phrase. To entertain the idea that the diversity of custom in time and space is not a matter of appearance, of stage settings and comedic masques, is to entertain, also, the idea that humanity is as various in its essence as it is in its expression. And with that reflection some well fastened philosophical moorings are loosed and an uneasy drifting into perilous waters begins.

For to discard the notion that Man, capitalized, is to be looked for "behind," "under," or "beyond" his customs, and to replace it with the notion that man, uncapitalized, should be sought "in" them, is to incur the risk of losing sight of him altogether. Either he dissolves into his time and place, or he becomes a conscripted soldier in a vast Tolstoian army, engulfed in one or another of the terrible historical determinisms which have plagued us from Hegel onward. We have had, and to some extent still have, both of these aberrations in the social sciences—one marching under the banner of cultural relativism, the other under that of cultural evolution. But we have had also, and more commonly, attempts to avoid them by seeking in culture patterns themselves the defining elements of a human existence which, while not constant in expression, is yet distinctive in character.

Attempts to locate man amid the body of his customs have taken several directions, but they have virtually all proceeded in terms of a single overall intellectual strategy: the "stratigraphic" conception of the relations between biological, psychological, social, and cultural factors in human life. In this conception, man is a composite of "levels," each superimposed upon those beneath it and underpinning those above it. As one analyzes man, one peels off layer after layer, each such layer being complete and irreducible in itself, revealing another, quite different layer.

. . . One way of doing so is to utilize "invariant points of reference." To quote one of the most famous statements of this strategy—the "Toward a Common Language for the Areas of the Social Sciences" memorandum—"these are to be found in the nature of social systems, in the biological and psychological nature of the component individuals, in the external situations in which they live and act, in the necessity of coordination in social systems. In [culture] . . . these 'foci' of structure are never ignored. They must in some way be 'adapted to' or 'taken account of'." Cultural universals are viewed as crystallized responses to unevadable realities.

Analysis consists, then, of matching assumed universals to postulated underlying necessities. On the social level, reference is made to such irrefragable facts as that in order to persist all societies must reproduce their membership or allocate goods and services—hence the universality of family and of trade. On the psychological level, recourse is had to basic needs like personal growth—hence the ubiquity of educational institutions; or to pan-human problems, like the Oedipal predicament—hence the ubiquity of punishing gods and nurturant goddesses. Biologically, there is metabolism and health; culturally, dining customs and curing procedures. The task is to try to look at underlying human requirements and then to try to show that these aspects of culture which are universal are, to use Kluckhohn's figure again, "tailored" by these requirements.

Again the problem is not so much whether this sort of congruence exists, but whether it is meaningful. It is not difficult to relate some human institution to what science, or commonsense, tells us are requirements for human existence, but it is very much more difficult to state this relationship in an unequivocal form. Any institution serves a multiplicity of social, psychological, and organic needs, but there is no way to state in any precise and verifiable way what the inter-level relationships are. There is no theoretical integration here at all, but merely a correlation. Even by invoking "invariant points of reference," we can never construct genuine functional interconnections between cultural and non-cultural factors.

However, the question still remains whether such universals should be taken as the central elements in the definition of man. This is a philosophical, not a scientific question. Is it in grasping general facts, such as that man has everywhere some sort of "religion," or in appreciating the richness of religious phenomena that we grasp him? Is the fact that "marriage" is—if it is—universal as penetrating a commentary on what we are as Himalayan polyandry, or Australian marriage rules, or the bride-price systems of Bantu Africa? It may be in the cultural particularities of people that some of the most instructive revelations of what it is to be generically human are found; and the main contribution of anthropology to the construction—or reconstruction—of a concept of man may then lie in showing us how to find them.

The main reason anthropologists have shied away from cultural particularities and taken refuge in universals is that, faced with the enormous variations in human behavior, they are haunted by a fear of historicism, of becoming lost in a whirl of cultural relativism. And there is some occasion for such fear: Ruth Benedict's *Patterns of Culture*, with its strange conclusion that anything one people is inclined toward doing is worthy of respect by another, is perhaps only the most outstanding example of the awkward positions one can get into by giving oneself over rather too completely to what Marc Bloch called "the thrill of learning singular things." The critical issue is not whether phenomena are empirically common in science, but whether they can be made to reveal the enduring natural processes which underlie them.

In short, we need to look for systematic relationships among diverse phenomena, not for substantive identities among similar ones. We need to replace the "stratigraphic" conception of the various aspects of human existence by one in which biological, psychological, sociological, and cultural factors can be treated as variables within unitary systems of analysis. The establishment of a common language in the social sciences is not simply a matter of coordinating terminologies nor of imposing a single set of categories. It is a matter of integrating types of concepts so as to formulate meaningful propositions embodying findings in separate fields of study.

To launch such an integration from an anthropological base and thereby to attain a more precise image of man, I propose two ideas. The first is that cultures are best seen not as complexes of concrete behavior patterns—customs, usages, traditions, habit clusters—but as sets of control mechanisms—plans, recipes, rules, instructions, what computer engineers call "programs" for the governing of behavior. The second is that man is the animal most desperately dependent upon such extragenetic control mechanisms for ordering his behavior.

Neither of these ideas is new, but a number of recent developments in anthropology and in other sciences—cybernetics, information theory, neurology, molecular genetics—have made it possible to state them more precisely and to lend them a greater degree of empirical support. Such reformulations of the concept of culture and its role in human life lead to a definition of man which stresses not the empirical commonalities in his behavior, but the mechanisms whereby his inherent capacities are reduced to the narrowness and specificity of his actual accomplishments. One of the most significant facts about human nature may be that we all begin with the natural equipment to live a thousand kinds of lives and end having lived only one.

The "control mechanism" view of culture starts with the assumption that human thought is both social and public, that its natural habitat is the houseyard, the market place, and the town square. Thinking consists not of "happenings in the head" but of a traffic in what have been called significant symbols—words for the most part, but also gestures, drawings, musical sounds, mechanical devices like clocks, or natural objects like jewels—anything, in fact, which is used to impose meaning upon experience. To any one individual, such symbols are largely given data. They are already current in the community when he is born and they remain, with some modifications, in circulation after he dies. He uses them sometimes deliberately, most often spontaneously, to put a construction upon events, to orient himself to "the ongoing course of experienced things."

Man needs such symbolic sources of illumination because the nonsymbolic sources ingrained in his body cast so diffused a light. The behavior patterns of lower animals are more rigidly tied to their physical structure. Man has the innate capacity for general responses; these make possible greater plasticity, complexity, and effectiveness of behavior, but are much less precisely regulated.

This, then, is the second face of our argument: undirected by cultural patterns man's behavior would be virtually ungovernable, a chaos of pointless acts and exploding emotions, his experience virtually shapeless. Thus, culture is not just an ornament of human existence, but an essential condition for it.

Some of the most telling anthropological evidence for such a position comes from new understandings concerning the emergence of *Homo sapiens* out of his general primate background. Of these advances three are of critical importance: (1) the discarding of a sequential view of the relations between his physical evolution and his cultural development in favor of an overlapping or interactive view; (2) the discovery that most of the biological changes that produced modern man took place in the central nervous system, especially in the brain; (3) the realization that man is an incomplete, unfinished animal; that he is set off from non-men less by his sheer ability to learn than by the sorts of things he *has* to learn in order to function at all. Let me take each of these points in turn.

The traditional view of the relations between man's biological and cultural advance was that the biological was completed before the cultural began. This was a stratigraphic view. At some particular stage in his phylogenetic history a marginal genetic change rendered man capable of producing culture and thenceforth his

men there can be no culture, certainly, but the converse is equally true.

We are, in sum, incomplete animals who perfect ourselves through highly particular forms of culture: Dobuan and Javanese, Hopi and Italian, upper class and lower class, academic and commercial. Man's capacity for learning, his plasticity, has often been emphasized, but what is more critical is his extreme dependence upon certain kinds of learning: the development of concepts, the apprehension and application of specific systems of symbolic meaning. Beavers build dams, birds build nests, bees locate food, baboons organize social groups, and mice mate on the basis of forms of instruction encoded in their genes and evoked by appropriate patterns of external stimuli. But men build dams or shelters, locate food, organize their social groups, or find sexual partners under the guidance of instructions encoded in flow charts and blueprints, hunting lore, moral codes, and esthetic judgments: conceptual structures which mold formless talents.

We live, as one writer has put it, in an "information gap" between what our body tells us and what we have to know in order to function. There is a vacuum we must fill ourselves, and we fill it with information provided by our culture.

Between our inborn behavioral capacities and what we actually do lies a complex set of significant symbols under whose direction we transform the first into the second. Our ideas, values, action, even our emotions, are, like the nervous system itself, cultural products.

The approaches to the definition of human nature adopted by the Enlightenment and by classical anthropology have one thing in common: they are both basically typological. They endeavor to construct an image of man as a model, an archetype, a Platonic Idea, or an Aristotelian Form. The individual is but a reflection, distortion, or approximation of this image. During the Enlightenment the prototype had to be uncovered by stripping man of his cultural trappings to reveal the hard core of natural man. Classical anthropology factors out the commonalities in culture to arrive at consensual man. In both cases the result is the same: the differences between individuals or groups of individuals become secondary. Individuality is seen as eccentricity, distinctiveness as accidental deviation from the underlying, unchanging, normative type. Living detail is lost; we seek a metaphysical entity: Man.

The sacrifice is, however, unnecessary and unavailing. There is no conflict between general theoretical and circumstantial understanding, between synoptic vision and an eye for detail. If we want to discover what man amounts to we can only find the answer in what men are; and what men are is various. An understanding of that variousness—its range, nature, basis, and implications—will lead us to a concept of human nature which, more than a statistical shadow and less than a primitivist dream, has both substance and truth.

It is here that the concept of culture has its impact on the concept of man. Seen as a set of symbolic devices for controlling behavior, culture provides the link between what men are intrinsically capable of becoming and what they actually in fact become. To become human is to become an individual, and we become individual under the guidance of cultural patterns, systems of meaning which give form, order, point, and direction to our lives. The cultural patterns involved are not general but specific—not just "marriage" but a particular set of notions about what men and women are like; not just "religion" but belief in the wheel of karma, the observance of a month of fasting, or the practice of cattle sacrifice.

Man is to be defined not by his innate capacities alone, as the Enlightenment sought to do, nor by his actual behavior, as contemporary social science seeks to do, but rather by the way in which the first is transformed into the second, the generic potentialities focused in specific performance. It is man's *career*, in its characteristic course that we discern his nature. Although culture is only one element in determining that course it is hardly the least important. As culture shaped us as a single species, so too it shapes us as separate individuals.

. . . We must, in short, descend into detail, past the misleading tags, the metaphysical types, the empty similarities, to grasp firmly the essential character of the various cultures as well as the various sorts of individuals within each culture. In this area, the approach to the general, revelatory simplicities of science involves concern with the particular, the circumstantial, the concrete; but concern organized and directed in terms of theoretical analyses—physical evolution, nervous system functioning, social organization, psychological process, cultural patterning—and especially in terms of the interplay among them.

Cultural Anthropology and Biology

Roy A. Rappaport

Editor's Note

This selection is taken from Rappaport's long essay, "Desecrating the Holy Woman: Derek Freeman's Attack on Margaret Mead." Rappaport, a cultural ecologist, has devoted sustained thought to the interaction of biology and culture, being the author of *Pigs for the Ancestors* (1968) and *Ecology, Meaning, and Religion* (1979). He vindicates the dominance of culture in cultural anthropology on the grounds that language and symbolic meaning constitute the human, non-biological domain of human existence. At the same time he contests Freeman's claim that anthropology dogmatically repudiates the biological dimension of human life and culture.

In a section of the essay omitted here, Rappaport took issue with Freeman's assessment of Franz Boas' antagonism towards the Darwinian biological anthropology of his time. Rappaport read Freeman as vindicating Darwinian anthropology against Boas' supposed opposition, while rejecting the eugenic and racist elements of that anthropology as merely "insufficient in scientific terms." Rappaport protested that this rebuke failed to register the essential point that in perspective of contemporary biology, it was Boas, not the Darwinians, who were right about the absence of evidence for racial differences in behavior. Freeman rejects this criticism, noting that he commended Boas' "remarkable prescience" in warning that eugenics "was not a panacea that would cure human ills, but rather a dangerous sword" whose "expedient of eliminating 'the unfit' would soon reach a terrible culmination in National Socialist Germany."

The exchange on eugenics occurred prior to the publication of Donald J. Kevles' *In the Name of Eugenics: Genetics and the Uses of Human Heredity* (1985). Kevles shows that eugenic thinking was more wide-spread among leading biologists than either Rappaport or Freeman believed; and that eugenics was and remains closely connected with respectable causes such as family planning, population control, birth technologies, and genetic engineering.

"Desecrating the Holy Woman" appeared in *The American Scholar* 55 (1986):313-347. The selection is reprinted with permission of *The American Scholar.*

The assertion that Kroeber was espousing a "doctrine of absolute cultural determinism" . . . is falsified by any serious reading of the article.[1] Kroeber argued, in effect, that culture, an exclusively human possession, is grounded in the possession, unique to humans, of language. Language, in turn, is grounded in a mental capacity that is an organic product of evolution by natural selection. As Kroeber states in *The Nature of Culture:*

> To deny that something purely animal [i.e. biological] underlies human speech, is fatuous; but it would be equally narrow to believe that because our speech springs from an animal foundation, and originated in this foundation, it therefore is nothing but animal mentality and utterances greatly magnified. A house may be built on rock; without this base it might be impossible for it to have been erected, but no one will maintain that therefore the house is nothing but improved and glorified stone.
> Although culture is erected upon an organic foundation, it itself is not genetically transmitted.
> Heredity saves for the ant all that she has from generation to generation. But heredity does not maintain and has not maintained because it cannot maintain one particular of the civilization [culture] which is the specifically human thing.
> Although individuals vary in their abilities to contribute to culture, to transmit it, or even to learn it, 'the difference between the accomplishments of one group . . . and another . . . is of another order from the difference between the faculties of one person and another.'

Kroeber's general conclusions are that culture, although an order of phenomena distinct from the organic and mental, stands upon or is rooted in them; that culture is not, because it cannot

---

[1]Kroeber's essay, "The Superorganic," seems to be meant. Rappaport is challenging in this context Freeman's historical researches reported on pp. 5-6, 38-48 of *Margaret Mead and Samoa.*—Ed.

be, transmitted genetically; that it is, and can only be, transmitted through language and modes of communication contingent upon language; and that no differences between "racial" groups in their genetically given capacities to create, maintain, learn, or transmit culture are known. How Freeman could have so misread the positions of Boas and his students on the relations among race, culture, and biology as to represent them as forms of "absolute cultural determinism" is not easy to understand. Deliberately or not, his account misrepresents the Boasians and, inasmuch as he asserts that the imaginary sins of ancestors afflict their descendants, it also misrepresents subsequent developments in American anthropology.

It is difficult to generalize about the orientation of contemporary American anthropology. The discipline has expanded enormously since Boas' time. The American Anthropological Association has more than eight thousand members now, and the variety of their concerns reflects the complexity of the species that constitutes their subject matter. Medical anthropology, which is directly concerned with the interaction of cultural and organic processes, is an expanding speciality nowadays, and ecological theories that take human individuals and groups to be organisms adapting to environments through cultural means are also influential. The limits of various specialties are such that many anthropologists are not directly concerned with the interaction between organic and cultural processes. Even so, it would be hard to find any who would subscribe to a "doctrine of absolute cultural determinism." Moreover, "a view of human evolution in which the genetic and exogenetic are distinct but interacting parts of a single system," as Freeman puts it in his book, has long been part of American anthropology's received wisdom. Freeman's vague concluding suggestions for "a more scientific anthropological paradigm" are as inapposite as the critique that proceeded them is obtuse.

It is safe to say that most American anthropologists, following Alfred Kroeber, and later Leslie White and others, take culture to be an order of phenomena based upon symbols in Charles Sanders Peirce's sense. (A symbol is a sign related "only by law"—that is, convention—to that which it signifies.) American anthropologists also generally agree that the symbol and culture emerged in the hominid line, through processes of natural selection, as part of the adaptive apparatus of our forebears. Although some other species may make limited use of symbols, it is apparently only among hominids that full language—with its capacities to predicate, to name, to generate an infinite number of utterances at once novel and comprehensible—has emerged. Language and the cultural usages contingent upon it leave no unambiguous fossil evidence, but hominid evolution from the *Australopitheci-nae* to the present is generally conceived as a "mutual causal," "dialectic," or "positive feedback" interaction between "genetic and exogenetic" (linguistic and cultural) components of an emerging humanity. The culmination in genetically endowed linguistic and cultural capacities was almost certainly reached with the appearance of *Homo sapiens sapiens* around forty thousand years ago, but perhaps earlier with the appearance of *Homo sapiens neanderthalensis*, or even with late *Homo erectus*. Thus, the enormous elaboration of culture over the past forty thousand years has been unaccompanied by anatomical indications of commensurate changes in mental capacity. In the absence of such evidence, cultural differences prevailing among the many societies into which the species has been and is divided can be better explained by history than biology.

Language and culture must have emerged through processes of natural selection as part of the adaptive apparatus of the hominids, but their significance transcends the human species. Leslie White claimed in *The Science of Culture* that the appearance of the symbol—by which he meant language—was not simply an evolutionary novelty enhancing the survival chances of its possessors but the most revolutionary innovation in the evolutionary process itself since life first appeared. If he was exaggerating, it was not by much. The symbol may have been no more than the most far-reaching advance to appear in evolution since the advent of sex. The recombination of genetic information in each generation not only accelerates by magnitudes rates of evolutionary change over what is possible in asexual reproduction, but also lays the ground for sociability. Transmission of information through language is yet more elaborate, comprehensive, and rapid; but the significance of language is not confined to the transmission of information. With language, whole new universes (composed, in part, of meanings) evolve. Conceptions unimaginable to nonverbal creatures—Truth, Honor, Sin, Evil, the Possible, the Impossible, Heaven, God, Equality, Kinship, Race—are created out of language. The universe inhabited by humans is in part constituted by lawful evolutionary processes—

galactic, tectonic, ecological, and genetic—and in part culturally constructed out of concepts imagined into being.

Such conceptions are not simply the possessions of the particular human groups in which they emerged. In the course of evolution the relationship has become, in part, inverted. The conceptions have come to possess those who have conceived them. As cultural constructions have continued to serve human organisms as central elements in their many modes of adaptation to the physical world, so, conversely, have humans come to serve and perpetuate the conceptions that provide them with meaning.

Natural law and conventional meaning, the lawful and the meaningful are not coextensive, and they are differently known. If the laws of nature and the states of affairs they constitute are to be known, they must be discovered. In contrast, humankind's meanings must be constructed and accepted. Discovered laws and facts may provide some of the materials out of which meanings are made, but by themselves they do not constitute meaning, nor can they do meaning's work of organizing human action. Conversely, although constructed meanings are often represented as discovered law, they do not constitute nature. The laws of nature and the states of affairs contingent upon them are the case, whether or not they are known.

The lawful emergence, in the course of evolution, of the ability to construct meaning provided humanity with no exemption from natural law, but it did increase by magnitudes their capacity not only to conceive the world but to misconstrue it as well. Evolutionary advances always create new problems as they respond to older ones, and culture itself was no exception. It must have emerged as part of the adaptive apparatus of a particular species, but it has not remained unambiguously adaptive. The cost of perpetuating some of culture's conceptions—fatherland, free enterprise, the True God, socialism, racial superiority—always great, have become greater as technology has become ever more powerful and the dangers following from misconstructions of the world have grown ever more deadly.

Contrary to what Freeman has written, contemporary American anthropology does not divorce culture from biology. It is, in fact, centrally concerned with a species that must live by meanings it itself must construct, only loosely constrained by its nature from fashioning self-destructive or world-destroying follies, in a world devoid of intrinsic meaning but subject to incompletely understood causal laws.

If law and meaning have different places in the world and if they are differently known, it follows that the consideration opposite to the assessment of scientific texts—verisimilitude, inclusiveness, parsimony, elegance, productivity, and perhaps even falsifiability—are not necessarily appropriate for the judgment of texts devoted to the construction of meaning, a class into which myth falls. If myths are texts in which problematic aspects of the world are represented and in which conventions are both sanctified and naturalized, it seems reasonable to judge them by the courses of action they justify or inspire and by the nature of the societies they edify.

But the matter is not so simple. Some texts cannot be assigned exclusively to one category or the other. As Margaret Mead knew better than any other anthropologist of her time, ethnography should make available to humanity as a whole what it discovers about law and meaning in individual societies so that humanity as a whole, through some of the individuals composing it (including, perhaps, ethnographers), can construct larger conceptions of itself and its place in nature.

Coming of Age in Samoa stands up well to the criteria against which both classes of text are to be judged. A pioneering work in culture and personality, Mead's study was sensitive and filled with insight, even if unidimensional. Not so much incorrect as thin and in need of enrichment, it did make a modest contribution to Samoan ethnography.

The "main lessons" Mead drew from her ethnography for American society, or even for humanity as a whole, have borne up better. That relations between generations under conditions of accelerating culture change would become increasingly difficult was an accurate prediction . . . . The insistence upon human plasticity and educability upon which her didactic chapters are founded still conforms to scientific consensus about the lack of relationship between race and cultural capacity. The meanings she constructed were not then, nor are they now, in violation of discovered fact or law, as were those of the eugenicists. Her position was, and remains, better science than theirs.

And better myth. Matters might not have been so clear in the first decades of the century, but the results are in now, and from the the end of the century we can see where both myths led. Looking back through the successful assimilation into American life of the south and east Europeans whose immigration so alarmed [the eugenicists], through the continuing emancipation of blacks and women, through changes in the conventions of sex and through the Holocaust, one finds it is easy to choose the myth derived from Mead's vision of Samoa over the naturalization and sanctification of hatred and oppression intrinsic to the eugenicist's myth of a northern European herrenvolk.

Its work being done, Mead's Samoan revelation and her exegesis of it are fading from the American mythos. It will be replaced by other texts, of course. The world is always full of candidates for canonization, and the choice, if choice there is, for any individual or society is not between myth and no myth but among accounts contending for mythic status. We will be well served if those we choose are as humane and liberating as the text Mead gave us.

Against Cultural Determinism

The Disunity of Anthropology
and the Unity of Mankind

Robin Fox

Editor's Note

Robin Fox is a leading exponent of interactionist anthropology. His study, *The Imperial Animal,* co-authored with Lionel Tiger in 1974, was an early attempt to synthesize the ethological and anthropological literature into a picture of human social behavior in evolutionary perspective. The present selection is taken from a lecture that Fox delivered at the University of Notre Dame in 1986. He begins with a description of the theoretical diversity of contemporary anthropology, traces this condition to historical wrong turns that separated the social from the biological, and sketches a framework for interactionist anthropology that redresses what he claims is a false dichotomy. The crux of Fox's critique—that human social interaction lies no less in the plane of biology than does individual psychology—is based on the ethologist's reductive analysis of social interaction into adaptive social behavior, whose patterns are observable cross-culturally and cross-species. Fox's essay was published in *Waymarks: The Notre Dame Inaugural Lectures in Anthropology,* ed. Kenneth Moore, pp. 17-41, Notre Dame University Press, 1987. Reprinted by permission of the Notre Dame University Press.

. . . Specialization is only healthy within a science unified by an accepted general theory (or paradigm, as it has become fashionable to call it). The life sciences, unified by the theory of natural selection, can specialize merrily with profit. They can argue about and modify the theory itself without damaging consequences. Anthropology, however, is unified only by a concern with culture, not by a general theory of it. Any disputes about this subject matter, turning as they do on points of definition and ideology, are preludes to even further fragmentation. The affluent hordes of new anthropologists seized on each new fragment and elaborated it. The result is the present chaos and darkness over which Notre Dame is brooding like the biblical dove. Can order be brought out of this chaos? Perhaps, but certainly not in seven days.

One of the consequences of this recent history is that most anthropologists have given up the idea of a unified anthropology and have accepted the necessity of fragmentation as a virtue. Anthropology simply becomes an employment convenience—a useful fiction that administrators accept as valid and which provides a suitable cover for intellectual espionage. Departments go on stubbornly appointing the quota of linguistic anthropologists, symbolic anthropologists, physical anthropologists, archaeological anthropologists, mathematical anthropologists, medical anthropologists, applied anthropologists, ecological anthropologists, primatological anthropologists, psychological anthropologists, feminist anthropologists, cognitive anthropologists, structural anthropologists, marxist anthropologists, urban anthropologists, and, in California, paranormal anthropologists. They do this knowing that they are simply housing these people in the same corridor and with no real expectation that they will do more than preach to each other. Their professional organization, which started as a learned society and was one of America's most distinguished, has now become simply a trade union and lobbying operation for all those who call themselves "anthropologists" and pay their dues. They have nothing left in common, it seems, except the prospect of unemployment. They are a vested academic interest to be protected, not a collegiate body which exists for learned disputation. The ultimate irony is that a group of concerned members have now founded a new society within the American Anthropological Association called the "Society for Cultural Anthropology"! It's that bad.

So much for fragmentation and the institutional problems. I have alluded also to the "ideological quagmire" and this is, of course, a contributor to the fragmentation. I have argued elsewhere and at length on this subject and it gets dangerously close to original sin, so I shall merely summarize here.

Anthropology is an heir to the humanist, empiricist, liberal tradition that started with the Renaissance, coalesced in the Enlightenment, and became a serious political force in the nineteenth century. Darwin added fuel to this position; he did not, as is often wrongly assumed, start it for anthropology. It is indeed curious today to see Darwinism so freely associated with reaction, when in its origins it appeared as a revolutionary materialism threatening the whole Establishment. But anthropology was ambivalent during its formative period. In England it split apart on the slavery issue: there was always a reactionary wing. In America it found itself having to take a stand on eugenics. How quickly we forget our intellectual history. How many anthropologists could give a coherent account of the once powerful eugenics movement and its alliance with the Progressive Party? This presented a real dilemma to anthropology. The "split mind" I have referred to elsewhere began here. Tylor had uncompromisingly declared anthropology "a reformer's science"—particularly in its role as sweeper away of "survivals," as in religion. The Darwinian theory of evolution gave anthropology an uncompromising materialist base. Yet there was much hesitation on this score. Matthew Arnold in fact elaborated the modern concept of "culture" for the middle classes to fill the gap left by the receding tide of faith. These two notions of culture sat uncomfortably side by side: Tylor's materialistic, reformist view, and Arnold's integrative and uplifting notion of sweetness and light. Strangely, it was a view of culture more like Arnold's that prevailed in social science, although this again has not been recognized, except by George Stocking.

Anthropology had banished faith and raised the specter of race. It had to accept evolution, and human variation was real. But how could this be reconciled with its liberal, reformist stance? Anthropology temporized. It mitigated the harshness of its potential materialism and banished the eugenicist/racist specter by elaborating the concept of "culture" as non-genetic, superorganic, *sui generis*. Even Huxley had felt driven to make the distinction between "cosmic evolution" and "ethical evolution," and anthropology seized on this distinction to restore the uniqueness of man. In fact anthropology recast itself in the role of defender-of-the-faith in the uniqueness of man, and thus usurped the church which was still floundering with the concept of the "soul."

In America Kroeber elaborated the doctrine of culture as superorganic, and cultural determinism was launched. Boas sweepingly declared genetics irrelevant and invented the implicit formula:

$$genetic = race \neq culture$$

thus preserving culture from contamination and launching cultural relativism. All this happily coincided with the rise of behaviorism and this seemed to clinch the issue.

In Europe, in a related development, but one with different roots, the answer was to follow the explicit formulations of Durkheim on society and social facts. No one knows quite whether to claim Durkheim for liberalism or conservatism, and he was indeed ambivalent. He ended life as a guild socialist and admired Saint Simon. But he too was torn between his adherence to the scientific, i.e. materialist, positivist tradition, and a concern, like Arnold's, for the anarchistic consequences of the failure of traditional institutions like the church. Comte, the father of sociology, solved the problem by founding his own church. Durkheim was more subtle. His answer: society was God, and its members constituted a church. But this had to be phrased in positivist terms. Thus "society" became for him (as "culture" had become in America) a reality *sui generis*, to be examined scientifically through the study of social facts. These were (a) exterior to the individual, (b) general in the society, and (c) exercised constraint on the individual through the "collective conscience." Thus Durkheim's political concerns, and the supposedly positivistic science of society, ended in a kind of sociological mysticism. Society was reified, and Durkheim, in his eagerness to carve out a piece of reality for his science, consigned psychology and biology to the individual, producing his basic equation:

$$\text{individual} = \text{biological} \neq \text{social}$$

If we put the two formulae together, then we get:

$$\text{individual/biological/genetic/racial} \neq \text{social/cultural}$$

This became the ideological linchpin of the social sciences. And for sociology it was not so bad. But for anthropology it created the schizophrenic situation to which I have alluded. For anthropology's distinctiveness lay in its grounding in the theory of physical evolution. The ideological formula, however, sundered this from the study of culture/society.

While we are on the concept of culture, it is worth noting that Boas, Kroeber, and Kluckhohn, for example, were particularly influenced by the German formulation of the idea which had its origins in Hegel and the rise of nineteenth-century nationalism. This was clearly more influential than either Tylor or Arnold (although Arnold was not himself uninfluenced by it). Its clearest expression was probably in the work of the German Romantic Nationalist, Herder. It is ironic then to follow the fortunes of the idea in American anthropology, for one of its major consequences was the doctrine of cultural relativism: each culture was an entity unto itself, understandable on its own terms, judged only by its own standards. This was conceived as a liberal onslaught on the racists and eugenicists. Genetics was not responsible for cultural differences, culture was. Papa Boas trained various attractive young ladies at Columbia to go out and pursue this, and they dutifully did so. With Benedict it was transparent, and that Mead was more influenced by ideology than ethnography has been recently demonstrated by Freeman (although to her credit she acknowledged this herself). Cultural relativism attacked the twin sins of "ethnocentrism" and "racism," and it became another fixed dogma that this was the only answer possible. In effect, this "answer" played right into the hands of the very ethnocentrism it sought to combat. It said that every culture had the right to be ethnocentric. What it was attacking was European ethnocentrism, not ethnocentrism as such.

The real answer to the problem they were addressing—as to all problems of the growing social sciences—was of course "species-centricism," if we can coin a phrase: Marx and Feuerbach's "species being"; and the precious store of variation. The tragedy is that anthropology by its very nature as a distinctive science, that is, by its commitment to man's biological being through the study of his evolution, was the perfect science to insist on this. It threw away the chance. The ideological and methodological traps it set itself with the Durkheimian and Boasian formulae led in the opposite direction. The steady, and at times hysterical, attempts to separate the social and the biological have eroded that special position, erected a new dogma, and fragmented a promising science. Cultural anthropology, with its rampant doctrine of cultural relativism, is in fact a bastard child of German Romantic Nationalism. As such, it is paradoxically closer to the racism and fascism it fears than is a biologically based science, whose basic tenet is Washburn's empirically established position that all human races share 97% of their physical traits in common.

The only real opposition to relativism has come from those anthropologists interested in universals of culture. But the majority of these were themselves cultural determinists. The closest they came to a notion of culture as biology was the doctrine of the "psychic unity of mankind"—itself developed in opposition to diffusionism. Thus, if similar institutions or traits appeared in all societies, it was because of standard human responses to similar problems.

They didn't want to take it further than that, and those like Wissler who insisted that the logic of this was that cross-cultural uniformities were "in the genome" were politely dismissed as cranks. Much of the weakness of this school lay in the difficulty it had in defining the units by which to measure universals. Very often, as in the case of "the nuclear family" the question was begged by definition. In other cases the proposed universals were so vague—"a system of social control"—as to be simply part of the definition of the social order itself. Almost all attempts concentrated on what linguists came to call "substantive" universals. And the parallel search by linguists had some important lessons: the search for substantive universals seemed barren; if there were universals they were at the level of *process*.

[Clifford] Geertz has been lauded for having given the death blow to the search for universals. This argument: the "universal" capacity that distinguishes man is his capacity to learn culture; thus when we see people displaying the unique behavior of their particular cultures we are in effect witnessing the universal. Thus we can forget the problem of universals and get down to the real business of examining the particular cultures. A neat argument that slips in relativity by the back door and allows anthropologists to continue business as usual. No wonder they like Geertz.

But while it is the truth and nothing but the truth, it is not the whole truth, because the acquisition of culture is not arbitrary: Why are cultures acquired in the way they are and not some other way—or infinitely different ways? They may be unique at the level of specific content—like languages—but at the level of the processes there are remarkable uniformities—like language again. Geertz wants to confound the varied manifestations of the processes with the processes themselves. Thus each outcome of a universal process can look very different. But it is nowhere written that universal processes should have identical outcomes; in fact it is in the nature of such processes that they should *not*.

. . . What then of the nature of the process? This is where I believe the search for universals ties in with the problems presented by the Boas/Durkheim formulae. Let me try it this way: it was correct to emphasize the reality of the social collectivity as more than the sum of the individuals and their actions; it was wrong to insist that this collectivity could not be biological in nature. It was correct to say the collectivity could not be reduced to the sum of its individuals, but wrong to assign the individual to the biological sphere and cut off society and culture from their biological roots. It was a mistake to assume that the biological basis of local variations could only arise directly from genetic, i.e., racial sources.

Anthropology as Anti-Science

J. Timothy O'Meara

Editor's Note

O'Meara's essay undertakes to describe and refute the "critical reflexivity" widespread in anthropology and the social sciences today. Its temper opposes the firm and decisive knowledge implied by the concept of refutation. Freeman's unhesitating willingness to "speak in the name of the real" produced a sense of astonishment and aversion among those who think themselves authorized to speak only in the name of appearances. From their perspective his study was wayward and out-of-step (see Ivan Brady's Addendum, above, and Freeman's Letter to G. E. Marcus below). O'Meara notes that the clashing epistemologies are old hat and "should not have to be debated again." Most of the arguments do indeed occur in classical sources, so that, notwithstanding the aura of timeliness, we are probably, in this dispute, witnessing yet another recycling of *philosophia perennis.* The protagonists in this debate each claim that a specific subjective benefit accrues from their respective philosophies: calmness, or relief from anxiety. Just this benefit, *ataraxia,* was claimed by the protagonists of antiquity.

Returning recently from an extended period of fieldwork in Samoa, I was surprised to find anti-science sentiments still gain-ing in popularity as the critics make ever bolder declarations. Labelled the "romantic rebellion" by Shweder (1986), more and more anthropologists are rejecting the empirical basis, logical methods, and explanatory goals of science as being inappropriate for the study of human affairs. They are, as Tyler says, "dedicated more to honesty than truth" (1984:335). The rebels hail their rejection of science as a liberation. I find it rather more distressing.

My purpose here is to defend the validity of scientific anthropology by showing that the critic's anti-science arguments are invalid. Whatever benefits their own approaches may offer, such benefits neither derive from nor imply that the application of the scientific method to the explanation of human affairs is either impossible or undesirable, as the critics maintain.

The Anti-Science Position

Critics believe that the goal of science (i.e., lawful explanation) and the "scientific" method are inappropriate for the study of social phenomena. Reasons differ, but their doubts generally stem from difficulties arising from the role of choice in human affairs and from subjectivity in the observation and interpretation of social phenomena. Because of these problems, some anthropologists argue that we must abandon science and turn instead to the humanities for guidance. For example, Shweder (1984:28) states:

> A central tenet of the romanticist view holds that ideas and practices have their foundation in neither logic nor empirical science, that ideas and practices fall beyond the scope of deductive and inductive reason, that ideas and practices are neither rational nor irrational but rather nonrational.

Leach (1984) ridicules anthropologists for even speaking of their work as "science." He denies the "underlying assumption that the ethnographic 'facts' recorded by anthropological observers in the field have some kind of objective reality," claiming instead that "the data which derive from fieldwork are subjective not objective" (ibid:3-4).

The most strident critic is Stephen A. Tyler. He believes that all science is impossible because "there is no origin of perception, no priority to vision, and no data of observation" (1986:137).

He claims that "scientific discourse, particularly in the social sciences, is deeply mendacious" (1984:335). Tyler advocates ethnopoetics or the post-modern ethnography, an "emergent fantasy" whose goal is "neither description nor production, but evocation"—which places it "beyond truth and immune to the judgement of performance" (1986:125,123).

While the anti-scientists differ in many of their views, most are united by a belief that the study of social phenomena is unlike the study of purely physical phenomena in two fundamental ways. First, they assert that the most interesting and distinctive aspect of social and psychological phenomena is their "subjective nature"—i.e., people's thoughts and other actions are characterized by sensations, feelings, and emotions that are experienced privately by individuals and are thus not directly observable. Consequently, they argue, it is not possible to analyze social phenomena using logical methods that require objective proof. As Vendler concludes, "science has no foothold on subjective states."

Second, anti-scientists argue that social phenomena have multiple meanings, and that "knowledge" or "understanding" is gained by discovering those meanings rather than by scientific explanation of the phenomena themselves. They acknowledge that this method leads different researchers to different, though equally "valid," interpretations. Some authors . . . believe that this is their method's greatest strength—producing a Babel of voices that expresses, evokes, or enriches the world of experience. Other anti-scientists seem more embarrassed by this slippery state of affairs.

For example, [Clifford] Geertz states that "the besetting sin of interpretive approaches to anything . . . is that they tend to resist . . . systematic modes of assessment. You either grasp an interpretation or you don't" (1973a:24). Other than his prescription to maintain a hold on the minutiae of ethnographic description, however, Geertz doesn't propose a criterion by which different interpretations might be "appraised." He suggests only that "we must measure the cogency of our explications . . . against the power of the scientific imagination to bring us into touch with the lives of strangers." Thus, Geertz and other anti-scientists believe that statements about "subjective" phenomena can only be assessed subjectively.

A Critique of the Anti-Science Position
    In order to evaluate the critics' rejection of science, we first need to accept a working definition of what they reject. I will use "science" to mean the systematic description and classification of objects, events, and processes (both particular and general), and the lawful explanation of those events and processes by theories testable against publicly observable data.
    We should also acknowledge at the outset that "subjective" and "objective" are relative terms. All of our perceptions and thoughts, and all of our verbal and physical expressions are filtered through and formed by our senses, our knowledge, our culturally formed "tropes" and "frames," and a host of private perversions. As D'Andrade says, all "facts" are interpretive (1986:24-25). While this recognition damages an earlier, naive inductionist philosophy of science, it supports the necessity of a deductionist philosophy (Jarvie 1986:214-215, 224). We will also have to be content with inferring what our fellows' thoughts and experiences are from observation of their overt actions. But since these restrictions on objectivity are characteristic of human beings as observers rather than the things we observe, they provide no basis for distinguishing between inquiries into physical and social phenomena, as the critics believe.
    The debate over the unity of logical methods in the social and the physical sciences is an ancient one. The current rebellion is but a minor skirmish in a battle ignited by John Locke over three hundred years ago, the war itself having begun centuries earlier. Many of the arguments raised by the modern rebels have been dealt with adequately in previous campaigns and should not have to be debated again. Some anthropologists have recently attacked social science on points that are sufficiently novel, however, to warrant inspection. I will examine five arguments, beginning with one concerning the nature of refutation, upon which hinges much of the anti-science position:
    ARGUMENT 1: Use of the scientific method is inappropriate in anthropology because statements about social phenomena, unlike statements about purely biological or physical phenomena, are not susceptible to refutation or disproof.

REJOINDER 1: THE IMPOSSIBILITY OF DISPROOF
    It is axiomatic among pro-science anthropologists . . . that while one can never prove that a particular statement is true, "one single observation may falsify it, serving logically as a counter-

example to it" (Ember 1985:911). This is the method used by Margaret Mead in her famous "negative instance" where she argued that her cultural data on Samoan society disproved the then-current theory that adolescent rebellion is caused by the biological process of puberty. And 55 years later Derek Freeman used the same logic, based on the writings of Sir Karl Popper, to refute Mead's original argument.

Popper states that no accumulation of positive cases can ever justify the acceptance of a theory as true, a position that is now universally accepted. He also contends, however, that "the assumption of the truth of test statements sometimes allows us to justify the claim that an explanatory universal theory is false," (1972:7) an overstatement that has confused both pro- and anti-science factions. This confusion, in turn, underlies much of the debate of the use of the scientific method of anthropology, and the specific debate over Freeman's refutation of statements made by Mead in her Samoan ethnography.

In rejecting Freeman's refutation of Mead's Samoan work, many American anthropologists simply deny the applicability of refutation in anthropology. For example, Shore denies that "social 'facts'" are amenable to "simple refutation in the Popperian sense." He argues that "simply bringing to bear on a statement *evidence that is contradictory* is not in the human sciences sufficient to disprove that statement" (1983:943, my emphasis). The import of this view is that the truth of statements about social phenomena—unlike purely physical phenomena—cannot be tested against empirical data.

I believe that the anti-scientists' rejection of refutation in social analysis is based on the misunderstanding of two logical limits of disproof, limits that apply equally to the analysis of social and physical phenomena. Understanding these limits will show why the rejection of refutation, because of a supposed uniqueness of social phenomena, is unwarranted.

LIMIT 1: In order to disprove a statement, we would first have to prove that the object or event is indeed a "negative instance." But no accumulation of evidence can prove this to be true. Thus we can never prove that we have found a negative instance that would, in turn, prove the statement to be false.

LIMIT 2: Even assuming that the descriptive test statement is true and that it contradicts the prediction of the explanatory theory, it still does not allow us to mechanically reject that theory as necessarily false. For contradictory evidence tells us only that *at least one* of the premises of the explanatory argument is false, but not which one.

There are always many stated and unstated premises to an argument, any of which might be false. But the number of these premises is not just very large, it is infinite. The premises of any explanatory argument include not only an explicit statement of all those conditions that are thought to cause the particular event (and perhaps an explicit statement of various auxiliary hypotheses, assumptions, or boundary conditions), it also includes the implicit assumption that every other condition not stated is irrelevant. This assumption, of course, has an infinite number of parts, for there is always an infinite number of conditions that we think are irrelevant to the argument at hand. Unfortunately, later experience may show that one or more of these conditions was relevant after all.

Since there is an infinite number of premises, no accumulation of "negative instances" can ever narrow the field to a single premise that must, of logical necessity, be false. Therefore, even if we assume that we have a negative instance, this does not necessarily imply that the theory itself is false, rather than one of the other premises. As Paul Feyerabend says, "theories cannot be refuted by facts."

But the import of this conclusion is not, as the anti-scientists believe, that hypothesis testing is pointless. The import is simply that nothing is known to be absolutely true or false. We may only know things with greater or lesser certainty, or, as some would say, with higher or lower probability.

Given the same data, different people may calculate the probability of truth or falsity of an argument differently. This is one area where subjectivity enters into all scientific research. Sometimes the subjective element is large. For example, when judging the veracity of the tales of sexual intrigue told to Mead by her young informants, different people hold widely different opinions on the probability that Mead was duped. But another test of the same question may have a very small subjective element. For example, there would be more unity of opinion on the probability that twelve menstruating and presumably fertile girls could have engaged in sex for periods ranging from two months to four years without a single pregnancy occurring, as Mead reported.

The critics are correct, then, in noting that contradictory evidence can not disprove a descriptive statement or a theory. But this has nothing to do, as they suppose, with a presumed uniqueness of social inquiry. The reasons for the impossibility of disproof are formal and logical and apply equally to all descriptive and explanatory statements, rather than being specific only to statements about human affairs. Therefore, the logical limits of disproof provide no justification for rejecting the use of refutation in the social sciences when it is demonstrably successful in the physical and biological sciences.

Since refutation is never "mechanical" or "absolute," but requires in every case the informed judgement of individuals, it obviously follows that all science is practiced within a social, historical, and psychological matrix . . . . This may inhibit progress in both the physical and social sciences, but the difficulties require not the rejection of refutation or of science itself . . . but rather the adoption of refutation as a method for controlling and eliminating human bias.

Many critics would advance two additional arguments to support their rejection of refutation in anthropology:

ARGUMENT 2: Science is not appropriate for cultural analysis because the primary subjects of cultural analysis—"frames, paradigms, absolute presuppositions, or constitutive premises" (Shweder 1984:40)—are nonrational or arbitrary, and therefore not subject to true-false testing.

For example, Shweder notes (correctly) that not all kinds of statements are subject to true-false testing. Declarative statements, for example, which include classifications and statements such as "God blesses men in the sign of their prosperity," are neither true nor false. Shweder argues that "the conceptual underpinnings of a social order are (ultimately) nonrational and . . . many of the customary practices of a society . . . are symbolic expressions of those nonrational choices [sic]" (ibid, 46). He concludes by defining "culture as arbitrary code" whose study is outside the realm of science.

Shweder's argument thus moves from correctly noting the existence of particular nonrational statements to an erroneous conclusion that the entire "domains" about which those statements are made are themselves nonrational. These views are broadly shared by other critics.

REJOINDER 2: CULTURE AS ARBITRARY CODE

I have three objections to this argument that culture is "arbitrary" and therefore outside the realm of science.

1) The view that culture consists of various forms of symbolic meaning is an artifice designed to exclude by definition the more obviously rational and mundane affairs of human existence, such as technological, political, and economic thought and activity.

2) The semiotic "world view" that certain broad classes of human behavior are arbitrary and thus without cause is a hypothesis that can be tested by empirical research, i.e., by science. In effect, the anti-scientists illicitly maintain the *a priori* assumption that the null hypothesis (no relationship between variables) is *always* true in certain broad domains, and furthermore that this a priori assumption should not be tested.

3) Statements such as "God blesses men in the sign of their prosperity" are non-falsifiable, as Shweder says. But Shweder's argument does not spring from this truism. Instead, he has confused the rationality status of belief in and action upon a statement with the rationality status of the statement itself. His implicit and illegitimate argument is that if a *statement* of belief is nonrational, to *believe* in and *act* upon that statement must also be nonrational. But the latter is an open question that cannot be decided a priori by the researcher.

ARGUMENT 3: Human cultures, personalities, and behavior are composed of contradictory elements. Since contradiction is inherent in our cultural world, no contradictory empirical evidence can refute a statement about culture. For example, adding to the Mead/Freeman debate, Shore states:

> What is wrong, in the end, with the kind of absolute, formal refutation that is the hallmark of Popperian science and that informs Freeman's book is that it pretends that the "facts" of human existence operate like some bloodless, mindless machine according to the strictest principles of Aristotelian noncontradiction. And yet human life is riddled with contradiction . . . . Simply bringing to bear on a statement evidence that is contradictory is not in the *human sciences* [my emphasis] sufficient to disprove that statement. Does the Samoan orator refute the dignified *ali'i*? Does the passive in us refute the aggressive, or our virtue refute our vice? Does Lucifer, the highest of archangels, refute Lucifer the devil? (1983:943).

REJOINDER 3: THE "TRUTH VALUE" OF THINGS

This argument confuses the truth value of statements made about worldly things with a supposed truth value of the things themselves. Descriptive and explanatory *statements* concerning the real world are always either true or false. As statements they are refutable, keeping in mind the limits discussed above. But Samoan orators and *ali'i*, the passive and aggressive in us, Lucifer, archangels, and the devil are all *things*. As things, they are neither true nor false—they simply are or are not.

In addition to their arguments rejecting the method of science (i.e., refutation), critics present two arguments rejecting the goal of science, i.e., lawful explanation. The first of these arguments rejects the possibility of determining causes of human affairs. The second advocates the interpretation of meaning as the proper way to understand those affairs.

ARGUMENT 4: Science is inappropriate for the study of human affairs because those affairs have "meanings," rather than causes. And since these "meanings" vary with context, the understanding of human affairs is achieved by interpreting those meanings and giving detailed (or "thick") descriptions of those contexts; or as Frankel says, by "describing patterns rather than discovering causes" (1986:356).

REJOINDER 4: DENIAL OF CAUSE AND INTERPRETATION OF MEANING

The Denial of Cause. The major arguments supporting the denial of cause in human affairs have been identified and refuted by Nagel, Brodbeck, and Gellner, among others. I will not repeat those arguments here. I will, however, comment briefly on a common but erroneous argument that confuses causal explanation with prediction. According to this argument, the test of any causal explanation is whether it allows the accurate prediction of the explained phenomenon in the future; and since the accurate prediction of future events is regularly achieved in some of the physical sciences, but less often in the social sciences, it is therefore impossible to explain human affairs causally.

This conclusion might seem to follow from Hume's classic argument that "cause" is not some strange force that impels things to occur, but is instead simply the "constant conjunction" of certain conditions. According to critics, since the "conjunctions" found in explanations of human affairs are rarely "constant," causal explanations are therefore inappropriate for human affairs. But this conclusion is in error on two counts:

1) While an explanatory argument states the conditions under which a certain phenomenon will (always) occur, that statement includes not only an explicit list of the (few) "causal" conditions, it also includes an implicit, *ceterus paribus* list of the remaining (infinite) conditions that—in their present states—are thought to be irrelevant (or are incompletely understood, such ignorance resulting in imperfect prediction—hence the appearance of so-called "statistical explanations"). A change in any of those "irrelevant" conditions, however, might confound the effect of the original "causal" conditions. For example, the conditions that caused the Russian Revolution might have occurred again under Stalin's reign of terror, but in that case the increased military power of the central government prevented another revolution from occurring.

2) A related error is that the argument confuses the valid requirement that an explanation correctly predict the occurrence of a phenomenon *when* its causal conditions occur with an invalid requirement that we be able to predict when those conditions themselves will co-occur.

Anthropology's romanticists also feel that causal explanations of human affairs somehow "dehumanize" people, and that to do so is thus either immoral or impossible. But this ostrich-like behavior is misplaced, being apparently a reaction left over from earlier debates with knee-jerk behaviorists.

Causal explanations state the conditions under which specified events or processes will occur, together with the mechanism through which those conditions have their effect. But there is certainly no requirement that all of those causal conditions must be external to the human actors. Indeed, recognizing that no matter how severe the constraints on our lives, the choice remains how or whether we choose to act. Thus, in order for an explanation of human affairs to be valid, its causal conditions *must* include the hopes, values, emotions, or ideals of individual human beings. Furthermore, in order for us to comprehend the explanation of another person's behavior (let alone another society's behavior), we must share at least *some* of that person's basic psychological conditions.

In addition to including some internal psychological states among the *causal conditions*, the *causal mechanism* through these conditions have their effect must *always* be the minds of individual human beings. Superorganic entities such as "culture," "symbols," or "structures" are unacceptable. To accept causal mechanisms other than the minds of individuals certainly would "dehumanize" people.

References

Clifford, James and George E. Marcus, eds. 1986. *Writing Culture: The Poetics and Politics of Ethnography*. Berkeley: University of California Press.

D'Andrade, Roy. 1984. Cultural meaning systems, in Shweder and Levine, 1984:88-119.

Ember, Melvin. 1985. Evidence and science in ethnography: Reflections on the Freeman-Mead Controversy, *American Anthropologist* 87:906-917.

Fiske, Donald W. and Richard A. Shweder, eds. 1986. *Metatheory in Social Science: Pluralisms and Subjectivities*. Chicago: The University of Chicago Press.

Frankel, Barbara. 1986. Two extremes on the social science commitment continuum, in Fiske and Shweder, eds., 1986:353-361.

Geertz, Clifford. 1973a. Thick description: toward an interpretive theory of culture, in Geertz, 1973:3-30.

Geertz, Clifford, ed. 1973b. *The Interpretation of Cultures*. New York: Basic Books.

Jarvie, I. C. 1986. *Thinking about Society: Theory and Practice*. Dortrecht: Reidel.

Leach, Edmund. 1984. Glimpses of the unmentionable in the history of British social anthropology, *Annual Review of Anthropology* 13:1-23.

Popper, Karl R. 1972. *Objective Knowledge: An Evolutionary Approach*. London: Oxford University Press.

Shweder, Richard A. 1986. Divergent rationalities, in Fiske and Shweder, 1986:163-196.

Shweder, Richard A. 1984. Anthropology's romantic rebellion against the enlightenment, or there's more to thinking than reason and evidence, in Shweder and Levine, eds., pp. 27-66.

Shweder, Richard A. and Robert Levine, eds. 1984. *Culture Theory: Essays on Mind, Self, and Emotion*. Cambridge: Cambridge University Press.

Shore, Bradd. 1983. Paradox regained: Freeman's *Margaret Mead and Samoa*, *American Anthropologist* 85:935-944.

Tyler, Stephen A. 1984. The poetic turn in postmodern anthropology: The poetry of Paul Friedrich, *American Anthropologist* 86:328-336.
Tyler, Stephen A. 1986. Post-modern ethnography: From document of the occult to occult document, in Clifford and Marcus, pp. 122-140.

The Significance of Freeman's Refutation[1]

George N. Appell

In 1916 [John] Bennett published a critically important article
on anthropological explanation. He detailed the contradictory interpretations of Pueblo culture that had appeared in the ethnographic literature and advanced an explanation for this. However, in the reviews of Freeman's book there has been no mention of the possible relevance of this study for understanding the
Samoan controversy.
  Bennett (1946) distinguishes two approaches to socio-cultural
reality: the "organic" or "configurationist," and the "repressive."
He agues that the "configurationist" approach has certain biases
which has resulted in presenting Pueblo culture and society as
being "integrated to an unusual degree, all sectors being bound
by a consistent, harmonious set of values. Associated with this
integrated configuration is an ideal personality type which
features the virtues of gentleness, non-aggression, cooperation,
modesty, tranquility, and so on" (1946:362-363). The other
interpretation, which he terms "repressive," is that "Pueblo
society and culture are marked by considerable covert tension,
suspicion, anxiety, hostility, fear, and ambition" (1946:363).
  The bias of the organic, or configurationist, approach, Bennett argues, is to be found in the assumptions with which they
approach non-literate societies. These assumptions lay stress on
"the organic wholeness of preliterate life in contrast to the hetero-
geneity and diffusiveness of modern civilization" (1946:364);

---

[1]This excerpt is taken from Appell's study, "Freeman's refutation of Mead's
Coming of Age in Samoa: The implications for anthropological inquiry," *Eastern
Anthropologist* 37 (1984):133-135. Reprinted with permission.

"there is an implicit value orientation toward solidified, homogeneous group life" (1946:366). Mead was part of the configurationist school through her association with Ruth Benedict and her interest in cultural patterns. One might speculate that this might be part of the explanation of why she dealt with deviants in a separate section of her *Coming of Age in Samoa*.

But this argument misses the point. Freeman's refutation of Mead's depiction of Samoan culture cannot be simply viewed as the differences between an "organic" and "repressive approach," as some have implied in their criticism of Freeman's work. For Bennett makes a very important point. He says of the Pueblo controversy, "there is no argument over or challenging of fact. In most cases the contrasting parties work with the same raw data" (1946:362). Freeman's refutation, on the other hand, is just that. It is over the facts; it is entirely concerned with showing that Mead got the facts of Samoan culture wrong.

Reference

Bennett, John W. 1946. The Interpretation of Pueblo culture: a question of values, *Southwestern Journal of Anthropology* 2:361-374.

Inductivism and the Test of Truth

Derek Freeman

Editor's Note

In these selections Freeman states what he meant by "absolute cultural determinism" and its antithesis, the "interaction" of genetic and exogenetic variables. The variables correspond to the units of analysis sought by Murdock and discussed by Robin Fox. Freeman nominates attachment behavior as such a unit or variable, and adverts to his observations and experiments in Samoa which showed it in operation. These remarks were written in response to multiple reviews of *Margaret Mead and Samoa* published in *Canberra Anthropology* 6 (1983):1-100. Reprinted with permission from "Inductivism and the test of truth," *Canberra Anthropology* 6 (1983):101-192.

Boas and Absolute Cultural Determinism

As I have documented in my book (1983:47), in his address on "The Mind of Primitive Man" given during the year following his appointment in 1899 to the chair of anthropology at Columbia University, Boas explicitly argued for culture as a construct to which the laws of biology did not apply. To this view he adhered for the rest of his life. In 1916, just before Kroeber and Lowie formally propounded their doctrine of absolute cultural determinism, Boas (1916:473ff.) declared that it had to be assumed that "all complex activities are socially determined" and that "in the great mass of a healthy population, the social stimulus is infinitely more potent than the biological mechanism." Boas is here directly comparing exogenetic and genetic variables; his belief that the first of these two sets of variables is in general "indefinitely more potent" than the second is but a short step from the absolute cultural determinism of his students and followers Kroeber and Lowie with its total exclusion of biological variables.

Mead's conclusion in *Coming of Age in Samoa* that biological variables are of no significance in the etiology of adolescent behavior was in complete concordance with Kroeber's and Lowie's doctrine of 1917, and Boas in accepting Mead's conclusion without qualification was, in this instance, however much Holmes might wish to deny it, explicitly a proponent of absolute cultural determinism.

Of Dabbling

I have but two points to make in response to Marilyn Strathern's [*Canberra Anthropology*] review, which is written from the vantage point of one possessing no firsthand knowledge of Samoa, and of a British social anthropologist trained in a tradition, stemming ultimately from Durkheim, that insists (Corning 1983:127) that "the biological substrate is essentially irrelevant to the explanation of social phenomena."

It is characteristic of many of those who take this stance that, while possessing no expert knowledge of either animal or human ethology, they do not demur from making their own exclusively sociological interpretations of behavior, the etiology of which obviously involves biological variables.

There is an instructive instance of this in Strathern's review (1983:73) where she advances the apparently commonsense proposition that as the punishment of Samoan children is some-times severe this might be expected to result in a child owing "no emotional allegiance to its father and mother," as Mead (1939a [orig. 1930]:239) has claimed.

As it happens, this is a subject that I investigated in Samoa (Freeman 1973) in great detail during the years 1966-67, as at that time there was a widespread interest among behavioral scien-tists in attachment behavior and the primary bond, stemming in the main from the seminal researches of John Bowlby that culmi-nated in his now classic volumes of 1969 and 1973 on attachment behavior. As I report in my book (p. 202), my inquiries showed "that attachment behavior in Samoan infants has all the character-istics described by Bowlby."

The unfactual assertion that in Samoa a child "owes no emo-tional allegiance to its father and mother" was made by Mead long before research on the ethology of attachment behavior had begun and without any systematic study of Samoan children. After I had taxed her about this matter, Dr. Mead confessed in a letter dated New York, 2 December 1964, that "unfortunately" in Samoa she "did not study infancy or early childhood". Her assertion is thus no more than an unverified impression which she advanced, in inductivist style, in support of her overall depic-tion of Samoa.

If Strathern had known anything about attachment behavior she would have realized that it occurs specifically during the first year or so of an infant's life, and that an infant's bond to his (or her) mother (or other caretaker) has thus been formed well before he (or she) begins to receive any kind of severe punishment. Further, had she studied the scientific literature on attachment be-havior she would also have known that once a primary bond has been formed, in Samoa as elsewhere, it is fundamentally unaf-fected by punishment, although the bond itself, in such circum-stances becomes marked by ambivalence.

So, while all of my psychological inquiries revealed ambiva-lence, and often high ambivalence, towards their parents in Samoans, this ambivalence was joined with intense attachment. Thus, adult Samoans will travel great distances at great cost to be with their parents when the need arises.

In recent decades social anthropology, like cultural anthropol-ogy, has, because of its doctrinaire exclusion from consideration of all biological variables, become a preserve to itself. This, however, is no justification for the kind of uninformed dabbling in which Strathern has engaged in her attempted defence of Mead's uninformed and preposterous assertion that in Samoa "the child owes no emotional allegiance to its father and mother." During the last two decades there have been such significant advances in our knowledge of human genetics and ethology that the time has come when such dabbling will no longer do, and it is now plainly incumbent on all behavioral scientists, including cultural and social anthropologists, to acquaint themselves with and take fully into account all of the phylogenetically given elements in our behavior of the kind that are summarized in, say, Richard Passingham's *The Human Primate* (1982).

References

Boas, Franz. 1916. Eugenics, *The Scientific Monthly* 3:471-478.

Corning, P. A. 1983. *The Synergism Hypothesis: A Theory of Progressive Evolution.* New York: McGraw-Hill.

Freeman, Derek. 1973. Kinship, attachment behaviour and the primary bond, in Jack Good, ed., *The Character of Kinship.* New York: Oxford University Press.

Freeman, Derek. 1983. *Margaret Mead and Samoa: The Making and Unmaking of an Anthropological Myth.* Cambridge: Harvard University Press.

Mead, Margaret. 1939 (orig. 1930). Growing Up in New Guinea, in *From the South Seas.* New York: Morrow.

Strathern, M. 1983. The Punishment of Margaret Mead, in *Canberra Anthropology* 6: 70-79.

Evaluations

Malosi: A Psychological Exploration of Mead's and Freeman's Work and of Samoan Aggression

Jeannette Marie Mageo

Editor's Note
Mageo's study represents an effort to allow the lessons of the Samoa controversy to inform new ethnographic study. The author has taught in the Samoan-Pacific Studies Program at the American Samoa Community College in Pago Pago, and is an American married to a Samoan—a fact that constitutes part of her data. This essay is abridged from *Pacific Studies* 11 (1988):25-65. Reprinted with permission.

This article's intent is to take a step toward clarifying the nature and the place of aggression in Samoan social life. Aggression has always had a focal place in Samoan culture. In pre-Christian times, Nafanua was the only divinity who was worshipped throughout the Samoan islands (Stair 1897:220). Nafanua was a war goddess.

Exploring the real nature of Samoan aggression is a pressing matter in current Pacific ethnography, because a great deal of confusion about the Samoan psyche, and specifically about Samoan aggression, has arisen as a result of the Mead/Freeman questions. These questions concern the nature of child development in Samoa and its effects, both on the tenor of Samoan adolescence and on the prominence of aggression in adult personality.

Mead offers Samoa as a radical alternative to socialization in our own society. In her Samoa the social environment is so tolerant and non-threatening that aggression has lost is *raison d'être* and is as invisible as a phantom (Mead [1928] 1973). Freeman portrays Samoan childhood as extremely violent and intimates that this violence leaves a smoldering aggressive undercurrent in the personality that expresses itself in "outbursts of uncontrollable anger," "acts of suicide," and states of possession

(Freeman 1983a:219-221). Shore disapproves of Freeman's book, but says its value lies in presenting the "darker strain" of the Samoan psyche (Shore 1983:937). Others accuse Freeman of slandering Samoans. They argue that Freeman replaces an extremist view of Samoan personality as exceedingly erotic with a view of Samoans as wildly fierce (Ala'ilima 1984:92-92; Wendt 1984:92-99). Felix Wendt, of Western Samoa, complains that Freeman makes Samoans "appear like the gang hoods in Charles Bronson's 'Death Wish II'" (1984:95) and contends "that the overriding characteristic of the Samoan ethos is *alofa* (love)" (ibid:96). Leacock tells tales of nineteenth-century fire-and-brimstone missionaries who were aghast at the permissiveness of Samoan parents toward their children (1987:182-183).

The tendency in American anthropology has been to divide the two sides of this controversy into the good guy (namely Mead) and the bad guy (namely Freeman) and to dismiss the bad guy. Goodness knows Freeman, in his manner of writing gave us ample excuse (McDowell 1984). However, now that the dust has settled, it is time to admit that this manoeuvre is too easy. In the analysis of culture the issue is how to combine a cacophony of information into a harmonious perspective in which apparently contradictory elements make a common sense. In the present case, what is wanting is a perspective from which these conflicting statements about Samoan aggression dovetail.

To resolve the enigma of Samoan aggression, two kinds of inquiries are necessary, inquiries that I will undertake in the pages to follow. First it is necessary to bring to light the psychological biases implicit in both Mead's and Freeman's work and the stance on aggression entailed in these biases. When their positions on psychology in general, and on Samoan psychology and aggression in particular, are elucidated, it becomes possible to adjudicate the merits of their respective arguments.

However, to truly fathom Samoan aggression, a further study of Samoan culture itself is in order. My analysis will draw on the copious ethnographic data that exist on Samoa and on my own six years of residence and research in Samoa. My experiences as the wife of a Samoan, as a member of a Samoan *'aiga* (extended family), and as a teacher at a Samoan college will also provide a source of data. In the course of this analysis, I will show that while (as Freeman vehemently argues) Mead's work is marred by her unwillingness to acknowledge the presence and importance of Samoan aggression, Freeman's is marred by his tendency to assess and judge Samoan aggression in Western terms. Freeman is right that, socially, aggression finds its roots in and takes it character from early relations with authority figures. However, what is needed is to understand these relations in Samoan terms. Only then can we ferret out the place of Samoan aggression in adult personality.

I will begin at the historical origins of this controversy, by unearthing the psychological biases of Margaret Mead. Within these biases we can discover her stance on Samoan aggression.

Mead's Psychological Biases

Boas' influence on Mead has been the subject of much comment over the past few years, but Freud was another major influence on her early work. Mead's career as a whole had its genesis in psychological concerns. At Barnard College Mead majored in psychology. Her circle at Barnard has been described as "intensely involved in Freudian psychology" (Sheehy 1977:334). In the 1920s, Freudian ideas represented a major, if not the major, theoretical paradigm for those anthropologists who, like Mead, were concerned with psychological development.

Mead discusses the initial relationship between Freudian and anthropological influences on her thinking in *Blackberry Winter*: "I entered my senior year committed to psychology, but I also took a course of psychological aspects of culture given by William Fielding Ogburn, one of the first courses in which Freudian psychology was treated with respect" (Mead 1972:111). Clearly Ogburn was not alone in his respect for Freud: Mead shared Ogburn's admiration. Ogburn had a lasting influence on Mead's work.[1] He and his wife were her lifelong friends. Ogburn himself, Mead says in her autobiography, was one of those who "left their mark on my life forever" (ibid:287).

---

[1]Freeman mentions Ogburn's importance in this regard, stating that Mead conducted her research in Samoa inspired by Ogburn's "doctrines." However, Freeman never mentions Ogburn's psychological leaning, only his methodological ones. In private correspondence with me, Freeman has disputed Ogburn's belief in psychoanalysis because Ogburn counseled, "Never look for a psychological explanation unless every effort to find a cultural one has been exhausted." Freeman construes this sentence to mean that Ogburn "introduced his students to psychological theories only to reject them . . . ." This statement is in marked contrast to Mead's own comments that Ogburn treated Freudian theory with respect . . . . Mead, who was a psychology major . . . before and after she took Ogburn's course, would hardly have been sympathetic to such a rejection.

When she was halfway through her master's thesis, Mead decided to shift her focus to anthropology. Nonetheless the questions Mead took to the field were essentially psychological ones. Of her work in Samoa Mead says "the principal emphasis of my research was . . . psychological rather than ethnographic" (Mead 1969:3). In her own words she had merely switched the locale of her work from the psychology lab to the South Seas, but as she so eloquently clarifies in her introduction to *Coming of Age in Samoa*, only the "laboratory" had changed, not the substance of her psychological inquiry (Mead [1928] 1973:3-4).

From a Freudian viewpoint psychological problems, including those of adolescents, are born of an inherent conflict between social mores and individual instinct. In *Civilization and Its Discontents*, Freud writes: "The two processes of individual and cultural development must stand in hostile opposition to each other and mutually dispute the ground." Why? Because, Freud believed, society profits from individual frustration. Energy that cannot be released in immediate gratification is redirected, through sublimation, to higher social aims.

However, Freud also argued that, while a margin of profit was to be gained through the social exploitation of the individual, society had gone beyond the limits of that margin. Modern Western society had begun to damage the mental health and stability of its basic resource, upsetting the ecology of the self.

According to Freud, the superego (the internalized agent of the state) "in the severity of its commands and prohibitions . . . troubles itself too little about the happiness of the individual." Freud reasoned—and his reasoning has changed the course of Western social history—that civilization could demand less of the individual to the benefit of both. This is the position Mead takes up in *Coming of Age*.

Mead's Samoa

American society was not singular in marking off an intermediate phase between childhood and the established roles of adult life. In Samoa, according to Mead, incessant industriousness was required of the child and adult life was laden with heavy social responsibilities. But between childhood and adulthood there was an intermediate phase, often more prolonged than Western adolescence. As Mead described it, this Samoan adolescence was a moratorium in Erikson's sense of the word. Responsibilities lightened and possibilities for play and exploration opened.

Because Samoan society shared this phase of life with our own society, it offered a comparative frame of reference. Mead used this reference point to assay Freud's belief in the essential contrariety of the individual and the social order. In *Coming of Age* Mead is concerned with questions that are Freudian in nature. This is not to say that she always agreed with Freud about the answer to those questions. In fact *Coming of Age* is meant as a foil and a counterpoint to much Freudian dogma. However, Mead has no argument with Freud's basic premise. Freud believes that society's intolerance of instinct is internalized by the individual at key points in childhood and adolescence. These internalizations generate intrapsychic conflicts. The conflicts in turn lead to mental illness. If Mead's Samoa represents a saner solution to the problem of socializing the individual, it is precisely because Samoan society had resolved those problems of development that had been posed by Freud. Whereas Freud, more pessimistically, leans toward the idea that the conflict between the human body and the body politic is fundamental to the nature of society itself and is therefore universal, Mead sets out to prove that it is neither necessary nor universal.

Mead presents Samoa as a picture, call it a hypothetical picture, of how harmony between the individual and society could be achieved, and at what costs, for Mead was also aware of the costs. Whether or not Mead's portrayal of Samoa was accurate and, therefore, whether or not Samoa was in reality such a sane society is an issue I will consider later in this paper. For the moment, the issue is merely that Mead saw Samoa as a kind of vindication of those positive potentialities of human society which had been disparaged in Freud's work.

Freudian theory has, of course, been the object of decades of critique by both anthropologists and psychologists. Nonetheless we will see that Mead's use of Samoan society to explore certain of Freud's ideas is persuasive and that her specific developmental foci in *Coming of Age* are derived from her early work with Ogburn and his Freudian biases. Boas conveyed nothing to Mead as to what her methodological approach to the problems of adolescence should be and gave her but a half hour's advice before her departure for the field. In her 1959 memorial lecture to the Philadelphia Association for Psychoanalysis, Mead tells us who was responsible for the direction of her Samoan research:

Then in 1925, Franz Boas (who was, it must be remembered, a product of the German culture of his time and
who had, in fact, competed for a scholarship in psychology) set me a field problem on adolescence . . . I had
read quite thoroughly in the available psychoanalytic literature of the day, in the unique course through which
Columbia University students were introduced to psychoanalysis by William Fielding Ogburn. What this
provided me with as a background to research was primarily a directive to look closely at family life, at the
early relationships of parents of the same and opposite
sex, and at children's relationships to their own bodies; it
also alerted me to conflicts arising between the springing
sexuality of adolescents and the authority and jealousy of
parents and elders who sought to control them (Mead
1959:60).

In regard to Ogburn's clearly Freudian directive, Mead saw
Samoa as presenting a series of radical and appealing contrasts to
American society. For example, Mead says American adolescents of the 1920s were "denied all firsthand knowledge of birth
and love and death, harried by a society which will not let adolescents grow up at their own pace, imprisoned in the small, fragile
and nuclear family from which there is no escape and in which
there is little security" ([1928] 1973:ix). Samoans, however,
were acquainted with the facts of life from childhood: "All of
these children had seen birth and death. They had seen many
dead bodies. They had watched miscarriages and peeked under
the arms of the old women who were washing and commenting
upon the undeveloped foetus. There was no convention of
sending the children of the family away at such times . . . . In
matters of sex the ten-year-olds are . . . sophisticated, although
they witness sex activities only surreptitiously" (ibid:74-75).
These children, Mead writes, also had some firsthand familiarity
with sex. During latency children indulged in "homosexual play
as experimentation without any expectation of, or fear of, permanent object deflection" (Mead 1959:61). Thus "the facts of life
and death are shorn of all mystery at an early age" (Mead [1928]
1973:75), and the frightening misinterpretations and
mythification of these facts, which Freud associates with the
child's crises and complexes in Western society, could not arise.

For Freud, socialization is achieved through an Oedipal conflict between father and son. The boy loses the competition for his mother around the age of five. In lieu of possessing his mother, he identifies with the person who does, his father. However, his father represents moral authority to the boy. Hence when he internalizes his father, he also internalizes a set of social interdictions. In theory, the girl goes through a roughly parallel evolution vis-à-vis her mother. Mead thinks that in Samoa the Oedipus complex itself was undermined.

In Samoa, the nuclear family . . . was imbedded in an extended family; ties between mother and child were diluted by ties to other females who could succor and breastfeed the child. The close identifications necessary for the sort of super-ego formation which was recognized in our culture were diffused as young children were cared for by child nurses and many other members of the family. Authority was vested in a senior titled male—seldom the father of the young child—who presided over the whole group, not as a jealous head of a horde but as a responsible and honored organizer (Mead 1959:61).

Because childcare was turned over to a slightly older sister, the Samoan incest taboo was aimed at the brother/sister bond, rather than centering on the mother/son relationship. Mead says that Samoan development included a "conspicuous period of latency" (ibid:61-62). The onset of this period was marked by a new-found shyness between brothers and sisters and their consequent avoidance of one another (Mead [1928] 1973:24-25).

If the family did not lend itself to Oedipal conflict in Samoa, presumably socialization proceeded along another route. Mead realized that it occurred for the girl through her role as a sibling caretaker. The girl's primary responsibility was to keep the little imp quiet so adults were undisturbed. If the tot made noise, the sister was punished. This interdiction created a balance of power between the older sister and her *tei* [younger sib]. If adults were nearby, it was necessary to placate the child in order to control it. Thus she became something between the toddler's sovereign and a drudge. Her own willful behavior was mastered, not by one-to-one conflict with an authority figure, but rather by adjusting to the willfulness of her *tei*. Producing conformity in another brought temperance to her own behavior (ibid:14).

From Mead's description of the *tei* relationship, one might also reason that this childcare situation provided other mollifying elements that eased the process of socialization in Samoa. The sister had authority over her charge. Should she punish the youngster, elders would support her action unquestioningly. The necessary identification with authority was produced, not by a conflict with a parental figure, but by her role.

. . . The reader may well admit that Mead is preoccupied with Freudian issues in *Coming of Age*. However, she seems more interested in debunking Freudian views than in defending them. Indeed there was a great deal of Freud's work that Mead wished to argue with and did. As she comments in her lecture to the Philadelphia Association for Psychoanalysis, "I made my study in one of the few cultures in the world in which the vicissitudes to which children and adolescents are subjected were reduced to a minimum in just those areas which our early understanding of psychoanalytic theory had named as important" (Mead 1959:61). In what sense, then, can one say that *Coming of Age* was written under the sway of Freudian influences? Later in the same talk Mead asserts that "I believe that to the extent that psychoanalytic theory ascribes the Oedipus complex to the actual relationship between contemporary parents and children within a family, the Samoan findings confirm rather than dispute analytic findings" (ibid:64).

In *Coming of Age*, Mead is simply taking the Freudian argument to its logical extreme. Freud says that mental illness finds its genesis in society's unreasonable demands upon the individual, demands transmitted largely by parental figures and in opposition to human "nature." Mead replies that a society could be created, indeed had been created in Samoa, that was not against nature but in accord with it. In Mead's Samoa the civilized source of psychological discontent was thus eliminated and adolescence was, therefore, "freer and easier and less complicated" (Mead [1928] 1973:x).

It must be added, however, that Mead feared eliminating discontent would also undermine intensity, individuality, and involvement with life. These were the qualities she found missing in her Samoan model of social harmony (ibid). If Mead did not doubt that the conflict between the individual and society could be resolved, she had reservations about the wisdom of doing so. But while Mead had the sophistication to cast a critical glance at her own argument, it was nonetheless a psychoanalytical perspective from which the argument derived . . . .

Freeman on Mead and Samoan Aggression

In *Margaret Mead and Samoa*, Freeman portrays Mead as taking a cultural relativist position on human personality and in doing so underrating the importance of biological factors. Freeman does not ignore the centrality of psychological concerns in Mead's work. On the contrary, after constructing for the reader an anthropological polarity between cultural determinism and biological determinism, Freeman draws a parallel polarity in psychology between the "environmentalists" and the "instinctivists" (1983a:34-61)—and misplaces Mead within these polar sets.

Early in the twentieth century, Freeman tells us, the field of anthropology was dominated by a debate between the cultural relativists and the biological determinists. Biological determinism was, during the second decade of the century, taken up by the eugenic movement. Human nature, eugenicists argued, was hereditary and, therefore, biological. This claim was used to assert the genetic inferiority of certain races (ibid:8). Rallying against racism, says Freeman, Boas was forced into a cultural determinist position and therefore contended that biology, and with it instinct, were not determining factors in human nature. In Freeman's portrait, Mead is a defender of the faith of cultural determinism, that faith preached by Boas. As a result, Freeman argues, both Boas and his student, Mead, underrated the importance of biological factors. However, Freeman bases this "biological" censure of Mead's work on a recourse to the history of psychological theory.

In the twenties, Freeman tells us, psychology was the stage for a debate roughly parallel to the one that raged in the field of anthropology. On one side of the debate, he says, were the "instinctivists." Freeman argues that "instinctivist" theory was the psychological analogue of biological determinism. On the other side, Freeman places the behaviorists, who were, like Boas, in a battle against hereditarian ideas. "Limiting the purview of psychology to overt behavior . . . led to the rejection of theories of genetic determinism and gave rise, in about 1920, to the anti-instinct movement" (ibid:54). Freeman uses J. B. Watson to represent the behaviorists. Watson stressed the importance of environmental factors in determining human nature and was "almost savagely against the notion of human instinct" (ibid). Thus, Freeman suggests Boas, and Mead with him, are anthropological versions of J. B. Watson.

However, precisely which psychologists should be taken as representative of the "instinctivists" remains a mystery in *Margaret Mead and Samoa*. In light of the polarity that Freeman establishes, one can only presume Freud. Watson considered Freud his intellectual adversary, referring to psychoanalytic theory as a "mentalistic fiction." Freud certainly is responsible for forwarding the idea that human behavior is instinctually motivated.

Freeman's implication, that Boas and Mead with him are behaviorists, is far from accurate. In fact, Mead crusaded against behaviorism. In the preface to the 1973 edition of *Coming of Age in Samoa*, Mead says that "the pleas for a harsh, manipulative behaviorism among some psychologists make me wonder whether the modern world understands much more about the significance of culture than was known in 1928: ([1928] 1973:x-xi). Mead goes on to say it is, "alas," still necessary to stress the concept of culture "when psychologists dream of substituting conditioning for cultural transmission, just as the crudest behaviorists did in 1920" (ibid:xi).

If *Coming of Age* represents one side of a dialectic (is Freeman really the synthesis?), this dialectic is surely not based upon a simple dichotomy between instinct and environment. For in *Coming of Age*, alongside her belief in Boas and cultural relativism, Mead was preoccupied with Freudian theory.

Freeman implies that the nature/nurture controversy of the 1920s centered on whether psychological problems stemmed either from biology or from culture. "If . . . these problems were caused by the biological processes of maturation, then they would necessarily be found in all human societies. But in Samoa . . . life was easy and casual, and adolescence was the easiest and most pleasant time of life" (Freeman 1983a:xi). Mead, like Freud, never says that psychological problems are either cultural or biological. She did not take issue with the universality of biological processes but with the necessity of a concomitant spiritual storm. Mead does not insinuate that biology fails to function in Samoa. The pubescent girls of whom she writes are surcharged with erotic feelings, but these biological impulses do not put them in opposition to their society.

It is not the biological element of human nature that Mead portrays as fluctuating from one culture to another, but only the nature of the clash between the vicissitudes of the body and those of custom. The question is whether the culture at issue takes a stance that is essentially opposed to or in harmony with instinct. Mead's queries pertain not to biology, but rather to our Western civilization ([1928] 1973:6-7). Like Freud, Mead believed that the degree of dissonance between culture and nature suffered by our own society, and particularly by adolescents in our society, was unnecessary.

Freeman accuses Mead of favoring environment over instinct in the formation of human personality and, therefore, of ignoring the "genetic" for the "exogenetic" (Freeman 1983a:25, 29, 31). We have seen that this characterization of Mead is incorrect. However, Freeman's argument has yet another flaw. He is extremely vague about the nature of the "biological" factors that Mead purportedly neglects. Because his definition of biology is never explicit in *Margaret Mead and Samoa*, it must be deduced.

We do know that Freeman sets out to correct Mead's "deficiencies" through his own research. In the chapters where he attempts to supplement Mead's work, Freeman discusses sexual repression, evidence of social maladjustment such as suicide, and various forms of aggressive behavior. One can hardly argue that either sexual repression or social maladjustment are genetic problems or due to "phylogenetically given impulses" (ibid:300). Thus one is left to conclude that Freeman sees aggression as the biological element missing from Mead's account.

In a few pages toward the end of the book Freeman's real position becomes fleetingly visible. Culture, Freeman believes, imposes conventional modes of interaction over "highly emotional and impulsive behavior that is animal-like in its ferocity" (ibid:301). "Ferocity" and "animal-like" are the key words here. Freeman, sitting cross-legged for endless hours in the Samoan *fono* (chiefly assembly), observes the overlay: "incensed chiefs, having attained to pinnacles of elaborately patterned politeness, would suddenly lapse into violent aggression" (ibid:300).

Thus Freeman's position on human aggression is ethological. Inasmuch as we are aggressive we are "animal-like." While he implies, however, that Samoan aggression is merely a local version of a universal and ethological phenomenon, Freeman most often traces Samoan aggression to child-rearing practices. I would like to disentangle Freeman's propositions and consider each separately: (1) that Mead underplayed Samoan aggression in *Coming of Age*, (2) that when humans are aggressive they are "animal-like," and (3) that Samoan aggression is tied to the strictures placed upon children.

Mead acknowledges the place of aggression in her other works on Samoa, works in which she was not painting Samoa as a model of mental health. Like the early Freud, Mead links aggression with conservative attitudes toward sexuality. These attitudes Mead finds in Samoan hierarchical contexts. In *Coming of Age* Mead only hints this conservatism exists by telling the reader that the adolescent girl is extraordinarily careful to conceal her affairs from all elders ([1928] 1973:38, 51). But in Mead's other works on Samoa, when hierarchical relations are involved, attitudes toward sexuality are not represented as indulgent, nor is aggression depicted as inappreciable.

In *Cooperation and Competition Among Primitive Peoples*, for example, Mead says, "Any man committing adultery with the chief's wife was put to death by village edict," and she attributes intervillage hostilities principally to adultery, especially when the adulterer was younger or of lower status than the cuckold (1937:284, 302, 303). In an appendix to *Coming of Age* Mead discusses attitudes toward sexuality in pre-missionary times, reporting that in those days, if an ordinary girl was discovered to be unchaste, she was cruelly beaten and her head shaved ([1928] 1973, pp. 3:153). Mead goes on to indicate that the higher one's place in the Samoan hierarchy, the more extreme this attitude toward sexuality became. Before the Navy prohibited the ceremony in which the *taupou* (village ceremonial virgin) was ritually deflowered, a *taupou* who failed to bleed was stoned to death (ibid).

Christianity, Mead says, softened the Samoans' treatment of their children. Nonetheless, if Samoan methods of punishment for sexual indiscretion were moderated by Christianity, it is unlikely Christianity liberalized Samoan sentiments about it. The fact that premarital sex was publicly disapproved of during pre-missionary times implies that it was also publicly disapproved during missionary times. It should also be added that heads are still being shaved and girls beaten today, not only for actually having sex but for being caught in a situation that might be interpreted as leading in that direction. In *Coming of Age*, Mead does not give aggression the weight it bears in her other works on Samoa, nor could she, for it would not support her Freudian argument.

Aggression and Ethology

Even allowing that Mead failed to discover a society lacking significant aggression, it does not follow that she, therefore, neglected the animal side of human nature. Freeman's ethological perspective on aggression requires scrutiny, both in regard to how well it becomes an extremely vocal proponent of "interactionism" and as to how just a characterization of human aggression it produces.

Like Lorenz in *On Aggression*, Freeman traces an "apposition between the genetic patterning of animals and the cultural patterning of human beings" (Freeman 1983a:300). In an earlier essay, "Aggression: Instinct or Symptom," Freeman clarifies the nature of this apposition. He gives examples of Samoan behavior that he believes directly parallel aggression in animals (Freeman 1971:70). For example, Freeman describes Lagerspetz's experiments with mice in which, once the mice had begun to fight, they tended to persist in aggressive behavior (ibid:69-70). Here, Freeman says, the physiological state itself appears to function like a drive. Likewise in Samoa, "when serious fighting was stopped by chiefs, the aroused opponents commonly displayed a marked tendency to re-instigate attacks upon one another" (ibid:70).

If this parallel seems to imply that aggression is an instinct, Freeman is quick to assure the reader that aggression involves the interaction of "both internal and external variables" (ibid:71). However, the interaction to which he refers is between biology and those social factors that are precultural. Thus Freeman tells us that dominance hierarchies among animal and humans limit aggression, while crowding and learning can stimulate it, but he bases these conclusions on various experiments carried out with rhesus monkeys and with laboratory mice (ibid:69-71). Freeman mentions two experimental studies of human behavior. In both cases, however, they exemplify similar findings in work with animals (ibid:68-69).

In the field of psychology this parallel with animal behavior has been overused for decades. What those who work with our animal brethren fail to recognize is that new abilities emerge at the human level. Human beings have language and construct symbol systems—such as cultures—and because of this fact our behavior does not necessarily resemble that of other species. Needless to say, we have something to learn from animal studies. However, it would seem that an interactionist model should take human culture into account, and culture is not reducible to those social behaviors we share with our evolutionary predecessors.

Animals are, it is true, genetically programmed to respond when their vital interests are threatened. But this disposition is not toward violence *per se*. Fight, flight, or submission are equally likely to follow such a threat, depending upon the adaptiveness of each reaction in the environment (Fromm 1973:16-32).

Biological research does imply that some human aggression can be interpreted as an analogue to this animal reaction, but this is a distorting comparison and one that culture often turns back against biology. Humans, like animals, will rally when their vital interests are threatened, but to a great extent these interests are defined by society. For example, stratified Mediterranean societies have a concept of honor, although the definition of this concept varies. Men, women too, will fight if they honor is in jeopardy. But as Falstaff points out in *Henry IV*, honor is a cold bedfellow, especially when the bed one shares with it may well turn out to be a grave. One wonders: is this analogue or antinomy?

Furthermore, human aggression ranges far beyond the scope of the dubious parallel with nonhuman animals. Unlike animal instinct, human aggression is not merely reactive in nature, but often gratuitous and malignant. The source of this latter form of aggression may be cultural or, as Erich Fromm suggests, it may be existential (1973:218-433), but Freeman is wrong to trace it to the animal in us. In regard to aggression, as in so many other areas, humans appear to be an unnatural animal; or in the terminology of many traditional cultures, one might say we are, for better or for worse, not raw but cooked.

References

Ala'ilima, Fay. 1984. Review of *Margaret Mead and Samoa: The Making and Unmaking of an Anthropological Myth*, by Derek Freeman, *Pacific Studies* 7:91-91.

Freeman, Derek. 1983a. *Margaret Mead and Samoa: The Making and Unmaking of an Anthropological Myth*. Cambridge: Harvard University Press.

Freeman, Derek. 1983b. Inductivism and the test of truth: a rejoinder to Lowell D. Holmes and others, *Canberra Anthropology* 6:135-142.

Freeman, Derek. 1971. Aggression: Instinct or Symptom, *Australian and New Zealand Journal of Psychiatry* 6:66-73.
Fromm, Erich. 1973. *The Anatomy of Human Destructiveness.* New York: Holt, Rinehart and Winston.
McDowell, Nancy. 1984. Review of *Margaret Mead and Samoa: The Making and Unmaking of an Anthropological Myth,* by Derek Freeman, *Pacific Studies* 7:99-140.
Mead, Margaret. [1928] 1973. *The Coming of Age in Samoa: A Psychological Study of Primitive Youth for Western Civilization.* New York: William Morrow.
Mead, Margaret. 1937. The Samoans, in *Cooperation and Competition among Primitive Peoples,* 283-312. New York: McGraw-Hill.
Mead, Margaret. 1959. Cultural contexts of puberty and adolescence, in *Bulletin of the Philadelphia Association for Psychoanalysis* 9.
Mead, Margaret. 1969. *The Social Organization of Manu'a.* Honolulu: Bishop Museum Press.
Mead, Margaret. 1972. *Blackberry Winter.* New York: William Morrow.
Sheehy, Gail. 1977. *Passages.* New York: E. P. Dutton.
Shore, Bradd. 1983. Paradox regained: Freeman's *Margaret Mead and Samoa, Canberra Anthropology* 6: 17-37.
Stair, Rev. John B. 1987. *Old Samoa: Flotsam and Jetsam from the Pacific Ocean.* London: Religious Society Tract.

Freeman's Quest
for an Interactionist Anthropology

Hiram Caton

Many were puzzled by Derek Freeman's assault on the "cultural determinist" paradigm in the name of interactionism. To them it seemed far off the mark to maintain that Franz Boas had denied the influence of biological variables on culture and that his culture-only paradigm remained to this day the presiding orientation of anthropology. The antitheses robustly asserted were that cultural anthropologists, Boas in particular, had in the main never denied the significance of biological variables in understanding human behavior. Anthropology was said to have diversified, in more recent years, into a variety of schools and sub-disciplines, including a number of approaches to the systematic investigation of biological variables.

Freeman rejected this account as missing his point. He maintained Boas' trimming biological variables down to physical anthropology and admitting physical anthropology into the anthropology department as one among four fields did not achieve effective communication between biology and cultural anthropology. In practice it was equivalent to sealing culture off from biological contamination, however much it might be protested that the distinction was merely a division of labor. His claim that this to him perverse state of affairs continued to dominate anthropology was not an inference obtained from study but was the constant experience of his professional life.[1]

My object is to review a portion of the professional experience that fostered Freeman's certainty that cultural anthropology repudiated biology. For about fifteen years he labored against the grain of his own training and in virtual isolation from his colleagues with a view to establishing the integration that he espoused under the banner of "interactionism." As it happened, he correctly identified research trends that from about 1975 blossomed into an array of fruitful biological approaches to human behavior and culture. Indeed, with the advent of sociobiology, Freeman got more biology than he had bargained for.

Defection from Conventional Anthropology

The years 1960-1961 were a watershed that neatly divide Freeman's theoretical allegiances into cultural determinist and interactionist phases. The consolidation of the second phase is marked in a letter of October 19, 1962 to his mentor, Meyer Fortes, to whom he wrote: "I am now convinced that anthropology, if it is to become the science of man, must be biologically based—we must begin with the human animal, and never let him slip from our sight when studying social systems." The watershed occupied the period July 1960 to March 1961, which he describes as "a momentous experience" and a "Kierkegaardian

---

[1]One such experience is detailed in the objections of Freeman's department head, W. E. H. Stanner, to the research he proposed for his Samoa fieldwork, 1966-1967. See Chapter VI.

earthquake."[1] The triggers were two confrontations with evidence for which he could find no explanation within conventional anthropology.

The first trigger was a concluding statement of a paper in which Victor Turner had unsuccessfully sought enlightenment about color symbolism from psychoanalysts. Turner queried: "Where psychoanalysts disagree, by what criterion can the hapless social anthropologist judge between their interpretations, in a field of inquiry in which he has neither received systematic training or obtained thorough practical experience?" Turner's plaintive statement "stuck in my mind," Freeman wrote, until he concluded that the anthropologist had no choice but to "get hap" by learning psychoanalysis himself. This was a formidable task, he thought, but with determination it could be done.

In February 1961 there was a second event. His duties as department chairman brought Freeman into contact with two persons, one of them a research scholar in his department, who presented psychopathic behavior. He was delegated by the Vice-Chancellor of the Australian National University to journey to Borneo, where the scholar was conducting field work, to investigate alarming reports and retrieve the distressed scholar. In Sarawak Freeman witnessed the scene, and later collected information on both individuals from senior government officials in Kuching. He wrote of this experience: "To my immense edification I was at the center of a complex social situation in which I was able to discern and document a whole series of deep psychological processes. For one who had reached my state of mind about the significance of psychological and behavioral variables for anthropological inquiry, this was an educational experience of the most fundamental kind, and it led to what I can only describe as a cognitive abreaction: faced by facts that I could not doubt I suddenly saw human behavior in a new light."

---

[1]The biographical information detailed here is drawn from "Derek Freeman: Notes Toward an Intellectual Biography," in *Choice and Morality in Anthropological Perspective: Essays in Honor of Derek Freeman*, edited by George N. Appell and Triloki N. Madan (Albany: SUNY Press, 1988):3-25, and the more extensive unpublished typescript from which this information was drawn, "Some Notes on the Development of My Anthropological Interests" (July 1986, pp. 63). I also use three other unpublished sources: Derek Freeman, *et al.*, 1987, *Transcript of Interviews by Frank Heimans for the Documentary Film Margaret Mead and Samoa*; Taped Interviews of Derek Freeman by Hiram Caton, July 1985 & January, 1987; and selected documents from the Freeman Papers.

As a result of these experiences, Freeman reorganized his research agenda. He cancelled his sabbatical leave and took steps
to arrange for study of psychoanalysis at the London Institute of
Psychoanalysis, which he attended in 1963-1964. At that time he
also established contact with Konrad Lorenz and Irenäus Eibl-
Eibesfeldt at the Max Planck Institute in Seewiesen. The link between depth psychology and ethology was the seminal work of
John Bowlby, of the Tavistock Clinic, on attachment in infants
and children. Bowlby used animal models in his decades-long
studies, and Freeman followed suit during his London sojourn
by devoting 96 hours to observation of primate behavior in the
facilities of the Zoological Society of London.[1] The final component of the *Wendung* was the commencement of study of Karl
Popper's philosophy, which had been commended to him by a
philosophy colleague a few years previous. In the next decade he
would record in a series of essays the critical and constructive
reasons why anthropology should abandon cultural determinism.
  Freeman's initial embrace of cultural determinism was as natural as mother's milk. In his years at the University of Wellington, New Zealand, he was a zealous reformer who fervently believed in the power of social conditioning. This faith was the advanced social thinking of the day, and his instructors cheerfully
reinforced it. On his first sojourn in Samoa as a school teacher,
he carried out research on child behavior modelled after the Polynesian anthropological publications of his mentors Ernest Beaglehole. His postgraduate work was completed at the London
School of Economics and Cambridge University, where he im-
bibed the Durkheimian assumptions of British anthropology and
the Boasian assumptions of American anthropology. His teachers and associates were Raymond Firth, S. F. Nadel, Max
Gluckman, Edmund Leach, Meyer Fortes. His ethnographic research in Samoa and Borneo, which consistently won commen-
dation, was conducted along orthodox structuralist lines. Indeed,
his skill in orthodox theory won him the Curl Bequest Prize of
the Royal Anthropological Institute for his essay, "The Concept
of the Kindred"—awarded, ironically, in the year of decision,
1960.

---

[1]This was not Freeman's first experience with observing primates. During his
field work on the Iban in Borneo, he and his wife Monica had the companionship
of a hand-reared gibbon who remained in the precincts of their house.

Freeman's thinking had been prepared for renovation by the clash between field observations and theory. Among the Iban of Borneo he encountered an elaborate dream mythology and ritual that he could not riddle in terms of social structure. Iban symbolism was prominently focussed on the head-hunting practices that they had only recently abandoned. He felt that a psychological analysis was required, but the doctrine of "levels" forbade the cultural anthropologist to enter that territory. Another preparation was the discovery, in 1942, that Margaret Mead's description of Samoan sexual customs was contrary to what he observed. Freeman had gone to Samoa expecting to confirm and augment Mead's ethnography, which his teacher Dr. Beaglehole had unequivocally endorsed. This discovery shook his confidence and put him in search of an explanation that he would not find for some two decades.

But perhaps the most serious scruple about theory was a philosophical point which was at the same time an empirical point. If human behavior is the product of culturally-shaped conditioning, what becomes of the phenomenon of choice? The seed of this question was planted by the Indian thinker Jiddu Krishnamurti, whose lecture in Wellington Freeman attended during his student days with a view to debunking. In the event, the thinker subdued the skeptic by explaining, in practical terms, how the shackles of social conditioning could be removed and a new state of free awareness attained. The Young Turk was so captivated by this enlightenment that he took two weeks leave from school teaching to associate with Krishnamurti. The encounter bolstered Freeman's propensity to be his own man; but the discovery of the phenomenon of choice was a slow fuse that translated into an explicit interrogation of anthropological theory only in the 1970s.

Recovering Nature for Anthropology

In 1970 Freeman published an essay, "Human Nature and Culture," which proved to be the anchor of another half dozen essays[1] elaborating the concept of an anthropology that would inte-

---

[1] Freeman's bibliography may be found in *Choice and Morality in Anthropological Perspective: Essays in Honor of Derek Freeman*, edited by George N. Appell and Triloki N. Madan (Albany: SUNY Press, 1988), pp. 27-30. Of particular significance to the present account are: "Aggression: instinct or symptom?," *Australian and New Zealand Journal of Psychiatry* 5 (1971):66-73;

grate natural givens into a "unified science" of Homo's culture-making capacity. In writing *Margaret Mead and Samoa,* Freeman drew substantially on the ideas developed in the essays and occasionally incorporated passages from them into his text. These essays exhibit certain common features. The most essential, if the goal was to be achieved, was the identification of the empirical and speculative scientific literature in which the latest research results and concepts were reported. This effort was by no means easy, as other social scientists who paralleled Freeman's course will testify. Empirical work is done by specialists, and specialists notoriously do not communicate beyond their circle. It was necessary to sift through journals devoted to a dozen specializations, from endocrinology to zoology, to locate research meaningful for theory construction in social science. Leading biologists who took a broad view, such as C. H. Waddington, Roger Sperry, Theodosius Dobzhansky, Konrad Lorenz, and G. G. Simpson, were unable to perform the required task of synthesis because they did not know, in detail and from first-hand experience, what the problems were that social scientists had to resolve. Freeman's essays identified key findings, and, pruning away all irrelevance, crisply wove them into a holistic concept of interactive anthropology.

For those engaged in theory construction the great temptation is to allow wish to father the science. Forewarned by the examples, as he believed, of Durkheim and Boas, Freeman abstained from inserting any element into the theory that was not supported by solid research. This was very different from browsing the literature to cull striking findings. It was the more demanding task of identifying significant findings that lay in research courses that would have a fruitful future. He proved to be remarkably astute in this undertaking

The foil of "Human Nature and Culture" is learning theory or Watsonian behaviorism, which he characterized as "extreme environmentalism." Discussing its origins in the Twenties, Freeman identified it as the psychologist's version of Boasian

---

"On Sociobiology and anthropology," *Canberra Anthropology* 1(1977):24-32; "Towards an anthropology both scientific and humanistic," *Canberra Anthropology* 1,3 (1978):44-69; "Sociobiology: The 'antidiscipline' of anthropology," in *Sociobiology Examined,* edited by Ashley Montagu (New York: Oxford University Press, 1980), 198-219; and "The Anthropology of choice," *Canberra Anthropology* 4 (1981):82-100.

cultural determinism. To display the sense of extreme environmentalism, Freeman pointedly quoted Margaret Mead's dictum that human nature was "the rawest, most undifferentiated of raw material."[1] This meant, in terms of learning theory, that animals are behaviorally a *tabula rasa,* that species differences are insignificant to behavior, and that all responses are equally conditionable to all stimuli.

This view of behavior was, when proposed, counter-intuitive to those experienced with animals and it was absurd to zoologists of the Lorenzian stamp. Nevertheless it was an empirical hypothesis and therefore could be tested against evidence that had accumulated to that time. Freeman's review of the evidence showed that the three cardinal theses of environmentalism were disproved by solid evidence. Species differences are bounded by distinctive phylogenetic adaptations (or repertoires of innate behavior) that mark the adaptive divergence of species as clearly as do anatomical, neurological, and biochemical adaptations. Animals are not then *tabula rasa* but present a predictable range of behaviors. Further, individuals of the same species are not interchangeable, as learning theory proposes, because the genetic variation built into the conditions of sexual reproduction of diploid species ensures that each individual is endowed with a unique combination of physical, behavioral, and motivational traits.

The hypothesis that all responses are equally conditionable could scarcely survive the first two rebuttals. Freeman cited Breland and Breland's anecdotal classic, "The Misbehavior of Organisms," as evidence against it. Breland and Breland made light of of learning research by pointing out, in a series of amusing animal stories, the transience of laboratory conditioned responses in contrast to the stability of natural behavior. For the explication of physiological and neurobiological mechanisms (innate signal detectors, neural circuits, and releasing mechanisms) that gave substance to the concept of natural behavior discussed by the Brelands, Freeman cited the research of Ernst von Holst, P. A. Weiss, Karl Lashley, Wilder Penfield, and Roger Sperry, among others. He laid particular stress on

---

[1] Freeman had at that time satisfied himself that *Coming of Age in Samoa* had been received into this intellectual milieu and had the galvanizing effect he later attributed to it in Chapter Seven of *Margaret Mead and Samoa.* Freeman himself was one of those recruited to this enthusiasm in remote New Zealand—a testimony to its global reach.

Lorenz's discovery of imprinting and G. R. Sackett's demonstration that rhesus monkeys reared in isolation are able to identify images of conspecifics although they have never seen them.

What had this to do with Homo? Had not our species, thanks to language, escaped the realm of necessity? Not if modern evolutionary theory is accepted. It was now understood, Freeman advised, that the morphological and other continuities observed in animal species are founded on the extraordinary informational density of the inheritance material, DNA. This information carried instructions for building animals and the behavioral programs enabling them to flourish in their respective niches. "And these are conclusions," Freeman declared, "which indubitably apply to all of us, for one of the facts of which we may all be sure is that all of our lineal ancestors . . . reached reproductive age."

To establish the empirical application of these principles to Homo, Freeman discussed recent discoveries about that seemingly most undifferentiated of all human raw material, infants. Citing the work of Teitelbaum on the spontaneous cyclic activity of infants, Freeman progressed to the discovery of sensitive learning times and their significance for understanding bonding or affiliation in mammals and humans—a subject he has investigated throughout his career. Here, he proposed, were the roots of that key element in the social organization of primitive societies, kinship. Biology reaches yet more deeply into the anthropologist's domain. Language, so often proposed as distinctive of the human species, turns out on investigation to be yet another system of animal communication replete with neural controls. He cited Hackett to the effect that the development of verbal behavior is "as inevitable as menarche" and invoked Lenneberg's authority to assert that the processes through which a natural language is expressed are "species-specific, innate properties of man's biological nature."

Having ascertained that kinship and language are biologically based, Freeman marched boldly forward to occupy the citadel. He took as the foil Alfred Kroeber's dictum that culture could not have evolved because there was nothing resembling it among animal species. It was Kroeber's view that the cultural capacity for the transmission of learned behavior originated by a sudden "leap into another plane." Freeman's triumphant rebuttal of this particular foundation of cultural determinism bears repeating:

The subsequent discoveries of prehistoric archaeology and of the ethological study of infra-human primate behavior have reduced Kroeber's theory to the status of a private fantasy, for it is now known . . . that rudimentary cultural behavior does indeed exist among infra-human primates; furthermore, both the palaeontological and archaeological evidence demonstrate an unbroken evolutionary continuity. Kroeber's theory, therefore, must be rejected, as also, on genetical grounds, must the Lamarckian theory of human domestication advanced by Boas . . . .

The meaning of these tidings for his anthropological conspecifics Freeman drew out in the voice of reckoning that would become the hallmark of his polemics in the aftermath of the publication of *Margaret Mead and Samoa.* "Culture is a purely natural phenomenon . . . [n]ot a few social scientists . . . trained in yesteryear now find themselves far out on a conceptual limb not of their own making," he noted gravely; ". . . no one who professionally concerns himself with the study of men and their ways can afford any longer to pride himself on his illiteracy in matters biological." The indignity of persisting in this error moved Freeman, in 1979, to write the Registrar of the Australian National University to state that he "renounced" his "profession of the academic discipline of anthropology," and to seek redesignation as Professor of Human Ethology.[1]

The Interactionist Synthesis
    The interactionist synthesis was to be "a unified science of man." The unification would bring together what Boas and Durkheim had put asunder. This was an ambitious project indeed. The new science had to be sufficiently broad to absorb input from the many biological and behavioral sciences of today and the future. It must enunciate the conceptual equipment that the interactionist would use to observe, analyze, classify, and explain cultural diversity. And not least of all, it must be proof

---

[1]The request was ignored. Recently Freeman renewed his request and the Australian National University conferred the designation Emeritus Professor in Human Behaviour.

against the shocks of the discovery of mechanisms that may vex the personal sense of humanhood.

The basis of interactionism is for Freeman the phenomenon of choice, considered in its double aspect as a behavior and as a phylogenetic adaptation.[1]

It is crucial to the concept that the phenomenon is equally well established in subjective experience as in scientific observation. Subjectively, choice simply means electing one of several alternatives that the conscious mind has recognized. It is, of course, a ubiquitous human experience. This experience is proof against the shock of discovery of ever new natural determinisms because no matter what the course of research may turn up, it cannot obliterate the experience of choice.

The objective foundation of choice is that latitude of behavior, found in all animals however primitive, by which the animal applies its set patterns of behavior to the immediate situation; for example, the fight, flight, or freeze responses. Learning, which is the acquisition of a behavior pattern or the adaptation of an innate pattern to recurring habitat circumstance, is of course the prime example of choice.

To establish the objectivity of choice was by no means easy in the 1970s. The rediscovery of cognition in psychology was only beginning. Ethologists, allies against cultural determinists, were preoccupied with behavioral mechanisms and preferred to relegate the indeterminacy of animal learning to the stochastic process of ontogenetic adaptation.[2] To obtain a scientific warrant for the central position ascribed to choice in the theory construction of a unified science, Freeman had recourse to the speculations of the grand men in biology. Taking the large view of human history in evolutionary context, he and they recognized that our species is distinctive for the degree of its dependence on culture, that is, on learned behaviors socially transmitted. This was of course one of the founding facts of Boasian anthropology. But now it recurred on the fruitful soil of modern

---

[1]In this discussion I omit, for the sake of brevity, what Freeman regards as the most important dimension of the anthropology of choice—its ethical dimension.

[2]Freeman injected the phenomenon of choice into an international symposium on human ethology, held at Bad Homburg, West Germany, under the sponsorship of the Werner Reimers Foundation in October 1977. It took some doing, since the participants, according to Freeman's report, were not disposed to consider this topic seriously.

evolutionary theory where it was possible to rethink the evolutionary novelty of culture as itself an evolved adaptation which permitted rapid change of socially organized behavior without needing genetic modification to support those changes.

This process, long familiar as "cultural evolution," was Lamarckian in character. It had to be given a Darwinian basis. From the several formulations available at that time, Freeman selected that of Sherwood Washburn. Washburn proposed that natural selection may in some cases act on behavior, rather than on an adventitiously advantageous physical trait, to induce orthodox Darwinian changes of gene frequency in a given population. This is a general possibility applicable to any species; it becomes particularly interesting when applied to man. If tool use, for example, were the behavior selected in our hominid ancestors, that behavior would drive selection for brains best adapted for it. Each increment of neural complexity would in turn improve dexterity, so that a feedback between a particular intelligent behavior and physical modification would be established. The adaptive advantage of a proto-human behavior would then prove to have driven the evolution of our species and one could say with René Dubos, somewhat poetically, that man is the self-made species.[1]

With choice thus identified on the evolutionary scale as the motor of cultural evolution, and on the ontogenetic level as a significant control of individual behavior, it remained to specify how the study of culture could be organized by these two cardinal principles.

This Freeman has not done; a book on the anthropology of choice is promised. However, there is a programmatic statement of intent in several essays, particularly "The Anthropology of Choice" (1981) and "Sociobiology: The 'Antidiscipline' of Anthropology" (1980).

---

[1]Freeman however meant this literally. In "Human Nature and Culture" he quoted C. J. Herrick to the effect that "man's capacity for intelligently directed self-development confers on him the ability to determine the pattern of his culture and so shape the course of human evolution in directions of his own choice." There can be no intelligent direction of cultural evolution without a concept of the same and without a knowledge of the relevant constituents that require direction. Such knowledge is still unavailable. The basic mechanism postulated—natural selection of behaviors rather than physical traits—might operate very generally, so that it could be said of tool-using eusocial insects that they too shaped their own evolution by their choices. Since behavior is not preserved in fossils, such hypotheses would seem to be permanently speculative.

In these writings Freeman extols choice as a creation of mind so free from natural constraints that empirical connections between biology and culture are difficult to discern. Thus, while the brain is held to be a complex mechanism, this has no consequences for the nature and character of mind because the brain is a "self-programming cybernetic system on two legs." Values, which Freeman had previously intimated are deeply influenced by the phylogenetically old limbic brain, are now said to "owe their very existence to the exercise of choice . . . [i.e.] our own powers of judgment . . . ." The range of choice is virtually unlimited; choice can and does override biologically given propensities, as may be seen in "the endless range of exogenetic phenomenon . . . found in the hundreds of differing cultures." Smartly rebuffing E. O. Wilson's pretension to reduce anthropology to the sociobiology of a single species, Freeman denied that any cultural phenomenon had been demonstrated to be tethered to the genetic leash. In words that echoed the tradition of Boas and Durkheim, Freeman declared that "it is the existence of conventional behaviors, in great profusion, in all human populations, that establishes, indubitably, the autonomy of culture."

The "bewildering variety" of variation, which in the years after 1962 Freeman wished to subdue to the regularities of science, now became a refuge against an aggressively reductionist science that he feared would diminish man. That variety, stemming from the "open program" or indeterminacy of choice, he used to spike the cannon of sociobiology. To Wilson's question, what is man's ultimate nature, Freeman responded:

> humans . . . cannot be said to have any kind of "ultimate" nature. Indeed, I would argue that because of the way in which humans are able to create and select their own values, Homo sapiens can only be defined as a *self-defining* animal.

Of the anthropologists who responded to the sociobiological challenge, none chastised it more vehemently than Derek Freeman. The clarion call of 1970, that culture is a purely natural phenomenon, was now trumpeted by entomologists, to his dismay.[1] The genetic menace drove him for a period of about four

---

[1] It was not only Freeman's dismay. At the 1977 annual meeting of the American Anthropological Association, there was much agitation against sociobiology and

years back to the conventional anthropological thesis of the autonomy of culture which he had previously seen to be inconsistent with a unified science of man. It was ironical then that in the Samoa debate, his solidarity with cultural anthropologists about erring sociobiology was ignored so that he could be stigmatized as a biological determinist and even a sociobiologist.

The cadres of anthropologists, primatologists, and others who regularly published "bioanthropological" research lent little public support to Freeman's advocacy. Some held back because of his negative evaluation of sociobiology; others felt that their established research paths would not be promoted by renewed controversy.[1]

These attitudes highlight Freeman's peculiar relation to the "unified human science" that he calls his "passion in life." That passion has been a quest to enunciate an idea or orientation, and to facilitate its scholarly ratification. He has not advanced a specific theory of cultural evolution, or of the interaction of a segment of human biology with a segment of culture; nor has he published empirical research describing some specific interaction. The students he trained were not given a distinctive interactionist methodology or problem. The Festschrift for his seventieth birthday bore the humanistic title *Choice and Morality in Anthropological Perspective*; none of the nine contributors were "bioanthropologists." His major contribution to the ratification of the new orientation was the refutation of the data and theoretical conclusion of a then fifty year old book regarded by most anthropologists as belonging more to their discipline's history than to its present. Had *Margaret Mead and Samoa* been published a decade before it was, its closing exhortation on the new horizon of unified human science would have been a harbinger. But coming after seven years of debate apprising the scholarly world of the new sociobiological dispensation, the call to reform was familiar. Freeman could maintain the harbinger posture through the years of controversy because his critics largely endorsed unregenerate cultural anthropology. But his polemics so antagonized colleagues that the net effect may be to retard the spread of interactionist research.

---

a motion was put to condemn it as racist, sexist, and unscientific. There was strong support for this action until Margaret Mead took the podium and strongly advised against the motion. It was defeated on a close vote.

[1] Personal communications from William E. Irons and Vernon Reynolds.

Between 1979 and 1981, Wilson arrived at a sociobiological interpretation of human evolution. In *Mind, Genes, and Culture* (1981) and *Promethean Fire* (1983), written in collaboration with Charles J. Lumsden, genetic evolution and cultural evolution were brought into systematic relation in a way that ascribed a central role to choice in the course of cultural evolution while yet holding choice on a genetic leash. This leash is epigenetic rules, which summarize, in the calculus of population genetics, the gene-culture interaction that assembles a human mind with distinct innate preferences that bias its choices.

Freeman withdrew his objections to sociobiology once Wilson incorporated choice as an element of theory. However, the sociobiology of the evolution of choice does not appear to be compatible with Freeman's formulation of interactionism. According to Freeman, interaction is between human phylogenetic endowments and culture, where culture is construed as an independent variable stemming from choice. In *Mind, Genes and Culture* (1981) and *Promethean Fire* (1983) Lumsden and Wilson devised a theory that interpreted culture as the *dependent* variable deriving from the choices made by the hominid brain. They purported to show how the mind of Homo sapiens was "assembled" through the interaction of somatic properties, behavior and natural selection. Natural selection operates on behaviors in such a way as to evolve minds constrained to choose in accordance with innate preferences, or epigenetic rules. This is the basic genetic model of the culture-making animal—an animal that makes culture because that activity is mandated by its genes.[1] It is, one might say, the last word in determinism: we have no choice but to choose according to rules natural selection has shaped.

As it happened, I had a discussion with Wilson one month after Freeman saw him during his 1983 American tour. *Promethean Fire* was just out and cultural evolution was on my mind as one theme of a book then nearing completion. Epigenetic rules seemed to me a major conceptual advance linking behavior *and* psychobiology with evolutionary change. Ethological research had suggested that something like epigenetic

---

[1]This theory, known as "co-evolution," was devised by William Durham. For a discussion of the background, see Lumsden and Wilson, *Promethean Fire: Reflections on the Origin of Mind* (Cambridge: Harvard University Press, 1983), pp. 48-50.

rules must exist, but a distinct idea of their content had not been formed. It was a decided encouragement that a theory was now available. My studies had impressed on me the repetitiveness of thought and behavior across cultures and through historical time; epigenetic rules were a way to interpret the uniformities. They could be used to exhibit the diversity human works and deeds as enactments of the species' genetic endowment. The enactments include numerous ways in which individuals and cultures have defined themselves through the elaboration of distinctive rituals, customs and beliefs. But the deep structures revealed by biology enable the social scientist to penetrate the often xenophobic differentiations to discern the common humanity forming the armature of the detail.

It is nevertheless true that the common humanity is a diminished humanity. Freeman's assault on sociobiology may be read as the expression of a highly differentiated human being, steeped in the lore of diversity, protesting reduction to the common denominator. This insight is no doubt essential; the new human science aborning will need to be equally conversant with life in all its petty or grand detail and with the deep mechanisms that contain us within the primate order.

Maintaining a dual focus on detail as well as generality is requisite for any sound knowledge. Peculiar difficulties arise in the present case owing to the perturbations stemming from a third focus—ourselves. We are prone to invest projects for self-knowledge with gravity, and in this mood we overlook the comic aspects of that elusive quest.

Chapter II

Method and Ethnography

Coming of Age Defended

Margaret Mead

Editor's Note
This letter, dated January 6, 1974, appears to be Mead's most
extensive unpublished defense of her Samoa work. It is to be
taken in conjunction with her published defense—to which abundant reference is made in the letter—Reflections on Later Theoretical Work on the Samoans, in the second edition of the *Social Organization of Manu'a* The letter to Goodman responds to his
questions and criticisms. Central among these is the matter of
Samoan aggression, which was said to be momentary and non-
lethal in *Coming of Age in Samoa,* a view which appears to be
unique among ethnographers of Samoa. As Mead records in this
letter, she had become aware of Samoan "touchiness" and sought
an explanation alternative to that proposed by Goodman and
Freeman, who derive it from the harsh punishment of Samoan
children. In the second edition of the *Social Organization of
Manu'a*, she preferred the theory of Gloria Cooper, who derived
touchiness from the inconsistency between public indulgence of
the child's misbehavior and severity toward the same in private.
The letter is printed with permission of Richard Goodman and
Mary Catherine Bateson.

I am afraid this letter may be too late to be of any further use
to you as I have been busier than I expected since I returned to the
United States last fall and have barely kept my head above water.
However on the chance that your book is not yet finished, or has

113

not been put into proof, I will add a few more points to our earlier discussion.

I assume that you have now looked at pages 226-228 of the paperback edition of the *Social Organization of Manu'a,* where I raise the whole question of how Samoans develop their intense vulnerability to small insults and present some hypotheses about it. These I assume you have included.

Since I spoke to you last, I have spent a week in Fiji, talking with Samoans and about Samoans to a good many people there, *papalagis* and other Polynesians. The main complaint about them is their pride and touchiness. This served to accentuate what I believe I may have mentioned to you on the telephone when we discussed the behavior of Samoans in the United States before and after World War II. I am more convinced than ever, that Samoans do not forgive what they regard as intentional slights. In 1925-6, they did not assume that any of the Americans with whom they came in contact knew enough to give intentional slights. Instead they laughed covertly at the ignorance of the Americans whom they could insult without the Americans ever guessing what was happening. "Do you think we get out a *taupou* for a paymaster." Similarly in their United States contacts with Americans, there was no reason for them to expect any detailed knowledge of Samoan custom. You asked, in your second letter (June 24, 1973) what I knew about Samoans abroad before World War II. I knew only three groups, those in Hawaii associated with Sua, those in San Diego associated with Ufuti's family, and the troop of Samoan dancers led by the Manu'an who later became the Tufele, who were in this country for several years after being brought here to make a film. What I think has happened is that Samoans abroad encountered after the war Hawaiians and other Pacific Islanders in Hawaii, (and in New Zealand, where they also have accumulated a reputation for extreme contentiousness) and began to assume that other Pacific Islanders were insulting them on purpose. That is, they expected a knowledgeable deference from Pacific Islanders which they did not expect from Americans or white New Zealanders. This is equally true at the University of the Pacific. They are in a state of irritable resentment at the failure of other islanders to treat them as they feel they should be treated. So the question comes back to: what is the basis for this extreme response to very slight cues? I see no theoretical basis for the "*uma* process"[1] as you call it, and as Freeman calls it, being explanatory. Gloria Cooper's interpretation, which I have published, but unfortunately she never has published her Samoan work, seems to me much more likely to provide a clue. There must be some experience of discrepant intent back of the intensity with which intended insult is experienced.

I also feel, after talking with Derek Freeman again in Canberra last fall, that Ta'ū in 1928 was something of a sheltered spot, no alcohol, only two enlisted men and one pharmacist's mate, a moratorium on the competition between parts of Ta'ū, and between Ta'ū and Fitiuta, etc. You are, of course, free—and I would think obligated—to publish those three concluding pages to the new edition of *Social Organization of Manu'a*.

I am also more convinced than ever that there must be a great deal of male fantasizing about what they would do to a girl who . . . which gets turned into memories of what young men said they did do.[2] I do not believe any Samoan girl who was not feeble minded would go out to a remote spot alone to meet a boy and then turn him down with the expectation that he would then knock her unconscious and rape her. But I do believe that Samoan young men, talking among themselves and to you, might well relate such exploits. We know of this kind of thing in many other cultures. In Bali, because a man is expected to give his daughter to his brother's son, marriages to other than parallel patrilineal cousins have to be disguised as marriages by capture. The bridegroom arranges an assignation with the girl, and takes along a group of young male kinsmen. If there are any spectators, they seize her and she screams; if there are none, she walks off with her intended husband. Occasionally a Balinese boy will believe that such marriages are accomplished by capture and attempt to carry off an unwilling girl and throw the whole com-

---

[1] *Uma* means "Be done!" The "*uma* process" is the utterance of this phrase while slapping the infant on the legs or buttocks, which makes the infant cry the more. The process continues until the infant chokes on its tears, as described by Goodman below. Freeman summarizes reported observations on the punishment of infants in *Margaret Mead and Samoa*, pp. 206-07. Mead had stated that Samoan children are not "carefully disciplined" until the age of five or six. Thereafter "summary chastisements" do occur, but "consistent and long disciplinary measures are absent." Augustin Krämer, writing in 1901, reported that Samoan children are not physically punished.—Ed.

[2] The ellipsis is Mead's.—Ed.

munity into an uproar. The boy has misheard the meaning of the behavior, which the Balinese will verbally describe as a capture. We have checked such accounts against the actuality.

Similarly, in Puerto Rico, men add to their machismo by seducing virgins and other men's wives, and by protecting their own virgin daughters and chaste wives. As a result, most men have to content themselves with loose women or prostitutes. There is the same kind of asymmetry as there is in Samoan village rivalries.[1]

Your description of how Samoan children are treated has to be considered against the treatment of children in other cultures. Both Holmes and Cooper thought it harsh when compared with middle class America, as it was. But nothing that I saw made it very harsh as compared, for example, with the treatment of lower class children by many groups in the United States who, nevertheless, do not end up with such touchiness and aggressive fantasies as the Samoans.

It may be that within urban contexts like Pago Pago or Apia, the very delicate set of hints and responses through which courtship is conducted within isolated villages is blunted, and as a result boys think girls have given them signals of assent, and are enraged to find that they are repelled, and "rape" results. This happens frequently in large American cities where people of different class, or region, or ethnic background, mistake the clues and "rape" results, often not accompanied by anger, initially, but rape is, of course, always retrospectively interpreted as having involved anger.[2]

As a matter of interest you might compare my account of post mortem caesarian on Ta'ū, performed by the medical assistant with the clinic equipment, with one published in 1940, by Donald Sloan. If his account was accurate, which I have no very good reason to believe it was, there was an extreme change in ethos in a period of some 12 years. I enclose his account as the book is hard to come by. My account is on page 93 of the American paperback.

---

[1] In _Coming of Age_, sexual rivalry of this high anxiety sort was said not to exist in Samoa.—Ed.

[2] By placing quotation marks around the word "rape," and ascribing the act to mistaken cues, Mead may be defending the view taken in _Coming of Age_ that in Samoa "rape is inconceivable."

I assume also that you will have corrected the variety of assumptions which you scattered through the book, such as (page 18) that I spent most of my time with nuclear families. And I also assume that you will stop implying that I ever misrepresented what I did. For example you say (page 16) that *Blackberry Winter* reveals that I lived with the Holts. If you will look carefully at the acknowledgements to *Coming of Age in Samoa*, you will find my statement of the four months residence in their home. In fact it's this continuous attempt to discredit me—in the face of my careful documentation of what actually occurred—that perplexes me. You assert your only desire is to add to our knowledge of human nature, and that of Samoan character formation in particular, and to correct my failures to study what I was not sent to study, namely the care of young children. As I demonstrated when Gloria Cooper went to Samoa (1961), and before I had met Derek Freeman, I knew that the extreme touchiness about insult was something which I did not understand and I asked her to work on it. Yet your work is subtly designed to discredit me, inferring that I used an interpreter when you quote my statement that I didn't,[1] or that I hid the fact that I lived at the Holts, or that I spent a lot of time on ethnography. (If you had read *Social Organization of Manu'a* carefully, you would realize how much of its "density" is based on the old literature, simply used as context for the Manu'an version.) The whole tone, in spite of your protestation of respect, looks like an attempt to discredit me, or at least to base your book primarily on using my name to sell it. You say neither of these are your motives. If they are, then you have to do some very careful work on your sources—my work—and stop making misstatements.

January 9, 1974

Here I decided to telephone you.

I am interested to hear that you plan to illustrate your own ethnographies.

I think I should add one note about the question of spellings in the *Social Organization of Manu'a*. I cannot reconstruct the whole setting of difficulties now, but I know that we had tremendous difficulties over discrepancies in spelling which I was unable to get the Bishop Museum to correct. When I wrote the new

---

[1] Mead's knowledge of the Samoan language is discussed on pp.158-161.—Ed.

chapter I asked that the spelling be corrected and regularized and this was finally refused. If I had had Derek Freeman's list of errors it might have been possible to persuade them at least to publish a list of errata.[1] The original text was done from *Pratt's Dictionary,* but there were all sorts of theories about Polynesian which crept in. For words which neither occurred in Pratt's dictionary nor in Churchill's manuscript, I would have to take responsibility. But I should have fought that battle harder. I was on the way to the field and very rushed and I seemed to be getting nowhere.

Queries to Boas on Method

Margaret Mead

Editor's Note
   In this letter, dated January 5, 1926, Mead sought the advice of on whether she ought to present her results in statistical form. Boas responded that a statistical presentation was undesirable because it would be misleading: "Statistical work will require the tearing out of its natural setting, some particular aspect of behavior which, without that setting, may have no meaning whatever." Boas encouraged Mead's preference for expressing meaning in a "rounded" account. The data Mead might have used for the statistical description found its way into the Appendix of *Coming of Age in Samoa.* This letter was first published in the *History of Anthropology Newsletter* together with a commentary by G[eorge] W. S[tocking] (vol. 14, 1987, 3-10). Mead's letter is printed with the permission of Mary Catherine Bateson.

---

[1]Freeman did call the Bishop Museum's attention to the more than 200 hundred spelling and transliteration errors in *Social Organization,* but without result. The *American Anthropologist* also declined to publish his list of errata. See below, pp. 160-161.—Ed.

Dear Dr Boas:

This will acknowledge your letter of November 7th. That for all your generous haste in answering it it reached me after I had been settled in Manu'a for six week[s]. Which very neatly demonstrates the hopelessness of trying to correspond about anything down here.

I am enclosing my report to the Research Council which is required by the first of March. I have sent them two copies under separate cover and registered. If by any chance they should fail to reach the Council and they should advise you of the fact would you see that they get a copy, please. I have to take endless precautions because there is no regular mail service here and we have to entrust our mail to the good nature of a series of irresponsible individuals. I realize how irregular it is for you not to have had an opportunity to criticize and approve this report. But if I had sent it earlier, I should have two weeks instead of five to report on and furthermore there would have been no time for your criticisms to have reached me. It therefore seemed advisable to send my report directly to the Council [with] a definite statement that you had neither seen nor approved it in any way. And I hope that I said nothing in the report of which you would actively disapprove.

As to the content of the report, I have, as you see, made it exceedingly brief and tentative. While making absolutely no showing in conclusions at all, I could hardly enlarge further than I have done. Every conclusion I draw is subject to almost certain modification within the next ten days and is therefore pretty valueless. If the report satisfied the Council that I am working with passable efficiency, it will have accomplished as much as it could under the circumstances.

And now what I need most is advice as to method of presentation of results when I finally get them. Ideally, no reader should have to trust my word for anything, except of course in as much as he trusted my honesty and averagely intelligent observation. I ought to be able to marshall an array of facts from which another would be able to draw independent conclusions. And I don't see how in the world I can do that. Only two possibilities occur to me and both seem inadequate. First I could present my material in semi-statistical fashion. It would be fairly misleading at that because I can't see how any sort of statistical technique would be of value. But I could say "Fifty adolescents between such and such ages were observed. Of these ten had step-mothers, and five of ten didn't love their step-mothers, two were indifferent and three were devoted. Fifteen had some sex experience, five of the fifteen before puberty, etc.'' All of which would be quite valueless, because whether fifty is a fair sample or not, could be determined only on the basis of my personal judgment. And saying you don't love your step-mother, or that you rebel against your grandfather but mind your older sister, or any of the thousand little details on the observation of which will depend my final conclusions as to submission and rebellion within the family circle, are all meaningless when they are treated as isolated facts. And yet I doubt whether the Ogburns[1] of science will take any other sort of result as valid.

Then I could use case histories, like this. "X L7-3 is a girl of 12 or 13 (ages have to be as doubt[ful] as that). She is just on the verge of puberty. Her father is a young man with no title and a general reputation for shiftlessness. Her mother is likewise young and irresponsible, given to going off visiting and leaving X with the care of her five younger brothers and sisters. X is nevertheless excessively devoted to her mother, showing an unusual amount of demonstrative affection for her. The girl is decidedly overworked and is always carrying a baby. They are quite poor and she never has even any passable respectable clothes. Her mother is a relative of the high chief of Y, and as poor relations a great [deal] of unpleasant work falls to the share of X and her sister of 9. Her younger sister is much prettier and more attractive and is the mother's favorite (the father is negligible). X is tall, angular, loud voiced and awkward, domineering towards all her younger relatives, obstinate, sulky, quick to take offense. She regards her playmates as so many obstacles to be beaten over the head. She has no interest in boys whatsoever, except as extra antagonists. All her devotion seems to be reserved for her mother and the pretty little sister" (etc.). I can probably write two or three times as much about each one of them before I leave. But to fill such case histories with all the minutiae which make them significant to me when they are passing before my eyes is next to impossible. And the smaller the details become, the more dangerous they become if they are to be taken just as so many separate facts which can be added up to prove a point.

---

[1]The reference is to William Ogburn, a leading proponent of quantitative methods. Mead had attended his courses at Columbia University.

For instance, how many other little girls carry babies all the time, and how many other mothers go visiting. Facts which possess significance in one case but which are mere bagatelles of externality in another would have to be included in each case history or they would not be comparable.

As I indicated in my report I am making a thorough personnel study of the whole community. These provided me with a tremendous background of detail.

. . . As rank does not depend on primogeniture nor necessarily upon being the son of a chief rather than a relation, one must know in addition who are the favorites, and why, etc. But you see what type of information this gives me, and the numerous questions I can answer on the basis of it. I had to have it anyhow in order to thread my way through the mass of gossip and village happening.

But how to use it. If I simply write conclusions and use my cases as illustrative material will it be acceptable? Would it be more acceptable if I could devise some method of testing the similarity of attitudes among the girls, in a quantitative way? For instance no Samoa[n] who knows I'm married ever fails to say "have you any children?" NO. Talofai. Poor you. This is the universal response from men and women, except in the case of the boarding school girls. Now would it be more convincing if I could present an array of such responses indicating attitudes with actual numbers and questions—as "Of the fifty girls questioned, 47 said they hoped to marry soon and 45 wanted at least five children." I wouldn't feel any wiser after collecting information in that style but maybe the results would be strengthened. It will of course be fairly easy to demonstrate a fairly dead level of background and information.

I am sorry to bother you with so much detail, but this is a point on which I am very much at sea. I think I should be able to get an answer in time to get some help. On second thought, I'll not enclose my report in this letter (the report contains nothing which I haven't written you) but send it air mail. If you could dash off an airmail answer I might get it sometime in March. You see that is quite late and will perhaps forgive my importunity.

The hurricane, no. II, has messed everything up nicely, but as Tutuila and Western Samoa were equally wrecked, I shan't make any change in my plans.[1] It will considerably lessen my chances of getting ethnological information by observation, as nothing important can occur without a feast and there will be a famine here for months where every morsel of food will have to be hoarded. My health continues to withstand the onslaughts of the tropics.

Mead's Configurationalism

Marvin Harris

Editor's Note

Marvin Harris' quest for a materialist anthropology set him apart from the culturalist orientation of most of his contemporaries but especially from the psychological orientation called "configurationalism." This comment, which appeared in *The Rise of Anthropological Theory* (1968), was commonly considered to be the most energetic published criticism of Mead until the appearance of Freeman's book. Nevertheless, Harris saw no merit in Freeman's refutation when it appeared and indeed penned an aggressive critique of it (Chapter IV). Printed with permission of Harper & Row.

Configurationalism, the identification of salient cultural characteristics and their presentation in a familiar psychological idiom, was the forerunner of the rapprochement between historical particularism and psychoanalysis. We see this quite clearly in the case of Margaret Mead, who as a student of both Benedict and Boas made extensive use of the configurationalist frame during her formative period.

Coming of Age in Samoa (1928), the first major product of Mead's prodigious outpouring of field-based books and monographs, bore the subtitle A Psychological Study of Primitive Youth for Western Civilization. Although this book was far richer in psychologistic phrasings than the usual ethnographic report, it cannot be said to reflect an interest in the summing up of a

---

[1] Mead did not mention this natural disaster in her depiction of Samoa as unstressed by "poverty or great disasters."—Ed.

whole culture in terms of a few dominant categories. Mead's mission, chosen for her by Boas, was to emphasize the existence of biopsychological plasticity in human affairs sufficient to permit the cultural conditioning of adolescent behavioral patterns along lines which contrast with the stereotype of adolescence in middle-class Euro-American culture. The use of the phrase "for Western Civilization" in the subtitle and the inclusion of two chapters concerned with the comparison of the Samoan adolescent girl with her counterpart in the United States indicate the importance which Boas and Mead attached to the simple demonstration of the power of cultural conditioning in this area of life. The fact that Samoan sex patterns turned out to be strikingly less inhibited than their Western analogues could not have been unanticipated. That adolescence was not necessarily a stormy and awkward biological age was additional support for Boas' emphasis upon the influence of culture as opposed to biology. And it also corresponded well with the contemporary interest in Freudian psychology and the role of sex in pathological personalities. The Samoan's relative freedom from sexually inspired frustrations was eagerly incorporated into the scientific foundation of the "sexual revolution" which the American middle class was in the process of experiencing. There was also a strong feminist moral in *Coming of Age in Samoa*, highlighted by the description of a carefree premarital sex life for adolescent girls. But the most important moral proposed by Mead was very similar to that which Benedict was to urge in *Patterns of Culture* six years later: Knowledge of the spectrum of possibilities of enculturation should be made to contribute to our own process of sociocultural change. Like Benedict, Mead found an antidote for cultural determinism in the prospect that once a knowledge of alternative patterns become widespread, significant changes in the Euro-American way of life would necessarily ensue:

> . . . it is unthinkable that a final recognition of the great number of ways in which man, during the course of history and at the present time, is solving the problems of life, should not bring with it in turn the downfall of our belief in a single standard.

Coming of Age in Samoa did not attempt the configurationalist synthesis of the sort on which Benedict was working. But there are many points of similarity between Mead's and Benedict's early writings, especially from a methodological perspective, and these resemblances increased as time wore on. Mead as much as Benedict succumbed to the temptation to exaggerate the decisiveness with which both individual and cultural personality types can be identified and contrasted. Although the proposal to find out what is going on "inside of peoples' heads"—to find out how they think and feel—is perfectly respectable, it must be admitted that other forms of cultural investigation are decidedly less risky. No one would wish to assert that even a matter so simple as counting the members of a household is without its methodological pitfalls, but the problems associated with developing verifiable statements about how a man feels toward his mother or his wife are more numerous and much more exposed to the observer's moods and fancies.

Mead has recently argued that the adherence to a physicalist model of science in anthropology is premature, and she has underscored the "need for waiting until appropriate theories and methods have been developed to fit our exceedingly complex materials into an evolving framework." Yet it cannot be said that her own launching into the domain of culture and personality was anything less than precipitous. In the absence of operationally acceptable research techniques, it might very well be argued that the entire configurationalist approach was premature and that the attempt to sketch the typical Samoan girl's feelings and emotions during the transition from puberty to marriage was entirely too ambitious an undertaking.

In this regard it should be stressed that ethnography can easily become overcautious and obsessed with a passion for verifiable minutiae. That is also a grave threat to scientific standards, and I would certainly not wish to be associated with a point of view which demeans the role of impressionistic, nonstatistical data in cultural anthropology. But the most important consideration regarding the appropriateness of research methods, which are relatively "soft" in terms of verifiability, is the nature of the articulation between the data and the corpus of orienting theory. If the data-collecting process is designed to maximize the opportunities for continuous correction in relationship to a set of cross-culturally relevant hypotheses, one may tolerate a considerable amount of guesswork and nonquantitative generalization out of the conviction that some data is better than no data and that the errors will call attention to themselves during the process of cross-cultural comparison. Yet it is precisely the development of systematic cross-cultural comparisons which Mead believes is premature for culture and personality studies and which she believes involve a "violation of the actual complexity of the materials."

Let us consider what this means in terms of one of the sweeping ethnographic generalities which leave many of her colleagues in a state of wide-eyed wonder. Samoan girls, according to Mead, move through puberty and adolescence without major psychological conflicts, and this is especially true in the area of sexual development. The result is that "the girls' minds were perplexed by no conflicts, troubled by no philosophical queries, beset by no remote ambitions." For a generalization which is at once so sweeping and so thoroughly dependent upon "getting inside of heads," Mead's style conveys an unnerving degree of conviction. To be sure, Mead does take up several cases of girls "in conflict." But these are treated as deviants and as requiring no modification in her major point. It is not possible to bring this picture of a serene, even apathetic, passage to maturity into line with a corpus of interrelated and testable hypotheses of cross-cultural and causal significance. There is some evidence from other Oceanic societies which suggests that Mead's Samoan findings were exaggerated. As Barnouw points out, studies in Truk and Ifaluk by Gladwin, Sarason, and Spiro indicate that premarital sexual freedom and an apparently placid and leisurely life is no guarantee that deep inner frustrations and anxieties are not also present.

The Oceanic Ethnography of Margaret Mead[1]

Nancy McDowell

The fundamental premise that data are always raw material to be used to further understanding of human behavior and to improve the quality of life is explicitly behind all of Mead's work and explains its dual nature. Simply, data can be used in two ways: (1) to enlighten nonanthropologists, educated laypeople, and professionals in other fields, and to inform social-policy deci-

---

[1]Reproduced by permission of the American Anthropological Association from *American Anthropologist* 82:2, (1980):278-303. Not for further reproduction.

sions; (2) to provide the material for professional scientific work and theory-building on the nature of human behavior.

Many of Mead's ethnographic publications are specifically designed for use by the general public, e.g., *Coming of Age in Samoa, Growing Up in New Guinea,* and *Sex and Temperament in Three Primitive Societies.* They are meant to inform and enlighten, to educate on the nature of human cultural diversity. Further, she holds the mirror in which we, specifically Americans, might see and understand ourselves better. In *Coming of Age in Samoa,* for example, she informs us that adolescence need not be traumatic, that such a stormy period is a cultural creation. Her work on Manus provides a platform upon which she makes astute comments on the American educational system and recommendations for changing it, and allows her to test then-contemporary educational theories. She uses ethnographic data to debunk current myths, such as "mother-right," as well as to illustrate more general theoretical arguments. Her data, however, are useful as a mirror not only for us but also for the people studied and the developing countries in which they live. She does not fear to make recommendations in this direction: she advocates, for example, using the best teachers at the early levels in Papua New Guinea schools, rather than "saving them" for the secondary levels; she makes suggestions on the establishment of courts in Papua New Guinea; she is critical of the way in which the Australian colonial government instituted the council system for local government in the Admiralty Islands. Always aware of the social and political context within which anthropology is practiced, she has the main goal of documenting human plasticity and variability so that we might better understand ourselves: "From these contrasts, which are vivid enough to startle and enlighten those accustomed to our own way of life and simple enough to be grasped quickly, it is possible to learn many things . . ."

Mead is also keenly aware of the scientific use of data. She frequently makes reference to other societies as "natural laboratories" but goes beyond by explicitly ensuring that her data are of use to other, perhaps later, scholars with more advanced theories. In 1961, in a new preface to *Coming of Age in Samoa,* she wrote: ". . . but because each generation must begin anew and, in doing so, must stand on the shoulders of the one before, there is perhaps a continuing usefulness in this book . . . ." She once chided participants in a conference for being inadequately aware that data must be in a form useful to researchers in the future.

She directs readers to alternative ways of using and analyzing the data she published, and frequently suggests areas needing future investigation.

Most significant is her concern for the precision and accuracy of the data she gathered, unsound and weak data are of use to no one:

> When field data are so good that they can be used retrospectively, especially by other investigators, it is a genuine tribute to the thoroughness of the field-work, and incidentally, a validation of the accuracy of the cultural interpretations.

. . . In presenting her material accurately and precisely, Mead is a careful and exceptionally honest ethnographer. She describes the conditions within which fieldwork was conducted, including the extent to which the presence of the investigator might warp the material. Reasons for choosing a particular field site are explicit. When photographs are used, especially where they provide the basis for analysis . . . the reader is told the conditions under which the photographs were taken, who took them, whether they were in any sense "posed," and which if any had been retouched.[1] She is also careful to record those situations in which she intervened. When she is unsure of the data, she explains why.

---

[1] According to Lola Romanucci-Ross, Mead refused to allow her crew to film an altercation in Pere village because she had written that there is no fighting in Manus. Derek Freeman, *et al., Transcript of Interviews for the Documentary Film Margaret Mead and Samoa* (Sydney, 1987), Tape 28, p. 40.—Ed.

Mead as Ethnographer and Mythmaker

Lola Romanucci-Ross

Editor's Note
The author of this essay collaborated with Mead in Manus and for two decades was of the inner circle of what Mead called her "family." Her experience is thus particularly relevant to the evaluation of Mead's ethnography. Romanucci-Ross published two essays on Mead's field methods prior to the commencement of the Samoa controversy (see the bibliography of this volume). The present selection appeared in _Reviews in Anthropology_ 10 (1983):85-92 under the title, "Apollo Alone and Adrift in Samoa: Early Mead Reconsidered." Printed by permission of the author.

In finding ethnographic flaws in a "negative instance" of stressful adolescence, Derek Freeman hopes to demonstrate that his refutation of Mead's thesis has implications for the future of research in anthropology.
. . . We can rightly reject as inappropriate to our discipline the experimental model of research on myocardial infarct size reduction. But if our researches are to be considered in any sense a scientific endeavor we cannot reject the concept that phenomenologies must, at least in some basic ways, converge to validation by consensus even if subject to change over time. Short of this, we must reconcile ourselves to producing libraries of idioversal anthropoetry. Are anthropological investigations subject to any rules of scientific inquiry or is it really impossible to ever prove anyone wrong?
. . . I have written on Margaret Mead as a fieldworker, having observed her in Manus and elsewhere, and through the reading of most of her field notes. But some remarks on the disparity of the conclusions of two fieldworkers in the same area might be addressed in addition, here.
Although Mead's fieldwork methods became more sophisticated in time, one "basic" remained constant. She went into a field situation to find an answer to a question of vast importance to the times. (She often criticized my notes because of my great "unrealistic" concern with "what was really there" rather than having a problem orientation.) To give some examples of Mead's approach: the answer to sex and repression was to be found in

Samoa; to the high cost of stereotyping sex roles, in New Guinea; to dilemmas of child-rearing in Bali; and to the best pacing for culture change (as well as child-rearing), in Manus. Equally important to her was the exchange of information with other researchers elsewhere and their insights at the time of her field researches. Malinowski in 1927 had declared the absence of neuroses in the Trobriands raising the question, for Mead, for neuroses in Samoa.

On several continents discussions of ethos were "in the air" and Mead's correspondence with Ruth Benedict, who was busy misinterpreting Nietzsche (Romanucci-Ross 1980:306) brought her the Apollonian/Dionysian sorting device which Mead found a "revelation." This Benedictine revelation dragged Apollo from Olympus through ancient Greece (as a 19th century English invention), through the Southwest U.S.A., and to Samoa: an Apollo deprived (by Benedict) not only of the necessary presence of Dionysius for his own proper identity, but his name as well. Thus, the Samoans came of age as mild-eyed lotus eaters passing their days in sexual dalliance with no pater- nor mater-familias to recognize the value of a woman to exchange.

This accomplished some good things for tormented pre-maritals back home and for professionals who gave lectures on human behavior. Mead, who did think of herself as an educator (and not just parenthetically so), was indeed a mythmaker in the best and most profound sense of the word. Myths are morality tales, embodying the most basic of predictions that people can become what they "ought" to a remarkable degree. In the late 1920's: if parents could only believe that repression is bad, constraining, contra-creative and pathology-inducing! If individuals could be freed from sex-role stereotyping slavery! In the 1950's: if administrators could only believe that rapid culture change works! (Others had earlier called it "the privilege of historical backwardness"). Mead, as a muse of the clinical experience on the outposts of Western Empires found "instancings" of these possibilities. She had every confidence that somewhere along the way she would be proven correct. And I submit that Margaret Mead did prove her point that cultural beliefs determine behavior at least in the American society she so greatly influenced. Did we not, from the late 1930's to the late 1960's, move from socially repressed and denied sexual impulses to a socially approved sexual freedom? (With, to be sure, sequelae that she would not have predicted from her early writings).

Mead's Samoa and Freeman's Samoa are not simply a matter of divergent views nor did she see it that way nineteen years ago. There is such a thing as getting more information and more accurate information over a long period of time. Dr. Mead knew that, even though some of her current self-appointed "public defenders" argue as if they do not know it. In a three year intensive study of a Mexican village I would not have discovered the conflict, the violence, nor the mismatch of moral codes if the investigation had been restricted to the first year. I would have had a different analysis in the subsequent year also from the psychological tests and interviews and from diurnal affairs. Villager insistence on their style of conflict resolution as non-violent was unassailable until I went through thirty years of court records and began to get involved in all group activities of day and night year-in and year-out. My "view" from the first year would have been descriptively incorrect of the culture even though it was true to the time, true to my experience of it, true to the way it was presented to me.

. . . We have no shortage of the problematic in drawing conclusions from our own observations without the inclusion of undocumented accounts of events. Interpretation of cultural materials demands recognition that we are confronted with a series of personal inventions: the culture-bearer invents as he/she "acts out" and further invents in reportage. Up to this point, as we begin to describe (read "interpret") we can at least count on the convergence of probabilities within a manageable range. But this is then followed by the inventiveness of the investigator in linguistic and cultural translation (with increased intensity if a problem of grand proportions is being addressed by the exercise). In some areas (e.g., sex and cannibalism), asking a question is the best way to engender tactical evasions, or shocking confessions as a strategy by the informant for future manipulation and control. (There is a person behind the cultural mask, one who is not usually unprepared for the intruder, benign or malignant.) Silence, time, and blending in will bring "facts" tumbling your way, however, if factual material is really what you are seeking.

. . . Margaret Mead towered above many of her generation with her multitudinous talents which would loom larger rather than diminish as one learned to know her in greater degrees of intimacy. She has never been accused, however, of having been the most meticulous and persistent of linguists, historians or ethnographers. If, as Freeman says, she was not prepared to cope with that area where biology and culture interact, it can be asserted that no one from either discipline was or is. If, in our times, we note a flimsy movement in this direction, it is still fashionable to fragment both anthropology and biology into more specialized fields: symbolic, political, economic, macro-, socio-, cryo-, and a host of other hyphenations. Perhaps this current hyphenation process is an attempt to engage the gains of other disciplines into anthropology (an act of intellectual reciprocity). Or, perhaps it manifests an unexpressed recognition that any one concept (e.g. "culture") that explains everything, must, of logical necessity explain nothing.

Although the early cultural determinists did not deny that the culture-bearer is an organism that shares much with similar organisms, this belief was not usually reflected in their works. "Culture" as the exclusive explanatory principle is found in description, analysis, and explanation of the same corpus of data. In the past thirty years we have seen anthropological works that employ other paradigms to validate or qualify the cultural explanation. Such research can lend itself to intersubjective testability and to more accurate description. The propriety and necessity of formal refutation of an argument based on multiple observations by different observers is what the scientific process is all about; but it is not acceptable to close the loop back to a hopeless irreconcilable set of solipsisms.

This is not to belittle "insight" . . ., but the test of appropriateness of an "insight" is that it proceed from and lead to accurate description. Benedict's "patterns" insight did neither. . . . We are or should be concerned with reliability, i.e., a sufficient degree of confirmation. Freeman's volume does address concerns related to completeness of description and reliability. But there have been other anthropologists since 1928 (from the briefly serenaded to the unsung) who have also addressed these concerns in their works. And for that reason, the weakness of the Freeman volume, though not central to his main argument, lies in this area of non-acknowledgement. Progress in anthropological methods is glossed over in silence in that "leap" in the end of the book from Freeman's conclusions based on his refutation of Mead's early Samoan research to the uses of these in criticism of anthropology today. This unfortunately leads him to have us turn to latter day evolutionists for guidance in the study of culture. Anthropologists who have worked diligently and responsibly (as Freeman did himself!), though not all producing colorful copy, have carried the discipline forward to better ethnologizing and more accurate description. Through the development and refinement of our own methods we are sometimes somewhat closer to validity, reliability and authenticity.

There have long been those among us who follow David Hume and have therefore always been skeptical of those early Mead Samoans whose encoding of moral accommodations are or were described as beyond the periphery of human variation (as ever noted by any serious reporter). Freeman's persistent scholarship should have been welcomed.

It seems, however, that after being offered the demolition of a myth, the reader deserved more than the prescription that we look to one latter-day evolutionist's speculation on how "genetic programs open up" to "incorporate personally acquired information." Since this is not at present known or knowable, we may relegate such a statement to fiction science as a concept that may or may not join the evolution of testable ideas. We do not need to barter the fictions we discard for those of other disciplinarians whose words show they do not understand our methodological problems and at times do not even understand their own.

. . . Margaret Mead, was, among many other things, an enchantress. The uses of enchantment cannot be underestimated as generators of scientific knowledge. But it does not become anthropologists, makers of the myth of tolerance, to imitate Galileo's detractors; disenchantment can often reveal new galaxies in the firmament. Dr. Mead would not oppose a general inquiry into the cybernetic nature of "sciencing," even for anthropologists. To the contrary, convinced of the importance of such a message, she would set about her task of enticing a world to listen.

A Tale of Two Studies

Lowell D. Holmes

Editor's Note

Of all those who challenged Freeman's refutation of *Coming of Age in Samoa,* Lowell Holmes proved to be the most tenacious. Holmes stated in his Ph.D. thesis, which was a restudy of Mead's Samoa work, that the reliability of Mead's Samoan ethnography is "remarkably high," and he maintained this position in numerous statements critical of Freeman. Holmes' views are of particular importance since he has devoted three decades of fieldwork to Samoa. This reading is drawn from the *American Anthropologist's* 1983 Special Section on *Margaret Mead and Samoa.* Reproduced by permission of the American Anthropological Association from *American Anthropologist* 85:4 (1983):929-935. Not for further reproduction.

In 1951 Margaret Mead had commented that "there is no such thing as an unbiased report on any social situation . . . . All of our recent endeavors in the social sciences have been to remove bias." On another occasion she went so far as to suggest that a fieldworker be psychoanalyzed before going into the field in order to assess bias. Although Margaret Mead never maintained that her field methods were infallible, she is on record as expressing doubt concerning the value of restudies. She argued that one drawback of the restudy is that the second observer must work within the frame of reference of the first, either trying to prove or disprove the former's material. This, interestingly enough, seems to be a rather accurate description of what Derek Freeman has attempted to do in his book . . ., although it is my impression that Freeman has worked much harder at trying to refute the Mead data than trying to confirm them. My own view is that a restudy is not necessarily conducted with a sharp pencil in one hand and a checklist in the other. A restudy should be a holistic analysis of the total culture configuration, always taking into account, insofar as it is possible, of course, the events that have taken place since the earlier research took place. Nor should a restudy be confined to the limits of the scope of the earlier study; it is desirable if the second investigator can apply new methods and perhaps a frame of reference somewhat different from that which oriented the first

study. Each anthropologist will view the culture in terms of his
or her own personality, interests, and methodological training. It
is inevitable that the results of the two studies will be somewhat
different, but there is nothing wrong with this. It does not necessarily mean that one ethnographer is "right" and the other is
"wrong." It means that the two have come to the culture from
different perspectives, at different times and with biases that grow
out of their unique backgrounds and life experience. As the classic Japanese film Rashomon illustrates, several people viewing
the same situation will invariably interpret it differently. Freeman
chooses to believe, in spite of the fact that he was a middle-aged
man living with his wife in a Western Samoan village more than
40 years after Mead worked in the Manu'an village of Ta'ū in
American Samoa, that any discrepancies between his assessments
of Samoans and Samoan culture and Mead's are due only to her
inability to use the language properly, her inexperience in field research, her naiveté, and her cultural deterministic bias. Margaret
Mead was, according to him, duped by her young informants,
and believe it or not, Freeman's documentation is Nicholas von
Hoffman's (1976) spoof of Mead, Samoa, and anthropology,
Tales from the Margaret Mead Taproom.[1] It is interesting to note
that in an earlier debate about Samoan culture that Freeman had
with Melvin Ember, Freeman suggested that Ember's work was
incorrect because he was "an inexperienced ethnographer, lacking
a command of the Samoan language and residing in a village for
only a few weeks or months." If one were to ask Derek
Freeman why he has been able to obtain the "truth" about Samoan
culture from these people he characterizes as being masters of
duplicity, he would probably respond, as he has on numerous
talk shows, that it is partly because he is a Samoan chief. He is
not the first anthropologist, however, to be made a chief. My
title, awarded in Ta'ū village in 1954 is Tuife'ai (King of Fierce
Cannibals), but I have never considered this honor anything more
than a friendly gesture (or perhaps a good joke) that is not to be
taken seriously by anyone. Since holding a title involves both
family responsibility and a certain amount of control over family
property, including land, it is hardly something that Samoans
seriously grant foreigners. I am not certain, but I doubt if it is
even legal for someone without Samoan ancestry to actually hold
a title. Being known as the "King of Fierce Cannibals" has done

---

[1]On the duping issue, see pp. 162-164.

little for me anthropologically other than permitting me free access to fono (village council) deliberations.

Laughter and Anger: On Samoan Aggression

Richard A. Goodman

Editor's Note
This selection is drawn from the author's monograph, *Mead's Coming of Age in Samoa: A Dissenting View* (Oakland: Pipperine Press). The study was written in 1973 but remained unpublished until 1983, when the news of the forthcoming publication of Freeman's book prompted Goodman to go to press. Neither had known about the other's research; they were pleased to discover that their findings were concordant. In the ensuing debate, Freeman cited Goodman's study as a rebuttal to critics who treated the ethnographies of Mead and Freeman as expressions of two strong personalities. Goodman's view on Samoan aggression may usefully be compared with Jeannette Mageo's ethnography and analysis (Chapter I). Printed with permission of Richard Goodman.

To understand the expression of aggression in the Samoan personality, it is necessary first to penetrate one aspect of Samoan life that beguiles almost all visiting foreigners and that apparently beguiled even Mead. She had written:

> Whenever people ask me, as they often do, who are the happiest people I have ever known, I answer unhesitatingly: 'the Samoans.' As I knew them, they were a people who brought up their children to expect the kind of life they would live, and for the most part, adult life fulfilled their expectations. From childhood they moved slowly and easily into an adult world that was wholly familiar and enjoyable. Year after year from childhood on they could sing the same songs and dance the same dances—and watch one another dancing the same dances—with pleasure.

Life in Samoa had a very real quality of happy and contented tranquility. Watch the way Samoans interact. They do an extraordinary amount of smiling. In their everyday, casual activities, it is almost impossible for one Samoan to look another in the eye without smiling. While I have nothing that would be considered "hard" data about the frequency of smiling among Samoans, certain stereotyped notions in the culture do support my observation. Samoans believe that *Papalagi* (Caucasians) scarcely smile at all and are, in fact, rather sour people. Most Europeans—even those who have lived in Samoa for years and who should know better—will tell you that Samoans are always laughing and smiling and that, like children, they cannot remain serious for long. Neither of these characterizations does either group justice, but they both underline the same difference between the two groups. Samoans do, in fact, smile a good deal more than Americans, New Zealanders, or people of European extraction.

Samoans are required to. A Samoan who does not smile often is neither trusted nor liked. Children are taught to laugh and smile at an early age by being lavished with attention whenever they do so and by being criticized when they act unpleasantly. This training begins just as soon as the child can perceive and respond to other people. For the rest of his life, his cheerfulness will be encouraged. . . . A particular aspect of the training of young Samoan children provides a clue to many of the secrets of Samoan personality. . . . After a child has reached a certain state of robustness—at about six months of age—the parents, aunts, uncles, brothers, sisters, and all other adults he comes into contact with in the course of his daily life begin to discipline him. When he starts to cry, the person looking after him will take a fan, a belt, the strap from a fishing slingshot, or perhaps even a bare hand and will smack him sharply on the arm or leg, saying at the same time, "Uma!"—"Be done!" Naturally the child cries still more loudly. The parent figure responds by smacking him again.

Westerns witnessing this kind of training interpret it as a brutal treatment. In reality, the blows are carefully measured, and the person delivering them is fully aware of what the infant can safely withstand. Further, the adult is normally calm, deliberate, and not angry. The smacking of the crying child normally continues until he is so choked up he can no longer make a sound. Then it stops. Repeated over and over, this kind of discipline soon makes an impression. The child learns to bury emotions that others consider bothersome. Before long, a parent just has to raise a hand and say "Uma!" to silence a fussing child. When he has reached this stage, the child is well on his way to having learned two lessons he will find valuable for the rest of his life: to control himself and to repress his disagreeable emotions.

When asked, a Samoan may not be able to articulate the function of this stress on good humor, but it serves a definite purpose. Samoans are intensely communal. They prefer living in groups and normally dislike being alone. (This predilection sometimes causes them difficulties in New Zealand and the Unites States when their *Papalagi* landlords take it upon themselves to determine what is an appropriate number of tenants for a house or an apartment.) When fifteen or more people share one residence, which is not at all uncommon, sour dispositions and unpleasantness make communal living very difficult. The Samoan solution to this problem has been not to reduce the number of people living together, but to eliminate as much of the unpleasantness as possible. They do not allow themselves the luxury of the dozens of small, scarcely noticeable explosions of dissatisfaction that characterize the daily emotional life of the average Papalagi. The sourest expression of disapproval normally given is a light shake of the head accompanied by a click of the tongue. If Samoans disapprove strongly of someone, they may comment that what he needs is a good *moko* (fist in the face), whereupon they may start laughing. Laughter and humor are the grease that eliminates much of the friction in relationships. Obviously, however, while a person goes on smiling, unsettled and painful emotions may lurk beneath the surface.

The extraordinary good humor of Samoans makes them very pleasant to associate with, a fact that must have struck Mead strongly because it is reflected in a good deal of *Coming of Age*. Naturally there are exceptions among Samoans, just as there are exceptions among any people a generalization is applied to. In the past five years, I have met a few Samoans who do very little smiling. These persons have always proven to be cultural deviants and have been disliked by other Samoans. In general, the rule holds true that Samoans feel compelled to display a smiling exterior much of the time, even when people of many other nationalities would not.

The strong discouragement of unpleasant emotions is important in the Samoan way of life, as an examination of some of the culture's principles of status shows. American and Western

Samoans alike live under the *matai* system, which delineates many of the lines of authority within their '*aiga* extended families. Each '*aiga* normally has one or more *matai*, or titleholders. One of these, who ordinarily bears a title name reflecting the name of the extended family itself, is recognized by the family as its paramount authority. This man makes many of the important decisions within the '*aiga* such as those relating to land tenure, work schedules of various members of the kinship group, and serious discipline. He also represents the '*aiga* at important ceremonies and acts to smooth over and settle disputes. In addition, with the other *matai* of the village, he meets at least once a week to make important policy decisions that affect all the people of the village. Though it is showing some signs of strain, the *matai* system is still strong throughout Samoa. It forms the core of Samoan existence, providing structure and dictating the way society functions. In the *matai* system, the untitled man (*taule'ale'a*) takes orders from his *matai*. It is the *matai*'s role to give orders and the untitled man's role to follow them.

. . . Despite this freedom, the *matai* system can weigh heavily on the shoulders of the untitled men. After all, they are following orders and doing the '*aiga*'s work. One anthropologist, Edwin M. Lemert, has noted that in their relationship with the *matai* the *taulele'a* have no way of disagreeing with him either symbolically or openly. This situation, which Mead failed to note, produces a strong buildup of repressed anger and frustration. In ways that we shall later examine, aggressive feelings often explode violently.

Another status principle important in Samoan culture consists of the subordination of younger people to their elders. This is not just a matter of a twenty-year-old being subordinate to someone several decades older. In many cases, even a year's difference in age can be decisive. One often hears Samoan youngsters jokingly telling each other to "respect your elders" when they disagree about what to do. Often, these remarks are meant seriously. In Samoa, when a small group forms, leadership frequently falls upon the eldest unless other status considerations outweigh age. The way older children take care of younger children in Samoa undoubtedly prepares the way for easy acceptance of this status principle in adult life.

A third major status principle in Samoan society dictates the subordination of women to men. Samoa is unquestionably a man's world. The women's liberation movement of contemporary America would be scorned in Samoa by both men and women alike. Normally the men make decisions and order the women about. The women serve their families. Being accustomed to this idea of service undoubtedly helps make them outstanding nurses when they choose to go into that profession.

. . . The obedience required in Samoan society—of women to men, of younger people to their elders, and of the untitled people to *matai*—is not easy. Within most individuals, frustrations and dissatisfactions built up. These pressures cannot build up forever. They must be released.

. . . Within the *matai* system, an untitled man will not ordinarily disagree with a *matai*. Not wanting to do what he has been told to do, he has several options, but open disagreement is not one of them. He may follow instructions properly, though this may leave him feeling frustrated and dissatisfied. Or he may express anger by following orders precisely without using his brain, thus purposely botching the job. If he is told to be somewhere at a particular time, he may simply not show up. Anyone who has ever been in an army is probably reminded by this of the way enlisted men sometimes act when they have been given orders they dislike. The Army is divided into status groups that resemble those of Samoan society. Both cultures are strongly authoritarian. Both environments understandably foster passive-aggressive behavior.

. . . Male or female, Samoan children are taught at an early age to be aggressive and not to fear fighting and physical violence. At the age of four or five, for instance, they are made to fight each other. Parents, aunts, uncles, or even older siblings select two children and push them toward each other with cries of "Fusu! Fusu! Po le guku!"—"Fight! Fight! Hit the mouth!" A younger child is normally recalcitrant and may require a smack from an adult to be made to fight. Within his first few years, he will learn, however, to prefer taking his chances in a fight with a sibling to be certain of an immediate spanking from an adult. Often he takes zealously to fighting.

. . . There can be no reasonable doubt that Samoans today also have difficulty controlling their aggressive impulses. I have been told this by police in San Francisco and Honolulu. I have learned from leaders of the Samoan community in the San Francisco Bay Area that it has become almost impossible for the Samoans there to secure a police permit to hold a gathering where liquor will be served.

. . . It is not only when Samoan men drink, however, that they show these impulses. A good deal of fighting takes place at night among the young men who have not had any alcohol. What seems little realized by non-Samoans, including anthropologists, is that a good deal of this takes place between gangs. Every Samoan village has at least one gang, usually several, comprised of young men ranging in age from their mid-teens to their mid- or late twenties. These gangs recruit members and are sometimes formally organized enough to have names, such as "Tamaiti ole itu ole vaitfe," "The Riverside Gang." A Samoan boy grows up with a group of children of approximately the same age, and the emergence of a gang from such a group is common. Gangs are strongly territorial, often causing trouble for young men from neighboring areas who pass through their territory. They fight particularly over girls. When members of one gang have caused trouble for members of another, brawls may ensue. Guns and knifes are not normally used. Often, young men resort to stone throwing, at which they are adept from years of killing chickens with this technique. Samoans tend to prefer bare fists, however, and most often simply resort to fist fights. It is no wonder that boxing is a favorite sport in the Archipelago. The practice and training gloved fighting affords later comes in handy in a young man's personal life.

. . . I have traced [gangs] back half a century in Savai'i and more than that on Tutuila. As long as *Papalagi* observers have known them, Samoan villages have been characterized by their political autonomy and the resistance of their *matai* when the autonomy has been threatened. In this setting, gangs of young men accustomed to and unafraid of fighting must have been useful. It seems probable that gangs and gang warfare remain as a residue of Samoa's pre-contact culture. At any rate, my informants report gangs as a part of the Manu'an cultural landscape during and shortly after the time of Mead's visit, as well as ever since then.

A tendency toward violence can be found in much of Samoan life. The usual way of punishing a child is to give him a good beating, whether he has done something naughty, stupid, or merely clumsy. In discussing the subordination of women to men, I have already indicated that Samoans consider it proper to correct a wife's misbehavior with a few blows of a stick, an open hand, or even a closed fist. To a Samoan, it is permissible for a man to beat his wife provided he does not do her great bodily harm. A family in which the sons beat their wives now and then without comment from the sons' parents will probably be disturbed, however, if their daughter is beaten by her husband, who would naturally be from another *'aiga*. There is, here, something of a double standard.

. . . Nonconformist behavior is likely to be branded as *ulavale* [reprehensible] and corrected by a sound beating, too. A young man who openly swaggers around town is likely to end up fighting. I knew of one *taula' ale' a* [untitled man] who, when he felt angry, put on a hat, decorated it outlandishly with leaves and blossoms, and went downtown, spoiling for a fight. He knew that his nonconformist behavior would lead him into one, and he was also reasonably sure of being the victor because he was one of the better boxers in Western Samoa. Samoans exhibit this same attitude toward nonconformity in the United States, especially among their own people.

. . . A person unacquainted with Samoa may have a mental image of the village *fono* . . . as a gathering characterized by great reserve and solemnity, at which wise village elders sit and discourse quietly on the problems of the village, drawing upon the wisdom they have accumulated over the years. The wisdom is often there. But rippling subtly under the surface is an enormous amount of aggression. Sometimes this can escape the notice of a non-Samoan observer. But at other times the aggressions of *fono* participants are loudly and overtly expressed.

The political emphasis in Samoan life is well known and has been commented upon by a good many people. For instance, Dr. Roland W. Force, Director of the Bishop Museum in Honolulu, has commented that he finds the Samoans "among the most politically sophisticated and astute people in the Pacific. Political oratory, political intrigue, and the enjoyment of political behavior are clearly vital aspects of Samoan culture. It may not be amiss to say that politics provides the mortar which binds Samoan culture together." This is not confined to the life of the matai, but extends to most of the untitled people, including many adolescents. A visitor spending any length of time in Samoa cannot help but note that Samoans devote a good deal of their efforts and energies to trying to manipulate others to their own advantage. Until recently, those who did not have titles spent much of their time trying to get them. And even these days, those who already have titles constantly strive for new and higher ones. This background in itself should be enough to convince anyone that life in

Samoa is hardly stress-free, for stress is a natural by-product of politics.

. . . What makes life in Samoa *look* easy is the malleability of the human personality and the smoothness with which, to an inexperienced outsider, the Samoan system appears to run. We might use an analogy from the arts to clarify this. The performance of a great ballet dancer gives a spectator the impression of absolute ease. All great art does this. But the ease is an illusion. Behind it lie years of difficult practice. So it is, too, with life in Samoa. This illusion appears to have mislead Mead.

A Criticism of Falsification[1]

Roy A. Rappaport

The question to ask is: In what sense does Freeman's discussion falsify Mead's? Does he show her observations to have been false, or her interpretations to be erroneous, or does he accomplish something much more modest—namely, to demonstrate that there was more to it than she told us? If his goal was to show her account not to be altogether wrong but one-sided, it would also have been incumbent upon him to face the problem of contradictions, which completion of the picture would make obvious: how, for instance, casual sexuality, a cult of virginity, and high frequencies of various forms of "rape" can coexist in one small society. He does not address this problem, explicitly stating that his aim is simply to refute her. But he really can't get away with this. The term refutation tacitly contends that Mead's account is not simply inadequate but erroneous; it also claims that his facts and interpretations are not only correct in detail but are themselves "complete" or "adequate." If this is the case, he has presented us, despite his disclaimers, with an alternative view of Samoa. Where Mead's view emphasized gentleness, coopera-

---

[1]This selection is drawn from "Desecrating the holy woman: Derek Freeman's attack on Margaret Mead," *The American Scholar* 55 (1986):313-347. Reprinted by permission of *The American Scholar*.

tion, passivity, and casualness, his view emphasized aggressiveness, prudishness, guilt, and obsession. His account is even more oversimplified than the account to which it is reacting, for, in claiming to be no more than a refutation, it denies itself a unifying structure of its own. It is no more than a heap of observations constituting half-truths.

Formal falsification may also come close to being illusory, either by being too difficult to be practicable or too easy to be meaningful. It demands—although this is not reflected in Freeman's practice—that the statements to be falsified be framed in rigorously falsifiable terms. It also assumes either the irrelevance or constancy of contexts. This requisite may not set insurmountable problems for categorical assertions of such generality that they hold true across all contexts, but with respect to ethnographic data this condition may be very difficult to meet. All ethnographic observations are made in complex contexts that, unlike those in some laboratory experiments, cannot be excluded or even controlled. If, however, statements are fully hedged by context qualifications, their claims may lose so much in generality as to be applicable to no more than particular events. On the other hand, if standards are relaxed to admit into the category of falsifiable statements those as loosely formulated as "The Samoan attitude toward sex is easy-going," other problems arise. For instance, the occurrence of some rape cases, or the presence of a cult of virginity, or frequent moralizing statements by pastors, parents, and village elders—any of these might be taken to contradict that assertion about the Samoan attitudes toward sex. But contradiction is not falsification. How many rape cases would be sufficient to falsify the characterization of Samoan attitudes?

It could be argued that the fault here is not so much that of falsification as it is of the literature to which the procedure is applied. Ethnographies are never composed of tightly articulated sets of assertions, each of which is framed in sufficiently rigorous terms to be itself falsifiable, let alone part of a comprehensive account that is falsifiable as an integrated whole. Whether anthropologists should strive to write ethnographies in such a manner is another matter. I myself think not. The increase in formalization requisite to unambiguous falsifiability would exact too high a price in breadth, richness, informativeness, significance, and readability. Rigorous accounts, rich mainly in jargon, about narrowly defined matters of little significance to anyone, might become the order of the day in anthropology, as perhaps they already have in some other social sciences. Such accounts might accommodate a limited number of statements based upon objectively derived data, but they would accommodate with difficulty, or not at all, the hermeneutically derived component of ethnographic knowledge—what I earlier called "inside knowledge."

Good ethnography arises out of the tension between two opposed but mutually dependent endeavors. The one, objective in its method and aspirations and inspired by the sciences, seeks explanation and is concerned to discover causes and, possibly, even laws. The other, subjective in its orientation and influenced by the humanities, attempts interpretation and seeks to illuminate meanings. Ethnography at its best is a richly textured, highly informative, and very complex form that has as much in common with interpretive as with scientific texts. Good ethnographies will likely include some unambiguously falsifiable statements but are never, and should never be, composed entirely of them.

This is to say that ethnographies are invulnerable to the effects of contradictory data or alternative accounts and interpretations. It is to say that rigorous formal falsification is not possible and that, even in a looser sense, it is no simple matter. The main difference between good ethnography and poor ethnography is not the former is true and the latter is not. Even poor ethnography usually gets its facts straight. It is that good ethnography illuminates non-obvious aspects of experience and culture; it exposes and possibly accounts for the apparent contradictions that pervade all societies; and it tries to explain why particular ways of life have developed where and when they have. The knowledge of humanity that emerges from ethnographies and their comparison does not grow or advance mainly through a program of hypothesis generation and falsification but through a complex process of modification, qualification, confirmation, elaboration, deepening, and synthesizing. The part that out-and-out falsification has to play is a small one.

I am not applying for a special exemption for anthropology from falsification. It isn't necessary. Jonathan Lieberson, following Thomas Kuhn, Imre Lakatos, and others, have observed that even though the technique of falsification has a long history it has never been of great importance in the practice of any science. Even in sciences as "hard" as physics, adverse test results need not always be taken to falsify a generalization but may simply clarify its scope. Moreover, the nature of scientific theories is such that they require auxiliary assumptions to predict observational results. Disconfirming tests may falsify these connecting assumptions rather than the hypotheses. Testing, critics of Popper say, helps us to locate shortcomings in our initial formulations and to correct them, but the claim that falsifiability is the criterion for distinguishing science from non-science is, according to Lieberson, "just a logical toy," simply "one more instance in the depressing attempt of so-called philosophers of science to squeeze and warp the teeming variety of scientific attitudes and inquiries . . . into severe logical calculi and 'rules'." In light of the dubiety of falsification's methodological validity, Freeman's claims for its usefulness in anthropology are not only scientistic and pretentious but also misleading and destructive.

The Limits of Popperian Metascience[1]

Allan Patience and Joseph Wayne Smith

We now extend our critique of Freeman's work by arguing for the untenability of Popperian metascience. Popperian metascience must be understood as arising as a response to Hume's problem of induction. Hume's logical problem is: how we can justify reasoning from repeated instances, of which we have had experience, to other instances, the description of which serves as the conclusion of an argument of which we have no experience? Hume argued that attempts to justify induction involve circular reasoning, for they presuppose the inductive principle itself. This vitiating circularity is present, Hume argued, even if the conclusions of such empirical arguments are taken to be merely probable rather than certain. Hume's psychological problem is: why do human beings believe that instances of which they have no experience will conform to those of which they have had experience? Hume's answer to the psychological problem of induction is that

---

[1]The title of the article from which this selection is taken is "Derek Freeman and Samoa: The making and unmaking of a biobehavioral myth." Reproduced by permission of the American Anthropological Association from *American Anthropologist* 88:1 (1986):157-162. Not for further reproduction.

we are conditioned by custom or habit to believe that the future will be largely like the past.

Popper reformulates Hume's problem in the following terms: "Can the claim that an explanatory universal theory is true be justified by 'empirical reasons'; that is by assuming the truth of certain test statements or observation statements (which, it may be said, are based 'on experience')?" His answer is the same as Hume's: "No, we cannot; no number of true test statements would justify the claim that an explanatory universal theory is true" (Popper 1972:7). Popper, unlike Hume, does not believe that this answer leads to irrationalism. The *falsificationist* position is summarized in the proposition that "*the assumption of the truth of test statements sometimes allows us to justify the claim that an explanatory universal theory is false*" (Popper 1972:7, emphasis in original). Popper believes that his principle enables us to solve another problem: "Can a *preference* with respect to truth or falsity, for some universal theories over others ever be justified by such 'empirical reasons'?" For Popper, theory choice can be made if luck is on our side, for "it may happen that our test statements may refute some—but not all—of the competing theories; and since we are searching for a true theory, we shall prefer those whose falsity has not been established" (Popper 1972:8). Empirical theories remain "conjectures" or "guesses" and it is not possible to establish, or even give adequate justification or good reasons for belief in the truth of any universal theory. "The number of *possibly* true theories remains infinite, at any time and after any number of crucial tests" (Popper 1972:15).

Truth then stands as a regulative ideal for Popperians. There is an objection which should have been made to Popper in 1934 which shows that Popperians are genuine irrationalists. If we cannot justify or give good reasons for any purported truth-claim, then how can *truth* serve as a regulative ideal? In our opinion Hume's argument, which Popperians accept, shows that it cannot. If we cannot justify any purported truth-claim, then truth is an *inaccessible* notion. It is pointless to have an inaccessible notion as a regulatory ideal, because the very point of any regulative ideal is to enable the harmonious, consistent and systematic evaluation and classification of data. Truth in Popperian epistemology cannot play such a role. Such a position seems to us to be no more than a form of irrationalism, inconsistent with the bulk of the work done by empirical scientists. It is only by a series of literary devices, well documented by Stove (1982), that Popperians are able to conceal the fundamental contradiction in their epistemology:*that they have taken science to be the pursuit of truth, but have made truth an unattainable phantom.*

Freeman has also been deceived by the logical hypocrisy of the Popperians, given his incorporation of Popperian epistemology into the very fabric of his work. As we reject Popper's epistemology as being to any degree rationally acceptable, we find that the principal epistemological motivation for Freeman's work collapses.

[Freeman's Biobehavioral Foundation]
Let us suppose for the sake of the argument of this section, that Freeman's critique of Mead is successful. What alternative foundation does Freeman offer to the Boasian paradigm? *We make no accusation here that Freeman is in any way committed to the position of biological determinism.* He tells us that the genetic and the exogenetic systems are part of an interacting system and that specific cultural behaviors "need to be related to the phylogenetically given impulses in reference to which they have been evolved, and in apposition to which they survive as shared modes of socially inherited adaptation" (Freeman, 1983a:300). We find fault with the brief sketch of Freeman's views of a theoretically adequate and scientific anthropology and shall document a very serious inconsistency in Freeman's recent work on the foundations of anthropology and outline inconsistencies that are produced by the application of Freeman's accepted Popperian metascience to this matter. Interactionism is in Popperian terms, we will argue, a *metaphysical* rather than *scientifically falsifiable* position.

In his discussion of Wilsonian sociobiology Freeman is prepared to grant that "it is the existence of . . . conventional behaviors, in great profusion, in all human populations, that establishes, indubitably, the autonomy of culture" (Freeman 1980:215). Shankman has argued that Freeman's description of rape in Samoa leads one to believe that the causes of rape are primarily culturally transmitted male practices. Freeman (Freeman 1983b:156) replies by stressing that all behavior has a biological, and especially a genetic, basis. In support of this he cites a controversial survey paper (Velle 1982). The bulk of this paper's contents have been criticized by one of us elsewhere (Smith 1984). Here however we will show that Freeman's biobehavioral foundation of anthropology conflicts with his own Popperian metascience.

We are to suppose that rape in Samoa is best explained genetically and hormonally, even though information about how to perform effective rapes is transmitted by males via cultural mechanisms. Presumably the biological mechanisms are such that the incidence of rape will be high, a prediction Freeman claims to have confirmed. Let us suppose however that the number of rapes in Samoa per unit population per unit time was exactly as Mead said that it was; i.e., very low relative to the number of rapes in America over the same time and same units of population.[1] If Freeman's position was scientific in Popper's sense, then we would expect his position to be falsified. However nothing prevents Freeman from repeating here the same reply which he gave to Shankman, that all behavior has a biological basis.

That *all* behavior has a biological basis cannot explain why some particular behavior B is observed in culture C at time T *rather* than B. As both B and ~B are both behaviors, both must have a biological basis. This does not, and cannot, explain why B occurs in C *rather* than ~B. It is interesting to note that the proposition that Freeman wishes to make as the foundation of his anthropology, that all behavior has a biological basis, is quite resistant to possible falsification. What is an example of a possible human behavior which does not have any biological basis at all? How would we know it when we came across it?

Anthropologists in the Boasian tradition have not denied the significance of biology. Mead never denied that there is a biological, especially a hormonal, basis to adolescence. She did however reject the view that adolescence is itself simply a period of physiological puberty, arguing that adolescence is the beginning of mental and emotional maturity. The cultural causes of the turbulence of adolescence are described clearly by Mead.

The autonomy of culture, even if based upon biological structures, is a thesis which Freeman himself has accepted (Freeman, 1980:215). We can only explain Freeman's desire to abandon culturology and replace this paradigm by a biobehavioral paradigm, by admitting that Freeman is inconsistent in his

---

[1]Mead did not give an estimate of the rape rate in Samoa because she held that "the idea of forceful rape or of any sexual act to which both participants do not give themselves freely is completely foreign to the Samoan mind."

thought about this basic issue. For a Popperian this is the ultimate logical sin because, through their acceptance of classical logic, any inconsistent position must be regarded as being trivially false.

References

Freeman, Derek. 1983a. *Margaret Mead and Samoa:the Making and Unmaking of an Anthropological Myth.* Cambridge: Harvard University Press.

Freeman, Derek. 1983b. Inductivism and the test of truth, *Canberra Anthropology* 6:101-192.

Freeman, Derek. 1980. Sociobiology: the 'antidiscipline' of anthropology, in *Sociobiology Examined*, edited by Ashley Montagu (New York: Oxford University Press), 198-219.

Mead, Margaret. 1981. *Coming of Age in Samoa.* Harmondsworth: Penguin.

Popper, Karl. 1972. *Objective Knowledge.* Oxford:Clarendon Press.

Smith, J. W. 1984. *Reductionism and Cultural Being: A Philosophical Critique of Sociobiological Reductionism and Physicalist Scientific Unificationism.* The Hague: Martinus Nijhoff.

Stove, David. 1982. *Popper and After: Four Modern Irrationalists.* Oxford:Pergamon.

Velle, Weiert. 1982. Sex hormones and behavior in animals and man, *Perspectives in Biology and Medicine* 25:295-315.

Rejoinder to Patience and Smith

Derek Freeman

Patience and Smith, it is important to realize, are fervent latter-day believers in the pre-scientific ideology to which Margaret
Mead adhered in the 1920s. That is, Patience like Smith, is "a
thorough-going Culturologist," convinced, as is Smith, that "all
social action is culturally derived and only sensibly compre-
hended in purely cultural terms" (Patience 1984). And so,
alarmed at my demonstration of the errors in Mead's account of
the Samoans, Patience and Smith, lacking any experience of
Samoa, have sought to counter the refutation contained in my
book . . . by resorting to "metascientific and logical" arguments.

As I shall document, Patience and Smith's arguments are a
muddled mishmash of mis-information, their highly unphilo-
sophic method being to attribute to me positions I do *not* hold,
which they then convince themselves they have demolished . . . .

(1) *"Mead's principal conclusion."* Patience and Smith are in
clear-cut error in asserting of Mead's Samoan researches that her
"principal conclusion" was that "coming of age in Samoa is relatively easier than coming of age in the United States." As Mead
repeatedly documented (1977:19; cf. also 1962:122; 1959:60),
and is clearly indicated in *Coming of Age in Samoa*, she went to
Samoa at Boas' behest "to investigate to what extent the storm
and stress of adolescence" is "biologically determined and to what
extent it is modified by the culture within which adolescents are
reared." The outcome of this investigation is recorded in the
fourth paragraph of the thirteenth chapter of *Coming of Age in
Samoa*, where Mead concludes that biological variables are of no
significance in the etiology of adolescent behavior; "we cannot,"
she asserts, "make any explanations" in terms of the biological
process of adolescence itself . . . .

(7) *"Popperian metascience"* Patience and Smith claim that my
work "collapses" because of its reliance on what they term
"Popperian metascience," which, after advancing a truncated and
tendentious argument, they brashly pronounce to be "untenable."
Once again this claim is misinformed and misconceived.

My refutation of Mead is *not* coextensive with, and does *not*
depend on, "Popperian metascience" *in general*. In my book I in
fact do no more than follow what Popper has called "the critical

method of error elimination,'' which is fundamental to all scientific disciplines. This critical method is of great antiquity, being traced by Popper to Anaximander (*ca.* 610-540 B.C.) of Miletus, who criticized the cosmology of his teacher Thales.

As Bunge observes (1964:viii), "criticism can be applied to fact-gathering, to description, and to theory-building" and "must" be so applied "if these activities are to be rational.'' Accordingly, it is Popper's view that the "rationality contained in the development of science is to be found in testing and criticism.''

This same view was taken by numerous scientists and philosophers of both the 19th and the early 20th centuries . . . . Over a hundred years ago T. H. Huxley declared that "the essence of the scientific spirit is criticism,'' and today I would suppose it is universally recognized among scientists that "all assumptions and claims made in science may in principle be questioned and refuted by publicly presented evidence" (Niiniluoto 1984:5).

It is from this general ethos of science that my refutation of Mead's erroneous conclusions stems, and the tendentious philosophical argument advanced by Patience and Smith is obviously altogether too vaporous to invalidate either this firmly grounded general ethos or the scientific prepotency of "the critical method of error elimination.''

(8) "*A biobehavioral paradigm.*" As Patience and Smith would have it I am intent on an anthropology with "a biobehavioral paradigm.'' This, once again, is a quite false assertion. Nowhere in my book or other writings have I used the term *biobehavioral*; nor have I ever advocated the adoption of "a biobehavioral paradigm.''

Instead, in conspicuous contrast, I have proposed a fully interactionist paradigm in which "the genetic and the exogenetic are distinct but interacting parts of a single system.'' At the same time I have made it clear that in my view in anthropology (as in any science) *all* determining variables should be taken into account, with the identification of these variables, of whatever description, being a matter for open-minded and impartial scientific investigation.

(9) "*Rape in Samoa.*" I do *not* hold, as Patience and Smith, with their chronic disregard for factual accuracy, mistakenly report, that "rape in Samoa is best explained genetically and hormonally.'' What I in fact say is something quite different (Freeman 1983b:128), that is, that "while it is true that certain

elements in rape behavior in Samoa are cultural . . . it is also clearly evident that this whole behavioral complex cannot adequately be understood unless the relevant biological variables are also taken into account.''

(10) *"The Boasian tradition."* Patience and Smith's assessment of the "significance" that Mead, "working within the Boasian tradition," gave to biological variables in the etiology of adolescent behavior is far from historically accurate. The conclusion reached by Mead in *Coming of Age in Samoa* was, as I have documented, that biological variables are of no significance in the etiology of adolescent behavior. Moreover, this conclusion was an explicit exemplification of the doctrine of absolute cultural determinism, formulated by Kroeber (1915:284-285; 1917:194) and Lowie (1915:218; 1917:66), which had been enthusiastically embraced by Benedict and Mead in the early 1920s.

. . . For the benefit of Patience and Smith, let me reiterate that there is *"no* logical connection between my refutation of Mead's classing of Samoa as a negative instance, and my advocacy *on general scientific grounds* of an interactionist paradigm for anthropology.'' Thus, it is open to any cultural anthropologist (as it is to Patience and Smith) to advance some other purported "negative instance" in support of the preposterous notion that biological variables are of *no* significance whatever in the etiology of adolescent behavior and of the scientifically unwarranted doctrine of absolute cultural determinism that Mead and others championed in the 1920s and 1930s.

This, however, is an unlikely happening. Today, as Stephen Jay Gould has observed, "every scientist, indeed every intelligent person, knows that human social behavior is a complex and indivisible mix of biological and social influences.'' And if this be true—and all the pertinent evidence indicates that it is indeed true—then it is plain that anthropology has no rational alternative to the acceptance of a scientifically informed interactionist paradigm.

If I have been able, in some way, to contribute to this necessary development, I am content.

References

Bunge, Mario. 1964. Preface, in *The Critical Approach to Science and Philosophy,* ed. M. Bunge. New York: Free Press.

Freeman, Derek. 1983 Inductivism and the test of truth, *Canberra Anthropology* 6:101-192.

Kroeber, A. L. 1915. Eighteen professions, *American Anthropologist* 17:283-288.

Kroeber, A. L. 1917. The Superorganic, *American Anthropologist* 19:163-213.

Lowie, R. H. 1915. Psychology and sociology, *American Journal of Sociology* 21:217-229.

Lowie, R.H. 1917. *Culture and Ethnology.* New York: McMurtrie.

Niiniluoto, I. 1984. *Is Science Progressive?* Dordrecht:Reidel.

Patience, A. 1984. Letter to Derek Freeman, 30 November.

Tweny, R. D., M. E. Doherty, and C. R. Mynatt, eds. 1981. *Scientific Thinking.* New York: Columbia University Press.

Inductivism and Refutation

Derek Freeman

Editor's Note
The present selection is drawn from Freeman's monograph-length reply to critics, "Inductivism and the Test of Truth," which appeared in *Canberra Anthropology* 6 (1984):101-191. Freeman was invited to reply to critics who had filled the previous number of the journal. This he did; but he also used the occasion to reply to criticisms that appeared in the Special Section of the *American Anthropologist* December 1983 issue. This monograph was his most extensive and perhaps his most concise rejoinder. Printed by permission of Derek Freeman and the editors of *Canberra Anthropology.*

In her characterization of the background which, so she claims, makes growing up in Samoa "so easy, so simple a matter," Mead roundly asserts (1961:198) that "neither poverty nor great disasters" threaten the people of Samoa. In fact, the Samoan archipelago is regularly visited by devastating hurricanes, one of which Mead herself lived through at Luma, on the island of Ta'ū, Manu'a, in January 1926, and which in another context where no theoretical conclusion is at stake, she described as "terrific storms which strip the coconuts from the trees and blight the growing crops with salt spray, so that the available food supply is radically reduced and it is necessary to take communal measures against famine" (1969a:16). Indeed, as Gray reports, so severe was the devastation of the great hurricane of January 1915 that "two-thirds of the population of approximately 2,000" of Manu'a had to be evacuated as refugees to the island of Tutila. Yet when Mead had a particular theoretical conclusion to "prove," such facts . . . are simply ignored.

. . . Inductivist methods of the kind I am here discussing are not at all uncommon in cultural and social anthropology, and are conspicuously present, as we shall see, in the writings on Samoa of both Holmes and Shore. They are methods that may be attributed, in my judgement, to the fact that each of these disciplines is based on arbitrary assumptions about the nature of the phenomena being studied, with the result that, in inductivist style, evidence in support of these assumptions is ever being sought and found.

With the dangers of inductivism having been made apparent by David Hume and others, and particularly by Popper in his *Logik der Forschung* of 1934, the time is due, I would argue, for the adoption within anthropology, as in all other sciences, of critical or scientific rationality, or falsificationism, according to which our assumptions and theories are not dogmatically upheld, justified or defended, but rather are subjected to (Miller 1982:24) "the most ruthless and uncompromising attempts" to show that they are "not true." Only when this is done can we rationally place tentative credence in the scientific objectivity of our suppositions.

On Refutation

. . . Although Karl Popper is, in P. B. Medawar's judgement, "incomparably the greatest philosopher of science that has ever been," and although Popper's crucial work *Logik der Forschung* appeared in English as *The Logic of Scientific Discovery* as long ago as 1959, the influence of his thought on cultural and social anthropology has, because of the inductivist and relativistic leanings of these disciplines, been but slight. Indeed, so innocent is Lowell Holmes of these seminal developments in twentieth-century scientific thought that he naively supposes (1983b:11) that anyone who does not follow inductivist methods is not a "serious scientist." And somewhat similarly Bradd Shore and Paul

Shankman mistakenly persist in treating my refutation as an alternative "portrait" of Samoa, which it specifically is not. Nor is it, as Shore supposes, a general critique, in which case it would be incumbent on me to appraise all aspects of Mead's Samoan writings. Rather, as I have made abundantly clear, my book contains a formal refutation, the specific object of which is to advance "test statements" about Samoa that effectively falsify Mead's widely accepted conclusion of 1928.

As Bartley (1982:264) notes, "there is a basic asymmetry between the verification and falsification of a theory," for while "no amount of observations" can ever "verify a theory logically, one single observation may falsify it, serving logically as a counterexample to it." The same point is made by Quine and Ullian (1978:102) when they observe that "a generalization with even a single false instance . . . is irremediably false." It is this logical situation that makes the refutation of Mead's generalizations about Samoa feasible. For example, when Mead asserts (1928a:487) that "the idea of forceful rape or of any sexual act to which both participants do not give themselves freely is completely foreign to the Samoan mind," all that one has to do to refute this absolute generalization is to adduce a test statement in the form of a single verified case of rape that occurred in Samoa during the period of Mead's researches. And this same logical situation holds with Mead's other inductively derived generalizations, all of which, because they refer to supposedly empirical realities, are entirely open to refutation by the advancing of verified counter-instances.

In this process the content of a refutation is obviously determined by the content of the generalizations to which it refers. Thus, in the case of my refutation of Mead, I necessarily must deal with her generalizations about such things as the supposed unaggressiveness, uncompetitiveness, and free love of the Samoans. In so doing, however, I am doing no more than attempting to refute these generalizations, and I am, in no sense, as I make clear on p. 278 of my book, presenting a general depiction of the Samoans. It is thus quite illogical, and no rebuttal of the cogency of my refutation, to argue, as does Shore, that it does not amount to an adequate "alternative ethnography" of Samoa. This is just not what a refutation is about.

Again, I do not claim, as Shore mistakenly supposes, that my refutation is "absolute" for the obvious reason that (Miller 1982:25) "all test-statements are themselves fallible and open to dispute." I would surmise, however, that the test statements I

have advanced and the factuality of which has not been rebutted
are sufficiently cogent to falsify Mead's general conclusion of
1928.

If [I had . . .] written a general treatise on Samoa, Mead's
widely accepted theoretical conclusion would most certainly not
have been revealed as erroneous and would, in all likelihood,
have remained part of the ideational fabric of cultural anthropology for generations to come. That outcome has already become
highly improbable. In science, as Charles Darwin remarked
. . . "to kill an error is as good a service as, and sometimes
even better than, the establishing of a new truth or fact."

. . . [Marilyn] Strathern's principal criticism of my refutation
of Mead's conclusion of 1928 turns on what she terms (1983:78)
"the social sources of data," an issue which she claims to be in-
imical to "Popperian science." "Falsifiability in the strict sense,"
she writes, "surely rests on the replication of experience." This
is by no means the case. As I have shown, the falsification of an
empirical generalization can be based purely on internal evidence,
on a combination of internal and historical facts, or as in the case
of Mead's generalizations about rape and warfare, on verified
historical evidence. Again, in the case of major persisting elements of Samoan behavior, such as competitiveness, one is certainly justified in advancing test statements derived from the accounts of other observers.

Such methods of falsification may certainly be validly employed while paying due regard to the context of the formulations
to which they apply, and to refrain from all attempts to falsify
suspect generalizations on the ground that all contexts are historically unique—a consideration that applies variously to all forms
of scientific investigation—would be to abandon the purposes of
science for mere idiographic inquiry.

Such a course, if followed, would reduce anthropological
monographs to a genre of descriptive literature and the science of
anthropology to a kind of exegesis of literary criticism, a trend
that has, alas, been clearly apparent in recent years.

I would argue then that the defensive plea that Strathern has
based on what she calls "contextualization"—the notion that
ethnographic accounts because they refer to finite and unreplica-
ble historical contexts are immune to falsification—is alien to both
the spirit and practice of science and an expression of a decidedly
obscurantist doctrine.

This same plea, interestingly enough, was repeatedly resorted to by Mead herself in attempts to shield *Coming of Age in Samoa* from skeptical attention. In 1961, for example, in discussing what she called "the . . . absoluteness of monographs of primitive societies," Mead described such monographs . . . as being "like well-painted portraits of the famous dead" that would "stand forever for the edification and enjoyment of future generations, forever true because no truer picture could be made of that which was gone" (Mead 1961:Preface). Again, in 1973, after Samoan students and scholars had challenged the accuracy of her account of Samoa and asked when she was going to revise it, Mead replied that any revision "would be impossible" and that *Coming of Age in Samoa* "must remain, as all anthropological works must remain, exactly as it was written" (Mead 1973:Preface).

If this notion of the "absoluteness of monographs of primitive societies" be adopted, these monographs become, as I have indicated, the equivalents of sacred texts and the minimal conditions of scientific inquiry are abrogated.

References

Bartley, W. E. 1982. A Popperian Harvest, in *In Pursuit of Truth*, ed. P. Levinson. New Jersey: Humanities Press.

Gray, J. A. C. 1960. *American Samoa*. Annapolis: US Naval Institute.

Holmes, Lowell D. 1983. On the questioning of as many as six impossible things about Freeman's Samoan study before breakfast, *Canberra Anthropology* 6:1-16.

Mead, Margaret. 1928. The Role of the individual in Samoan culture, *Journal of the Royal Anthropological Institute* 58:481-495.

Mead, Margaret. 1961. *Coming of Age in Samoa*. New York: Morrow.

Mead, Margaret. 1969. *Social Organization of Manu'a*. Honolulu: Bishop Museum.

Mead, Margaret. 1973. *Coming of Age in Samoa*. New York: Morrow.

Miller, D. 1982. Conjectural knowledge: Popper's solution of the problem of induction, in *In Pursuit of Truth*, ed. P. Levinson. New Jersey: Humanities Press.

Quine, W. V. and J. S. Ullian. 1978. *The Web of Belief*. New York: Random House.

Shankman, Paul. 1983. The Samoa conundrum, *Canberra Anthropology* 6:38-57.
Shore, Bradd. 1983. Paradox regained: Freeman's *Margaret Mead and Samoa, American Anthropologist* 85:935-944.
Strathern, Marilyn. 1983. The Punishment of Margaret Mead, *Canberra Anthropology* 6:70-79.

Did Margaret Mead Speak Samoan?

Hiram Caton

The Rashomon Effect, which occurs when two observers make very different reports about the same phenomenon, was often invoked to explain the contrasting ethnographies that many commentators believed to be implied by Freeman's refutation (Holmes 1983; Heider 1988). Thus arose the Doctrine of the Two Samoas, which holds that Mead's ethnography as well as the facts that Freeman used to refute it, are both in some manner warranted.

In this controversy the Rashomon Effect extends to matters that in everyday practice are subject to univocal decision. Language competence is one of these. This human ability is subject to precise measurement formally in the classroom and informally, just in speaking. The informal measurement is made intuitively, to an elaborate degree, by native speakers in probably all cultures where accent, diction, and expression differentiate social classes, ceremonial functions, special status, and so forth. In light of this experience, one would expect there to be no seriously conflicting evidence about the degree of Mead's facility in spoken Samoan. Yet the opposite is true.

The earliest evidence of Mead's command of the Samoan language dates to letters she wrote from Samoa. She claimed a mastery sufficient to allow her to dispense with interpreters. Thus she wrote of her visit to Vaitogi, her first stop after Pago Pago, that talking chief Lolo who "spoke no English . . . took it upon himself to teach me to speak the chiefs' language and to act as a Samoan lady . . . when the other chiefs learned that I could talk politely, which means being master of three sets of nouns and verbs and using the proper terms of address to each rank, they all came to see if it was true. Solemnly they addressed weighty questions to my royal highness and I answered each lord and duke as best I could, with Lolo watching for mistakes with a hawk eye" (Mead 1974:32-33). The precocious language student claimed in another letter that she "only tried an interpreter once and that was to use the native nurse, Mele, with an old midwife. But the old midwife stayed behind to tell me some stories she wouldn't tell Mele because she came from another village. So I gave up attempting interpreters and worked on everything from religion to medicines without them" (ibid 54). Mead leaves her American correspondents in no doubt of her fluency, so quickly attained, for she tells of engaging in conversations requiring that she "follow arguments closely" (ibid).

These claims, all made in letters to persons far away, were repeated many times over the years: all her fieldwork was done in "polished Samoan" and she resented the implication to the contrary (above, p. 117).

Her claims are backed by Lowell D. Holmes, who tells a remarkable story of Mead's fluency. He states that shortly before her death, he heard Mead converse "in Samoan for about twenty-five minutes. And so Margaret Mead . . . learned to speak Samoan well enough that in the late 1970s she was still able to use the language."[1] This amazing power of retention is as wonderful as the ease with which she mastered conversational Samoan. In only six weeks of her arrival in Pago Pago knowing no Samoan at all, she was, according to her reports, speaking the language fluently.

There appears to be no Samoan source to confirm these claims. The half dozen at my disposal state that Mead used an interpreter and that her knowledge of spoken Samoan was meagre. One of these sources is Napoleone A. Tuiteleleapaga, who claims to be the interpreter. He states that as a young teacher he translated what the girls and adults told Mead unless their English was good enough to communicate directly (Freeman *et al.* 1987, tape 32, pp. 35-36).

Napoleone's statements are supported by Samoans who remember her visit and by Samoans in close contact with the memories of Mead (ibid, tape 35, pp. 57-58; tape 36, p. 21). Several

---

[1]Derek Freeman, *et al.*, 1987, tape 15, p. 22. Holmes does not himself speak Samoan, although he understands it (ibid, Tape 15, p. 20).

Samoanists concur with these stories. Among them is Lowell D. Holmes, who states that Napoleone "is definitely known to have had close ties with Mead as both informant and interpreter" (Holmes 1987:138).

Mead's biographer, Jane Howard, also accepted that Napoleone was Mead's interpreter (Howard 1984:323). Howard states that "even her most fervent champions have not claimed that her many remarkable talents included a flair for languages. Few could assess authoritatively her command of the languages of the Samoans, Manus, Balinese, and the various New Guinea tribes she encountered, but several who closely followed her work spoke pidgin English . . . and insisted that Mead's pidgin, as they heard it, was merely passable" (ibid:207). This assessment agrees with Mead's collaborator and bosom friend for two decades, Lola Romanucci-Ross: "Margaret Mead *never* learned a language and did not know Manus" (Romanucci-Ross 1987). Another admirer who testifies to Mead's modest language ability is Mary Catherine Bateson, herself a linguist. Mead "didn't have a terribly good ear, . . . her French accent was horrible and there was no foreign language she spoke so that she sounded like a native" (Freeman *et al.* 1987 tape 11, p. 32). Mead acknowledged her modest language competence to her daughter, but stated that despite her want of fluency, she knew better than her language-competent collaborators "whose pig was dead."

In 1972 Freeman published his article, *"Social Organization of Manu'a* (1930 and 1969) by Margaret Mead:Some Errata." This study showed that there was about one spelling error of Samoan words per page of *The Social Organization of Manu'a*, not counting repetitions of the same error, making a total for the book of some two hundred errors. A number of these errors, Freeman reported, entered the anthropological literature. Since spelling errors often change the meaning of the intended word to quite another meaning, a corrupt language with expressions such as "defunct banana" and "coughing wound" came into existence under the imprimatur of the prestigious Bishop Museum, Mead's publisher (Freeman 1972:72). These errors may be due to Mead's pragmatic approach to language acquisition, for she wrote in the second edition (1969) of *Social Organization of Manu'a,* "I did not make any formal study of the language but simply used it as a means of communication" (p. 213).

When Freeman's corrective article came to her attention, Mead said that if she had had it when the second edition was prepared, a list of errata might have been published in the new edition. Her one comment on the large number of errors was that in preparing the work "all sorts of theories about Polynesian . . . crept in" (ibid). Yet it seems unlikely that the errata would have been published had it been available, since Freeman wrote the Bishop Museum, when he heard that a new edition was in preparation, to warn the Director of the multitude of errors, but to no effect.

The Errata article was submitted initially to the *American Anthropologist*. It was rejected with the explanation that "as a matter of policy, publication of errata in the articles section certainly seems most inadvisable" (Bohannan 1971). Freeman responded that the importance of his article lay in its demonstration of the fact that Mead's "control of the Samoan language in 1925-26 was of a kind inadequate to the proper investigation of the fundamental anthropological problems on which . . . she worked" (Freeman 1971).

The evidence reviewed presents but one independent witness to Mead's fluency in Samoan. But that witness also says that Mead, contrary to her own statements, *did* use an interpreter. To the philosophically uninstructed the inference would be that Mead's claims of language competence were either boasting or Münchausian fantasies. In this difficult circumstance the Rashomon Effect comes to the rescue.

References

Bohannan, Laura. 1971. Letter to Derek Freeman, March 2.

Derek Freeman *et al.* 1987. *Transcript of Interviews for the Documentary Film Margaret Mead and Samoa.* Sydney: Cinetel Films.

Freeman, Derek. 1971. Letter to Laura Bohannan, March 17.

Freeman, Derek. 1972. *Social Organization of Manu'a* (1930 and 1969) by Margaret Mead: some errata, *Journal of the Polynesian Society* 81:70-78.

Heider, Karl G. 1988. The Rashomon Effect: when ethnographers disagree, *American Anthropologist* 90:73-81.

Holmes, Lowell D. 1987. *Quest for the Real Samoa: The Mead/Freeman Controversy and Beyond.* Postscript by Eleanor Leacock. South Hadley, Ma: Bergin and Garvey.

Holmes, Lowell D. 1983. A Tale of two studies, *American Anthropologist* 85:929-935.

Howard, Jane. 1984. *Margaret Mead: A Life.* New York: Simon & Schuster.

Mead, Margaret. 1977. *Letters from the Field.* New York: Harper & Row.

Romanucci-Ross, Lola. 1987. Undated personal communication, received October 20.

Mead Was Teased; Was She Duped?

From *The Samoa Times*

Editor's Note

Freeman, Eleanor Gerber, and Bradd Shore among others reported the opinion among Samoans that Mead's report of casual sex in Ta'ū and Samoa derived from teasing by her informants. Freeman noted this opinion in his book, but stated that in the absence of direct evidence it could not be substantiated. Direct evidence was found accidentally when Frank Heimans visited Samoa to take footage for his documentary *Margaret Mead and Samoa.* The evidence is the testimony of Mead's chief informant, Fa'apua'a Fa'amū Togia. This interview with her appeared in *The Samoa Times*, January 6, 1989. A detailed report is being prepared by Freeman, who claims on the basis of Fa'apua'a's testimony that the debate on Mead's Samoa ethnography is closed. Critics retort that either Mead was duped or Freeman was. This edited version of *The Samoa Times* interview is reprinted with permission.

Fa'apua'a Fa'amū Togia, generally regarded as Margaret Mead's chief informant during her field trip to Manua in the mid-1920s, has poured scorn on Mead's general conclusions about Samoa, especially her view that Samoa is a free-love society.

Interviewed by Leulu F. Vaa, a lecturer at the National University of Samoa, . . . Fa'apua'a said she (and her companions, including the mother of the present lieutenant governor of American Samoa) had teased Mead when Mead asked her whether she slept with young men.

She had casually lied to Mead that she and her companions often did so, not knowing that Mead was an anthropologist or that Mead was going to publish what they told her. She did notice, however, that Mead was always going around with a notebook and writing things on it.

The fact, as Fa'apua'a, aged 87, told Leulu, was that young women were closely chaperoned in Manua in those days. There was no way that a young girl could go out with a young man without someone knowing about it.

"In those days," Fa'apua'a said, "if a young man wanted to take a girl to a village social, he had to go to the girl's family and formally ask permission . . . . The two would attend the [social] and after that the man would leave and the girl return to her own home. . . . Such was the behavior expected of the young people."

As for Mead, she said the American girl acted in a very free manner and often showed little respect for Samoan custom. She was always wandering from house to house and it was difficult to keep track of her movements. She did participate in Samoan ceremonies, such as the welcome by the [young men]. In such welcomes, it was customary to give away gifts and often Mead gave away a lot of her own personal belongings. When the young men left, she would cry and say she had lost everything.

"Yet she was the one who insisted on giving away her things," Fa'apua'a said.

She admitted, however, that while Mead was in Manua she and her companions had treated Mead as a sister and had tolerated a lot of her idiosyncrasies as a *palagi* and as an American.

But she was very displeased with Mead after she heard of the things she had said in her book. . . . She found it hard to believe the nasty things Mead had said (e.g., about free love) after the excellent treatment accorded her in Manua.

. . . Fa'apua'a's testimony . . . is of paramount importance in the ongoing debate involving Mead and Freeman . . . for it shows that Mead had been duped by her informants. They told Mead what she wanted to [hear],[1] little knowing that their innocent little game would be heralded around the world as the truth about Samoa.

Freeman's critics, of course, have another card up their sleeves. If Fa'apua'a told a lie . . . to Mead, what is there to pre-

---

[1]The text reads "know." Presumably this is an error in English idiom.—Ed.

vent her from telling a lie again, for instance, that she had merely kidded Mead?

At the end of the six hour interview, Leulu had offered Fa'apua'a a Samoan Bible and asked her to swear that what she told Leulu was true.

The old lady unhesitatingly placed her hand on the Bible and swore . . . .

Leulu said Fa'apua'a also gave much other valuable evidence about Mead and the social conditions of Manua at the time and that all this evidence had been sent to Professor Freeman, on whose behalf he had acted.

Editor's Afterword

Mary Catherine Bateson and Lola Romanucci-Ross have expressed the opinion that Mead was not duped. I asked the latter whether in light of Fa'apua'a's testimony she still maintained that view. The response was affirmative. While she did not doubt the truthfulness of Fa'apua'a's testimony, she stated that "Margaret Mead was not one to believe what people told her—she checks, triple checks, and goes to observe." The tease "gave [Mead] an 'out' for *what she wanted to write anyway* . . . her audience was the U.S. and what they wanted to *read.*"

For Romanucci-Ross the veracity of Fa'apua'a's testimony is warranted by a detail—Mead's distress at gift-giving. She writes: "When [Fa'apua'a] said that Margaret *hated* to give her things away—well, that settled it for me. She remembers that aspect of her personality in the field. *So do I.* We couldn't get her to give anything to the Manus . . . and she didn't like it when Ted [Schwartz] and I did . . ." (Personal communication, December 23, 1988).

Chapter III

History of American Anthropology

Introduction

Part of the objective of *Margaret Mead and Samoa* was to establish the significance of *Coming of Age in Samoa* in the history of anthropology. Freeman argued that Mead's Samoan study was perceived by Boas and his students to confirm the doctrine of cultural determinism that they advanced in the first and second decade of the century. By studying the reception of *Coming of Age in Samoa* in the fortnightlies and professional journals of the day, Freeman concluded that the celebrity of the book derived from its vindication not merely of Boasian theory, but more generally confirmed the environmentalist approach to social explanation then in fashion, not least among sex educators (*Margaret Mead and Samoa*, Chapter 7).

The second objective of Freeman's historical argument was to show that cultural determinism, or explanation of human behavior in purely cultural terms, originated from an explicit criticism of biological and evolutionary explanations of behavior. This interpretation was not novel. It had been advanced by the historian George F. Stocking, Jr. in his *Race, Culture, and Evolution* (1968), and was subsequently endorsed by Alexander Lesser. Both attributed to Boas a pivotal role in the history of anthropology, wherein, as Lesser stated, "the concept *cultural* replaced the concept *natural*. The culture concept did away at one blow with efforts to explain human nature biologically and physiologically (as with concepts of instinct or inherent drives)."

Freeman had studied these two historians of anthropology. Indeed, his chief characterizations of the Boasian orientation, "explanation purely in cultural terms" and "absolute cultural de-

165

terminism," were taken from Stocking. But Freeman went further than Stocking and Lesser in purporting to identify in Boas' writings an irrational animus against evolutionary theory and genetics. This animus, not an impartial criticism of the evolutionary anthropology of the day, was the reason why Boas abandoned the evolutionary orientation in cultural anthropology. Thus, contrary to the common impression that Boas' own contributions to physical anthropology, and his proposal of the four-field approach, showed him to be biology-friendly, Freeman's Boas was unfriendly. The contemporary meaning of this history appeared to be that Boas' dogged opposition to genetics, despite the potent evidence against his own Lamarckian views, is a legacy continued by contemporary anthropology in its opposition to the introduction of biological variables into cultural anthropology.

The brief selection from Eric A. Wolf states succinctly the perceived conjunction between the liberal reform agenda championed by New Dealers and the explanation of human behavior in terms of environmental factors.

The selection from Mead's 1929 article "South Seas Hints on Bringing Up Children," which appeared in *Parents' Magazine,* is the *Reader's* one example of Mead writing as social pundit. The article shows that Mead saw her Samoa research as supporting the culturalist explanation of adolescent behavior; and that this approach to behavior held many important liberal reform messages for the public.

Alexander Lesser's portrait of Boas as theorist, based on many years of study, undertook to resolve "pro-evolution" and "anti-evolution" statements scattered through Boas' writings into a coherent theoretical concept. Lesser concludes (as Stocking had) that Boas' "anti-evolutionism" was specifically opposition to the notion of biologically-driven evolution of cultures to higher types (evolutionary orthogenesis). Evolutionary anthropology, in other words, was dependent on the idea of progress in all domains of human culture. This concept, which enjoyed a broad consensus in Europe and North America, had racist implications merely in virtue of its classification of cultures according to a scale of increasing technical and social complexity. The scale identified hunters and semi-agriculturalists as "primitive" and ancient civilizations as "stagnant." Animated by his concern for the oppression of American blacks, Boas strove to differentiate between primitive cultures and primitive men, but could not sustain the distinction within his cultural determinist framework.

Surprisingly, few critics of Freeman's history of anthropology raised this point. One who did, Roy A. Rappaport, claimed that Boas' rejection of biologically-driven cultural evolution accorded then and today with fundamental genetical theory, so that it was Boas, not the Darwinian anthropologists Boas opposed, who got it right. This point is important to the argument about cultural determinism or explanation purely in cultural terms. The Boasians reasoned that if cultural variation has no evolutionary explanation, then only culture explains cultural variation. This inference has been challenged by Marvin Harris, who seeks to construe cultural change as adaptations to the physical environment (an explanation that Boas also rejected). Freeman for his part accepts that evolutionary biology does not explain cultural change; but he maintains that the agency of change, human choice, is itself a natural trait rich in biological implications that give ample scope for interactionist biology (above pp. 108-109).

Leslie White's study of Boas and the Boasian school is a debunking essay written by an anthropologist who, like Marvin Harris and Eric Wolf, rejected the idealist trait of anthropology based on explanation purely in cultural terms. Its value for the present volume is its tracking of the intricate mazeway of the Boasians, including the many startling inconsistencies of their testimony about Boas as teacher and theorist, the Boasian school, and the nature of anthropology. Contra Lesser, White maintains that Boas had no developed theory.

Freeman's critics dwelled on particular points. They objected to the anti-biological attitudes attributed to Boas and to the purported elimination of biological explanation from cultural anthropology. They claimed that Freeman had failed to appreciate the validity of Boas' objection to the evolutionary anthropology of his day. One critic, Stephen O. Murray, in correspondence with Freeman, disputed his claim that *Coming of Age in Samoa* was the validating text of Boasian anthropology. The editor's attempt to draw Murray's material into the *Reader* unfortunately did not succeed.

The Anthropology of Liberal Reform

Eric R. Wolf

Editor's Note

Wolf distinguishes three phases in the development of American anthropology. The second phase, the period of "intermittent Liberal Reform," he dates from the end of the last century to World War II. This corresponds to the Boas era. The public philosophy and uplifting endeavors of Margaret Mead were part of reform politics.

The selection is taken from "American Anthropologists and American Society," in Stephen A. Tyler, ed. *Concepts and Assumptions in Contemporary Anthropology*, Proceedings of the Southern Anthropological Society, pp. 3-11 (Athens: University of Georgia Press). Reprinted with permission of the Southern Anthropological Society.

The assertion of the collectivity of common men against the anarchistic captains of industry was represented by Beard, Turner, Veblen, Commons, Dewey, Brandeis, and Holmes; in American anthropology, the reaction against Social Darwinism found its main spokesman in Franz Boas. His work in physical anthropology furnished some of the initial arguments against a racism linked to Social Darwinist arguments. In his historical particularism he validated a shift of interest away from the grand evolutionary schemes to concern with the panoply of particular cultures in their historical conditioned setting. If we related these anthropological interests to the tenor of the times, we can say that the renewed interest in cultural plurality and relativity had two major functions. It called into question the moral and political monopoly of an elite which had justified its rule with the claim that their superior virtue was the outcome of the evolutionary process—it was their might which made their right. . . . For the intellectual prophets of the times the preeminent instruments for the achievement of this cooperative participation among new and diverse elements were to be scientific education and liberal reform achieved through social engineering. . . . The tool for discovery of the manifold educational processes—and hence also for a more adequate approach to the engineering of pluralist education—was science, that is, anthropology. The faith in social engineering and in the possibility of a new educational pluralism also underwrote the action programs among American Indians, who by means of the new techniques were to become autonomous participants in a more pluralistic and tolerant America.

But . . . the anthropology of Liberal Reform did not address itself, in any substantive way, to the problem of power . . . only rarely—if at all—did anthropologists shift their scientific focus to the constraints impeding both human malleability and malleability in socialization from the outside. . . . The culture-and-personality schools of the Thirties and Forties made a moral paradigm of each individual culture. They spoke of patterns, themes, world view, ethos, and values, but not of power. . . . Neither in the nineteenth century nor in the first half of the twentieth century, therefore, did American anthropology as such come to grips with the phenomenon of power.

South Seas Hints on Bringing Up Children[1]

Margaret Mead

There is a tendency in these United States to regard adolescence, "the teen age," "the awkward age," as one of the inevitable penalties of man's sinful nature. . . . So widespread is this belief that adolescence is inevitably a difficult period, that longer legs mean later hours and general bad behavior, that the first tender down on the boy's lips means the assumption of religious and political views different from his father's, that the first definition of the girl's figure means active revolt against parental standards—that even thoughtful Americans have gotten the mental and physical aspects of adolescence hopelessly mixed up. The physiological aspects are so obvious, the mental aspects are so prevalent, that one can hardly blame the theorizers for coming to regard the whole period much as they would regard an attack of a particularly virulent, but fortunately not permanent, disease. The next step, one which many of the wealthy have already taken, is to quarantine all these young people, these sufferers from "adolescence" until they get over it.

And certainly, according to this theory of adolescence, there is nothing else to be done. Just as one puts a fever patient to bed, supervises his food and keeps him quiet until his fever has run its

---

[1]This article appeared in *Parents' Magazine* 4 no. 9 (September, 1929):20-22, 49-52.

course, so, thinks many a modern parent: "Shut the young people up in nice, safe schools, with plenty of cold showers and athletics. Keep them away from cocktails and cigarettes and any knowledge of birth control or psychoanalysis, and after a while they will snap out of it, [and] grow up," that is, become physiologically mature and so able to behave as their parents behave—a doubtful blessing.

But suppose all this is a great mistake. Suppose by the very act of trying to keep our children safe we are unfitting them to meet life successfully. We Americans, children of pioneers though we are, have become singularly unadventurous in our thinking, limiting our observations to our own country, our own language group, insisting, blindly, that what is true of ourselves is necessarily true of the whole human race. At least, we insist that all races of men share our limitations and defects, although we may deny them some of our virtues.

But there is one group of students of human society that doubts this method which is content to generalize from what one sees in one's own front yard without ever looking over the fence into other civilizations. These are the anthropologists, the students of mankind at all times and in all places on this inadequately explored earth. The anthropologist, in the course of his investigations of all the diverse societies of the world, has found out some very queer things about human nature. He has come to believe that human nature is not nearly so fixed and inflexible as we used to think. Take such a fundamental human feeling as jealously, for instance. Even jealousy is shaped and defined by the particular civilization in which a man has grown up and learned what things to be jealous about. . . . The anthropologist began to wonder whether all these theories about adolescence were true either, whether its miseries and rebellions were as inevitable as all the well-meaning preachers and pedagogues believed. Maybe all these pains and pangs were due not to being young but to being young in America, in 1929. Maybe it wasn't the growing body which was responsible, nor the growing spirit, but rather, the ideas and attitudes upon which the growing spirit was fed. It was a good guess. But how really to find out?

It couldn't be done in America. We needed what the biologists call a "control group," that is, we had to have two sets of growing children, one in one kind of civilization and one in another. In both civilizations there would be adolescent boys and girls, passing through the same period of physiological change through which our children pass. If a society could be found in which the growing boys and girls missed out on all this storm and stress, then the anthropologist would know and the parents and teachers and preachers would know, that this storm and stress was not inevitable.

And so I set out to study the adolescents of a primitive community, a community so different from our own that there was a good chance of finding great differences in the young people who grew up in it. I picked a tiny volcanic island in American Samoa, an island inhabited by a few hundreds of brown South Sea Islanders. On the lee shore of this little island of Ta'ū there were three small villages, in which there were some fifty girls between the ages of ten and twenty. For nine months I lived among them, learned to eat their food and speak their language, go barefoot over the slippery trails and sleep upon a few mats laid on the pebbly floor. I listened to their secrets, played with their younger brothers and sisters, talked with their sweethearts, sat docilely at the feet of their elders, learned to know them and to know their way of life. And always I was trying to find out whether these Samoan girls were torn by conflicts, baffled by spiritual doubts and tormented by vague ambitions as are American girls of the same age.

To these questions, my answer is no, no and again no. The period of adolescence was unstressed in the girls' own lives. They changed without vexation from little girls whose main business in life was baby-tending to big girls who could be trusted with longer and more difficult tasks. No religious worries, no conflicts with their parents, no confusion about sex, vexed their souls. Their development was smooth, untroubled, unstressed. They grew up painlessly and almost unselfconsciously. And that left me with just one possible conclusion, that the woes and difficulties of youth can't be due to adolescence for adolescence brings no woes to the South Sea Islanders.

Parents will immediately ask: "What kind of an upbringing was it, if, as you say, it's the upbringing which is responsible? What education produced this painless 'awkward age' these unstormy teens? How did that South Sea Island society differ from our own?"

The first big difference is in the family. Our typical family, of father, mother and children, is hardly ever found in Samoa. There were just three such families in the three villages I studied. The Samoans live in great households of ten to twenty people, father and mother, aunts, uncles, grandparents, relatives in law, cousins—all housed in a cluster of round open houses, with high thatched roofs and no walls and no privacy. In such families there is no youngest child, not for long. Some sister or aunt or cousin will have a baby in the next few months. The baby's nose is put so quickly out of joint that it never feels it. In such families there is no only child, the spoiled indulged pet of a family of adults. And there is no room for the eldest child to wax self-important and arrogant. Similarly the sharp division between parents and children vanishes. A family is just a long series of people of different ages, all somehow related to one another, grading down from the grandfather to the new baby.

Over the whole group presides a head-man, who isn't necessarily the father of any of the children, but who commands the obedience of all the other men in the household. So for most children the actual father is one person, and the head-man who lays down the law and controls the purse strings is some other elder. The importance and prestige of the real father and mother are shared and diminished by the presence of a lot of other grown-up people. Furthermore, the mother takes very little care of her own babies after they are about six months old. At that age they are handed over to children of six and seven, who trundle them about everywhere, astride their hips. As often as not, it isn't mother who dries the baby's tears nor father who spanks the little mischief makers. And so the setting for parent fixations vanishes; the relationship between Samoan parents and children is too casual to foster such attitudes.

The advantages are surely on the side of Samoa. The family as we know it in America is unhealthily restricted, a narrow group instead of a community of households, in which the small child cannot experience many different kinds of fathers and mothers and older and younger children and new babies. And instead of attempting to minimize this danger, the self conscious parent in our civilization is forever sheltering the child from bad grammar, from the measles, from casual associates. He needs a change of heart; he needs to remember always that wholesome social intercourse is essential to the healthy development of a child.

Similarly the evils of quarreling parents economically unable to separate are eliminated. A woman can always be economically independent of her husband in Samoa, for she retains a claim upon the lands of both of her parents and she can go home without economic loss. Samoans would think the sacrifice made by two uncongenial, quarreling parents to stay together "for the children's sake," unnatural and unlovely.

Life and death and sex are no mysteries to the growing child in Samoa. The horror, the shock, the nauseated recoil of our protected, unsophisticated children is unknown. The only secrets kept from the children are matters of family pedigree which the parents do not wish bandied about the village. But there is no attempt to keep from children knowledge of the facts of life. Little toddlers peep under the midwife's arm at a birth, hover about the group which is preparing a corpse, and make an evening game of spying upon wandering lovers. In Samoa the amatory arts are freely discussed, and the whole village stands ready to mock the inept lover. And children, living in unwalled, unpartitioned houses, scouting freely about the village at night, listening to the conversation of their elders, experience often in imagination what they will much later experience in actuality. Samoa considers untimely, precocious participation in adult affairs the most heinous of sins, but this applies to actions, not to knowledge. The judgements of Samoan children upon the experiences of maturity are not complicated therefore by ignorance nor confused by false teaching. They have the best equipment in the world against shock, a long tested unemotionally-charged experience of the facts of life and death.

In this armoring of the children's nerves, quite as important a factor as the actual experience is the attitude of the parents. The grown people regard the whole course of human life simply, without recoil or reservation. They consider sex as natural, birth as important and unexceptional. The spectator children are surrounded by their parents' uncomplicated attitudes and protected by their parents' emotional calm. The American mother who, because she has been told that Tommy must learn about birth points out that the cat is going to have kittens, blushing hotly the while, is probably doing more harm than if she withheld the information and let Tommy pick up the news in the back alley. The facts of life learned young enough do not stagger nor particularly interest the young child but the affective tone which surrounds the moment when he learns the facts may permanently influence the whole attitude. If a matter-of-fact attitude can be managed about kittens but not about babies, the child is better off if his parent discusses the anatomy of kittens only. Although the Samoan material proves that small children can view the facts of life without harm, it does not prove that the average American parent is equipped to share these facts with a child and preserve the necessary serenity.

Pre-adolescent sex experimentation in Samoa is, nevertheless, rarer that it is here. A strict taboo separates brothers and sisters and girl and boy cousins. Little Samoan girls may not romp and play with their cousins, dress up in their brothers' clothes, nor may little boys smash their sisters' treasured possessions. All this is forbidden as disreputable. Against all the other small boys of the village, the little girls band together. It is unseemly for boys and girls to play together; hostilities of hurled coconuts are the only relations permitted between them. As a result girls in Samoa always think of boys as boys without learning to distinguish between personalities. The fact of sex is so emphasized that differences of temperament vanish. Of this more will be said later.

. . . The Samoan conditions are striking demonstrations of what good results can be gotten out of backward children when society is prepared to teach them with endless patience and encouragement. Inferiority complexes do not flourish where the more forward child is scolded rather than praised. Furthermore, the child which shows most natural proficiency is not given the next chance at the same activity; it is the duller child who is urged to try. So the differences in native ability are not increased by practice. But, although the Samoan system has much to teach of what may be done for the dull and backward, it gives only a warning as to the treatment of the gifted child. For a method like the Samoan can blunt the ambitions, dull the interest, blur the spontaneity of the gifted until the difference between the stupid who are encouraged and the bright who are discouraged is hardly to be noticed.

At about sixteen or seventeen the girl has passed through the most marked period of physiological adolescence. She is ready for a way of life which holds no mystery for her, for experiences even the emotional tone of which she knows. Her ambitions are simple and uniform; she wishes to live as a girl with many affairs and few responsibilities as long as possible, then to marry near home and have many children.

At two or three years past adolescence for the girls, except in the case of chiefs' daughters, and three or four years past adolescence for boys, sex experimentation begins. Although surrounded by the trappings which seem to us most romantic, moonlight and slender palm trees, the rhythmic beat of the surf, white with "coral milk" and the soft perfume of the frangipani blossoms, low-voiced protestations of love and flowery invocations of the stars and moon, these affairs of Samoan youth are not love affairs as we conceive of love affairs. The element of genuine personal relationship is entirely lacking. Samoan amours, although much more downright, are more like the petting conventions of the younger generation. Comeliness and technique are the two most important requisites. Friendships, appreciation of personality, passionate love with its strong connection between sex feeling and an awakened imagination, romantic love with its ideology of fidelity and chivalry—all are lacking. To the Samoan sex is play, an art to be learned with care and practiced with discretion. The emphasis is all upon the proper note of casualness, upon the fleeting hour. Strong attachments between young people whose parents' wealth and social position are unequal are regarded as being exceedingly bad form.

For Samoa is a formal society, based upon social classes, upon a recognition of rank, maintained, as most of such societies are, by the marriage of convenience. If the Samoan girl has ever learned the meaning of a strong attachment to one person, here would be cause for conflict. But she has not. Her early ideals were formed upon the model of a dozen older relatives, not upon an adored father. She has never known intimately a brother or a boy cousin or friend. She meets young men as lovers for brief butterfly affairs, which are born with the young moon and wane as it wanes. And she marries, seldom with an objection, some suitable youth who suits her parents' favor. She comes to marriage with no romantic dreams, but with a realistic knowledge of sex and pregnancy and child-birth. She marries not to satisfy vague, undefined desires, but because she is a little weary of the love that flits so lightly among the palm trees and wants the social position of a married woman and children of her own. And the boys who at twenty were marriage-shy and wary marry at twenty-five or twenty-six because they wish to settle down to the serious pursuits of manhood, house building and fishing and village politics.

The experience and perfection of sex knowledge in Samoa makes for happiness, but the absence of strong personal ties can only be deplored. The separation of the sexes, the dislike of strong emotion, the lack of respect for personality are principally to blame. On the one hand the segregation of the sexes and the emphasis upon prudent marriages denies personality; on the other, indiscriminate petting and its necessary suppression of any genuine emotion lead to a like disregard of the importance of personal relations. We can appreciate as the Samoans cannot the value of personal relations.

From start to finish it is a very different picture from our own. . . . All that children have learned of life and death and birth is scattered hearsay, sly comment from children nearly as ignorant as themselves, accidental experiences. All this surreptitiously acquired knowledge predisposes them to shock, rather than armors them against it. At the earliest age when they can possibly be expected to understand such matters—most incorrectly dubbed "years of discretion"—they are expected to make religious choices, hounded by movements and causes and crusades, hurried hither and thither by the thousand conflicting currents of modern life. And they are tempted to experiment with sex in a fashion for which we have no canons of responsibility and through which many come to grief.

It is indeed no wonder that we hear so much about the younger generation. Their pains and pangs are genuine enough. Scores of proud, ignorant youngsters are going down before experiences for which they are ill prepared, brought up as they have been to believe that one code of religion, of morals, of economics, of manners must be right and all others wrong. We may well be exercised concerning all this waste motion, this misery, the heavy spiritual casualty list. But our concern should not take the form of a group of self-sympathizing adults, commiserating with each other because the children are "adolescent." For if adolescence were to blame, the young Samoans would be generating the same difficulties, or ones of similar force, out upon their coral-trimmed island.

The old slogan, "You can't change human nature" and "girls will be girls," have justified many an indolent shoulder shrug, many a relieved sloughing off of adult responsibility. But the anthropologists, through their study of people in different cultures, the behaviorists through their study of babies with no culture at all, are demanding a radical revision of our conception of human nature. "Girls will be girls" will have to be modified to read: "Kansas City girls in 1929 will be Kansas City girls in 1929." All the universality has gone out of the lazy old formula, and with its universality goes its value as a salve for irresponsible consciences. For what kind of girls Kansas City will produce in 1929 depends much more upon Kansas City, its parents, its schools, its movies, its newsstands, than it does upon the fact that the girls are "adolescent."

We could not reproduce Samoan conditions if we would. A simple society where all share the same ideals and the world of one generation is so very like the world of the next generation is not for us. Our complicated society, which is coming to recognize personality as a value and cherish choice and individuality of thought, demands higher prices than are every paid by the graceful young Samoans in their shady, peaceful villages. It is our youth, those who have not yet made their choices, who must pay most heavily for this right to choose. Their young days can never be as untroubled, as unpoignant as the days of the Samoans.

In the light of this knowledge, first, that adolescence does not necessarily result in conflict, misery and storm, and second, that we are asking our young people to grow up in a very difficult and expensive world, we should look to our educational theories. A country thrust suddenly into war sets about preparing its troops for emergencies unknown in peace time. But we do not say: "All soldiers get typhoid" and fold our hands. We say: "Soldiers are particularly liable to typhoid" and proceed to inoculate them. So our youth are subject to more severe tests and greater strains than are the youth of old settled societies. The answer is not, "They are just adolescent! Oh, dear, how troublesome," but "They are growing up in a very difficult society. How can we best prepare ourselves and them to meet those difficulties?"

Franz Boas:
The Founder of American Anthropology

Alexander Lesser

Editor's Note
This selection is drawn from "Franz Boas and the Modernization of Anthropology," published in *Totems and Teachers*, edited
by Sydel Silverman, Columbia University Press, 1981, pp. 3-31.
Reprinted with permission of the Columbia University Press.

Modern anthropology begins with Franz Boas. It begins in the scientific skepticism with which he examined the traditional orthodoxies of the study of man, exposing and rejecting the false and unproven, calling for a return to empirical observation, establishing the truth of elementary fundamentals, opening new pathways and creating new methods. It begins in Boas' ways of thinking about man and his history, in his use of rigorous scien-tific requirements for data and for proof, in his rejection of old myths, old stereotypes, old emotionally charged assumptions.

Boas' contribution to the transformation of anthropology was therefore not a simple, single event, a formal statement of princi-ples, or a generalized theory at a certain point of time. Boas worked from problem to problem, consolidating the truth gained and asking the next question. The framework and principles of the modern subject matter are emergents from this ongoing process, in part the residue of truth left after traditional materials and ideas were reevaluated, in part the positive discovery of empirical principles by fresh and original observation.

Boas was aware of this critical character of his method from his early professional years. . . . But in the end he restructured anthropology and its branches, leading physical anthropology from taxonomical race classification into human biology, breaking through the limitations of traditional philology into the problems of modern linguistics and cognitive anthropology, establishing the modern anthropological meaning and study of human culture. . . . *[The Mind of Primitive Man]* provided general anthropology and its separable branches—physical anthropology, linguistics, ethnology—with a structural framework. Establishing the relative autonomy of cultural phenomena, it gave to the concept of culture its modern meaning and usage. Boas proved that cultures are diverse historical developments, each the outcome of a prior history in which many factors and events, cultural and noncultural, have played a part. He made the plurality of cultures fundamental to the study of man . . . . He showed how languages, both semantically and morphologically, are each a context of perception that affects human thought and action. Analogously, he showed how cultural environments, especially as contexts of traditional materials, shape and structure human behavior—actions and reactions—in each generation. In so doing he ended the traditional ambiguity in the term *culture* understood interchangeably as both humanistic and behavioral—an ambiguity perpetuated by endless quoting of Tylor's "culture *or* civilization"—and started the modern era of the concepts of *cultures, viewed as contexts of learned human behavior.*

Several of the theses of the book *The Mind of Primitive Man,* taken together, establish the relative autonomy of cultural phenomena, showing that there are *no independent variables* on which the cultural is dependent. First, establishing that race (physical type), language, and culture have relatively independent histories and are not interchangeable terms in classifying man, Boas showed that inner inborn traits ("race" or heredity) are not causal determinants of similarities or differences of cultures. Second, showing that geographical or natural environments are not neatly correlated with cultures as adaptations but always involve preexisting cultures, Boas proved that outer environmental conditions are not *the* causal determinants of similarities or differences of cultures. Finally, establishing that ideas of *orthogenetic* cultural evolution do not fit the facts of actual cultural sequences and history, Boas showed that no necessary predetermining process of changes makes similarities or differences of cultures expressions of unfolding stages of development. These theses became the principles of modern anthropology.

. . . I come now to my final theme, Boas as theorist. Far from being antitheory, Boas was himself, I would argue, the great theorist of modern anthropology, who established the core of anthropological theory on which the science is based.

Inescapably, discussions of Boas on theory must begin with his handling of the theory of evolution. Here are his words on the subject in 1888:

> The development of ethnology is largely due the the general recognition of the principle of biological evolution. It is a common feature of all forms of evolutionary theory that every living being is considered as the result of an historical development. The fate of an individual does not influence himself alone, but also all succeeding generations. . . . This point of view introduced an historical perspective into the natural sciences and revolutionized their methods. The development of ethnology is largely due to the adoption of the evolutionary standpoint, because it impressed the conviction upon us that no event in the life of a people passes without leaving its effect upon later generations. The myths told by our ancestors and in which they believed have made their impress upon the ways of thinking of their descendants.

Clearly, in his early anthropological thinking Boas (1) accepted biological evolution as scientifically valid, (2) understood evolution in *historical* terms, not as orthogenetic, and (3) affirmed evolution as a *first principle* of ethnology and anthropology.

These statements must be emphasized in view of oft-repeated assertions that Boas was anti-evolutionary. No statement could show more clearly that he not only accepted evolution but accepted it as basic. Yet he did reject the so-called evolutionary ideas of some anthropologists. What did he reject, as distinction from the evolution that he affirmed?

In *Primitive Art* he wrote:

> Evolution, meaning the continuous change of thought and action, or historic continuity, cannot be accepted unreservedly. It is otherwise when it is conceived as

meaning the universally valid continuous development
of one cultural form out of a preceding type.

Essentially he was opposing orthogenesis, which is defined
as follows by Webster's dictionary:

In biology, variations which in successive generations of
an organism, follow some particular line, evolving some
new type irrespective of natural selection or other external factor. Determinate variation or evolution. Sociologically, the theory that social evolution always follows the
same direction and passes through the same stages in
each culture despite differing external conditions.

Orthogenesis, by its very definition, is a contradiction of
Darwin's theory of evolution. Darwin based evolutionary change
on the principle of natural selection; among the vast number of
variations occurring in each new generation, some were
"selected" to survive and reproduce, others were not. Natural
selection in turn must be understood as historical in character.
Forms or species are subject to variation and change. So, too, is
the environment in which they occur. The interaction between
variations of form and the changing environment is an event of a
particular time, not predetermined by either system. In modern
biology, orthogenesis is not a fundamental evolutionary process.
The point is made in Simpson's *Meaning of Evolution* and in
various other treatments.

It was this distinction between orthogenesis and evolution in
its historical, Darwinian sense that Boas had in mind, as has been
noted by some. Washburn has written about this, referring to
"evolution" as the term was used by Tylor, Spencer, Morgan,
and their contemporary throwbacks. "There is no evolution in
the traditional anthropological sense. What Boas referred to as
evolution was orthogenesis, which receives no support from
modern genetic theory. What the geneticist sees as evolution is
far closer to what Boas called history than to what he called evolution." In an article on Boas I wrote, "Boas' critique was directed not against the principle of evolution as historical development, which he accepted, but against the orthogenesis of
dominant English and American theory of time. He opposed history to orthogenesis."

. . . In 1938, discussing problems of the laws of historic development, Boas wrote:

When these data are assembled, the question arises whether they present an orderly picture or whether history proceeds haphazardly; in other words, whether an *orthogenetic* development of human forms may be discovered, and whether a regular sequence of stages of historical development may be recognized.

Several aspects of this view of evolution help explain Boas' view of theory, and his work as a scientific theorist. First, he uses the fact of evolution as proof "that every living being is the result of an historical development." He understands evolution as history and as evidence of the historicity of living things. In effect, Boas' view is a major theory, both of culture and of man. It states that every culture is the result of a long history, and that every such history involves a great complexity of events, accidents of history, and interrelation of factors.

. . . As Darwin's theory of evolution expressed in a generalization both the continuity and change of living forms—*descent with modification*—so a similar theory of the historical evolution of cultures served to express their continuity through time and their diversification and change—the idea of *continuity with change*.

Additionally, Boas established the modern *theory* of culture. Stocking has shown that it was Boas who established the modern use and meaning of the term. But more than that, in doing so he established the central theory of modern anthropology.

When Boas showed that cultures and their diversities could not be explained by differences in outer environment, natural environment, or geography; when he showed that cultural diversity could not be explained by difference in inner makeup of human groups (the racial argument); and finally, when he showed that cultural diversity was not a matter of stages of predetermined development or orthogenetic evolution, he made cultures and their histories the primary determinants of diversities or similarities at any time. Cultures became the basic factor in the understanding of cultural man. In anthropological thinking and explanation, the concept *cultural* replaced the concept *natural*. The culture concept did away at one blow with efforts to explain human nature biologically and physiologically (as with concepts of instinct or of inherent drives).

I would suggest, then, that two great theories in anthropology were contributed by Boas: the idea that in culture history, culture is the primary determinant, rather than some noncultural independent variable; and the theory of culture in its modern sense, as learned behavior. Both of these are inductive theories, based on the comparison and contrast of human cultures.

Franz Boas and the Boasian School

Leslie A. White

Editor's Note:
White's essay was published as *The Social Organization of Ethnological Theory* , v. 52, no. 4 of the *Rice University Studies: Monographs in Cultural Anthropology*, pp. 1-65. White documents his statements by prodigious quotation and source citation. In editing the essay, many of the source citations have been deleted. The selection is drawn from the opening pages of the monograph. Reprinted with permission of the Rice University Press.

In cultural anthropology, as in other sciences, we find conceptual processes in operation in which premises and goals are determined, and results evaluated, by the concepts and logic of science. But we also find social organizations—schools—of ethnological theory which closely integrated such nonscientific factors as personality, nationality, and race with scientific concepts such as evolution, diffusion, independent development, integration, determinism, choice, and law. These schools are by their very nature deceptive. They make it appear and would have everyone believe that their choice of premises and goals has been determined by scientific considerations and that the value of their results is measured by the yardsticks of science alone.

This is definitely not the case, as we shall later demonstrate. We are not accusing members of schools of an intent to deceive; they are obviously sincere. Their sincerity and group loyalty tend, however, to persuade and consequently to deceive. It is impossible to understand much of the work in ethnological theory without taking social organization—schools—into account. Viewed in the light of social organization—of personalities organized into groups—things that are otherwise incomprehensible or even incredible become clear. We shall attempt to demonstrate our thesis by a consideration of two schools of ethnological theory, those of Franz Boas and A. R. Radcliffe-Brown.

In our examination of these schools, we undertake to appraise the scholarly accomplishments of their leaders and followers; to compare our appraisals with those offered by adherents and by scholars who are not members of the schools; to draw inferences concerning the nature of social relationships between leaders and followers; and to describe various aspects of the personalities of both leaders and followers.

The Boas School

Many voices have been raised in protest against use of the word "school" in connection with Boas. "There is no 'Boas school,' and never has been in the sense of a definable group following a definable, selective program" (Kroeber, Redfield). The "term 'Boas school' . . . is a misnomer" (Herskovits). "Herskovits' insistence that there was no 'Boas school' is especially commendable" (Lowie). " . . . there is no Boas school . . ." (Mead). " . . . I do not believe that there ever was such a 'school' . . ." (Strong).

But it is interesting to note that some of the very persons who have denied the existence of a Boas school have, along with others, spoken freely of such a group. Kroeber refers to " . . . the heart of the Boas school." Lowie discusses "The Boas school" in *The History of Ethnological Theory*. Others who have objected to this term but have nevertheless used it are Edward Sapir, Paul Radin, and Leslie Spier. Goldenweiser not only speaks of a "Boas school," but tells us who its members, "in the narrow sense," were: "Robert H. Lowie, Paul Radin, Edward Sapir, G. Speck, Truman Michelson, and A. A. Goldenweiser." In the third edition of their *Introduction to Anthropology*, Beals and Hoijer also refer to "Boas and his school."

Although Herskovits "insists" that there was no Boas school, he gives us a very good description of it:

> The four decades of the tenure of his professorship at Columbia gave a continuity to his teaching that permitted him to develop students who eventually made up the greater part of the significant professional core of American anthropologists, and who came to man and direct most of the major departments of anthropology in the United States. In their turn, they have trained the students who . . . have continued in the tradition in which their teachers were trained (Herskovits 1953).

Kroeber did not merely assert that there never has been a Boas school; he tells us why such a group could not have existed: "It is evident that for a school to be such it must have something of the quality of a cult. There must be a positive creed or dogma or slogan. The excess of negative component in Boas' intellectual make-up would have tended to prevent such a formation" (Kroeber). We may grant the "excess of negative component in Boas' intellectual make-up," but we believe elements of a cult are easily discernible.

In defining "cult," Webster's *New International Dictionary* uses such phrases as "a system of worship," "great or excessive devotion to some person, idea, or thing," "a body of followers, practitioners, or worshippers."

Kroeber, who denies the existence of a Boas school, nevertheless tells us that Boas "was literally worshipped by some of those who came under his influence." To Lowie, Boas was "my revered teacher." I have personally heard Lowie speak of Boas in these terms several times. Lowie also refers to " . . . all who sat at Prof. Boas' feet . . . ." Gene Weltfish "sat at the feet of the great Franz Boas" when she was a student at Barnard College. Boas was Herskovits' "revered master" says Lowie in his review of Herskovits' biography of Boas. Section III of Goldenweiser's "Recent Trends in American Anthropology" (1941) is devoted to the "Disciples" of Boas. Lowie speaks of Boas' disciples, and Radin refers to ". . . all Boas' disciples." Melville Jacobs uses the word "disciple" repeatedly. The Reverend Joseph J. Williams, S.J., who might be expected to be discriminating in his use of terms pertaining to religion, speaks of Boas' followers as "his disciples," whose "permanent loyalty" was "effectively established" by Boas. "Once the contact [between student and Boas] is formed," said Goddard, "a relation of master and disciple grows up and in nearly every case continues . . . men and women who were studying at Columbia, came within the field of Professor Boas' attractions, and forsook all to follow him." One recalls another revered Teacher for whom fishermen dropped their nets that they might follow him.

It should not be difficult to predict the conception of Boas' role in anthropological science held by his disciples. "In the beginning was Boas . . .," thus May Edel begins *The Story of People, Anthropology for Young People* (1953) in a chapter on "Papa Franz," one section of which is entitled "Anthropology Begins." "Although Herskovits occasionally refers to precursors and contemporaries, there are times when Boas is assigned the role of a mythical culture-hero, bringing light out of Cimmerian darkness." Goldenweiser is more explicit: "To anthropology in this country Franz Boas, the 'Man,' came as such a culture-hero." Benedict sees Boas bringing order out of chaos: "He found anthropology a collection of wild guesses and a happy hunting ground for the romantic lover of primitive things; he left it a discipline in which theories could be tested . . . ." Kroeber says that Boas "found anthropology a playfield and jousting ground of opinion: he left it a science . . . ." Spier says " . . . so far as anthropology is a science he [Boas] made it one." La Barré calls Boas the "father of American anthropology."

Members of the Boas school have advanced and reiterated the thesis that it was fieldwork that undermined the theoretical work of their predecessors, specifically, theories of cultural evolution. Thus, Steward observes that the fieldwork of twentieth century anthropologists "tested and cast doubt on the validity" of "the specific evolutionary formulations of such writers as Morgan and Tylor . . . ." Herskovits, Sapir, Hoebel, and others subscribe to this thesis. Members of the Boas school have often pictured their predecessors as armchair philosophers—or "closet philosophers," as Sapir called them. The field of cultural evolutionism was a "happy hunting ground for the exercise of the creative imagination."

"With Boas, anthropology planted its feet firmly upon empiricism." "Boas must be understood, first of all, as a field worker." So generally has this view been accepted that we find a British social anthropologist, Meyer Fortes, attributing "a change which determined the whole course of anthropological studies in the twentieth century" to Boas, who "by the end of the [nineteenth] century . . . had established the method of systematic field work by professional anthropologists as the basis of American anthropology" (Fortes). These statements disregard the fact that competent scientific field work had been established as a tradition in American anthropology long before Boas' influence was felt. Lewis H. Morgan did intensive field work among the Iroquois in the 1840's, and extensive work among plains tribes years later. At its inception in 1879, the Archaeological Institute of America asked Morgan to outline a program of field research. And the Bureau of American Ethnology emphasized field work from the start (1879). One need only mention such names as Frank H. Cushing, Matilda Coxe Stevenson, Albert S. Gatschet, Washington Matthews, J. Owen Dorsey, James Mooney, Adolph F. Bandelier, W. J. McGee, Alice Fletcher, and J. N. B. Hewitt to indicate how extensively field work was carried on in the United States before, or independently of, Boas' influence.

In the thousands of pages of Boas' monographs on the Kwakiutl we find an immense amount of raw material, but very little else. "The essence of his method," says Radin "was . . . to gather facts and ever more facts . . . and permit them to speak for themselves." Thus we find hundreds and hundreds of pages of texts and translations of myths, legends, descriptions of art and crafts, ceremonies, folk beliefs and practices, and just plain odds and ends. In the *Ethnology of the Kwakiutl*, we find 155 recipes for cooking fish, along with data on hunting and fishing, "beliefs and customs," and miscellany. But no interpretation is included. "It is easy to go through a thousand pages of his [Boas'] monographs without encountering a line of interpretation (Lowie).

Boas' admirers extol his intellectual powers in general and his scientific mind in particular. Boas, "the faithful recorder was, above all, a thinker," an "independent and erudite thinker" (Lowie). "What marked him out from others and made him a leader was the union of critical acumen with a still higher quality, to wit, originality" (Lowie). Indeed, he played a "revolutionary role . . . in the history of anthropology," according to Goldenweiser. Ruth Benedict, Marian Smith, C. K. Shipton, and Ernest R. Trattner likewise speak of the "revolution" wrought by Boas.

Boas "seemed to personify the very spirit of science"; he was "the champion of scientific method in all anthropological research" (Lowie). Goldenweiser speaks of him as "the natural scientist that he was." And Naroll tells us that "Franz Boas was ferociously [sic] determined to make anthropology a science"— and then repeats the much-used phrase about "rigorous testing."

In fact, Boas spurned primary and fundamental procedures of science; namely classification and generalization. He was "fundamentally impatient of all classifications," according to Kroeber; he had a "deep-seated reluctance to generalize, summarize, or classify" (Kroeber). "Under his [Boas'] stimulation," says Radin, "ethnologists set to work to describe facts 'as they really were,' to make no judgments and scrupulously to avoid generalizations." According to Lowie, Boas "abhorred facile generalizations and all-embracing systems." In another connection, however, Lowie could write: "We cannot blame Tylor for striving to bring the greatest possible number of phenomena under a single formula, for that is the aim of all science."

As for original and creative thought, Lowie has testified that "one might well read a thousand pages of his output without finding more than a faithful, intelligent collector of raw detail." Radin tells us that under Boas' leadership "an exaggerated distrust of theories of whatsoever description" was engendered. Berthold Laufer, in a review praising one of Lowie's books, declared that he "would no longer give a dime to anyone for a new theory." Indeed, so great was the aversion to theory among the Boasians that Kluckhohn was moved to observe that "to suggest that something is 'theoretical' is to suggest that it is slightly indecent."

The Mind of Primitive Man is largely concerned with the subject of race and its relation to mental ability and to cultural development. It also contains an attack upon, and a rejection of, theories of cultural evolution. *Anthropology and Modern Life* consists of essays on various aspects of modern Western society and culture: race, nationalism, eugenics, criminology, education, etc. It ignores completely one of the most fundamental and important factors in modern culture, namely, the industrial and fuel revolution and its impact upon social, political, and economic institutions. The great cleavage in Western society between capital and labor is not touched upon. Phenomena such as the Paris Commune, the I.W.W. and the House of Morgan receive no mention. And the emergence and establishment of the Soviet system, as an instance of social evolution as well a revolution, find no place. In reviewing this book Sapir calls Boas "rigorous," but observes that he cannot "give himself."

Boas' distinctions between race, nationality, language, and culture were designed to oppose the racist doctrines of Gobineau and Houston Stewart Chamberlain, and of later writers such as Madison Grant (*The Passing of the Great Race*, 1916) and Lothrop Stoddard (*The Rising Tide of Color*, 1920), and no doubt they had a salutary effect in certain quarters. But we may well question the value of his contribution to the problems of race conflict.

Boas, who was "of Jewish extraction" (Lowie), had been intensely concerned with anti-Semitism since his "formative years" (Kluckhohn and Prufer). He wrote voluminously on racial problems, as did some of his prominent students. As I have argued elsewhere, however, he never got to the heart of the matter. Much of his argument was based upon anthropometry and anatomy, which were largely irrelevant because race prejudice and conflict do not arise form lack of knowledge of facts of this sort. In addition to citing anatomical evidence, Boas postulated a psychological basis of race prejudice: "The prejudice is founded essentially on the tendency of the human mind to merge the individual in the class to which he belongs, and to ascribe to him all the characteristics of his class." Boas did "not wish to deny that the economic conflict may be a contributing cause. . . . It would, however, be an error to seek in these sources the fundamental cause of the antagonism; for the economic conflict . . .

presupposes the social recognition of the classes." What then is the remedy? The "only fundamental remedy . . . is the recognition that the Negroes have the right to be treated as individuals, not as members of a class." This is undoubtedly true, but it is also a tautology. "Strong minds" might "free themselves from race prejudice . . ." but "the weak-minded will not follow their example." Education, Boas reasons, cannot "overcome the general human tendency of forming groups that in the mind of the outsider are held together by his emotional attitude toward them." What, then, can eradicate the conflict between races? Boas' answer was miscegenation:

> Intermixture will decrease the contrast between the extreme racial forms, and in the course of time, this will lead to a lessening of the consciousness of race distinction. If conditions were ever such that it could be doubtful whether a person were of Negro descent or not, the consciousness of race would necessarily be much weakened. In a race of octoroons, living among Whites, the color question would probably disappear.
> It would seem therefore, to be in the interest of society to permit rather than to restrain marriages between white men and Negro women . . . .

Thus it would seem that man being what he is, the Negro problem will not disappear in America until Negro blood has been so much diluted that it will no longer be recognized just as anti-Semitism will not disappear until the last vestige of the Jew as a Jew has disappeared.

Boas' reasoning is, of course, flawless: if one cannot distinguish a Negro from a white, or a Jew form a Gentile, then prejudice and conflict between them will cease to exist. However, advocacy of intermarriage between Negro and white might well accentuate, rather than diminish, race prejudice and conflict; nothing arouses the hostility of white supremacists more than the prospect of intermarriage. This is recognized by Negro leaders, one of whom recently sloganed: "We want to be the white man's brother, not his brother-in-law." An explanation of race conflict along social, political, and economic lines might have had more effect, but this Boas never offered.

Boas had virtually a closed mind, if we may trust Kroeber's judgment on this point:

Those [ideas] that he had grown up with and accepted,
that he had originated, dealt with, or appropriated—that
he held some ownership in, in short—he adhered to un-
flinchingly and persistently and would have died for.
Other ideas, those that came into his orbit from outside or
late, that impinged on his 'tree' of personality, instead of
having been created or annexed by it, he tended to react
to with reserve or even suspicion.

Smith remarks: "Born in the same year which saw publication
of the *Origin of Species* [he was in fact born one year earlier],
Boas could profit from the first great intellectual response which
greeted man's entrance into the world of nature." But Boas "was
not much interested in biological evolution" (Kroeber); Kluckhohn and Prufer speak of his "relative lack of interest in Darwinian evolution." And he was "skeptical about Mendelian
heredity" (Kluckhohn and Prufer). According to Kroeber Boas
"demonstrated that some human traits are not transmitted according to simple Mendelian rules." He "flatly rejected" historical
linguistics (Kroeber). Boas was "consistently anti-Freudian"
(Kroeber); Bunzel speaks of his "unalterable opposition to Freud
and psychoanalysis." Boas himself gives us the best picture of
his attitude toward "ideas that he had not grown up with." He
speaks of the "doubtful—and in my mind fanciful—interpretations of psychoanalysis." He also observed that "the elaborate
theories of psychoanalysis seem also unnecessary for the purpose
of explaining the wonderful elements of folk tales or of mytho-
logical figures. The free play of imagination operating with everyday experience is sufficient to account for their origin," Radin
observes:

Of the great intellectual events in Boas' lifetime, as-
suredly the two most significant were the theory of
evolution and the economic interpretation of history.
To the first Boas always took a prevailingly antagonistic position. The second he never so much as mentioned until the 1938 edition of *The Mind of Primitive
Man*. There he dismissed it in a paragraph as of only
secondary importance. . . . Marx and Engels are never
referred to.

Although Boas was "not much interested in biological evolution," he was intensely concerned with cultural evolutionism.
The evolutionist theory established in ethnology by Tylor "was

challenged, notably by Boas . . . and a good part of his energies and those of his school had to be devoted to disproving it" (Radin). Radin also reports that "to all Boas' disciples Morgan has since remained anathema and unread." "But if Boas and his school rejected the developmental schemes of Tylor and Morgan this must, in no sense, be ascribed to the inadequacies and crudities of those schemes, but rather to the fact they rejected all developmental sequences" (Radin). In a laudatory essay, Father Williams has much to say of the "initiative and indefatigable effort" of Boas in "the attack on cultural evolution" which he led "for more than a quarter of a century." The harm done to cultural anthropology by this campaign, waged by Boas and his disciples for years against one of the most fundamental and fruitful theories in all science, now seems incalculable.

". . . With the death of Franz Boas," said Kroeber, "the world lost its greatest anthropologist." There have been many who have thought that Boas was "the greatest." In what did his greatness consist? A satisfactory answer is difficult to find, and this difficulty is experienced by his followers as well as others. "It has long been notoriously difficult to convey the essence of Boas' contribution in anthropology to non-anthropologists" (Kroeber); " . . . no label fits him." Radin has observed that "others, besides myself, have found it difficult to define Boas' position." Kroeber undertook to interpret Boas in "History and Science in Anthropology" (1935), to which Boas replied: "I wish to express my complete disagreement with his interpretation." This difficulty, this uncertainty, is perhaps not surprising inasmuch as Boas himself is described as being "at a loss to explain his position in terms intelligible to the members of schools" (Kroeber).

. . . The picture now becomes clear; the enigma of Boas' reputation is solved. Boas has all the attributes of the head of a cult, a revered charismatic teacher and master, "literally worshipped" by disciples whose "permanent loyalty" has been "effectively established." We now understand such things as calling *The Central Eskimo* "monumental," and the inclusion of Boas in a series with Marx, Freud, and Einstein. We see in a new light the assertion, so contrary to fact, that Boas' unsparing mind insisted on definite proof. We face what Freud, in characterizing religion, has called a "delusional transformation of reality." Boas' personality and character are so confused with his anthropological work that his disciples cannot distinguish one from the other.

Historical Glosses

Derek Freeman

Editor's Note

The energy with which Freeman's history of anthropology was attacked is a measure of its polemical intention to exhibit American anthropology's persistent cultural orientation. The title "Historical Glosses" has been supplied because Freeman's rejoinders are extensions and elaborations of the history written in *Margaret Mead and Samoa*. Freeman wrote three sustained rejoinders to critics of his history. The first appeared in *Canberra Anthropology*, vol. 6, no. 2, 1984, from which the present excerpt is taken. A second statement appeared in his rejoinder to Nancy McDowell in *Pacific Studies* 7 (1984):140-196. The section on history, pp. 148-158, repeats the *Canberra Anthropology* essay, pp. 135-142. A third statement was composed as an Open Letter to the *Scientific American*. The Open Letter was prompted by that journal's coverage of Roy A. Rappaport's lengthy article in the *American Scholar*, "Desecrating the Holy Woman: Derek Freeman's Attack on Margaret Mead." The *Scientific American* billed its report "Untrashing Margaret Mead" [v. 225 (November 1986, 58-58B], and credited Rappaport with exonerating Mead and American anthropology from Freeman's charges of doctrinaire exclusion of biological variables. Freeman's first letter was published (February 1987, vol. 256, p. 6; see Rappaport's response in the same place). His second letter, dated February 9, 1987, was "for the record." It is printed here for the first time. The numerous references in both selections have been deleted.

If Mead had merely published a tolerably adequate account of Samoa and left it at that, there would be no substantial ground for subjecting her account to any intensive critical scrutiny. In fact, she went far beyond this to reach a quite general theoretical conclusion that came to be very widely accepted by the educated public and by cultural and social anthropologists alike.

As Mead herself has described, she went to Samoa in 1925 "to carry out the task" which had been "given" to her by her professor, Franz Boas, "to investigate to what extent the storm and stress of adolescence" is "biologically determined and to what extent it is modified by the culture within which adolescents are reared." In 1928, in the fourth paragraph of the thirteenth chapter of *Coming of Age in Samoa*, Mead came to the preposterous conclusion that biological variables are of no significance in the etiology of adolescent behavior; "we cannot," she asserted, "make any explanations" in terms of the biological process of adolescence itself.

I am here using the word preposterous in its dictionary sense of "contrary to nature, reason or common sense" for, in the light of modern scientific knowledge, human behavior is characterized by the interaction of cultural and biological variables, and, as Konner has put it, "any analysis of the causes of human nature that tends to ignore either the genes or the environmental factors may be safely discarded."

On this ground alone, any knowledgeable behavioral scientist would reject Mead's extreme conclusion of 1928, which, in asserting that biological variables are to be totally excluded from any explanation of the "storm and stress" associated with the behavior of adolescents, is clearly an example of absolute cultural determinism. Yet Boas accepted Mead's preposterous conclusion without question or qualification, and in his *Anthropology and Modern Life* announced to the world that in Samoa "the adolescent crisis disappears." And a few years later, in her *Patterns of Culture*, Ruth Benedict, Mead's other mentor at Columbia University, declared that among Samoan girls the adolescent period was "quite without turmoil." These unfactual assertions were associated with the belief that human nature was "the rawest, most undifferentiated of raw material," and with the movement "toward an explanation of human behavior in purely cultural terms."

In this movement Mead's extreme conclusion of 1928 was of quite pivotal importance and, although most of my critics have evaded the fact, it is specifically with the refutation of this crucially significant conclusion of Mead's that my book is concerned.

On the Doctrine of Cultural Determinism

While the movement "toward an explanation of human behavior in purely cultural terms," of which Mead's *Coming of Age in Samoa* was a principal expression, may be traced back at least as far as Boas' vice-presidential address of 1894 to the Anthropology Section of the American Association for the Advancement of Science, its first unequivocal formulation is to be found in Kroeber's "Eighteen Professions." This paper . . . may, as Stocking has noted, in many respects be regarded as "a kind of manifesto of Boasian anthropology." As Stocking also notes, because of his sensitivity to its Germanic associations in time of war, Kroeber avoided the word "culture" in the phrasing of his "eighteen professions," writing rather of "history," "civilization," and the "social." His "manifesto" remains, however, a quintessential expression of absolute cultural determinism. His ninth profession, for example, declares that "heredity cannot be allowed to have acted any part in history," and is the direct precursor of Mead's extreme conclusion of 1928. Absolute cultural determinism was thus a fully articulated doctrine at the time Mead began attending Boas' lectures on anthropology at Barnard College in 1922.

At this same time, one of the graduate students completing his Ph.D. under Boas at Columbia University was Melville Herskovits, who later became Boas' biographer and an ardent proponent of both cultural determinism and cultural relativism. As Vaughan has noted, culture was for Herskovits an "inclusive concept . . . comprehending the behavioral and the ideational, the group and the individual." And so, for Herskovits enculturation became the process, by which "all adjustment to social living" is "achieved," which yields "a profound sense of the plasticity of the human organism." He therefore had no hesitation in accepting Mead's extreme conclusion of 1928, and early in his *Man and His Works: The Science of Cultural Anthropology* of 1948, Herskovits cited Mead's assertion that the "puberty crises" of adolescent girls was "absent" in Samoa, and added, following Mead, that the "only conclusion" to be drawn from this finding was that "such emotional reactions are culturally, not biologically determined."

Here we have a clear example of inductivist thinking, for Herskovits is advancing evidence that, as he would have it, demonstrates the truth of a doctrine—that of cultural determinism—which he had derived from Boas and Kroeber, and to which he had given credence since his student days at Columbia University.

It is such inductivist thinking that I discuss briefly in the next section of this rejoinder. First, however, let me note that it was as a graduate student at Northwestern University who had been thoroughly enculturated by Herskovits into acceptance of cultural determinism and of Mead's conclusion of 1928, that Lowell D. Holmes first went to Samoa in 1954, and that, as he himself notes, Holmes remains, to this day, among those who "follow the Boasian theoretical frame of reference."

Boas, Biology and Cultural Determinism

Because of the profoundly important role that Boas played in the devising and supervising of Mead's researches in Samoa, and because of his unqualified endorsement of her conclusion of 1928 that biological variables are of no significance in the etiology of adolescent behavior, it becomes crucially important to assess in some detail Boas' attitudes both to biology and to the doctrine of cultural determinism.

The opinions of Lesser and Herskovits on which Holmes has relied are uncritically eulogistic and do not accurately report Boas' stance. The crucial issue is not whether Boas took biological variables into consideration at all, but whether given his undoubted prejudice against biology he took these variables adequately into account.

As Krogman has noted, Boas made notable contributions to the study of race, growth and development, and to biometrics. These fields, however, are peripheral to biology proper and particularly to evolutionary biology, and in considering the issue I have just posed it is essential to view Boas and his beliefs in the context of the scientific knowledge of his own day, and especially in relation to biology as it was during the first four decades of the twentieth century.

As I describe in the second chapter of my book, before he went to America Boas had derived a belief in Lamarckian inheritance from [Theodor] Waitz, and from [Rudolph] Virchow a marked disbelief in and antipathy to the theory of biological evolution.[1] These then were the attitudes to the great biological issues of the day that Boas had firmly espoused by the time he became professor of anthropology at Columbia University in 1899.

The following year three separate investigators, de Vries, Correns and von Tschermack (all of them engaged in studies of plant hybridization), stumbled on Mendel's classic paper of 1866. With that rediscovery what Garland Allen has called "the age of genetics" began. Boas was to live until December 1942, and so the last forty-two years of his professional life saw both the formation of the science of genetics and the emergence from the early 1930s onwards of the evolutionary synthesis, both of which are central to twentieth-century biology. It thus becomes possible to assess Boas' attitudes in relation to these historic developments.

---

[1]The views of Theodor Waitz are discussed by Kenneth Bock in Chapter 5, History and Cultural Differences, of his *Human Nature and History: A Response to Sociobiology* (Columbia University Press, 1980). Waitz was a vehement opponent of the cultural evolution or progress of society concept. He also opposed any notion of natural causes for social change. Freeman lays great stress on this source of Boas' thought.—Ed.

On Biological Research During the Last Four Decades of Boas' Life.

As early as 1902 Sutton had pointed to "the strong similarity between Mendel's hypothesis of segregation and the microscopically observable separation of homologous chromosomes during meiosis." By 1910 it had become evident that chromosomes were cell structures that acted as the vehicles of heredity: over the next five years T. H. Morgan and his associates (working in the same university as Boas) laid the foundations of modern genetics in a series of brilliant experiments. In particular, in their book, *The Mechanism of Mendelian Heredity*, published in 1915, Morgan and his associates developed the theory that factors in the Mendelian sense were physical units, genes located at definite positions, or loci on chromosomes. By 1920, as Allen notes, these discoveries were "almost fully accepted throughout the biological community."

In his *The Theory of the Gene* published in 1926, Morgan presented further evidence to show that the gene represented "an organic entity." In reviewing this book Jennings noted that the day had gone when in respect of heredity "one man's fancies seemed as good as another's," while Dunn remarked that "the theory of the gene or of inheritance by discrete units" was as secure as any was likely to be and was "ready to take its place as one of the major generalizations of biology."

These major advances in genetics also had a profound effect on the theory of biological evolution. As Huxley has noted, "about 1920 biologists began to be interested in how natural selection would operate on organisms with Mendelian (particulate) inheritance, and started applying mathematical methods to the problem." This problem was effectively solved with the publication in 1930 of Fisher's *The Genetical Theory of Natural Selection*, followed in 1937 by Dobzhansky's *Genetics and the Origin of Species*, a book which, as Mayr records, signalled the emergence of the synthetic theory of biological evolution.

All of these crucial advances within biology had occurred before the appearance in 1938 of the textbook *General Anthropology*, edited by Boas and containing a section by him on the "biological premises" of anthropology, and the publication in that same year of the second edition of Boas' *The Mind of Primitive Man*, originally published in 1911. The way in which Boas reacted to the seminal developments within biology that had taken place during the years of his professorship at Columbia University between 1899 and 1937 may thus be gauged with some precision.

The Scientific Status of Lamarckian Theory in the 1930s.

First, however, let me refer briefly to the way in which the attitude of informed biologists toward Lamarckian inheritance (in which Boas had long believed) changed during these same years. Whereas belief in Lamarckian inheritance had been not uncommon during the first decade of the twentieth century and lingered on in some quarters into the 1920s and beyond, it did not survive the epoch-making researches of T. H. Morgan and his associates to which I have already referred. Thus, in an article on Lamarckism published in the fourteenth edition of the *Encyclopaedia Britannica,* Morgan noted that "the most complete disproof of the inheritance of somatic influence is demonstrated in almost every experiment in genetics," and concluded that "the facts are positive and unquestioned and contradict thoroughly the claim that germ cells are affected specifically by the character of the individual." And the following year in his book, *The Biological Basis of Human Nature,* H. S. Jennings, the Henry Walters Professor of Zoology at Johns Hopkins University, referred to the fact that by that time an experimenter who put forward a claim that he had "proof of the inheritance of acquired characters" was classified "in the 'lunatic fringe' of biology." It was to this "lunatic fringe" that Boas belonged throughout the 1930s and until his death in 1942.

Boas' Attitudes to Biology.

Kroeber, who at the time he was formulating his doctrine of absolute cultural determinism went so far as to refer to those "infected with biological methods of thought," has recorded that Boas, whom he knew well, "was not much interested in biological evolution or in genetics both of which he used or related to his own work very little." This is an understatement.

Although Boas must have had some inkling of the momentous advances that took place in the theory of biological evolution during the first four decades of the twentieth century, he was antipathetic and indeed opposed to this theory, as he was to evolutionary theory in general, including, particularly, cultural evolutionism, throughout the whole of the time he exerted such a decisive formative influence on American anthropology. Radin, another of Boas' students, has recorded that Boas "always took a prevailing antagonistic position" to the theory of evolution, while Stocking, on the basis of his study of the historical evidence, states that Boas was "quite skeptical of natural selection," the central mechanism of biological evolution discovered by Charles Darwin.

Boas' pronounced lack of interest in Darwin and the theory of evolution by means of natural selection was actively communicated to others. As Vidich has described, Boas was "personally, a powerful figure which did not tolerate theoretical or ideological differences in his students." Indeed, Mead herself, in a vivid phrase, has written of how Boas' influence "spread through American anthropology like an animated veto." Kluckhohn and Prufer record that according to Boas' students he "did not discuss biological evolution in his seminars," and so marked was his influence that as Professor J. J. Williams noted in 1936 Boas had by that time succeeded in "suppressing the classical theory of evolution among practically the entire group of leading American ethnologists."

Boas' Prejudice Against Genetics

Boas' "prevailingly antagonistic position" to evolutionary theory on which Radin remarked in 1939 was joined by what Kluckhohn and Prufer have called "a skepticism about Mendelian heredity." Again, in recording that "a relative lack of interest in experiment remained with Boas all his life, and seems to have been a deep-seated quality of his mind," Kroeber also noted that Boas was "long inclined to be suspicious of Mendelian heredity, evidently trusting more in statistical analysis than in experimental findings on selected characters." Boas maintained these deeply seated attitudes, it is important to realize, as long as he lived, and in the face of ever mounting evidence that his beliefs had no scientific basis. As I have already indicated, by about the mid-1930s the science of genetics had through a series of elegant and precise experiments conducted during the previous two or three decades decisively illumined the problem of heredity, and Morgan, in recognition of his work in establishing the chromosome theory of heredity, had been awarded the Nobel prize in physiology in 1933. In his book *The Physical Basis of Heredity* Morgan had demonstrated that the presence of genes in chromosomes was "directly deducible" from his experimental results, a conclusion he further explicated in 1926 in *The Theory of the Gene*. Thus by 1930 Jennings in surveying the progress of genetics during the previous three decades could write: "positive and inescapable evidence proves that the chromosome is a structure composed of many diverse parts, each part, or gene, having a definite effect on development, and therefore a definite effect on the characteristics of the individual produced."

However, despite the "positive and inescapable experimental evidence" that had been widely published by the 1930s, there were still some obscurantists (Boas among them), most of them idealists who were opposed to the materialistic implications of genetic research, who in defence of their antiquated beliefs argued that genes were no more than figments. It was to this supposition that Boas gave voice in 1935 in suggesting that if genetic methods were applied to the study of human growth there was a danger that "the number of genes" would "depend rather upon the number of investigators than upon their actual existence." Understood in historical context, this remark by Boas in a serious scientific paper is the clearest evidence of the obscurantist antipathy to genetics which colored his thinking throughout the 1930s.

By 1930, through the researches of Landsteiner and others it had become apparent, as Jennings put it, that humans had "the same genetic system, operating in the same manner, as have other higher organisms," and further, that for many human characteristics there was "no doubt of the applicability of modern genetic science," with these characteristics "being inherited in the same way as are the characteristics of other organisms."

It was to these propositions, which have been fully substantiated by subsequent research, that Boas was rootedly opposed, as is evident in a brief article he contributed to the November 1939 issue of the journal of the New York Association of Biology Teachers. According to Boas, although the study of genetics had "attracted so much attention in recent times," the subject received "perhaps more attention" in the school curriculum than a "well rounded presentation of the facts of biology" justified. There was little doubt, Boas thought, that as time went on and the novelty of the study of genetics wore down, other aspects of the "problem presented by life" would receive "greater attention." It was "particularly unfortunate," Boas considered, that "the data of genetics obtained from the study of lower forms are too readily applied to man." "The application of genetic data to man," Boas declared, "should on account of its social implications be made most guardedly."

These statements are direct expressions of the suspicion about Mendelian heredity and the "actual existence of genes," that ruled Boas' thinking throughout the 1930s, and are evidence both of an antipathy to genetics in general and of opposition to scientific research on humans based on Mendelian principles.

From the Open Letter

In my letter to you of 5th February, 1987 I presented evidence to show that Professor Roy A. Rappaport's construing (in his rejoinder on p. 7 of the February, 1987 issue of *Scientific American*) of a paragraph on p. 197 of Margaret Mead's *Coming of Age in Samoa* is inexact, and that Mead's answer to the question "Are the disturbances which vex our adolescents due to the nature of adolescence itself or to the civilization?" which she had been sent to Samoa by Boas to investigate was indeed that "we cannot make any explanations" in terms of "the nature of adolescence itself," this being the conclusion which, having been endorsed by Boas, has been repeated in a long succession of anthropological textbooks.

Professor Rappaport, as I have already noted, asserts that neither Boas "nor any of his students ever propounded" the notion "that human behavior can be explained in purely cultural terms."

In fact, Alfred Kroeber, who was Boas' first Ph.D. student at Columbia University, propounded in 1915, in the *American Anthropologist*, a series of "eighteen professions" in which, in Robert Lowie's words, he outlined "the sole end of ethnology as the study of culture regardless of organic phenomena."

Biology, Kroeber asserted, had nothing whatsoever to do with human history, which "involved the absolute conditioning of historical events by other cultural events." There was thus, according to Kroeber, a total separation between history and biology, and his eighteen professions were specifically directed to the elimination of any kind of continuity or interaction between biological and cultural processes.

In 1916 Boas himself declared that "the social stimulus is infinitely more potent than the biological mechanism." The following year, Kroeber proclaimed that between cultural anthropology and biology there was an "eternal chasm" that could not be bridged, an uncompromising stance to which Lowie, another of Boas' students, at once gave vigorous support in his *Culture and Ethnology*.

As *The New International Year Book* for the year 1917 recorded (p. 32), it was the contention of both Kroeber and Lowie that "the domain of culture constitutes a distinct sphere of investigation, from which follow the complete autonomy of ethnology and the necessity of interpreting the data of civilization through other facts of a cultural character rather than by merging them in data of a supposedly more general nature."

From this doctrine propounded by Kroeber and Lowie in 1917 that cultural anthropology constitutes "a distinct sphere of investigation" wholly removed from the operation of biological variables it logically followed that for the cultural anthropologist the explanation of human behavior could be in terms of cultural variables alone.

The adoption by Kroeber, Lowie and other of Boas' students of this quite explicit doctrine, in which, on principle, biological variables are totally excluded from consideration was very much part of what George Stocking, the distinguished historian of anthropology, in discussing this period of the history of cultural anthropology, has referred to as "the movement toward an explanation of human behavior in purely cultural terms."

Indeed, the phrase "in purely cultural terms" is one that I adopted following Stocking. I would merely comment that it is a usage which, in that the doctrine propounded by Kroeber and Lowie in 1917 explicitly excluded all biological variables from the purview of the cultural anthropologist, is fully warranted in the context under discussion.

This doctrine of Boas' students Kroeber and Lowie, was adopted by Ruth Benedict when in the early 1920s she also became a student of Boas, as is evident in her review of 1924 of Kroeber's *Anthropology*. It was a doctrine, as I have already noted, that logically led to the theory that human behavior could be explained in terms of cultural variables alone, or, as Benedict, who in 1923 became Mead's mentor, herself put it: "the traditional patterns of behavior set the mold and human nature flows in it."

The testing of this theory was implicit in the question "Are the disturbances which vex our adolescents due to the nature of adolescence itself or to the civilization?" that Boas sent Mead to Samoa to investigate in 1925. The answer Mead gave was that "any explanations" of the "disturbances" of adolescence in terms of "the nature of adolescence itself" (i.e. in terms of biological variables) could be excluded.

This conclusion, which was wholly compatible with the doctrine of Kroeber and Lowie, was accepted without question, as their writings of the time show, by Mead's mentors, Boas and Benedict.

My Relations with Margaret Mead

Derek Freeman

Editor's Note

This is Freeman's most complete published statement on his relations with Mead. It is meant, among other things, as a reply to the objection that he waited until Mead's death to publish his findings. The source of this view seems to be the fact that in 1971, prompted by inquiries from publishers who had word of his Samoan studies, Freeman submitted two draft chapters of his book to Holt, Rinehart and Winston for consideration. One of the chapters was "Human Nature and Culture," which had just been published in *Man and the New Biology* (A.N.U. Press 1970). Three reports were received. Their strong strictures made Freeman realize that he had much more preparation to do. The passage printed here is usefully read in conjunction with Freeman's reply to Professor Stanner (Chapter VI), in which he discusses the preparations for his fieldwork of 1966-1967; and "Derek Freeman: Notes Toward an Intellectual Biography, in Appell and Madan," *Choice and Morality in Anthropological Perspective* (see Bibliography). The text is drawn from *Canberra Anthropology* vol. 6, no. 2, pp. 109-112. Reprinted by permission.

As Holmes would have it, I am someone who being "absolutely convinced that Margaret Mead was wrong . . . set out to prove it." This is very far from the truth. In fact, I began my study of anthropology as a student of Ernest Beaglehole, who had studied anthropology with Sapir (himself a student of Boas) at Yale. Beaglehole's whole approach to anthropology, as Gladwin has noted, was "in many ways similar to that of Margaret Mead," with his attention being focused, as was Mead's, on "the shaping of personality by the totality of expectations and pressures exerted on and communicated to a person by other persons sharing the same culture."

It was this approach that I also initially adopted. In an article entitled "Anatomy of Mind," published in 1938, I had declared that "the aims and desires which determine behavior" are all derived from "the social environment." As this article indicated, when I reached Samoa in April 1940 I was very much a cultural determinist. *Coming of Age in Samoa* had been unreservedly findings was complete. Indeed, at that time my inductivist aim, once I had gained sufficient command of the Samoan language, was to confirm Mead's already celebrated finding in researches of my own.

It was, then, not until several years after my arrival in Samoa and after I had become fluent in the Samoan language, had been adopted into a Samoan family and, having had a manaia title conferred upon me in Sa'anapu (a settlement on the south coast of Upolu in Western Samoa), had begun attending *fono manu*, village courts, that I gradually became aware of the extent of the discordance between Mead's account (in which I had hitherto unquestioningly believed) and the realities that I was regularly witnessing.

The discordance was further emphasized in my subsequent intensive researches into the history of Samoa, including Manu'a, in the manuscript archives of the London Missionary Society that I undertook in London during the years 1946-48. During these same years I completed a dissertation entitled *The Social Structure of a Samoan Village Community* for an Academic Postgraduate Diploma in Anthropology of the University of London, and it had been my intention to return to Samoa in the late 1940s to continue my investigations there. However, because of my involvement in other anthropological interests, in particular in the Iban or Sea Dayaks of Borneo, I took the matter of the discordance between Mead's findings and my own observations no further until 1964, when, during a visit that Dr. Mead made to the Australian National University, I placed before her the empirical and historical evidence that had led me to reject her conclusions about Samoa.

Immediately after this meeting, on 10 November 1964, I wrote to Dr. Mead as follows:

> It is plain to me that our conclusions about the realities of adolescent and sexual behavior in Samoa are fundamentally at variance. For my part I propose (as in the past) to proceed with my researches with as meticulous an objectivity as I can muster. This I would suppose, is going to lead to the publication of conclusions different from those reached by you, but I would very much hope that, however we may disagree, there should be no bad feeling between us. You have my assurance that I shall strive towards this end.

Dr. Mead replied in a letter dated New York, 2 December 1964 that ended with the exemplary words: "What is important is the work." During our subsequent correspondence, which extended from 1964 to 1978, Dr. Mead continued to behave in this exemplary manner. In a letter to *The New York Times* of 13 February 1983, Mary Catherine Bateson observed that although her mother was "vehement in the defence of her views," she did not descend to "the clangorous exchange of insult" precisely because "she believed that anthropology was evolving in her lifetime toward an increasingly exact science, and that science is everywhere the cumulative work of many minds."

In my judgement it is because Margaret Mead held these views and because she grappled, throughout her life, with anthropological problems of fundamental importance that she is assured an honored and secure place in the history of anthropology.

In 1964, then, I had informed Dr. Mead personally both of my misgivings about the conclusions she had reached in Samoa and about my future intentions. By this time I had become deeply interested in the bearing of human ethology on anthropology, and when I returned to Samoa in 1965 it was with problems in this emerging field that I was much more concerned than with Mead's findings of 1928. This situation began to change, however, as I once more explored the facts of Samoan existence, and in particular, as I shall presently explain, as a direct result of my correspondence with L. D. Holmes from April 1967 onwards, so that by the time of my return to Australia in February 1968 I had firmly decided that I would one day write a refutation of Mead's conclusions.

Soon after this, on 25 May 1968 at a meeting of the Australian Branch of the Association of Social Anthropologists of the British Commonwealth, I read a paper, critical of Mead's conclusions, entitled "On Believing as many as Six Impossible Things before Breakfast." By this stage my inquiries had revealed that the complexities of the history of cultural determinism from the late nineteenth century onwards were such that much further research was needed, particularly in relation to the biological theories of the day. This was indeed the case, and my historical researches on both anthropology and biology lasted well into the 1970s.

At this same juncture Dr. Mead herself introduced a further complexity by arguing, in her addendum of 1969 to the second edition of *Social Organization of Manu'a*, that while there was a "serious problem" of reconciling the "contradictions" between her reports and those of other observers, it was possible that Manu'a at the time of her fieldwork "might have represented a special variation of the Samoan pattern, a temporary felicitous relaxation" of the behaviors that others had recorded. Historically implausible as this conjecture was, it was nonetheless plain that before I could complete the refutation I had in mind I would have to test Mead's conjecture by locating relevant documentary evidence on American Samoa in the mid-1920s.

Having been occupied during the intervening years with quite other anthropological interests and academic responsibilities, it was not until 7 March 1978 that I was able to return to serious work on my refutation of Mead's conclusions. In August 1978, as soon as I had completed a draft chapter of my book (the present Chapter 16), I wrote to Dr. Mead asking if she would like to see this draft. In reply I received a letter dated New York, 14 September 1978 in which I was informed by an assistant that Dr. Mead had "been ill" and that if she had "an opportunity to read and comment on my manuscript" I would be notified. I heard no more from Dr. Mead's office before her death in November 1978.

As I proceeded with the writing of my book from 1978 onwards I became involved in further protracted research, especially on the history of Samoa in the 1920s and 1930s. A first draft of its text was not completed until August 1981.

With this draft I returned to Samoa in September 1981, to submit what I had written to the critical scrutiny of Samoan scholars and to test Dr. Mead's "felicitous relaxation" conjecture of 1969 by further archival research on American Samoa, without which my refutation would have remained conspicuously incomplete. This research in the archives of the High Court of American Samoa and in the manuscript holdings of the Bernice P. Bishop Museum in Honolulu—sources that had been unavailable to me in Australia—yielded information that greatly strengthened my refutation. By November 1981 I was ready to submit my revised typescript to various university presses. If I had not systematically completed my researches in the way I have described, my refutation would certainly not have the cogency that it has . . . .

Chapter IV

The Controversy

What the Fighting Was About

Hiram Caton

The circumstance that evaluation of Freeman's study commenced after it had become an international *succès de scandale* bears significantly on why its reception had the character of a controversy; and why the controversy sometimes took bizarre turns.

The promptings of the controversy were numerous. The theme that Mead's defenders sounded most overtly and indignantly was Freeman's "attack on Mead." Freeman was said to have unfairly or even maliciously criticized Mead's first writing, and sullied the reputation of a woman who had attained revered status in American culture. This misdemeanor was highlighted by chastising Freeman's own book against the backdrop of homage to Margaret Mead. The response was, as Ian Jarvie put it, the tribal defense of its desecrated totem.

Defending the totem proved to be awkward because Mead, despite her prestige, was not reckoned among anthropology's great scholars. Thus Robert I. Levy, ruminating on the furore in the pages of *Science*, wrote that "neither [Mead's] theory nor her method nor her data are at the center of current discussion." Mead's contribution to anthropology, he thought, stemmed from her effects on the profession as a shaker and mover. Roy A. Rappaport, in his discerning appreciation of Mead as mythmaker and social pundit, would allow *Coming of Age in Samoa* to have been no more than "a modest contribution" to Samoan ethnography. And Robert A. Paul, reflecting on the valorization of Mead at the annual meeting of the American Anthropological

Association in 1983, wrote that "maybe it was just a case of the seven cities vying for Homer's bones . . . but I would have sworn that if someone had asked most of the people in that room a year earlier what they thought of Margaret Mead's field research, the collective answer would have been 'not much'." The provocation, then, was not that Mead's most celebrated book had been "refuted." The provocation lay, initially, in the media interpretation of Freeman's deed, and subsequently, in Freeman's success in parlaying his criticism of Mead into a damaging critique of cultural anthropology.

The media treated the story as a scandal. The startling revelation that Mead's carefree Samoans were just folks who experienced the stresses and tensions familiar to us all was the basis: it seemed that Mead had perpetrated a hoax. The deeper scandal was that the anthropology profession had not set the record straight, and Freeman appeared to be a whistle-blower. His credibility in this role was enhanced by anthropologists who declared in interviews that anthropologists had "long known" that "Mead was wrong" about Samoa. Such remarks may have been meant to dampen the glitter of Freeman's sudden celebrity. But their effect was to magnify the scandal by tacitly acknowledging that anthropologists had sat on information deemed by the public to be of great moment. Alternately, anthropologists were represented as being as much in the dark about the real Samoa as the public, implying that the profession had been taken in by the hoax. However the matter was viewed, stigmata appeared on the professional body of anthropology.

The sensation that the scientist who had "assumed the mantle of omniscience" had been wrong was heightened by the ambience of other recent revelations of scandal in high places. Two years before the publication of *Margaret Mead and Samoa*, the first reports of fraud in science began to reach the public. In 1982, William Broad and Nicholas Wade published their best-seller, *Betrayers of the Truth: Fraud and Deceit in the Halls of Science,* in which they maintained that falsification of evidence and other forms of cheating were not uncommon in the laboratories of blue ribbon universities. Such aspersions upon the honor of venerated persons and institutions would scarcely have been credible a decade previous. But the public had accepted the fracture of a great political idol, the integrity of the Presidency, in the agony of the Watergate revelations. And beyond Watergate there was the suspicion, fuelled by a steady flow of independent studies, that the truth about the Kennedy assassination had been covered up by a commission headed by the Chief Justice of the Supreme Court. There seemed to be no limit to webs of deceit. This was the ambience that lent Freeman's book its punch. It was not a pleasant experience to be accosted on campus by colleagues who sought explanations or jibed at one's embarrassment. Anthropologists got angry less because of the insult to Margaret Mead than because of the damage he was believed to have inflicted on the credibility of the profession.

No small part of the damage was due to what anthropologists labelled "the media blitz." This expression referred to the velocity of the travel of Freeman's story, the massive coverage it received, and to Freeman's success in dominating reportage.

The media bomb was ignited by Edwin McDowell's front page story in *The New York Times* on January 31, 1983. His story was a masterpiece of investigative reporting which found the profession's dirty linen and displayed it through the words of named sources whose credentials lent the account authority. McDowell also recognized the hoax angle, and displayed it ever so delicately. He detected the "vendetta" rumor among anthropologists as well as Freeman's reputation as a "difficult man." These ingredients were skillfully stirred together.

McDowell's article made all the wire services within hours; columnists were commenting within a day. In forty-eight hours, hundreds of millions throughout the world had been exposed to the story and wanted to hear more. Thus anthropologists awoke one morning to find their territory ravaged and their citadel under siege by a solitary invader leading the natives into rebellion. They were shocked and perplexed. "Who is Derek Freeman?," was the first question most would ask; "why did he do it?" was the second. Since the book causing the ruckus was not yet in print, anthropologists were required to provide commentary literally without knowing what they were talking about. The media blitz, for those on the receiving end, had the quality of Blitzkreig.

Resentment was compounded when the Harvard University Press brought Freeman to the United States to promote his book in rounds of interviews, seminars, and talk shows. Reporters covering the story were struck by his towering confidence and his relish for taking on all comers. Anthropologists were dismayed by his aggressive attacks on cultural anthropology in the name of interactionism. His impulse to dominate opponents—the "dark side" of his personality—was also evident in televised debates and added credibility to the story that he was on a vendetta.

Attempting to comprehend these unprecedented events, some antagonists hit on an explanation that surfaced in a resolution put to the Northeastern Anthropological Association. It was said that the *New York Times,* the Harvard University Press, and Freeman clubbed together in a bid to slander Mead and preëmpt scholarly debate by using the tricks of press agentry, not the least of which was coat-tailing on Mead's reputation. Such "yellow anthropology," the objection went, discredited the author and his sponsors.

My investigations of the origin of the media blitz indicate that the seismic effect was not foreseen by any of the principals. McDowell stated to me that his story was not prompted by anyone. He sensed a story in a routine perusal of university press announcements of forthcoming books. He requested and received a prepublication copy from the Harvard University Press; the rest, including persuading the editor to place his story on the front page, was his own doing. Harvard was surprised and embarrassed by the appearance of McDowell's article because it had given an exclusive on *Margaret Mead and Samoa* to freelance journalist Robert Minton. Freeman states that he was not consulted by Harvard in any way concerning publicity for his book.[1]

These facts are of more than anecdotal interest. What, after all, are the selection criteria for the big stories? Anthropologists recalled another case—Boyce Rensberger's front page *New York Times* article on E. O. Wilson's *Sociobiology,* which launched Wilson to celebrity and sociobiology to years of controversy. It seemed to some that political motives were likely to be behind both "media events." According to Wilson, however, neither he nor Harvard made any approach to the *New York Times.* Like McDowell, Rensberger saw in Wilson's *Sociobiology* the stuff of a good story.

If the idea of collusion was fictitious, it was nevertheless an apposite fiction. McDowell played on popular anxieties in cultural politics by conjuring the menacing distinction between the overt and covert meaning of *Margaret Mead and Samoa:*

---

[1]This account is based on information provided by Edwin McDowell, Robert Minton, Derek Freeman, Benson Saler, and George Appell.

"Beneath the surface," he wrote, "Professor Freeman's book could intensify the often bitterly contested 'nature versus nurture' controversy, the argument over whether human beings are shaped mainly by environment or by heredity." After mentioning that Freeman's findings earned the approval of evolutionary biologist Ernst Mayr and ethologist Niko Tinbergen, McDowell inserted a riposte from "defenders of Miss Mead," who maintained that many of Freeman's supporters were "longtime champions of biological determinism." *Times* readers were advised that this doctrine had been advancing among academics over the past decade. Sociobiology was not mentioned, but anthropologists required no reminder. The fat of cultural politics was in the fire, and this issue, perhaps more than any other, provoked sharp words.

Mead's totemic status derived from her standing as the expositor and arbiter of the values to which Boas had attached American anthropology (see Eric Wolf, Chapter III). The "attack on Mead" sounded the tocsin that the faith of liberal cultural politics was yet again under attack (see Appell, Lefkowitz, Rappaport, this Chapter). The defense of this credo turned out to require at least a qualified defense of the legendary Samoa: once the stakes were clear, it could not be admitted that Freeman had shown Mead's Samoa ethnography to be decisively flawed.

The critics construed the cultural politics issue in current stereotypes. The nature/nurture theoretical dispute translated politically into public policy contests that polarized opponents according to whether they favored cultural or natural explanations of mores and institutions deemed to be in need of reform. The IQ debate, with its direct bearing on education and affirmative action, was an example. The drive for sexual equality was another. Laura Nader voiced this concern when she said that Freeman's book

. . . came at a time when there was a backlash on cultural determinism or explaining things in terms of environment . . . It was a political backlash, and out comes his book which supports a right wing political backlash and gives reasons why we should be following biologically based national policies. That's extremely threatening.[1]

Freeman declined to be drawn into the American political culture debate. He attempted to neutralize the issue by avowing his long-standing abhorrence for racism—the first article of faith in Boasian reform liberalism. As for biological determinism, which the controversies of the 1970s established was the alleged doctrine of the new scientific conservative apologia, Freeman protested that he rejected it together with every other determinism. His own belief, which characterizes the distinctly human as capacity for choice, was fully compatible with reform liberalism.

Critics found it hard to accept this self-description at face value. If he indeed accepted the values of Boasian reform liberalism, what animated his attempt to discredit the culturalist or environmentalist tilt of Boasian theory? What would be the political culture agenda of an interactionist anthropology? Regardless of how Freeman might answer these questions, by 1983 most social scientists believed that the renovation of their disciplines from the direction of biology (generically labelled "sociobiology") tended to close the open horizon of choice characteristic of the liberal reform movement in the United States. "Sociobiology" was therefore deemed to be conservative in tendency regardless of the personal preferences of its advocates (Harris, this Chapter).

Where then does the political question rest? Does the projected union of the social and biological sciences ineluctably serve conservative ideology, regardless of the intentions of individuals? While this is not the place to discuss this question, I may be allowed one or two observations.

The history of alliances between science and political doctrine suggests that they are usually make-shift. This is partly because science can furnish only some elements of political culture; the remainder are drawn from heterogeneous sources distinct from the scientific enterprise. And partly it is because the practical conclusions of scientific models are subject to different, even opposite interpretations. Cultural determinism will serve as an apt example.

---

[1] Derek Freeman, *et al., Transcript of Interviews by Frank Heimans for the Documentary Film Margaret Mead and Samoa*, Tape 25, p. 11.

When Boas spoke of the cultural determination of behavior, he meant specifically the power of custom over human action. This power has been a mainstay of conservative thought since Edmund Burke. Its polemical function in that quarter was to rebut the tumultuous radicalism of the model of the human nature endowed with "natural rights." In view of this history, protagonists of interactionism may claim that the restoration of the human nature concept to political culture will make that culture more open, more "radical," than under the environmentalist auspices. One need but think of the broad vistas of genetic engineering and biomedicine to realize that this prospect is not merely academic.

New Samoa Book Challenges
Margaret Mead's Conclusions[1]

Edwin McDowell.

Two months before its official publication date, a book maintaining that the anthropologist Margaret Mead seriously misrepresented the culture and character of Samoa has ignited heated discussion within the behavioral sciences.

The book is *Margaret Mead and Samoa: The Making and Unmaking of an Anthropological Myth* by Derek Freeman, professor emeritus of anthropology at the Australian National University in Canberra.

On the surface, the book— to be published in April by Harvard University Press—is a critical analysis of Miss Mead's *Coming of Age in Samoa,* the best-selling work of anthropology, which on its publication in 1928 established her national reputation.

"On that level, Freeman's book is an extremely important piece of work," said Robert C. Hunt, Chairman of the department of anthropology at Brandeis University, who evaluated the book for Harvard University Press.

---

[1]Copyright © 1983 by The New York Times Company. Reprinted by permission.

Beneath the surface, Professor Freeman's book could intensify the often bitterly contested "nurture versus nature" controversy, the argument over whether human beings are shaped mainly by environment or by heredity. Moreover, the book raises important questions about scholarship and ideological commitment.

Miss Mead described the Samoan people as gentle, peaceful, free of religious conflicts and devoid of jealousy. They condoned adolescent free love, she said, and as a result adolescence in Samoa was without the turmoil or stress that accompanies adolescence in the United States and elsewhere—demonstrating that adolescent behavior had to be explained in purely cultural terms. By contrast, Professor Freeman asserts that:

> The Samoan people are intensely competitive. They have high rates of homicide and assault, and the incidence of rape in Samoa is among the highest in the world. Samoan children, adolescents and adults live within an authority system that regularly results in psychological disturbances ranging from compulsive behaviors to hysterical illnesses and suicide. They are extremely prone to fits of jealousy.

Not only are Samoans not given to casual lovemaking, but also "the cult of female virginity is probably carried to a greater extreme than in any other culture known to anthropology."

Scholars are already commencing on the book. "If Freeman is correct, it raises the question of how many other people were collecting incorrect information and putting it out as fact," said Sherwood L. Washburn, a past president of the American Anthropological Association. "The question his book raises is how one assesses validity in a profession where people's field work and field notes are regarded by most people as unassailable."

The Freeman book contends that many of Miss Mead's assertions about Samoa "are fundamentally in error and some of them preposterously false." This re-evaluation comes 58 years after Miss Mead, then 23 years old, embarked in 1925 for the South Pacific to study adolescence there at the suggestion of Franz Boas, her professor at Columbia University, and 55 years after the publication of the resulting *Coming of Age in Samoa*.

The book, the first of almost two dozen by Miss Mead, helped turn the tide for the cultural determinists, who believe that culture determines personality, in their battle with the biological determinists. The book also helped vault the author to the forefront of her profession, where she remained until her death in 1978. It has sold millions of copies in 16 languages, including Urdu and Serbo-Croatian, and has had impact far beyond academe. Its message has influenced laws, social policy and, said Professor Washburn, "influenced the way people were brought up in this country."

"The entire academic establishment and all the encyclopedias and all the textbooks accepted the conclusions in her book, and those conclusions are fundamentally in error," the author said in a telephone conversation. "There isn't another example of such wholesale self-deception in the history of the behavioral sciences." Few scholars will go that far, but many are convinced that Professor Freeman, a New Zealander with a doctorate from Cambridge University, has written an important book. Ernst Mayr, professor emeritus of zoology at Harvard, and a leading behavioral scientist, said the book "is not only a contribution to cultural anthropology, but it will also have a major impact on psychology and other aspects of human biology." Nikolaas Tinbergen, the behavioral scientist who won the 1973 Nobel Prize for medicine, said the Freeman book is "a masterpiece of modern scientific anthropology."

Defenders of Miss Mead say that many scholars who have lined up behind Professor Freeman are longtime champions of biological determinism, a doctrine that has gained considerable strength and credence within the academic community during the last decade.

The author says that both nature and nurture are always involved in shaping human behavior, yet he asserts that many anthropologists still give insufficient recognition to the significance of biology. That aside however, he said that his book is not so much intended to address that longtime academic dispute as to rectify the wrong that has been done to Samoan society.

One of the Freeman book's admirers is Le Tagaloa Leota Pita, dean of development at the University of Samoa, who said that while the book does not tell the Samoans anything new about themselves, "for the first time an outsider writes about Samoa as a Samoan would write and describes the reality of his living culture."

Samoa Not Idyllic

That reality, according to Professor Freeman, who has spent a total of six years in Samoa since 1940, is wholly at variance with the idyllic picture conveyed by Miss Mead in her book and in subsequent writings about Samoa. The author attributes many of Miss Mead's "errors" to her unfamiliarity with the language, her absence of systematic prior investigation of the society and its values and to her choosing to live with expatriate Americans rather than in a Samoan household. He writes that Miss Mead's depiction of adolescent free love is probably the result of the young anthropologist being deliberately misled by her adolescent informants, who wanted to tease her.

His major allegation, however, is that Miss Mead's professional shortcomings derived from her doctrinal baggage. There is the clearest evidence, he writes, that "it was her deeply convinced belief in the doctrine of extreme cultural determinism, for which she was prepared to fight with the whole battery at her command that led her to construct an account of Samoa that appeared to substantiate this very doctrine."

"I think Margaret may have gone to Samoa with a cultural bias," said Theodore Schwartz, professor of anthropology at the University of California, San Diego. "She always had a theme; she addressed current preoccupations and brought back from the field something that would reverberate in society. And I don't doubt that Margaret knew very little of the language and didn't have the total immersion one would want." Professor Schwartz, who was a field assistant for Miss Mead in New Guinea in the 1950's, has not read the Freeman book. But he said that even if Miss Mead made errors in Samoa, "I would find it hard to believe that she was 180 degrees wrong." He said that she made some errors about the Manua people, the subject of *Growing Up in New Guinea,* her second book, "but overall, she was brilliant and perceptive."

Miss Mead's Defenders

Miss Mead was a curator at the American Museum of Natural History for more than 50 years. David Hurst Thomas, chairman of the museum's department of anthropology, said: "It would bother me if aspersions were cast on her integrity or honesty, but it doesn't bother me that her research findings may have been superseded. I am an archaeologist, and we learn that dealing with a culture 10,000 years old in 1983, it is not the same 10,000 year-old culture studies in 1923. It doesn't mean that the research is any less valid."

Several of Professor Freeman's professional colleagues note that his own personality has complicated the dispute. For example, Professor Washburn, a former chairman of the anthropology department at the University of California, Berkeley, said: "He is, unfortunately, a difficult person and he's using this anti-Mead data to attack Boas." (Miss Mead's late mentor, Professor Boas, was the intellectual leader of American anthropology. He wrote the foreword to *Coming of Age in Samoa.*)

"People who work on Samoa know Margaret Mead was wrong, and Freeman's book shows that beyond doubt," said Bradd Shore, professor of anthropology at Emory University and author of the recent book *Sala'ilua: A Samoan Mystery* (Columbia University Press). "But if she suppressed the dark elements, Freeman painted all those dark elements in his book. She generated a myth out of opposition to eugenics, he generated a distorted picture out of opposition to Margaret Mead. But on the whole, his book is brilliant."

Professor Freeman acknowledges his unpopularity within the profession but he attributes much of it to the hostility of colleagues who resent the mere suggestion that anyone would take issue with a virtual "goddess of anthropology," whom he describes as "a very remarkable woman of quite considerable achievement."

When he decided to return to Samoa in 1965, he said "I was refused research funds by my own department head on grounds that I shouldn't try to go against Margaret Mead." Moreover, he asserts in his book that so dominant were Miss Mead's position and reputation that anthropologists who subsequently went to Samoa and found errors in her research not only did not question her findings but, because of the prevailing intellectual climate, actually praised their "remarkably high" reliability.

Professor Freeman also denies conducting a vendetta. His book is a necessary corrective, he said, because Miss Mead "never revised in any way" the original text of *Coming of Age in Samoa,* despite its inaccurate picture of the Samoan ethos, and its conclusions continue to be regarded by anthropologists and others "as though they were eternal verities."

"What's involved here are two things—Freeman's arguments about Margaret Mead and Samoa in the 1920's, and Freeman's position on the relative strengths of nature-nurture," said Professor Hunt of Brandeis.

"You could write a book on either subject," he said, "without more than a paragraph or two referring to the other. His position on Margaret Mead is an attempt at intellectual history to put her in the context of events in academe. If that is controversial, it will be controversial not as a question of faith but of accuracy and interpretation. His position on nature-nurture amounts to a matter of faith. That he has put the two together will confuse the interpretation of both, but it's his book."

"I had a meeting with her in 1964 in Australia and laid my cards on the table at that time," said the author, who describes himself as having been a strong believer in Miss Mead's findings when he first went to Samoa. "I was in correspondence with her since, and when I finished a preliminary draft in August 1978, I wrote and warned her that it was highly critical, asking if she would like to see a copy. I did not get a reply, and she died that November."

Although he published a number of papers about Samoa on technical subjects, Professor Freeman said, not until 1981 was he finally granted access to the archives of the High Court of American Samoa. "I had tried in the 1960's but was refused, and when I was finally allowed in, the evidence was conclusive," he said, referring to the statistics about rape, assault and other crimes that appear in both the text and in the book's 55 pages of notes.

Media Sensationalism[1]

Sir Edmund Leach

... The result [of advanced publicity] was, as I can personally testify, that by mid-February in localities as far apart as Dunedin (New Zealand), New Orleans, and San Francisco, wherever a congregation of anthroplogists might be gathered together, "Derek Freeman's vicious attack on Margaret Mead" was a prime and passionate topic of conversation, made all the more heated by the fact that at that time hardly anyone had read the book.

On this side of the Atlantic, where the name of Margaret Mead carries none of these cult figure associations, the reception of Freeman's book is likely to be more sedate. It is a genuine contribution to the history of 20th century anthropology couched in a very polemical style, but the focus of discussion is extremely narrow and the excitement that has been generated in the United States can in no way be justified on academic grounds.

Annette B. Weiner

... Freeman's major thesis is to prove that Mead not only misrepresented Samoan society but that her fervent belief in cultural determinism blinded her to the reality of Samoan life. This reality he contends is more correctly illustrated by his own data, which record numerous cases of aggression, rape, competition, and authoritarian control. Freeman's refutation of Mead's ethnography is not only an attempt to discredit the research of the most famous woman scientist of this century, but his book is grounded in issues that call into question the scientific integrity of Franz Boas.

---

[1]These excerpts are drawn from Sir Edmund Leach's article, "The Shangri-la that never was," *New Society* 24 March 1983, 477-478 and Annette B. Weiner's essay, "Ethnographic determinism: Samoa and the Margaret Mead controversy," *American Anthropologist* 85:4 (1983):909-919.

The Times coverage was lengthy by any standards, and in the same week, three additional *Times* articles appeared, including an editorial. Interest grew rapidly as other newspapers, magazines, radio, and television broadcasts took up the controversy. Given the potentially damaging effects of this book, not only to the integrity of Margaret Mead but to both ethnographic methodology and the discipline of anthropology, anthropologists were momentarily caught in an unfortunate position. The book would not be available until April; only a few scholars who had either reviewed the manuscript or had read advance proofs sent by the publishers were familiar with its contents. Yet, in the days and weeks that followed the January 31 story, many anthropologists, most of whom had not yet read the book, were interviewed and asked whether Margaret Mead had been lied to by her informants and whether Mead's errors proved that nature rather than nurture controlled the socialization and sociability of human beings.

Anthropology's Adolescent Dilemma

Richard Basham

When news of the imminent publication of Derek Freeman's *Margaret Mead and Samoa: The Making and Unmaking of an Anthropological Myth* first broke on the front page of *The New York Times,* I was not surprised. My experience as a student and lecturer in America had led me to give little credence to Mead's early scholarly work; Mead seemed someone who was always at the center of anthropological ceremonials but at the periphery of its scholarship. Thus, although it might surprise members of the general public, I felt Freeman's book would create few ripples among anthropologists. My quoted comments in *The New York Times* the day after the controversy broke reflected this sentiment: "A lot of us had already discounted the scientific work of Dr Mead. To the extent that we assign her books, it is to show how anthropology has developed." At the time, I paid little notice to a jocular, but strangely prophetic, comment made by Berkeley Professor George DeVos: "This will be a real test of whether or not there is an afterlife."

When I read the book some weeks later, I was impressed by the manner in which Freeman effectively dismissed—at least for

Samoa—Mead's central conclusion that "adolescence is not necessarily a time of stress and strain, but that cultural conditions make it so." My only real reservation was that I thought more attention should have been devoted to her social "philosophical" agenda. On the whole, however, I found the book a powerful statement with ramifications for the entire field of anthropology.

But already before the book's publication, I noted that anthropologists who had not read Freeman's manuscript and who, like myself, were not Samoan specialists were nevertheless developing an apologia for Mead. Mead, the story went, was only 23 years old when she went to Samoa, her research was conducted nearly 60 years ago when field methods were in their infancy, and she presented evidence in the body of her work which supported Freeman and contradicted her own conclusions. But, perhaps in recognition that these formed a weak basis for her defence (and defence, not incorporation of Freeman's yet-to-appear findings, was already the order-of-the-day), they seemed advanced largely to deflect the spotlight from Mead; already it was Freeman the man, not Mead's work, which had become the issue. And the questions asked about Freeman were many: Who was he? What were his motives for attacking Mead? Was he a "racist" in guise of an ethologist? Why, if he had been skeptical of Mead's work for so long, did he not publish his criticism while she was still alive and give her a chance to reply? And, most importantly, was Freeman a stable and reliable witness of Samoan life?

Thus, when I attended a faculty seminar at Berkeley devoted to Freeman's work in mid-April, I was not particularly surprised at its condemnatory tone. What did surprise me was the failure of the speakers to explain the substance of his critique of Mead to an audience largely made up of students. Indeed, the session seemed almost designed to convince the students that there was little of substance to Freeman's attack; anthropology had nothing to fear and they—and their parents—could relax. All the speakers debunked his book as a piece of shoddy scholarship. To this end, *Margaret Mead and Samoa* was presented in brief caricature as the work of a biological reactionary soft on racism; one speaker commented that the adjectives Freeman used to describe Boas and the cultural determinists tended to be neutral or negative while those used for the eugenics movement tended to be either neutral or positive,[1] reminding the audience that eugenics-style thinking helped lead "to the holocaust." Thus, despite his own clear condemnation of the eugenics movement and praise of Boas for the "remarkable prescience" with which he warned that eugenics "was not a panacea that would cure human ills, but rather a dangerous sword" whose "expedient of eliminating 'the unfit' would soon reach a terrible culmination in National Socialist Germany," Freeman was tarred with the brush of racism before an audience who, almost to a person, had not read his book.   If this speaker had his way few did, as he pronounced its reading a waste of time before turning to consideration of the sinister motives which might have impelled Harvard University Press to publish such a poor piece of scholarship in the first place.

. . . Although the book was deemed controversial only because it had been "presented as such in the popular press" the association's journal, *American Anthropologist*, devoted a special section of some 40,000 words to it in its December 1983 issue. In his prefatory remarks, the review editor noted that Freeman's book "has raised questions of authenticity and viability in ethnographic research.   Most importantly, it has subjected the work of anthropology's best-known public representative to critical reappraisal in the popular press."[2] Of the five scholars who offered reviews of the book, four were highly critical; only one, Theodore Schwartz—who had had by far the closest relationship with Mead and who had worked with her in New Guinea—offered a generally favorable assessment of Freeman's work, noting among other things that Mead "did very likely go into the field looking for and expecting to find the cultural contrast in adolescence that she later reported . . . [and that] Samoa, or its representation in anthropology, social science, and the public's understanding will never be the same."[3] Derek Freeman was not permitted opportunity of simultaneous reply; when his reply appeared, he was limited to 4,000 words.[4]

---

[1]This assertion is untrue. See D. Freeman, *Margaret Mead and Samoa* (Cambridge 1983), pp. 3-61.

[2]Ivan Brady, Introduction, *American Anthropologist*, 85 (1983):908; emphasis mine.

[3]"Anthropology: a quaint science," *American Anthropologist*, 85 (1983):923, 925.

[4] See Ivan Brady's response below, 277-278.—Ed.

Clearly, there seems more to the Mead-Freeman controversy than a simple concoction of the popular press. For whatever reasons, Derek Freeman's book hit hard and hurt American anthropology.

The Oracle Profaned[1]

Roy A. Rappaport

... Let's first recall the event. The weeks following the appearance of the *New York Times* story were uncomfortable ones for professional anthropologists. It was difficult for us to walk across any campus in the United States without being accosted by economists, physicists, and historians who wanted to know what we thought about Freeman's book. They all, it seemed, assumed that anthropology had been thrown into some sort of crisis by it. Most of us had difficulty reacting. For one thing, the book was not yet available. For another, few of us had looked at *Coming of Age in Samoa* since our own undergraduate days. As Robert Levy put it in his review in *Science*:

> Whatever [Mead's] ... importance to a many-headed, vigorously developing present-day anthropology may prove to have been in some future retrospect, neither her theory nor her method nor her data are at the center of current discussion—which is not to belittle her enormous contribution to the organization, vitality, and morale of the profession during her lifetime.

... If anthropologists had been inclined in the winter of 1983 to scoff at suggestions that their discipline had been thrown into crisis by the Freeman book, they were not so confident later that spring. With, or very soon after, the book's publication, articles

---

[1]This selection is drawn from "Desecrating the holy woman: Derek Freeman's attack on Margaret Mead," which appeared in *The American Scholar* 5 5 (1986):313-347. Reprinted by permission from *The American Scholar*. Title supplied by the editor.—Ed.

about it began to appear in such national mass circulation journals as *Time, Newsweek,* the *Wall Street Journal,* and in more specialized magazines, such as *Natural History* and *Smithsonian.* The daily press carried simplified versions of Freeman's contentions to many times more readers than those sufficiently interested and well-to-do to pay twenty dollars for his book, and his appearances on national television programs brought to additional millions the word that Margaret Mead was being discredited.

If anthropology was not thrown into public disrepute, it was shadowed by public doubt. As the *Denver Post* stated on February 15 in an editorial entitled "Anthropological Crisis":

> This is more than just another academic teapot tempest; anthropology is a science often accused of being a haven for social theorists manipulating facts to prove their preconceived points . . . . Mead . . . made major contributions to U.S. social attitudes. Her reputation is secure. The real loser may be anthropology's reputation as a science. If its methods haven't made quantum jumps forward since Mead's day, the whole discipline might find a better home in creative literature.

The generation of a crisis in the public's confidence in anthropology, and consequently in anthropology's influence (such as it ever was) on public affairs or public opinion, may have been an unavoidable side effect of a scientific attempt to overthrow that Freeman called "the Boasian Paradigm." But his comments to Jane Howard, one of Mead's biographers, at least suggest that he counted on embarrassing American anthropology (as well as discrediting Mead) among the rewards of his enterprise. Two years prior to the publication of his book, Howard reports in *Smithsonian,* Freeman had predicted that his book might cause Mead's reputation to "do a thirty-two," a phrase referring to the rate at which the velocity of falling bodies accelerates. He later wrote to Howard: "I rather suppose that I may have written a book that will create the greatest denouement in the history of anthropology so far, not excepting Piltdown Man!" In a telephone interview around the time of publication, Howard reports him to have said: "I have succeeded, haven't I, in staggering the [American anthropological] establishment."

It depends upon what Freeman meant by "staggering." If, as his Piltdown remark implied, he meant that he had, so to speak,

knocked American anthropological theory off its factual underpinnings, his claim was not only an immodest exaggeration of the
importance of his own book but an inflated judgment of the
enduring theoretical significance of *Coming of Age in Samoa.* If
he simply meant that he had succeeded in getting the goats of a
good many American anthropologists, he could not have been
more correct. In an early review, in *The New York Times. . .*
George Marcus declared Freeman's book to be "a work of great
mischief," and the preponderance of American anthropologists
agreed.

Anthropologists' anger was at least as much a reaction to the
manner of the book's publication as a reaction to the book's contents. Accustomed to the sedate pace of academic disputation—at
least a year, usually more like two, elapses between the publication of a book and the appearance of its reviews in the professional journals—and more or less comfortable in what they believed the world regards as exotic subject matter, anthropologists
were astonished by the attention their discipline was suddenly receiving, disconcerted by the tone of much of it, and, quite simply, outraged by the professionally orchestrated hype that apparently animated it and defined its object as scandalous. Here, for
example, is a portion of David Schneider's review in the June
1983 issue of *Natural History*:

> This is a bad book. It is also a dull book. To make
> matters worse, the book has been promoted in ways that
> seem to me to have precluded whatever useful, serious
> discussion it might have provoked. I do not know
> whether the publisher should take the burden of the
> responsibility for this or whether the author shares a
> large part of the responsibility by virtue of the
> inflammatory statements he has made to the media. I do
> know that I was invited to discuss Freeman's work with
> him on a television show and also on a radio show,
> hardly suitable situations for the thoughtful discussion of
> scientific matters. But the real trouble with the hype . . .
> is that the problems the book purports to deal with have
> been oversimplified, distorted and sensationalized.
> Thus, instead of a work of scholarly significance, the
> book is now a media event. . . . If Freeman wants his
> book to be remembered and discussed as the book that

said Mead made errors in reporting Samoan ethnography
. . . he has succeeded, even though this has long been
known throughout the profession.

Provoked, possibly, by a prepublication draft of Schneider's
review or by similar reactions from others, Joy Pratt, then the
director of publicity at Harvard University Press, responded in
the *Chronicle of Higher Education* of May 11, 1983:

Academics don't understand publishing . . . . We have
a responsibility to make money and generate sales for
books as well as publish books with something
important to say. What shocks me about the reaction to
the book is the scholars who say Mead was a great
humanitarian and scholar, and it's mean to publish a
nasty book about her . . . . Whatever became of
scholarship and looking for truth? . . . People say it's
been known in the field for years that Mead made mistakes in interpreting Samoa, but the general public
hasn't known that.

Questions about the very nature of Freeman's book are raised
by this confrontation. Schneider's remarks suggest that his
understanding of *Margaret Mead and Samoa* is, curiously, closer
to Freeman's than is Pratt's. Schneider seems to accept
Freeman's claim that the book (however bad and dull he deemed
it) is an attempt at scientific refutation, a form of discourse for
which its mode of promotion was inappropriate. Pratt seems to
justify the book not so much as a contribution to anthropological
scholarship as an attempt to disseminate to a wider public what
anthropologists already knew. In her interpretation, the ways in
which the book was promoted were quite appropriate, the book
and its promotion inseparable.

Whatever Freeman's intentions may have been, Joy Pratt's
understanding of the book's nature and significance was, I think,
closer to the mark than Schneider's. For one thing, the book was
not addressed to a scholarly audience but to the social
descendants of the readership of *Coming of Age in Samoa*.
Although its promotion irritated anthropologists, it would be a
serious mistake to dismiss the book's significance as no more
than the media's creation. The play given to it in the press and on
television indicated journalists' judgments of public interest in its
contents, and the journalists, it turns out, were right. *Margaret*

Mead and Samoa may not be a major contribution to the anthropological understanding of Samoa, to the elucidation of the relationship between biology and culture, or to the improvement of anthropological method and theory, but its publication was, nevertheless, a cultural event of genuine importance. Public excitement arose because *Coming of Age in Samoa* had been a significant book and Margaret Mead a significant public figure. If anthropologists were surprised by the stir, it was because they had forgotten, if indeed they had ever fully understood, either the public significance of *Coming of Age in Samoa* or the nature of Margaret Mead's public status.

A Sad Day for Anthropology[1]

Lowell D. Holmes

I think it is a sad day for anthropology and science in general when an individual who studies another's work states in a nationally published interview . . . that as a result of his efforts he expects Margaret Mead's reputation to "do a 32" (32 feet per second per second being the rate at which falling bodies accelerate toward earth). Not only am I disheartened by the professional demeanor Freeman has shown, but am also depressed by the actions of some of my colleagues in American anthropology who eagerly reported to media people that the Freeman volume was "brilliant" and a great contribution to anthropology. Many of these people have never set foot on Samoan soil and obviously had not stopped to consider the ethical conduct and the methodology of Freeman's study. I have even found some people taking Freeman's side in the controversy because they didn't like Margaret Mead as a person. I don't think anthropology has done itself very proud in this debate.

I have also been greatly disillusioned by the action of a university press that I have long respected. The Harvard University Press promotion of this book involved virtually every

[1]From "A Tale of two studies." Reproduced by permission of the American Anthropological Association from *American Anthropologist* 85:4 (1983):929-935. Not for further reproduction.

shoddy trick known. Never before have I heard of a university press flying someone half way around the world to appear on television talk shows, and never before have I heard of an academic press circulating bound page proofs of a forthcoming book so that a raging controversy would be created to increase sales. While I did not receive a copy of the page proofs until I telephoned Harvard University Press and made a special request, the book was apparently sent to such sympathetic readers as Ernst Mayr (zoologist), Niko Tinbergen (zoologist and ethologist), Bruce Mazlish (historian), Eibl-Eibesfeldt (zoologist and ethologist), and John Pfeiffer (physical anthropologist and prehistorian), none of whom has done research in Samoa. These people must have had the book well in advance, since they were quoted in early promotion ads and in early interviews in the popular media long before the book was published.

The Dangers of Freeman's Book

Bob von Sternberg

Editor's Note
This text is abridged from an interview with Lowell D. Holmes which appeared in the Wichita *Eagle-Beacon*, February 20, 1983 under the title "Wichitan Defends Margaret Mead's Samoan Findings." It is of interest because of its visceral statement of what was perceived to be at stake in the cultural politics of the controversy. It also contains the first public reference to Freeman's letter of October 10, 1967, concerning Mead's behavior in Samoa (see Chapter VI for the text of this letter). © The Wichita Eagle and Beacon Publishing Company. Reprinted by permission.

. . . **H**olmes believes Freeman's book could inspire "dangerous ideas." "It's not just a matter of Margaret Mead being right. It's the whole nature vs. nurture thing I thought was settled in the 30s."

Holmes is concerned about a rekindling of the theory, espoused by Freeman and others, that behavior is influenced more by genetics than culture. A similar belief formed the basis of Nazi racial theories a half-century ago. A decade ago, Nobel laureate William Shockley attracted publicity and hoots of condemnation for arguing that race determines intelligence and that blacks are genetically inferior. "It's an elitist, racist point of view," Holmes said, "It becomes easy to say the poor are never going to be any better, so why help them?"

Cultural anthropologists like Mead and Holmes "basically have a democratic point of view, that everyone has the same potential, that racial differences are negligible. Einstein could have a black skin or a yellow skin."

. . . Until her death in late 1978, Mead made a good target during her celebrated half-century career. "She was a popularizer of science, a gadfly and she made a lot of money—those things don't make you popular with your colleagues," Holmes said.

During the 1960s, Freeman corresponded with Holmes, an exchange that still rankles the Wichita State University professor. "I sent him some of my work, but it was obvious from his letters that he was on a vendetta against Margaret Mead." In one letter, Freeman wrote that he had heard from a Samoan that Mead had "gone native," sleeping with Samoan men and appearing in the village bare breasted

"I was so appalled I never wrote to him again," Holmes said.[1] "When I told Mead about the letter, she wasn't worried. She said everyone knows Derek Freeman's crazy."

---

[1] Holmes did write again, a number of times. But he did not reply to the letter mentioned until a year later. Freeman prompted Holmes' response by reminding him, in a letter of October 3, 1968, that he awaited a response. Freeman wrote: "[i]f there is some emotionally-based reason why you do not wish to acknowledge my letters to you, I would be grateful if you would let me know of this so that I may be relieved of the obligation of writing to you further." Holmes' letter of October 9 begins: "I am sorry that you took personally the fact that I had not answered your last letters. The fact is that I am a very poor correspondent. . . . I must admit that I thought that your methods were a bit unusual in regard to Margaret Mead's activities back in 1925-26."—Ed.

Two Resolutions

Editor's Note

These two resolutions document the feeling among anthropologists in the first year of the controversy. The hostility directed to the Harvard University Press is particularly notable. According to reports, the Press received numerous communications chastizing its publication of Freeman's book. These interventions are said to have had a traumatic effect on the Press. The first of these resolutions was proposed and defeated at the Northeastern Anthropological Association meeting in March, 1983. The second was passed at the business meeting of the American Anthropological Association in November, 1983. In his response to the AAA resolution, Freeman stated that "this condemnation, by *institutional authority*, of a book based on empirical and verified evidence . . . is contrary to the values of science, and a regression to the days of Calvin . . . ." (*Anthropology Newsletter* 25 [1984], no. 4, p. 2). The second resolution appeared in the *Anthropology Newsletter*, 25 (1984), no 1, p. 5.

While the following resolution was NOT adopted, the membership voted to have the Executive Board [of the Northeastern Anthropological Association] communicate its substance to the *New York Times*, Harvard University Press and the AAA Newsletter. The authors of the resolution will use the NEAA Newsletter to encourage NEAA members to write individually in the ways described.

The following was NOT passed:

Whereas the *New York Times* published in one week three articles about Derek Freeman's book on Margaret Mead prior to its publication; and whereas such massive pre-publication publicity hampers the ability of the anthropological community to respond seriously to the issues raised in the book; and

Whereas the book and articles appear to promote the view that conflict, tension, and warfare have their origin in a biologically determined human nature rather than in specific cultural relations; and

Whereas such publicity actions tend to undermine scholarly consideration of Dr Mead's work and even create the appearance of ideological manipulations; therefore be it

Resolved that the Northeastern Anthropological Association condemns such action on the part of Harvard University Press, the *New York Times*, and Derek Freeman; and be it further

Resolved that the NEAA request information from Harvard University Press regarding what policy changes it has undertaken to insure that such publicity campaigns will not take place in the future; and be it further

Resolved that the NEAA insist that Harvard University Press sponsor and underwrite a conference, organized under appropriate scholarly auspices on the work of Dr Mead and relevant social and theoretical issues.

The members of the American Anthropological Association, at their 82nd Annual Meeting in Chicago, have noted with dismay *Science 83*'s recommendation of Derek Freeman's *Margaret Mead and Samoa* for holiday gift-giving.

We are surprised that a magazine of the caliber of *Science 83* would choose, from among the many scientifically respectable popular books now available in the social sciences, one which has been consistently denounced by knowledgeable scholars as being poorly written, unscientific, irresponsible and misleading. It not only distorts the work of Margaret Mead, but it misrepresents the entire field of anthropology. The book is "controversial" only because it has been presented as such in the popular press, including *Science 83*.

A review of such a book is always appropriate, but your special recommendation for purchase is a disservice both to your readers and to social science.

Comment on the American Anthropological Association Resolution[1]

Robert A. Paul

The vicissitudes of fortune of Margaret Mead . . . reflect, in a highly dramatic way, the rise, fall, and rise of interest in

---

[1]From the Editorial, *Ethos* 12 (1984):100-101.

psychological anthropology. A world-class superstar from the 1920's through the 1950's, her lustre faded in the discipline and languished throughout the 1960's and 1970's. Last November witnessed the end of that era, when what seemed like half the anthropologists in the world crowded into a grand ballroom in Chicago to cheer while everyone from cultural relativists to sociobiologists to cultural materialists defended Mead's honor against Derek Freeman's attack. Maybe it was just a case of the seven cities vying for Homer's bones after he was dead; but I would have sworn that if someone had asked most of the people in that room a year earlier what they thought of Margaret Mead's field research, the collective answer would have been "not much."

The Barnard College Symposium

Cheryl M. Fields

Editor's Note

During 1983, a number of symposia were organized to debate the issues. This report is of the first, held at Mead's alma mater Bernard College in April. The last, held at the annual meeting of the American Anthropological Association in November, attracted about 1000 people. Freeman states that he was not invited to any of these meetings nor was he notified of them.

This excerpt from an article entitled "Controversial Book Spurs Scholars' Defense of the Legacy of Margaret Mead," is reprinted with permission from _The Chronicle of Higher Education_, May 11, 1983, pp. 23, 28. Copyright 1983.

A book by the Australian anthropologist Derek Freeman attacking the late Margaret Mead's famous field work in Samoa has upset many cultural anthropologists—for many different reasons.

Rarely, some scholars say, has one academic launched such a personal, critical attack on another—particularly a deceased colleague as Freeman has in _Margaret Mead and Samoa_.

Other anthropologists fear that anthropology may suffer because widespread attention to Mr. Freeman's book in the news media has "trivialized" the issues involved.

Some scholars are concerned that the book's stress on the need to consider the influence of biology on behavior could be used to feed social conservatism and racial backlash in the United States.

And others are somewhat embarrassed at having to defend Margaret Mead. Her very popularity and power prompted professional criticism and jealousy, and, because she was a pioneer among American anthropologists in doing ethnography in foreign locales, much of her work inevitably has been subject to reevaluation and revision over the years.

Even so, the controversy has prompted a number of scholars to vigorously defend her contributions to cultural anthropology.

. . . Mr. Freeman emphasizes that Mead spent only nine months in Samoa in 1925, and that she had to learn the language after she got there, and that she lived not with a native family, but with the one American family on the island that she studied.

Those were signs for poor field work, he says, that undercut any conclusions she drew about that society. Further, he says, she may have been teased by the adolescent girls she studied about their sexual lives and values.

That part of the Freeman book infuriates many anthropologists, who say such a personal attack on Mead is unwarranted. Few anthropologists argue that they would like their students to go out today and conduct research precisely the way Mead did, but many say she deserves far more credit than Mr. Freeman gives her for being one of the first American anthropologists to do field work in an exotic foreign culture such as Samoa's, instead of concentrating on ethnographic studies of Indians in the American West.

. . . In discussing the personal tone of Mr. Freeman's criticism of Mead, a number of anthropologists noted the strong, colorful, assertive personalities of both.

As one said, "Not far below the surface of the book there is a lot bubbling. These are two very strong personalities. Freeman has some very strong compulsion to go after Mead. That does not mean his criticism has no basis, but it does raise questions about his motivation.

"There is one sense in which a sex angle probably is operating. There are a lot of male anthropologists who had trouble with Mead, who were uncomfortable that any woman should be that strong. I saw her once when she had a room of 40 full-grown male anthropologists cowed. It's not easy to do that."

. . . Beatrice Whiting, an emeritus professor of anthropology at Harvard University, reflects the concern of some anthropologists that Freeman's book may be used to bolster what some see as a social and racial backlash in the United States.

"Freeman has some interesting things to say about how the pendulum is going to swing in terms of the importance of biology to behavior," she said.

"But he could have written an essay on that and included some information on Samoa without taking the axe to Margaret. He's attacking a 25-year-old woman on her first field work. She went to the field when race prejudice and genetic explanations of behavior were very popular. She was a social reformer, not just an anthropologist.

"Freeman is right in saying the cultural relativism of the 1920s and 1930s was carried too far. The problem is in not letting the pendulum swing to racism when you start talking about genetic explanations of things," she said.

. . . A number of other [symposiasts] who had worked in parts of the world where Mead had preceded them . . . generally said Mead had been known for conducting very quick field work compared to today's standards, that she had sometimes oversimplified things in an effort to fit them into a theoretical framework, and that she could be stubborn in defending her conclusions.

But, they added, she also was "brilliantly right" on some things.

. . . Mr. [Lowell] Holmes of Wichita State, who is talking to publishers about doing a book to refute Mr. Freeman's, said in an interview that "while there were errors in Mead's work—I saw the society as much more competitive and much less sexy than Mead described—my findings generally corroborated hers."

. . . Despite the support that many anthropologists are expressing for Mead, some are a bit embarrassed at having to defend her. George E. Marcus, chairman of the anthropology department at Rice University, said in an interview, "In the current mood there may be too much of an effort to defend her and not [enough] to be objectively critical. . . . outside of introductory courses, her work has not generally been read in recent years."

Margaret and the Giant-Killer[1]

Marvin Harris

Editor's Note
This essay was among the most vehement rejections of Freeman's study penned during the controversy. Harris manages to "reduce" the book to "no more than a futile personal vendetta." But of equal interest is Harris' defense of cultural anthropology against Freeman's "sociobiological" threat. As an exponent of cultural materialism in a profession that defines culture in terms of the ideality of symbol, Harris is more exposed to the rival sociobiological materialism than are the out-right idealists.

Edward O. Wilson's best-selling sociobiological thrillers have shown that there is no limit to the spasms scholarly books can stimulate in the press if they advance two propositions: one, social scienists are incompetent bleeding hearts who deny the existence of human nature; and two, hard-nosed, real scientists must assume control over the social sciences and reassert the importance of biological factors in human life. Harvard University Press, Wilson's publisher, has found that, by twitching certain nerves, nearly any book advocating neo-Darwinian forms of biological determinism can soar to best-sellerdom. Its most recent entry is Derek Freeman's *Margaret Mead and Samoa: The Making and Unmaking of an Anthropological Myth*, which two months before its publication was already front-page news.

To Wilson's tried and true formula, Freeman has added one new twitch: he discredits cultural determinism by heaping scorn on Margaret Mead, the world's most famous anthropologist. Because Mead remains news even after her death, Freeman was

---

[1]This article is reprinted by permission of *The Sciences*, from volume 23, July-August, 1983, pp. 18-21.

able to boost himself to prominence on the back of her fame. If Mead was wrong about the significance of culture in Samoa, imagine what havoc her epigones have wrought in the name of the great god culture. (An especially unsavory aspect of this whole affair is that Mead would have ably defended herself had Freeman not waited until after she was dead to launch his intellectually blighted attack.)

When she was only ten years past her own adolescence, Mead set out to prove that the storm and stress suffered by Western youth is culturally determined. She reported in _Coming of Age in Samoa_ that Samoan adolescents passed from childhood to adulthood without experiencing the trials and tribulations that befall teenagers in the United States. While young Samoans indulged in extensive erotic experimentation and premarital free love, and enjoyed easy-going relations with their parents, American youth did not. Mead explained that the differences were part of a larger cultural contrast—that Samoan culture, in general, was more easygoing and noncompetitive than American culture. Samoans, she claimed, didn't have very strong feelings about anything; they were "one of the most amiable, least contentious, and most peaceful people in the world."

Freeman attempts to upend Mead's portraiture point by point. Samoans, he says, are sexual prudes, with one of the world's most highly developed virginity cults. Girls live in dread of being raped; boys are sexually aggressive and in the past were trained to be fierce warriors. Parents beat their children mercilessly, and children respond with dry-eyed, repressed hostility. Samoans are touchy about protocol, rank, and titles, and intensely involved in village and island-wide political struggles.

Perhaps Mead overemphasized the bright and amiable side of Samoan life; but perhaps Freeman has overemphasized the dark and aggressive side. He, of course, is not the first anthropologist to have doubted Mead's conclusions. Back in 1968 I myself wrote, in _The Rise of Anthropological Theory_, that her conclusions conveyed "an unnerving degree of conviction," and that there is evidence that "Mead's Samoan findings were exaggerated." An ultimate reckoning will have to be made by experts familiar with Samoan culture. Yet insofar as Freeman's work bears on the issue of cultural versus biological determinism, it doesn't matter a whit which of the two versions is eventually vindicated.

I hope I will not be misunderstood. I am not saying that anthropologists can afford to be cavalier about the accuracy of ethnographic descriptions. On the contrary, ethnographic validity and verifiability are matters of the greatest importance, the sine qua non of a science of culture. What I am saying is that the particular theoretical conclusions Freeman identifies as the reason for writing his book in no way depend on upending Mead's version of Samoan culture. Rather, Freeman aims to refute the paradigmatic assumptions formulated by Franz Boas, Mead's mentor at Columbia University and the leading figure in early twentieth-century American anthropology.

Freeman claims that Boas and his students subscribed to a doctrine of "absolute cultural determinism," a belief that "human behavior can be explained in purely cultural terms." In Freeman's view, cultural determinists early in the century were the antagonists of equally doctrinaire scholars who, in the footsteps of Francis Galton, over-emphasized race and heredity. He writes that forty years after Galton declared that "all of the differences between 'savage' and 'civilized' societies could be explained by the 'innate character of different races'" and that "'a galaxy of genius' might be created" by uniting "in marriage those who possessed the finest and most suitable natures," Mead was sent out by Boas to prove that differences between societies could be explained in "purely cultural terms."

By showing that Mead was mistaken about Samoa, Freeman presumes to right the balance between the extreme hereditarian and cultural viewpoints. In good Aristotelian style, he claims the middle ground between "these two antithetical intellectual and scientific schools, . . . each insufficient in scientific terms, . . . the one overestimating biology and the other overvaluing culture." He portrays himself as a veritable paragon of scientific objectivity and common sense. But his portrayal is a sham, for in order to counterbalance these two extremes—the absolute biological determinism of Galton and the absolute cultural determinism of Boas—Freeman erects his own fable of Boasian anthropology.

To portray Boas as a dogmatic advocate of "absolute cultural determinism," with an "antipathy to biology and to genetics and evolutionary biology," is to distort beyond recognition Boas' vision. One of Boas' most important achievements was the creation of the distinctively American plan of graduate education in anthropology known as the "four-field approach," which unites coursework in physical anthropology with studies in anthropological linguistics, archaeology, and cultural anthropology. There are dozens of four-field introductory anthropology textbooks—including one edited by Boas himself—that devote from a fifth to a third of their pages to various aspects of physical anthropology.

. . . The trend toward specialization—the demand that students become expert at one particular branch of anthropology—has made it increasingly difficult to fulfill Boas' plan. But the fact that major anthropology departments in the United States offer various courses in physical anthropology, primatology, medical anthropology, paleodemography, human biology, human genetics, and human paleontology (all of which have strong neo-Darwinian components) is largely because of Boas, not despite him.

Neither Boas nor his students ever denied that Homo sapiens has a nature that is specific to the human species. Rather, they denied, first and foremost, in their struggle against the proto-Nazi racist eugenicists who dominated the social and behavioral sciences of the beginning of the century, that the enormous range of cultural variation within the human species is grounded in genetic differences. Unlike their eugenicist adversaries, Boasians insisted that even if one group of people practiced polygyny, lived in extended families, and worshipped ancestor spirits, while another practiced monogamy, lived in nuclear families, and worshipped a single high god, both groups could nonetheless share the same human nature.

The overwhelming number of variations found in human social life are not encoded in the genes before birth, but in the brain during life. No one will ever find genes for monogamy, circumcision, matrilineal descent, slavery, parliamentary democracy, capitalism, or punk rock. This, of course, is not to say that all cultural variations are encoded independently of genetic variations—obviously certain cultural specialties such as some adults' inability to digest milk may be linked to genetic differences. But these instances are the rarest of exceptions, and are wholly compatible with the basic Boasian paradigm.

The major task to which Boas and his students devoted themselves was not to prove that there is no human nature, but to prove that there is only one human nature that allows for an enormous amount of mentally encoded variation. Mead herself wrote, in *Male and Female*, that "we have a biological ancestry that we dare not flout." Her mission to Samoa was not to pursue (in Freeman's words) the nefarious "stark stratagem of arbitrarily excluding 'nature' from any kind of consideration whatsoever," but merely to show that adolescence in America is not typical of adolescence around the world, and, therefore, that human nature is, in Mead's words, "not rigid and unyielding" but allows for enormous variation.

In this perspective, the whole of Freeman's attack is reduced to a futile personal vendetta that leaves the nature-nurture balance exactly where it was when we had only Mead's version of Samoan adolescence; for Mead's argument rests only on the fact that different cultures are different, not on any particular kind of cultural differences. In Freeman's account, Samoan adolescence turns out to be every bit as exotic and distinct from our own as Samoan adolescence in Mead's account. Samoan boys and girls have more problems than Mead has indicated, but their problems are scarcely the problems of American teenagers. For example, both Mead and Freeman agree that Samoan youth practice a custom known as sleep crawling, but their interpretations are quite distinct. In Mead's version, a young man steals into a young girl's house at night to have coitus with her, and she enjoys the experience enough to keep quiet about it. But according to Freeman, a sleep crawler is a "finger rapist" out to deflower a virgin, which he does not by phallic force but by manually inserting one or two of his fingers in her vagina. The finger rapist is not out for sexual pleasure, but to force a girl of higher rank to marry a man of lower rank. And the girl keeps quiet not because she enjoys the experience but because public knowledge of the loss of her virginity would bring loss of status. Instead of denouncing the rapist, she promises to marry him at a later date.

Needless to say, Freeman's account is no more reminiscent of the customs of American teenagers, whose marriage prospects are not influenced by the condition of their hymens nor by their finger-raping "skills," than is Mead's portrayal of free love. So it is not at all clear in what way Freeman thinks his evidence refutes the Boasian view that cultural practices are primarily learned and not innate. Showing yet again that Samoan adolescence differs from American adolescence brings us no closer to explaining the sources of cultural variation. Or is Freeman suggesting that

Samoans have a gene for finger-raping? The mind boggles at such a notion.

Freeman's book ends without any discussion of how sleep crawling, status rivalry, the virginity cult, or any other aspect of Samoan adolescence can be better understood by invoking human nature any more than Mead did, when she asserted that there is one human nature that allows for unlimited cultural diversity. In the absence of such discussion, it appears that Freeman merely wishes to remind us that human beings have sex drives, capacities for aggressive behavior, and certain anatomical parts, like hands and legs, useful for sleep crawling and other activities. But aside from sharing these glad tidings, what is his point? Simply, Freeman wants to right the balance of nature and culture by giving each equal weight, a seemingly reasonable settlement. But his solution derives from a fundamental misapprehension shared by many biologists, including Conway Zirkle, of the University of Pennsylvania, whom Freeman quotes: "Any attempt to make nature or nurture more crucial than the other is as silly as trying to determine which is the more important product, the multiplicand or the multiplier." Charles J. Lumsden and E. O. Wilson also fall prey to this notion in "The Dawn of Intelligence," published recently in these pages [March/April]: "People are neither genetically determined nor culturally determined. They are something in between."

. . . Despite the immensity of the task, the attempt to discover what is culturally (as opposed to genetically) programmed in human social life is of the highest scientific and practical significance. It is not silly. Our entire democratic way of life is predicated on the scientifically established fact that enormous changes occur in human behavior when humans are socialized in conformity with different cultural traditions. What's more, the mathematical analogy for culture-nature interactions is not multiplier and multiplicand, which are equally important in a product, but factor analysis, in which each factor is routinely assigned a different weight.

The notion that cultural and biological influences equally determine cross-cultural diversity clouds the fact that, in countless aspects of human existence, cross-population variance is overwhelmingly a result of cultural programming. For example, if we compare Chinese reared in China who speak Chinese, venerate clan ancestors, and eat with chopsticks, with Americans who speak English, worship a Judeo-Christian God, and eat with knives and forks, the respective contributions of nature and nurture are readily identified. Culture accounts not for fifty percent of the variance but for one hundred percent. We know this because children of Chinese descent reared in American homes speak English flawlessly, worship the same Judeo-Christian God, and are as inept at using chopsticks as the rest of us.

Most anthropologists agree that during the earliest phases of hominid evolution, genes and culture evolved together, or coevolved. The brain's genetically determined capacity to store information and behavioral instructions evolved as increasingly complex cultural repertories evolved. Lumsden and Wilson state: "Genes and culture are held together by an elastic and unbreakable leash. As culture surges forward by means of innovation and the introduction of new ideas and artifacts . . . it is constrained and directed to some extent by the genes. At the same time, the pressure of cultural innovation affects the survival of the genes and ultimately alters the strength and torque of the genetic leash." However, Lumsden and Wilson fail to point out that there was a moment in evolution when gene-culture feedback ceased to play a significant role. We cannot say precisely when, but we can be certain that it occurred long before twelve thousand years ago. At that time, simple, band-organized, hunter-gatherer groups ceased to be the only form of human social life. Thereafter, different forms evolved, their pathways continually converging and diverging. Villages, chiefdoms, agro-managerial and feudal states, empires, and complex commercial and industrial cultures emerged. And along with each of these cultural types there appeared an immense diversity of technological demographic, ecological, economic, sexual, mental, familial, political, religious, philosophical, and ideological institutions and customs.

Explaining how these institutions and customs evolved lies entirely beyond the competence of theories based on Darwinian selection, for the simple reason that no new biologically distinct varieties of Homo sapiens have evolved since 10,000 B.C. Where are the genetic changes to match the dramatic cultural changes in human evolution? Where are the genetic shifts that would justify applying the concept of coevolution to these cultural transformations? Certainly genetic changes have not kept pace with the cultural changes that have occurred among industrial societies in the last one hundred years—the appearance of communist, socialist, and welfare capitalist political economies; the expansion of information and service sectors at the expense of goods production; the rise of multinational conglomerates; the fall of fertility rates; and the redefinition of male and female roles at home and in the workplace. These changes have all occurred within the lifetime of a generation that is still alive today, a generation possessing the very same genes they have had since birth. These developments must, therefore, be independent of any changes in gene frequencies and obviously equally compatible with our one human nature.

Sociobiologists have been accused of attempting to resurrect social-Darwinist forms of biological reductionism characteristic of the racists and eugenicists who dominated the social sciences at the beginning of the century. In order for modern day neo-Darwinists to rebut this accusation and avoid a bitter and scientifically counterproductive clash with the majority of present-day social scientists, they must concede two points. First, we are unable as yet to distinguish with certainty between genetically and culturally determined universals. And second, while human nature may account for such general features of human social life as aggression and sexuality, it cannot account for such variable features as finger raping or sleep crawling. The major variations in human social life during the past twelve millennia cannot be linked to any known variations in gene frequencies. Social scientists are as eager as biologists to identify the biopsychological constants of human nature and the rare cases of gene-culture coevolution among post-Paleolithic societies. But there will be no fruitful collaboration unless biologists acknowledge these limitations in an energetic and forthright manner, especially when they have the attention of the press.

Saint Margaret[1]

Mary Lefkowitz

B y the end of her life Margaret Mead wasn't merely America's most famous anthropologist; for many, and perhaps most of all for herself, she had come to symbolize anthropology. Virtually every moment of her life was spent in observing herself and others, in questioning, discerning, conversing, teaching. Clothed as an outsider in her own country, clad in a red cape and carrying a forked stick, she became the interpreter, healer, and prophet that she had once been for South Seas native cultures. She spoke to us about us as she had spoken to us about them, both descriptively and didactically. It was not enough simply to be ourselves; we must learn to understand, and wherever possible to improve, the patterns of our own lives and civilization.

How Mead was able to attain such extraordinary status has been the subject of much recent inquiry—first her own *Blackberry Winter*, which described her education, fieldwork, and three marriages; then the apologetic discussion that followed the publication of Derek Freeman's critical *Margaret Mead and Samoa*; and now her daughter's memoir and Jane Howard's detailed biography. Howard, an experienced reporter, provides a discerning documentary, full of specific information only alluded to in, or else omitted from, other accounts: she keeps at a distance from her subject, rather as in a fast moving film, without trying to recreate Mead's thoughts or indeed the process of the work that occupied most of Mead's waking life. Bateson, understandably, gets us closer to both her parents, but only for brief moments (Mead chose presents thoughtfully, found tampons liberating), as in family photographs separated widely in place and time; she knew her parents well, both as people and as scholars, though only at intervals. Neither of these books says much about anthropology, or goes into detail about Mead's

[1]This excerpt is taken from "Saint Margaret," *New Republic* 68 (October 1, 1984):34-36. Reprinted by permission of THE NEW REPUBLIC, © 1989, The New Republic, Inc.

methodology in the field. Once again the woman, not her work, takes center stage.

Perhaps Mead's most enduring legacy was herself. Although she and other prominent liberals spoke in favour of women's rights and other social causes, Mead was one of the very few who practiced what she preached. In her behavior she predicted what was to become common and even acceptable conduct in her daughter's generation. She was married three times; she broke up with her first two husbands in order to marry their successors; during the course of her first marriage she was emotionally involved with Ruth Benedict and Edward Sapir; she supported herself by her earnings as a curator and lecturer; she breast-fed her baby on demand (despite the vogue for scheduled bottle-feeding); she traveled widely—all this before people spoke openly about bisexuality, or committed serial polygamy, or took nursing babies to dinner parties.

What enabled her to do all this . . . was a quality most women lack: boundless self-confidence. Mead rarely looked back, and rarely blamed herself when things went wrong. Not only did she have faith in herself, but she believed that one could, with energy and understanding, change and improve the world around her. At the same time, she had virtually a poet's power to convince others of the reality of her visions, not only of other cultures but of our own. She thought of herself as a scientist, but it was more a novelist—that traditional female role—that she reached beyond family and colleagues to the general public.

Her writing was exciting, and still is, because it is at once personal and comprehensive. She explains how she felt when confronted with the strangeness of a foreign society, but at the same time proceeds fearlessly to say what we can learn from the disquieting differences. If she mentions the past, it is often to remind us how we have managed to progress over the years to some new level of understanding: "We know a great deal that we did not know then of how the swaddling of infants fits into the way Russian children first experience life and the way Russian parents later look upon children," she wrote in the preface to the 1975 edition of *Growing Up in New Guinea*, first published in 1930, implying that this "knowledge" not only helped citizens in the Soviet Union to be more responsible than their rebellious American counterparts, but would also further "understanding of relationships among different nation states."[1] She believed that anthropological studies, no matter how small the sample or how dated the material in them, would become the first course of stones in a pyramid that would lead to the improvement of all cultures—in short, to a Better World.

Such wishful thinking has had an almost irresistible appeal to intelligent American audiences, who long to make some sense out of the disorganized components of their education, and who have always been convinced that in their own society cultural differences can be tolerated, if not completely eliminated. And, of course, Mead put the imprimatur of her own authority and the force of her considerable will behind each statement. But the swaddling-clothes theory has long been discredited. And where is the evidence that cultural understanding can bring about progress of any kind, not to mention world peace?

Even in her own life, however consciously she sought to influence the environment in which she lived and worked, Mead could not always employ anthropology to bring about practical solutions. She most egregiously failed to demonstrate how two career marriages could work, especially if the woman is more successful.

Nor did she contrive to make her death symbolize what she stood for in life. Mead was unable to admit even to her own daughter that she was dying of cancer, although she had witnessed deaths that were not mitigated or postponed artificially by medicine, and had brought her daughter to see the dead body of her friend and mentor Ruth Benedict, so that she could see what most American middle-class children in 1948 were shielded from. In the past she had made dramatic use of discomfiture (the forked stick helped compensate for an ankle injured in New Guinea and broken years later in Chicago), but here, at the moment of greatest challenge, when, like the philosopher-poet-prophet Empedocles, she might have jumped into a volcano, inspiration failed her.

It is this failure to apply her doctrine of understanding to herself that makes both Bateson's and Howard's books depressing reading. Mead always suggested that others see

---

[1]The reference is to the swaddling hypothesis of Geoffrey Gorer, which Robert A. Paul has called "one of the most easily parodied theories in the annals of science."—Ed.

psychiatrists but refused to see one herself, on the grounds that the top 10 percent of the top 10 percent did not need such help. Although she had many friends and a large extended family, and never lost touch with her ex-husbands, she seems to have shown the people she knew only what she wanted them to see. She could be direct and intimate, but only, it seems, in spurts, lasting at most a few years, before some sort of punctuation, either in space or time, became necessary.

By concentrating on Mead's personal life, as if that could be separated from her intellectual life, both books fail to show why she was so successful and why, in the long run, some of her findings may be proved wrong, some of her methods need to be questioned, and some of her assumptions to be revised. Neither author compares her field methodology to anyone else's, though Howard is careful to call attention to narrative discrepancies and Mead's discomfort with learning languages, questioning by implication Mead's claim that she spoke "polished Samoan" by the time she completed her famous study. Because both books deal primarily with personalities, they tend to react with anger to the tone of Derek Freeman's allegations about Mead's work in Samoa, rather than to concentrate on the substance of his findings. Should Freeman (or any other critic) really be regarded as an enemy? When one scholar criticizes another's work, he implicates him or her in his criticism; this happens not because scholars are more malicious than other people, but because discoveries are made by intuition as well as by hard work, and so the product cannot easily be separated from the temperament or background of its producer. Thus inevitably Mead, because she was a woman working with girls, failed to understand some of the surrounding values of the world of Samoan men (just as Freeman himself, in his criticism of Mead, may not have taken sufficient account of the women). But what of Freeman's questions about the short duration of Mead's investigation (six months), her relative lack of training (she was a graduate student[1] who had never done fieldwork on her own), the small size of the sample she studies, or the nagging question of fluency in languages?

The "truth," however relative and unpleasant, may be that Mead will be remembered not so much as a scientist, but as a brilliant and sophisticated writer of travelogues. She described

---

[1]Mead's Samoa fieldwork was not part of her doctoral submission.—Ed.

not only lost and remote cultures that have now disappeared into the modern world, but the times in which she lived and in which we still live, and which her explorations, with all their now obvious limitations, may help us, even imperfectly to understand.

Middle American[1]

Sir Edmund Leach

To the European intelligentsia, Mead's social science is faintly ridiculous and the grounds for her fame fairly unintelligible. Among anthropologists likewise, the esteem for her work—never as international or unanimous as her public success—generally decreases in proportion to the square of the distance from middle America.

. . . What was it about this very energetic but intellectually undistinguished individual that turned her into a national heroine? What did she represent in the minds of those who put her on the pedestal she so joyfully adorned? Sahlins's Europe/Middle America antithesis is much to the point. European social anthropologists see themselves as heirs to the giants of sociological theory, Marx, Durkheim, Weber in particular. Cultural differences are not labels which attach to whole societies but are the markers of social class, or of regional ethnic differences within nation states. When scholars of this sort discuss cultural criteria it is mostly to very fine-grain differences that they draw attention: the difference between BBC English and normal Cambridgeshire rather than the difference between English and Chinese. Individuals are coerced into behaving as they do by the jural constraints which are implicit in their immediate cultural surroundings. Cultural environment does not determine "personality." When Mead came to maturity, however, the "melting pot" theory of American national identity was much to the fore. Culture and personal character were both considered to

---

[1]Reprinted by permission of the Sir Edmund Leach Estate and the *London Review of Books* from the *London Review of Books* 7, no. 4 (1985):17.

be infinitely flexible. Given appropriate procedures for child-rearing and education, the children of all kinds of European and non-European immigrants, no matter what might be their linguistic, ethnic and social-class origins, could be forged into true Americans: individuals who reverenced individualism, but who shared a common basic personality, a common "national character." With this background the kind of impressionistic anthropology that was served up by Ruth Benedict in *Patterns of Culture* (1934), by Mead in *Sex and Temperament in Three Primitive Societies* (1935), or by Mead in the truly awful *Male and Female* (1949), gave its audience just what they wanted to hear. Bring up your children in the right way and they will behave in the right way. Mead's ethnographic descriptions are laid on with a tar brush. In a celebrated instance she flatly declared that "warfare is practically unknown among the Arapesh" and went on to romanticise at length about the educational correlates of their lack of aggression. Derek Freeman was not the first professional anthropologist to find such slapdash generalization academically intolerable. One of Reo Fortune's first actions in his status as Mead's ex-husband was to publish an article on Arapesh warfare! While Jane Howard went to the trouble to verify that it was Fortune's ethnography rather than Mead's that was the more accurate, she defends Mead's thesis simply because it was more popular: "Fortune would disagree, but Mead would write (for a vastly larger audience than he would ever have) that rarely among the Arapesh was anyone very aggressive." Many of Mead's professional associates both in her own country and elsewhere have taken the view that they have other scholarly duties besides that of playing to the gallery.

The Samoa Myth as an American Legend[1]

Roy A. Rappaport

Freeman claimed that *Coming of Age in Samoa* recounts a myth. I agree with him and would suggest that his book generated excitement not because it constituted a scientific refutation but because it was, as its subtitle makes explicit, an attempt to invalidate an important myth. The two are not one and the same.

Myths are accounts bearing upon the origin and nature of the world's proper order and upon actions that conform to, and thus realize, that order (and as such are moral) or that violate and undo that order (and are, ipso facto, immoral). Myths tend to concentrate on issues that are cognitively or ethically problematic and to deal with matters that are ambiguous, contradictory, and that can generate ambivalence—for instance, the need both to fulfill and to constrain sexual drives.

Although analysts of myth usually treat each text as discrete, the myths of any society are usually loosely joined into a more or less coherent mythos, which, in its entirety, expresses or represents that society's Logos (its conception of the world's moral and natural order) and how it came to be.

Myths may seem to naturalize conventions, but they do not provide descriptions of the world as it is. Rather, they present enduring models, always idealized, against which current states of the world can be judged. In telling of the world before some fall, as many myths do, they do not describe what is but recount what was, and in recounting what was, they stipulate what should be. The state of the world, that is, should correspond to a state stipulated, implicitly or explicitly, in the myth; but if the world did in fact correspond there would be no need for the myth. Although it recounts the past, myth is oriented to the future, inspiring actions that transform what should be into what is.

---

[1]This selection is drawn from "Desecrating the holy woman: Derek Freeman's attack on Margaret Mead," which appeared in *The American Scholar* 55 (1986):313-347. Reprinted by permission of *The American Scholar*. Title supplied by the editor.

Questions are raised concerning myth's epistemic and ontological status. In contradiction of the usage that takes myth to designate accounts that "prove" empirically to be false, ultimate truth is claimed for, or by, myth understood as the representation of Logos, the world's proper order. The "ultimate truth" of myth is, clearly, neither the necessary truth of logic nor the empirical truth of science. Whereas internal consistency is the criterion of necessary truth and factuality is the criterion of empirical truth, propriety or morality, perhaps represented as an aspect of the natural or necessary order of things, is the criterion of mythic truth. Where there is disparity between fact—observable states of affairs—and the truth of myth, it is fact that is wrong. Physical facts themselves may even be understood to be lies or something like them. In Zoroastrian Persia, for example, the word *druj* designated both lies in the ordinary sense and acts, such as rebellion against the Sassanid emperors, that violated Asha, the world's proper order. Asha also glosses as "truth" and is the name of the persons of the Zoroastrian Godhead. In Vedic India there was a corresponding opposition between *anrta*, denoting lie, chaos, and dereliction of duty versus *rta*, denoting duty, order, truth.

If the truth of myth can be demonstrated neither by reference to the world's observable condition nor by rigorous logic, upon what does it stand? The matter is involved and ramifying and can be discussed only briefly here.

First, the accounts that make up the enduring core of any mythos are not only about extraordinary events but are themselves extraordinary. Some core myths seem to the living to have come down from time immemorial, and their origins are easily attributed to the times of origin of which they tell. In recounting the primordial, they themselves become Primordial Word. Others are brought to peoples at times known to history by prophets who have received them as visions, revealing to humankind eternal truths for the first time.

But the truth claims of myth stand upon more than the persuasive capacities of antiquity and revelation. Being neither necessary nor empirical truths, the truths of myth constitute a sub-class of a third major category at least as important in human affairs: the category of conventional truths, truths that are validated by their acceptance by a community. That core myths are often expressed in ritual is salient in this regard, for, as I have argued at length in my own book, *Ecology, Meaning and Religion*, participation in a ritual is a formal act of acceptance of whatever is represented in that ritual. Ritual acceptance does not guarantee compliance with whatever directives may be implied or explicit in the order encoded in the ritual, nor does it even entail the subjective state of belief in them. Acceptance is a public act, visible to the performer and others, constituting an agreement that the order represented in the ritual is legitimate, and as such embodies criteria against which the events of an errant world, including the behavior of the acceptor, can rightly be judged.

That core myths are represented in ritual and in scripture, both media of religious discourse, suggests that mythic truth is a species of the genus of conventional truth for which the designation "truth of sanctity" may be used. Its source may be in ritual, but, in its flow from ultimate sacred postulates, such as creeds, expressed in ritual, to other texts, sanctify—the essence of which is a generalized unquestionableness that assumes, in particular contexts, the more specific forms of truth, propriety, morality, legitimacy, or correctness—may escape from religious discourse altogether. If, to use a crass but perhaps apposite example, the United States is "one nation under God," a God in whom we trust and whom we accept in weekly acts of worship, and if, as Calvin Coolidge, sworn in the name of God into our highest office, said, "the business of American business," then business is highly sanctified. And, if business is sanctified, so is what is called "the Horatio Alger Myth."

This discussion suggests that myth may suffuse a society's literature and its oral tradition. But it is, perhaps, more accurate to put the matter inversely: Literature, oral tradition, popular culture, and discourse of all sorts, including that of the sciences, continually generate materials that may be assimilated into a society's mythic corpus.

I speak of the "assimilation" or "incorporation" of narratives or other materials into a mythos. Myths are seldom, if ever, composed as such. Myth is a status conferred by a public upon some, but not all, texts. Horatio Alger did not write myth. He wrote light inspirational novels for boys, and the ethos behind these novels became myth. Margaret Mead wrote an ethnographic account of adolescent girls in Samoa to which she appended a discussion of education in America. When this account entered the consciousness of an American public, that public canonized it. Freeman is correct in construing *Coming of Age in Samoa* as mythic but wrong in labeling it an "anthropological myth." It became an American myth. Anthropology is no more capable of establishing the mythic status of narratives than is chemistry. All anthropology can do is to offer to a public accounts from which that public can select some (as it can from other sources) to establish as myth, leaving the rest to anthropologists' arcane in-house conversations.

We may, in this light, consider *Coming of Age in Samoa*. It had a head start, so to speak, in the competition for canonization; it was an account of a part of the world that had long had a place in Western fantasies, at least those of males. Earlier accounts of the South Seas Idyll had offered only dreams of escape from the constraints of Western society, not moral principles bearing upon society's deficiencies, as did *Coming of Age in Samoa*. Mead's ethnographic chapters offered, to a society in which adolescence seemed especially trying, an account of a society in which adolescence was much easier for most people. To a society struggling toward more permissive conventions of sex and more egalitarian relations between men and women, Mead's book offered a picture of relatively carefree sexuality, making that vision of sexual emancipation available not only to young men but to young women at a time when the double standard held tacit sway. (Think how different would have been the significance to Americans of a *Coming of Age in Samoa* that focused upon the sexual activities of adolescent males.) The didactic chapters of Mead's book attempted to draw conclusions from the "main lesson" of the ethnography—"that adolescence is not necessarily a time of stress and strain but that cultural conditions make it so."

The Edenic description of island life from which this lesson was drawn may have led readers to draw a further mythic lesson; that the Samoan condition was one of either nature or of grace and that the contemporary American condition represented a fall into a state either unnatural or sinful or both. Mead said or implied no such thing; and, if it is characteristic of myth to represent the specifically cultural or conventional as both natural and sacred, her conclusions were anti-mythic. She understood "the main lesson" of her ethnography to be "that our own ways are not humanly inevitable nor God-ordained, but are the fruit of a long and turbulent history." Therefore, "we may well examine in turn all of our institutions, thrown into strong relief against the history of other civilizations, and weighing them into the balance, be not afraid to find them wanting."

The final chapter of Mead's book amounts to a manifesto in which she argued that education in contemporary society must fit children for choice rather than conformity. Such an education requires them to be taught "how to think, not what to think." No one of the many ways open to children is "sanctioned above its alternative," and, this being the case, they must be taught tolerance. These prescriptions were not imported directly from Samoa but were derived from a comparison of aspects of Samoan and American society.

I have suggested that texts assimilated into a mythic corpus reaffirm and revitalize enduring general values at the same time that they legitimate changes in specific conventions—rules, usages, understandings—by which social life is assessed or even regulated. *Coming of Age in Samoa* proposes that American conventions of socialization be changed not only to adapt better to specific changes occurring in our culturally heterogeneous society but to adapt also to the condition of unremitting change itself. The enduring values and understandings at once underwriting these changes and represented by them are patent—an assumption of the plasticity of human nature, a belief in the perfectibility of humanity and in humanity's ability to improve the natural and social condition of the world, a belief in freedom of individual choice. All of this obviously conforms closely to a main line of American ideology descending from Declaration of Independence. *Coming of Age in Samoa* was sanctified by its association with general values stipulated n America's founding document (itself highly sanctified because the very act of national creation was viewed as expressive of the "Laws of Nature and Nature's God"). The radical changes in specific conventions that Mead expounded were implicitly represented as conservative of those general values under changed circumstances.

For the audience that originally made *Coming of Age in Samoa* a best-seller, its account of an alternative to American sexual mores was, possibly, a revelation and its proposals for change no mere pieties. Falling short of setting out a specific social program, the book constituted a text of liberation, a myth of enlarged human possibilities. For later readers, the book was even more charged with meaning. If in 1928 the audience was mainly adult and educated, most of those who came later were, at the time of their reading of Mead's book, not long, or not yet, out of adolescence themselves and still passionately engaged in the struggles with which Mead was concerned. The book enjoyed substantial classroom adoptions for decades, and most readers during the past fifty years have probably been undergraduates still wrestling with the possibilities laid before them by their complex society and still agonizing about sex more than enjoying it. This is the public that, in the course of time, confirmed the mythic status of *Coming of Age in Samoa.*

Anthropology, then, particularly in the person of Margaret Mead provided a source of mythic materials to American society during the late 1920s and 1930s, but it was hardly a sole supplier. In complex societies there are always many texts vying for mythic hegemony, and sciences other than anthropology were providing some of them.

She did not, however, confine herself to bring us Good News from the South Seas. She spent the sanctified authority she won through journeys to other worlds in the controversies of this one. Speaking as a Holy Woman in a tone of voice that never seemed to betray any uncertainty about anything, she continued all her life to tell the world all manner of things for its own good—about relations between the sexes and the generations, for instance, and the legalization of marijuana. To the extent that these issues were controversial, they profaned her, but she could always replenish her sanctity by another journey into the wilderness. And so she became a unique cultural institution, our own national oracle who, the joke went, when visiting her senior colleague at Delphi, asked, "What was it you wanted to know?" In November 1978 hundreds of newspapers observed her death not only in their obituaries and on their front pages but in editorials with such headlines as: "More than a Scientist," "Grandmother to Us All," "World Loses Margaret Mead," "Farewell to a Matron Saint." She was a Holy Woman, and much of the excitement following the publication of Freeman's book was a reaction to her desecration.

Why Didn't You Warn Us?[1]

S.D. Cornell

Professor Rappaport's lengthy grinding of Derek Freeman into the anthropological turf was instructive to this lay reader, although I find its title misleading. Demolishing the Unholy Antipodean seems more apt and almost as catchy.

Even while fascinated by the Battle of Boas, I kept waiting for a résumé of critical publications by those American anthropologists who were said to have early recognized the true character of *Coming of Age in Samoa*. Did they try to warn a deluded public that it was largely myth, not science? Surely the least they owed to those swallowing the story and joyfully accepting it as gospel (good news!) was such a warning. Failure in that seems irresponsible of professionals in a field as closely related to human behavior as cultural anthropology.

Perhaps most of all, one could wish that the Holy Woman Herself had felt a responsibility to caution her vast public, supposing that as she matured she recognized the misleading nature of her juvenilia. She must have seen her book becoming the beacon for hordes of youth leaping gleefully on what seemed the scientific promise and justification of adolescent adjustment through sex-on-demand. She played a leading role, as this observer sees it, in creating a tragic illusion that has made adolescence more traumatic, and far more costly to society, than it was in the days of sexual restraint. "Humane" and "liberating" seem ill-chosen words to describe the Mead Myth.

But regardless of how one interprets the social consequences of the widespread public acceptance of her myth, I wonder whether we laymen can hope that the lesson she has taught will persuade more anthropologists than Freeman, and more promptly, to speak out when they discover that their work, or that of a colleague, presented as science, turns out to be myth. Clearly, such revelations are even more important to society

---

[1]Letter to *The American Scholar* 56 (Winter 1987):159. Reprinted by permission of *The American Scholar*.

when the work profoundly affects the lay public than when the matter is of concern only to those toiling in the science.

For now, the iconoclast's attack, too late to counter the damage, and even granting Rappaport's points in his damning critique, seems nonetheless a welcome stroke for the discipline of self-correction that is crucial to any science and that one would dearly hope would follow fast every myth-as-science.

Rappaport Replies:

S. D. Cornell asks why anthropologists didn't warn "a deluded public that it was largely myth, not science." I can make only two brief suggestions in the space remaining. First, I don't think that anthropologists have been aware that a few of their texts have played a mythic role in public discourse. The mythic significance of *Coming of Age in Samoa* and Mead's publicly sanctified status were matters that escaped us until Professor Freeman forced us to reflect upon them. Second, as I tried to make clear, the contrast between myth and science is not an opposition between truth and falsehood, but a distinction between discourse directed toward the *discovery* of law and fact and discourse devoted to the *construction* of value and meaning. The two may, but need not, be complementary. That epistemologies dedicated to the discovery of law may threaten the grounds upon which meaning and value are constructed could be at the heart of contemporary problems, but that is another matter.

Examination of Holmes' *Quest*

Thomas Bargatzky

Editor's Note
As the anthropologist who made a restudy of Mead's ethnography, Lowell D. Holmes' evaluation of her work had a more than ordinary claim to attention. Although Holmes endorsed the conventional view of Samoan behavior on a number of points on which Mead had been at variance, he nevertheless held throughout the controversy to the global evaluation announced in his doctoral dissertation (1957) that Mead's reliability is "remarkably high." The appearance of his book on the controversy, *Quest for the Real Samoa: The Mead/Freeman Controversy and Beyond* (1987), was therefore an event. Freeman's two reviews were predictably harsh (see Bibliography). Bargatzky's review is highly critical, but it is authored by a Samoanist free of the professional entanglements of Anglo-American anthropology. Like so many non-American commentators, the author is struck by the influence of American culture on the defense of Margaret Mead. Bargatzky lectures in the Institute for Cultural Anthropology and African Studies at the University of Munich. His review appeared in *Pacific Studies* 11 (1988): 131-151. Reprinted by permission.

The purpose of *Quest*. . . is to discuss the Mead/Freeman controversy that began with publication of Derek Freeman's book *Margaret Mead and Samoa*. The target proper of Freeman's criticism are those generalizations in Mead's works that portray the Samoans as an easygoing people, without deep emotions, almost free from jealousy, with easy solutions for every problem, living in a paradise of free love for the young people, and with an adolescence free from storm and stress. Though it was soon realized that there are contradictions between Mead's data and her own generalizations (see Raum 1967 [1940]:42-43, 293-294), the myth created by Mead became enshrined in the anthropological, sociological, and psychological literature. To explode this myth was Freeman's aim. To assess his achievement, we have to take into account not only his book, but also his sometimes very detailed responses to his diverse critics (see

Freeman 1983b, 1984a, 1984b). What is more, his critique is not a personal attack on Mead, as some critics who fail to distinguish between a personal attack and criticism of a doctrine would have it . . . . Under these circumstances, and considering that in the wake of the publication of his book Freeman was subjected to an amount of aspersions and vilification unprecedented in the history of anthropology—I return to this later—one is indeed anxious to learn what Holmes, one of the most resolute defenders of Margaret Mead, has to say in his new book. _Quest_, however, is a big disappointment. And it is depressing reading.

Very generally, I am dismayed that Holmes neglects to consider Freeman's detailed responses to earlier criticism. Holmes merely elaborates his criticism published elsewhere (Holmes 1983a, 1983b) and reissues charges to which Freeman had already replied (Freeman 1983b, 1984a). None of this is incorporated into Holmes' book. Holmes merely repeats what he has said elsewhere. During the three to four years between Freeman's responses and the publication of Holmes' book, there should have been ample opportunity to revise his manuscript and tackle Freeman's detailed and—to my mind—mostly convincing replies. Considering that we are concerned here with anthropological issues of fundamental importance, I can think of no excuse for such conduct, because I cannot bring myself to believe that Freeman's responses should have passed unnoticed by Holmes.

Holmes, it is true, differs with Mead on several issues and he is explicit on this in Chapter 8. Hence, he is far from being an uncritical admirer of Mead, taking her every word for holy writ. Yet, despite the conspicuous contradictions between his own and Mead's results, he has always been committed to the message that "the validity of her Samoan research is remarkably high" (p. 103). This view he had already professed in his Ph.D. thesis, _A Restudy of Manu'an Culture_ (1957:232, cited in Freeman 1983a:105, 325 n. 22). _Quest_ is a desperate attempt to buttress this general conclusion and, to do so, Holmes not only gets entangled in self-contradictions, but he also resorts to omission and evasion. First, let me present some examples of self-contradictions.

Self-Contradictions

Unwed Mothers and Children born out of Wedlock. Holmes writes that "unwed mothers face very little stigma, and their offspring are welcomed into the family" (p. 78). In the same vein, he holds that "an unwed mother faced only the short-lived anger of her parents and brothers" (p. 106). Yet we learn that "abortion . . . does occur when an unmarried pregnant woman feels that the man responsible for her condition will not marry her, or that family censure will be severe" (p. 81).

Virginity.

On one hand, Holmes writes: "As Mead says, 'Sex activity is regarded as play; as long as it remains informal, casual, meaningless, society smiles' (1930:84)" (p. 106), and young men and women "have had numerous affairs and flirtations" by the time they marry (p. 78). On the other hand, we are told that "Samoan society certainly did not sanction sex outside marriage" (p. 122), and "proof of virginity at marriage is applauded by the families of both the bride and the groom" (p. 80). In fact, virginity is applauded to such an extent that in cases of non-virgins, "many a girl has been saved embarrassment by the substitution of a membrane containing animal or chicken blood for that normally produced by a broken hymen" (p. 80). One may indeed be astonished at Mead's smiling society that goes to such lengths to uphold the image of virginity. There is yet more to say about it, however.

Though many parts of *Quest* are taken verbatim from articles and books already published, this is not always so. The passage just quoted, for example, is taken from an article (Holmes 1957), later published as a book by the Polynesian Society. In the article, what is now a "membrane containing animal or chicken blood," however, was "a chicken bladder full of blood" (Holmes 1957:413). The chicken, of course, has no bladder (see Freeman 1983a:353 n. 48). What do we make out of this? Metamorphosis? Another "Samoan mystery"? Or just a spoof by informants who told Holmes the chicken bladder story? There may be something in the contention, after all, that the Manu'ans sometimes dupe anthropologists!

On Freeman's Interactionist Viewpoint.

I have already commented on Holmes' neglect to take into consideration Freeman's responses to earlier criticism. Moreover, other sources relevant to an assessment of Freeman's stance are not considered either. This is vexing since Holmes seems intent upon labeling Freeman as a narrow-minded ethologist. For example, Holmes writes: "Although Freeman rejects the label sociobiologist, his main orientation appears to be ethological and his tendency is *to rule out the forces of culture* as an explanation of behavioral differences between young people in the United States and Samoa" (p. 13; emphasis added). Quite apart from the fact that there is no basis for such a charge in Freeman's *Margaret Mead and Samoa* (in which Freeman subscribes to an interactionist point of view of human evolution in which the genetic and the exogenetic [cultural] are interacting parts of a single system), a careful researcher intent upon assessing Freeman's position should also consult his other publications. Elsewhere, Freeman has taken pains to clarify his position in relation to the interaction of the genetic and the cultural (Freeman 1980, 1981), yet none of these papers is taken into consideration by Holmes.

On Holmes and His Witnesses.

To enhance the credibility of Mead's account, Holmes quotes some statements of indigenous Samoans. For example, he quotes the highly respected La'ulu Fetaui Matā'afa (whom he mistakenly believes to be the "wife of the Prime Minister of Western Samoa"), who stated in a letter to the editor of *Newsweek Magazine* (28 February 1983) that "neither Margaret Mead nor Derek Freeman represented our ancient land, its customs or its way of life" (p. 137).

But at least one Samoan authority fully supports Mead's conclusion, Holmes writes:

> One man, Napoleone A. Tuiteleapaga [sic], is definitely known to have had close ties with Mead as both informant and interpreter. He is quoted in the *Wall Street Journal* article (14 Apr. 1983) as saying, "Margaret Mead was 100% right in her book." And in an interview in the *Samoa News* (11 Feb. 1983), published in American Samoa, he stated, "She got to know people well and wrote an accurate analysis of what she saw. Why didn't these anthropologists condemn Mead's book when she

was alive? I'll tell you why, they waited until Mead is gone because they knew she knew what she was taking about" (p. 138).

Here we have the Samoan authority, after all, who personally knew Mead and who is incensed about those anthropologists who disagree with her. Who is this remarkable man? Tuiteleleapaga (not Tuiteleapaga) is, among other things, the author of a book titled *Samoa Yesterday, Today, and Tomorrow* (New York: Todd and Honeywell, 1980). This book was reviewed in *American Anthropologist* (84, n. 3 [1982]:715-716), and the reviewer records how he first met the author:

Since most of my informants up to this point were extremely reserved . . . I was somewhat astonished by this extroverted man who claimed, among other things, to be a Rosicrucian and a songwriter . . . . He . . . claimed to be interested in anthropological research and was at that time engaged in a study of Samoan sexual behaviour, primarily through participant observation. When I left Napo's house he gave me a copy of a study he had done of old Samoan "superstitions." The manuscript contained some very detailed and impressive information concerning Samoan charms, taboos, deities, and spirits. Mostly I was impressed by the fact that the paper turned out to be chapters IV and V of George Turner's *Samoa, A Hundred Years Ago and Long Before* (1984). . . . The introduction to the book is by Margaret Mead, and it is interesting because she has managed to reproduce Napo's style of writing almost exactly. But the most puzzling aspect, which surely can be chalked up to insufficient proof-reading, is Tuiteleleapaga's statement in the dedication (p. iv) that Margaret Mead wrote the introduction "after reading the whole manuscript in her office in New York shortly after her death."

Maybe it is this transcendental relationship with Mead that enables Tuiteleleapaga to assert that she was "100% right." I regret that Holmes has denied us this piece of information about his witness. The book review in question cannot have escaped his attention, because it was written by a certain Lowell D. Holmes from Wichita State University, who is identical, I presume, with Professor Holmes, the author of _Quest_.

On Competition and the Noble Art of Definition.

Holmes says that he saw Samoan culture "as considerably more competitive than Mead did" (p. 103). As areas of competition, he mentions, for example, boys' games (p. 75), the zeal of untitled men to distinguish themselves as good servants to their matai and family (pp. 76, 93), interest in the ceremonial and traditional aspects of Samoan life (pp. 93-94), competitive spirit in schooling, the wish to have the best carpenter, the best coxswain, the best dancer (ibid), oratory (pp. 50, 93) (p. 122). To this, Sunday donations must be added (p. 71). This is an impressive list indeed and Holmes cannot help saying that "in view of Mead's long discussions of competitiveness in the village political organization of Manu'a, it is surprising to find that she characterizes Manu'an culture as one where competition is disparaged and played down" (p. 122). In view of such an admission it is highly annoying to realize that Holmes classifies, among other things, "competitive spirit" and "sex activity data" under "ethos" (p. 119), because he later declares: "It should be noted that Freeman did not mention that my disagreements with Mead were over matters of ethos, an area which Campbell believes is so much a matter of emotional response that 'ethos may indeed be beyond the realm of scientific study' (Campbell 1961:324)" (p. 155).

This, then, is Holmes' strategy: where Mead's conclusions are so obviously at variance with the facts that they cannot be explained away, he classifies the areas of disagreement as aspects of "ethos" and declares that ethos is beyond scientific scrutiny. This is immunization strategy. I fail to comprehend, moreover, how a society like Samoa—where "rank and prestige constitute the focal point . . . to which all other aspects of life are secondary in importance," where "every installation, wedding, and funeral of a chief affords an opportunity to gain prestige and raise one's relative position within the village through the display of wealth" (p. 122)—how such a society should provide a "comfortable ideological environment, allowing a smooth and unrestricted maturation process" for young people (p. 34). What is more, not only chiefs' _rites de passage_ offer opportunities to gain prestige (Tiffany and Tiffany 1978). As every student of things Samoan knows, Samoan life consists of a never-ending series of *fa'alavelave* (trouble, family business) of different magnitudes, each *fa'alavelave* reopening the arena for status competition.

. . . *Quest* is slipshod as to ethnographic detail, fraught with contradictions, and omissive and evasive in its attempt to salvage Mead's conclusions and to discredit Freeman's refutations and his status as a scientist. To account for the fact that such a book could have been written and published in the United States, we must look at the intellectual environment. A scandal bigger than *Quest* itself is the fact that this book has been hailed as "a timely contribution to the picture of Samoan culture" (Bateson 1987), "fair and lucid . . . instructive and informative" (Theroux 1987:49), and helping "to set the record straight in a most illuminating manner . . . fascinating reading" (Montague 1987).

. . . Freeman's critique evoked vilification, opprobrium, and aspersion to a degree unprecedented in the history of anthropology, mostly on the part of anthropologists who would consider themselves to be firmly grounded in cultural relativism. In many of the reviews, there is a "right-or-wrong-our-Mead" attitude that is hard to comprehend for an observer outside the United States. Or, to quote Jarvie, who puts it more politely: "That some of the reviews written in the United States have been defensive not only of nurture, or culture, theory, but also of Margaret Mead's status, is hard to understand" (ibid.:83).

But this is not the whole story, alas! What I consider particularly shocking in this connection are statements by anthropologists such as Lieber (1983:15) and Ember (1985:910), who intimate that Harvard University Press should not have published *Margaret Mead and Samoa*, or that the book should have been immediately rejected by the anthropologists who read it in manuscript. Ember even went so far as to proclaim that Freeman "is not a scientist" (ibid:909) because he did not comply with standards that I consider to be so rigid and unrealistic that, should we decide to adhere to them, 90 percent of what makes up anthropology would not be science any more, I dare say. I cannot help feeling that, for some American anthropologists, criticizing Mead is tantamount to un-American behavior. If so, one may understand why Holmes—who, mind you, is very critical of Mead himself—should have felt it necessary to downplay the amount of disagreement between his own findings and Mead's conclusions. There is a telling article, "A Controversy on Samoa Comes of Age," in which the author has this to say:

> In 1970 anthropologist Raoul Naroll of New York State University at Buffalo asked Holmes to contribute a chapter to a handbook on methodology he was preparing. He wanted a chapter on Mead's mistakes in Samoa. Naroll remembers: "Holmes wouldn't do it. He was afraid to criticize her. He thought he would lose grants. That doesn't mean he would have, but he thought he would." Holmes says he declined because he didn't have time to write the chapter. Today he still agrees with Mead's basic observations about Samoa" (Marshall 1983:1043).

I repeat this passage since it has already been quoted by Freeman (1983b:176 n. 46) and remains unchallenged so far. Compare this with the fact that in *Quest* Holmes tries to convince the reader that he finds the validity of Mead's Samoan research is "remarkably high" (p. 103). Can we conclude from all this, then, that anyone who dares to criticize Mead's Samoan ethnography too openly in the United States may face hard times? I want to make it clear that it is not my opinion that Holmes should be assessed by his new book alone. To assess him, his other works have to be taken into account. As far as I am involved, I can only state at the end of this review that it makes me sad that Holmes, after a long career as a professional anthropologist, has seen fit to be the author *Quest for the Real Samoa*.

References

Bateson, Mary Catherine. 1987. Comment on the dust jacket of *Quest for the Real Samoa*, by Lowell D. Holmes. South Hadley, Mass.: Bergin & Garvey.

Freeman, Derek. 1980. Sociobiology: the 'anti-discipline' of anthropology, in *Sociobiology Examined*, edited by Ashley Montagu (New York: Oxford University Press), 198-219.

Freeman, Derek. 1981. The Anthropology of choice, *Canberra Anthropology* 4: 82-100.

Freeman, Derek. 1983a. *Margaret Mead and Samoa: The Making and Unmaking of an Anthropological Myth*. Cambridge: Harvard University Press.

Freeman, Derek. 1983b. Inductivism and the test of truth, *Canberra Anthropology* 6: 101-192.

Freeman, Derek. 1984a. 'O Rose Thou Art Sick!': rejoinder to Weiner, Schwartz, Holmes, Shore, and Silverman, *American Anthropologist* 86: 400-404.

Freeman, Derek. 1984b. Response to reviews of *Margaret Mead and Samoa,* in Book Review Forum, *Pacific Studies* 7:140-196.

Holmes, Lowell D. 1957. Ta'ū: Stability and change in a Samoan village, *Journal of the Polynesian Society* 66: 301-338, 398-435.

Holmes, Lowell D. 1974. *Samoan Village.* New York: Holt, Rinehart and Winston.

Holmes, Lowell D. 1982. Review of *Samoa Yesterday, Today, and Tomorrow,* by Napoleone A. Tuitelelepaga, *American Anthropologist* 84: 715-716.

Holmes, Lowell D. 1983a. A Tale of two studies, *American Anthropologist* 85: 929-935.

Holmes, Lowell D. 1983b. On the questioning of as many as six impossible things about Freeman's Samoan study before breakfast, *Canberra Anthropology* 6:1-16.

Marshall, Eliot. 1983. A Controversy on Samoa comes of age, *Science* 219:1042-1045.

Mead, Margaret. 1930. *Social Organization of Manu'a.* Honolulu: Bishop Museum.

Montague, Ashley. 1987. Comment on the dust jacket of *Quest for the Real Samoa,* by Lowell D. Holmes. South Hadley, Mass.: Bergin & Garvey.

Theroux, Joseph. 1987. Review of *Quest for the Real Samoa, Pacific Islands Monthly* 58 no. 6 (June): 49.

Letter to G. E. Marcus

Derek Freeman

Editor's Note

This letter is among a suite that Freeman commenced in 1987, taunting colleagues on their embrace of the romantic, post-modernist movement in anthropology. The letter to George E. Marcus, dated March 27, stands out because Marcus had published a disparaging review in which he dismissed *Margaret Mead and Samoa* as a "mere curiosity." In this selection Freeman lampoons the pretentious language of post-modernism. Freeman relishes the "highly ironical and intensely pleasing" circumstance that Marcus edited a special issue of *Cultural Anthropology* which surveyed work in the interactionist anthropology that he had dismissed four years previous in his review of Freeman's book. Printed by permission of Derek Freeman.

Dear George,

You really are a G. E. M.!

With all your highfaluten talk of "valorizing innovations," "intertexuality," and "the current spirit of experiment" in your Afterword to *Writing Culture,* when it comes in *Anthropology as Cultural Critique* to epitomizing the significance of the prime expression of what you claim to be a "key example" of the "critical spirit" in American anthropology, you do no more, even with the assistance of your post-modernist colleague, Michael Fischer, than tell us that *"Coming of Age in Samoa* was, and continues to be, an effective work of cultural criticism among a very large public"—a conclusion that must surely rank as one of the most vacuous in the entire literature of modern (or, should I say, post-modernist) anthropology!

What, in the name of the "salience" of your collaborating brains, are you trying to say?

"Effective," as you must know, is a word which is "applied to that which has the power to, or which actually does, produce an (often lasting) effect."

Are you then, I wonder, given your "professional credentials," and your standing as one of the young Turks of modern, if not post-modernist, cultural anthropology in the USA, able to dispel the mindless vacuity of your conclusion and inform me (with or without the assistance of Michael Fischer) what you consider to be the effect that *Coming of Age in Samoa* has, as "an effective work of cultural criticism," actually produced?

Please be quite specific in your answer, for I am most eager to know what it is that you and Michael Fischer, as leading lights in "the experimental moment in the human sciences" of which you write, can in the case of that "effective work of cultural criticism," *Coming of Age in Samoa,* possibly have in mind.

Please also accept my warm congratulations on whatever part you played in the bringing about of the February, 1987 issue of *Cultural Anthropology.* This account of Biological and Cultural Anthropology at Emory University is the most promising development in American anthropology for decades.

As you must have noticed, in Robert Paul's introduction two principles are enunciated: (i) "human phenomena are always to significant degrees admixtures of biological and cultural factors"; and (ii) "the genetic and the cultural must never be reduced to one or the other, but need to be studied in interaction . . . ."

These are precisely the anthropological principles for which I have been arguing for the last quarter of a century, and, for the adoption of which I quite explicitly argue in the final chapter of *Margaret Mead and Samoa.*

In that review of yours of 27th March, 1983 you angrily pontificated that "Freeman is far from the concerns of contemporary anthropology and biology," and claimed that *Margaret Mead and Samoa* in addition to being "a work of great mischief" was "merely a curiosity."

It is both highly ironical and intensely pleasing to me that now as I write this letter on 27th March, 1987, just four years later, I have before me a copy of *Cultural Anthropology* which proves that those judgments of yours were both purblind and wrongheaded, for the final chapter of *Margaret Mead and Samoa* in fact turns out to have been a harbinger of a quite outstanding issue of a journal of which you, of all people, are the editor, and which clearly indicates the direction in which anthropology must develop if it is ever to become, as I phrased it some years ago, "both scientific and humanistic" . . . .

I finally turn to another but directly related matter. On p. 3 of *Anthropology as Cultural Critique* you misinform your readers that in *Margaret Mead and Samoa* I make a plea for "biological rather than cultural explanations of behavior."

This erroneous assertion by Fischer and yourself, which is based on a crass misreading of the final chapter of *Margaret Mead and Samoa,* is wholly without foundation, and so, quite unprofessional, as I indicated to you, with chapter and verse, in my letter of 20th August, 1986.

As yet, however, I have received from you no reply whatsoever to that, to me, crucially important letter.

Might I suggest then that you should for a few brief moments give up your involvement in whatever "edifying conversation" you are at present immersed and give me a straight-forward answer to an ethical and professional issue that, if you are a responsible professional, you cannot but face.

Or, are you the kind of man for whom such an honest course as the admitting of error is just too daunting?

I suppose we shall see.

May the eye of heaven shine brightly for you and no planets strike!

Yours as ever,

Derek Freeman
Emeritus Professor of Anthropology

P.S.: Incidentally, after reading the Preface to *Anthropology as Cultural Critique* I now see why, given your ambitious aspirations for that book, you should have felt my "devastating refutation of Mead" (to use the words of Albert Wendt) to be a "work of great mischief," for it obviously spiked the very cannon (or, should I say canon) around which the whole discussion in *Anthropology as Cultural Critique* was planned to revolve. Your mood when you wrote that wild review now becomes much more comprehensible, and you have my sympathy. How poetic it is that our paths should have crossed at just that "experimental moment" in the history of anthropology!

Chapter V

Professional Ethics

Introduction

Although the question of professional ethics was implicit in the Samoa controversy from the beginning, the imputations of misconduct in this dispute were made without reference to the Statement on Ethics adopted by the Council of the American Anthropological Association.[1] To find an orientation in the complexities to be examined, it is perhaps apposite to draw attention to some of the principles proclaimed in this document.

Association members "owe a commitment to candor and to truth in the dissemination of their research results and in the statement of their opinions as students of humanity." They may not "knowingly falsify or color their findings." They "bear a professional responsibility to contribute to an 'adequate definition of reality' upon which public opinion and public policy may be based." Adverting to the ethical complexity that fieldwork may involve, the Statement requires Association members to anticipate problems and resolve them "in such a way as to do damage neither to those whom they study nor, insofar as possible, to their scholarly community." There is an obligation to anticipate harm that may come to subjects as a consequence of publishing findings. Association members are enjoined to protect "the dignity and privacy" of their subjects. Their conduct in the field should not jeopardize future research. Regarding relations to governments, Association members are forbidden to undertake secret research, and they must be "honest and candid" in their dealings.

---

[1]Statement on Ethics: Statements and Procedures of the American Anthropological Association. As Amended through 1976. Washington: American Anthropological Association, 1983.

Freeman's resolve to "set the record straight" implied negligence on the part of his colleagues in their commitment to candor and truth. His stronger statement—or implication—that Mead's Samoa was a "hoax" indicated that an allegation of serious misconduct was being made.

Critics were swift to retaliate with numerous accusations, many of which are expressed in Chapter IV. The most serious of these were that—

•*Margaret Mead and Samoa* was a malicious book because it mounted a personal attack intended to destroy Mead's reputation;

•the attack was a vendetta stemming from Freeman's envy of Mead's reputation as a Samoanist;

•he cravenly waited until Mead's death before publishing his results;

•he played a major role in stirring media sensationalism ("yellow anthropology" it was called) to create an atmosphere in which dispassionate criticism was impossible or difficult;

•the attack on cultural anthropology and the imputation of negligence in failing to correct Mead's errors harmed the profession;

•he used his new-found prominence to accuse a number of editors of bias and discrimination when they did not give him space that he imagined was his due as the main protagonist in a scientific debate; when the opponent refused to comply, Freeman was liable to fits of rage;

•the tactic of wrapping himself in the flag of Science and demanding acknowledgement of his "ineluctable truths" thwarted collegial communication and mocked Freeman's frequent eulogies to objectivity. Critics refer to this behavior as "histrionics" and they think it is dishonest.

The retaliation soon gave Freeman and his supporters a list of complaints to hurl at the anthropology establishment. Chief among these were—

•abuse, and irrelevancies such as "the attack on Mead," were used to divert argument from substantive issues and to intimidate those who might otherwise have endorsed his refutation;

•the calumny that Freeman "waited" until Mead's death to publish was repeated many times and was not repudiated by those of Mead's defenders who knew it to be false;

•the defense of Mead's Samoan ethnography was disingenuous since it was generally believed by anthropologists to be seriously in error.

In addition to these broad charges and counter-charges, a number of disputes between individuals developed. The most important of these is the contention between Lowell D. Holmes and Freeman. As a Samoanist with three decades experience and as the anthropologist who undertook a restudy of Mead's Samoan fieldwork, Holmes' tenacious defense of her is of crucial significant to the resolution of the factual ethnographic questions at issue in Freeman's refutation. The numerous detailed criticisms that these scholars have made of one another are listed in the bibliography. The selection chosen for the *Reader* is the unpublished correspondence which fixed in the minds of each that scholarly integrity was wanting in the other. The key communication is Freeman's letter to Holmes of October 10, 1967, in which he detailed the evidence he recently gathered concerning Mead's sexual affairs while in Samoa. This letter was conveyed to me by Holmes (January 2, 1986). He wrote then that

> I believe [Freeman] to be a very unprincipled individual who has been on a witch-hunt for Mead and Boas for years . . . . Although Freeman has repeatedly stated that he has nothing but the highest respect for Mead personally I believe that this letter brands that statement as a lie. When I went out to the field to do my method-ological restudy . . . I went with an open mind and I certainly didn't see my role to gather all the gossip I could dig up on Mead's sex life. I went as an anthropologist not a peeping tom.

Holmes added this comment on the credibility of Freeman's information:

> He only spent about a week in Ta'ū village so he must have started right off looking for salacious details. I also don't believe what he says, because I was very good friends with Mrs. Sotoa where Margaret lived a good share of the time and I have never heard any of these things. . . . I believe that [Mead] conducted her investigations with dignity and objectivity. I don't believe that Freeman's work can be similarly described.

The letter in question is printed in Chapter VI.

There is an extensive correspondence between Freeman and some dozen editors in which Freeman alleges bias against him-self. Three of these suites of letters pertain to two editors of the *American Anthropologist* and one book review editor, Ivan

Brady. From this material I have selected Brady's response, in the *Anthropology Newsletter*, to Freeman's allegations of his bias in preparing the Special Section of reviews of Margaret Mead and Samoa. To this rejoinder, published in 1984, Brady has added remarks written specifically for the *Reader*.

There is a bulky correspondence between Freeman and individuals whose integrity he challenged. The most significant is the exchange between Freeman and Alexander Kohn, author of *False Prophets: Fraud and Error in Science and Medicine.* In this work Kohn reviewed Freeman's refutation of *Coming of Age in Samoa* under the chapter title, Criticism or Slander? Kohn criticized various aspects of Freeman's criticism, and concluded his account by showering Mead with bouquets while not explicitly answering the question posed in the chapter title. Freeman identified many factual errors in Kohn's brief narrative, all tending to denigrate his reputation and to support the suggestion that he had slandered Mead. In his rebuttal Freeman gave his fullest reply yet to some common criticisms of himself, such as waiting until Mead's death before publishing. He demanded, under British defamation law, the complete withdrawal of the account and the insertion of an apology in subsequent printings or editions, and a letter of apology. The new paperback edition of *False Prophets* meets these demands.

This incident is significant at two levels of the ethics question. Kohn, an Israeli virologist with no professional stake in the controversy, is the only critic to withdraw and apologize. In withdrawing he stated that Freeman had "quite definitely shown" that Mead's conclusion in her book that "the behavior of Samoan adolescents was entirely determined by the social environment was in error."[1] This is a significant witness to the cogency of Freeman's refutation. The second level of ethical significance derives from the paradox that a highly acclaimed book about a major problem of professional ethics today commits the very kind of error that the author set out to diagnose and remedy. Kohn espouses the prevailing "rotten apple" theory of misconduct in science; that is, misconduct is an aberrant event arising from a combination of pressure to publish and individual psychopathology. But Kohn's lapses, including one case of groomed data, arose entirely within the accepted practice of normal science and scholarship. Considering that this case concerns a scientist who is regarded as an authority on fraud and blunder, the Kohn evi-

---

[1]*False Prophets: Fraud and Error in Science and Medicine* (Oxford: Blackwell Paperback, 1988), p. viii.

dence gives new support to the rival of the "rotten apple" theory, the "tip of the iceberg" theory. The editor's study of this question, which was prompted by the Samoa controversy, is included as a means of placing the ethical contestations of the controversy in a suitable context.

The correspondence between Freeman and Jeannette Mageo is included because of the manner in which she responded to Freeman's threats to bring her before the Ethics Committee of the American Anthropological Association for knowingly misrepresenting his published views. Her response, like Kohn's, is exemplary. But whereas Kohn withdrew and apologized on being persuaded of his error, Mageo answered Freeman's onslaught with a factual and temperate defense of her scholarship. Her response is all the more remarkable in view of the great disparity between the professional status of the two.[1]

In sampling the charges and counter-charges, I have not thought it necessary to repeat here charges against Freeman that are stated in Chapter IV, to which the reader is referred.

---

[1] Why Freeman threatened to take Mageo to the Ethics Committee of the AAA is puzzling, for the delicts with which he taxed her were much less serious than those he imputed to others, with respect to whom such threats were not made. Moreover, in 1984 Freeman had asked the Ethics Committee to consider his Open Letter to the President and Board of the AAA, concerning the motion reproaching *Science 83* for recommending his book and other matters. The Committee Chair Joan Cassell responded on behalf of the Committee that his complaint had been considered, but determined that it did not "fall within our mandate, as defined by the Principles of professional responsibility of the American Anthropological Association and consequently, we cannot act upon them as a committee" (Letter to Derek Freeman, December 5, 1984). If the Committee would not act on that complaint, it is difficult to imagine what complaint from Freeman might prod it to action. In the event, Freeman did not act on his threat, but Mageo preempted it, as she explains in her letter. The matter has lapsed.

Denunciation at Berkeley[1]

Richard Basham

During the weeks following onset of the controversy but before publication of the book, I noted that anthropologists who had not read Freeman's manuscript and who, like myself, were not Samoan specialists were nevertheless developing an apologia for Mead. Thus, when I attended a faculty seminar at Berkeley devoted to Freeman's work in mid-April, I was not particularly surprised at its condemnatory tone. What *did* surprise me was the failure of the speakers to explain the substance of his critique of Mead to an audience largely made up of students. Indeed, the session seemed almost designed to convince the students that there was little of substance to Freeman's attack; certainly, anthropology had nothing to fear and they—and their parents—could relax. Although one of the three lecturers who spoke granted off-handedly that Freeman's description of Samoa was probably more accurate than Mead's all the speakers debunked his book as a piece of shoddy scholarship. . . . To this end, *Margaret Mead and Samoa* was presented in brief caricature form as the work of a biological reactionary soft on racism; one speaker commented that the adjectives Freeman used to describe Boas and the cultural determinists tended to be neutral or negative while those used for the eugenics movement tended to be either neutral or positive, reminding the audience that eugenics-style thinking helped lead "to the holocaust." Thus . . . Freeman was tarred with the brush of racism before an audience who, almost to a person, had not read his book. If this speaker had his way few did, as he pronounced its reading a waste of time before turning to consideration [of] the sinister motivations which might have impelled Harvard University Press to publish such a poor piece of scholarship in the first place. . . . It is fair enough that anthropologists dispute whether or not their field is a science, a form of comparative literature, or, at different times, both. It is quite distressing, however, to watch it unify as a guild to ostracize a member who disagrees with the consensus. It is almost unbelievable that the annual meetings of the world's largest associa-

---

[1]This selection is taken from Basham's article "Science or literary guild: anthropology's adolescent dilemma," *Journal of Pacific History* 16(1985):37-43. Basham is a polynesian specialist teaching at the University of Sydney.

tion of anthropologists would become a paean of "good" to warn outsiders of the dangers of reading Professor Freeman's work. But I suppose it could have been worse: the message might have been that *real* scientists do not criticize the works of influential anthropologists or embarrass their colleagues before the public.

Astonishing Behavior[1]

Phyllis Grosskurth

As a scholar I am surprised that anyone could have taken *Coming of Age in Samoa* seriously, especially her peers. It's written in ridiculously heightened prose, more like a *Cosmopolitan* article than an essay. I am absolutely stunned by the way the American anthropological establishment has ganged together to crucify Freeman. The argument wasn't carried on at an intellectual level at all. It was *ad hominem*—how could this nasty man have attacked our wonderful Margaret so soon after her death. It's been on that kind of level. I am concerned as a university professor. Some of my students tell me that in their anthropology classes they are almost actively discouraged from reading Freeman's book. I find that absolutely extraordinary. I've heard anthropology colleagues speak critically of Margaret Mead, but they seem to fear that Freeman's book will bring their discipline into discredit; and—let's face it—I think they're a little nervous about getting grants.

---

[1]From Derek Freeman *et al., Transcript of Interviews for the Documentary Film Margaret Mead and Samoa* (Sydney 1987), Tape 15, pp. 24-25. Professor Grosskurth, Mead's most recent biographer, teaches at the University of Toronto.

Something's Rotten in Anthropology[1]

Richard A. Goodman

I was dismayed to see a communication from Dr. Nancy Lurie [as president of the American Anthropological Association, in accordance with a motion passed at the 1984 Business Meeting in the March issue of *Science '84*] . . . scolding the magazine for recommending Derek Freeman's *Margaret Mead and Samoa* for Christmas reading.

. . . Never have I seen such dishonesty from scholars as in the Freeman/Mead controversy. Never have I seen such unethical tactics as I have seen used by some of your association's members to put Freeman down. And never have I seen such a disregard for the methods of science from a group of people who consider themselves scientists.

Are you aware that a shorter critical examination of Mead's *Coming of Age in Samoa* was written during the same time Freeman was writing his? The shorter study, which I wrote, concerns not theory, but rather the facts of Samoan behavior.

. . . Several of Freeman's most vociferous critics have long had a copy of my manuscript. One even urged me, a decade ago, to publish it . . . . Yet mention of my study appears only with extreme rarity in their bibliographies or in their critiques of [Freeman's book].

When two observers see and report the same things, this would tend to indicate with fairly high probability that there is an objective reality out there. In science, corroboration has value. And, in the scientific process, there is something fundamentally dishonest about ignoring evidence that invalidates one's point of view, which some of Freeman's critics have done.

I've noted many strange things in this . . . controversy. I have seen three members of an anthropology department . . . call a press conference to denounce Freeman's book when one of them had never even been to Samoa. I've seen a respected Samoanist who wrote a glowing evaluation of Freeman's manuscript for [a university press] now take a public stance 180 degrees opposite. . . . I've seen another respected Samoanist,

---

[1]Goodman's letter was published as "An Outside perspective on the anthropology of Samoa," *Anthropology Newsletter* 25 (1984), no. 8, p. 2. Reproduced by permission of the American Anthropological Association. Not for further reproduction.

who states that "the reliability of Mead's account is remarkably high," admit that in his original Ph.D. thesis he disagreed with many points in Mead's *Coming of Age* and was forced by his faculty advisor to omit his strongest criticisms before his thesis would be accepted. And I've seen quite a few members of the American Anthropological Association who've never been to Samoa, including some very well-known people, passing themselves off as experts on Samoa and Samoan culture.

Something's rotten in the state of American anthropology. Have we reached the point where people value trendy theory over facts, and denunciation over the untrammeled working of the scientific process?

The Discouragement of Criticism[1]

George N. Appell

Mead's superficial and out of focus account of the consequences of change in Manus has had unfortunate repercussions in my own work on social change. In pursuing my interest in measuring the costs of social change I have been confronted from time to time by scholars who pooh-pooh my work on the basis of Mead's "conclusions" from her restudy of Manus.

Mead's confusion of her role as a scientist with her roles of prophet and propagandist for her vision of utopia, and her search for examples to justify her vision of utopia on a scientific basis, led her to neglect the one critical aspect of the role performance of the scientist, the habit of the truth. This became clear in a controversy I witnessed between anthropologists that were working in the same ethnographic region. One anthropologist, a protégé of hers, had written an ethnographic account that not only did not ring true to the experience of others, but which contained many internal contradictions as well as contradictions with other publications by the same anthropologist. And it was felt by the community of scholars that had worked in the region that not only was the ethnographic account in certain sections wrong, but that

---

[1]This excerpt is taken from Appell's study, "Freeman's Refutation of Mead's *Coming of Age in Samoa:* the implications for anthropological inquiry," *Eastern Anthropologist* 37 (1984):133-135. Appell has written extensively on ethics in anthropological research.

these errors could cause political difficulties in the region. When a review of the book was prepared by one of the scholars working in that area, Mead had withdrawn it from publication. Even though the anthropologists who had worked in the region agreed that the material was wrong, Mead assiduously worked to have criticism silenced and even threatened one scholar—that if he did not keep silent she would withdraw her support for the activities of his department. At no time in this controversy did I witness any interest on her part in what the ethnographic facts were. Reputation seemed to be her concern rather than searching for the truth of the matter and ensuring that the ethnographic record was correct.

The Fairness of *American Anthropologist* Editing

Ivan Brady

Editor's Note

In this selection, *American Anthropologist* book review editor Ivan Brady responds to Freeman's charges that in assembling the Special Section on *Margaret Mead and Samoa,* Brady persistently discriminated against him. Since the substance of most of the allegations are stated by Brady, Freeman's statement has not been printed. One allegation not mentioned is that Brady attempted to prepare the Special Section by stealth. Freeman maintains that he was not informed by Brady that the Section was in preparation; and that he was allowed a rejoinder only because of his persistence. This Brady denies (personal communication). The correspondence between Freeman and Brady constitutes one source of independent evidence and will no doubt in time be evaluated. It may be added that a person informed about this dispute expressed to me the opinion that Freeman's cries of prejudice were "showboating and really quite deceitful."

Brady's response was entitled "Rethinking the American Dragon: A Response to Freeman." Reproduced by permission of the American Anthropological Association from the *Anthropology Newsletter* 26 (May, 1985): 2, 14. Not for further reproduction.

Derek Freeman's letter (February 1985 *Anthropology Newsletter*, p. 2) complains about unfair treatment of his book,

Margaret Mead and Samoa, in what turned out to be a Special Section of *American Anthropologist* 85[4]:908-947). Some of his charges ought to be answered:

1. *The "Special Section" was unfairly critical, lacking a balanced spectrum of critical opinion.* Just as I did not seek people who would disagree with Freeman, so did I not comb the bushes for supporters to prop up an arbitrarily "even" argument. The fact is that I only commissioned one "review" per se, and that (Schwartz) was done explicitly on the premise of being "balanced." The Special Section was put together as a conglomeration of this review and commentary by other justifiably interested parties (see my Introduction to the section), some of which came to us unsolicited. *All* of these contributions (including those we rejected) were critical of Freeman's efforts in important ways. So my selection was never conscientiously "against" the degree of balance Freeman claims would have satisfied him. Even if I had wanted it, the possibility for equal pro/con commentary was never there in the first place.

2. *Denied the "fundamental scholarly right" of "simultaneous reply."* I think scholars subjected to extended criticism in print should always have the right to reply. I do not agree that the reply has to be "simultaneous." The *American Anthropologist* has two policies on this matter, as Freeman suspects. But they do not refer to the same things. One is that we publish book reviews and review articles as quickly as possible. When justified editorially in terms of intellectual content, length, possible importance to the discipline as a whole, etc. we publish rejoinders or rebuttal. The other policy pertains explicitly to criticism that originates as "commentary." We do not feel the same time constraints for publishing commentary that we do for book reviews. Subject to editorial justification, scholars whose works are criticized initially in commentary are invited to publish a "simultaneous reply." As a mixture, our Special Section could have been treated either way. I decided to do it the way we did to expedite publication. There was never any plan to leave Freeman out of the debate entirely. Since there is no point in soliciting a rejoinder to specifics that fail the test from first to final draft, Freeman's response was to be invited as soon as a clean and final copy of our section could be produced. Given all of the editorial changes initiated right up to press time, the first clean copy appeared as page proofs. It was mailed promptly in that form to Freeman.

3. *Deprived of the right of adequate reply because of inadequate space.* Keeping to the dictum that no one gets carte blanche

in our journal, taking into account the average length of replies to reviews and articles that we had published in the past, considering the fact that Freeman actually had the "first word" in the form of the book itself, given the real mechanical constraints of how much space we could afford to give up in the next available issue (June 1984), and knowing that a two-volume special issue of *Canberra Anthropology* on the Freeman/Mead controversy was in the mill—to which our readers could be referred for more detailed arguments—I told Freeman in October 1983 to "think about 12-15 pages" for his reply, suggesting that additional length had to be justified extensively. He refused to tell me how much space he actually needed and he had already made up his mind that he would be "replying at some length." So I drew a hard line at 15 pages. That forced the issue. In December, Freeman said he wanted at least 15,000 words. The Editor-in-Chief and I offered him the 15 pages plus another 1,000 words and the opportunity to justify more. He refused.

4. *We censored his complaints.* Normal editing can appear to be very subversive, especially if readers don't know what gets edited out and why but suspect that these things have been done to gain unfair advantage over an adversary. Freeman began his rejoinder to our Special Section with the following text:

> I am writing this rejoinder under duress. It is a basic principle of scientific controversy that one is entitled to answer succinctly all of the substantive charges that have been made against one. Yet, although the issues under discussion are of the most fundamental scientific importance, and despite my formal protests to the American Anthropological Association, I have been restricted to 15 pages of double-spaced typescript, or about one-tenth of the space given my critics.
> By this discriminatory policy, which is contrary to the spirit and practices of science, I have been deprived of the right of adequate reply, for, within the space to which I have been restricted, it is quite impossible for me to deal with all of the substantive points my critics have raised.
> Fortunately, I have had just right of reply to a range of virtually identical points accorded to me in other and more fair-minded journals, like *Pacific Studies* and *Canberra Anthropology* to which I shall in the duress imposed upon me by the *American Anthropologist* refer the readers of the present rejoinder.

The Editor-in-Chief and I had only one important question about these remarks: Where did they belong? Following the "meta-policy" that editorial policy should not be debated in the journal itself, I invited Freeman to submit his argument to the *Newsletter* instead and otherwise to make his complaints known to the AAA President. I also insisted that the *Canberra Anthropology* issue be cited in Freeman's published reply (AA 86[2]:400-405) so our readers would know where to find everything he wanted to say. I didn't see any need to reproduce that argument in all of its refractory detail (it turned out to be 91 printed pages!) in the AA. We made no effort to stifle Freeman's criticisms—only to put them in the proper forum.

Finally, a tidbit: (5) Freeman's comment about my being in favor of a "show of hands" to settle academic debates is wrong. My brief reference to such matters in the Introduction to the Special Section was a simple act of reporting, not a statement of advocacy.[1]

Freeman's book has received (and still is getting in commentary with "simultaneous replies") plenty of exposure. The debate over it may continue to shed new light on the old issue of credibility in anthropological writing and research. Certainly the idea of cracking the intellectual marrow of our ancestors to see what "we" are made of is essential to continued growth in the discipline. I am just not sure it needs to be done with a blunt instrument.

My Dealings with Holmes[2]

Derek Freeman

According to Holmes (1983a:930), I presented myself to him in 1966, in correspondence, as "a serious scholar of Samoan culture." In fact it was Holmes who first wrote to me, in February 1960, as one of a number of "polynesian specialists," seeking

---

[1]See Brady's note added October 22, 1988; above p. 42, n.1.

[2]From "Inductivism and the test of truth: a reply to Lowell D. Holmes and others," *Canberra Anthropology* 6 (1983): 101-182.

my opinions on field research in Polynesia. In my reply of 22 October 1960 I told Holmes that my advice to a novice would be:

> gain complete (as possible) fluency in the local lan-
> guage, making certain that you at least reach the point
> where you can understand the free converse of native
> speakers in complex social situations; e.g. for Samoa
> an argument about precedence by several *tulafale*, or
> talking chiefs at an inter-village *fono*; and see that your
> field research lasts for at least two years (continuously).

Although I did not know it then, these are requirements that Holmes himself has never met.

It is true, however, that I wrote to Holmes for Samoa in 1966 inquiring about his own researches and that this led to his sending me in 1967 a xerox copy of pp. 186-234 of his Ph.D. thesis, which, at that time, I had not previously seen. I was considerably interested to discover that there was in Holmes' thesis decisive evidence to show that Samoa is not as Mead has described it.

As Holmes would have it, during the course of his researches in 1954 he "systematically investigated and evaluated every word that Mead wrote in *Coming of Age in Samoa*." I am quite unable to believe him. Nowhere in his writings on Samoa of 1957 and 1958 (or, for that matter, thereafter) does Holmes even report correctly the nature of Mead's main conclusion of 1928. Further, it is clearly apparent from his thesis that he made no specific and systematic restudy of the problem that primarily concerned Mead in *Coming of Age in Samoa*, and, indeed, he explicitly states (1957a:186) that his research project of 1954 differed "in its orientation insofar as the life of adolescent girls was concerned."

In April 1967 Holmes had informed me that he doubted the "validity" of the "case material" on the lives of individual girls that Mead gives in an appendix to *Coming of Age in Samoa*, and that he did "not believe" that Samoan girls were "any more promiscuous than girls in America."

It was following this, in July 1967, after having listed ethnographic facts that Holmes himself had recorded . . . that I inquired of Holmes how, given these facts, he could possibly assert, as he had done in his Ph.D. thesis, that "the reliability of Mead's account is remarkably high."

Holmes replied that while he disagreed with Mead on "many points of interpretation," he believed that "the majority of her facts were correct." I would interpolate that if Mead's sweeping theoretical conclusion of 1928 is to be scientifically acceptable all of her facts must be correct and not just "the majority" of them.

Holmes then went on, *inter alia* (these being the exact words in his letter to me of 1 August 1967, which because of their significance for this whole controversy I have italicized throughout), to state:

> *I think it is quite true that Margaret finds pretty much what she wants to find. While I was quite critical of many of her ideas and observations I do not believe that a thesis is quite the place to expound them. I was forced by my faculty advisor to soften my criticisms.*

To which he added: "The only tragedy about Mead is that she still refuses to accept the idea that she might have been wrong on her first field trip."

Here, then, we have incontrovertible evidence of the kind of abject debasement of science to which inductivism can lead, as well as, given the pivotal significance for American cultural anthropology of Mead's conclusion of 1928, a scientific scandal of the first order.[1]

At that time, as now, as one who holds with Bronowski that . . . in science "the test of truth is the known factual evidence," and that "no glib expediency" can justify "the smallest self-deception" about this most crucial of values for any scientist, I was appalled at the implications of Holmes' extraordinary admission. Indeed, it was this admission by Holmes that, more than anything else, made it crystal clear to me in 1967 that both for the sake of Samoan studies and of the science of anthropology it was vitally important for me to continue with my investigation of the whole context of Mead's Samoan researches, and to publish my findings, when they were complete, whatever might be the obscurantism and opprobrium I would have to face from those for whom prophecy would have failed.

---

[1]Holmes' fullest response to this accusation is reprinted in his *Quest for the Real Samoa*, pp. 144-45. He denies that his mentor, Melville J. Herskovits, protected the "theoretical position of his teacher, Franz Boas. . . . I believe his recommendation was that I should be 'icily objective.' I will admit that in 1967 I might very well have written Derek Freeman that 'she still refuses to accept the idea that she might have been wrong on her first field trip.' My relationship with Margaret Mead was a very stormy one for several years after my restudy of her work. However, the statements I made about Mead 'finding pretty much what she started out to find' was not in any way meant to imply that she falsified her data."

In the event, the obscurantism and opprobrium on the part of some cultural and social anthropologists have indeed been intense, but my integrity, I would hope, remains intact, and I in no way regret behaving in this whole affair as I have behaved. But then, I am in complete agreement with the stirring words that Franz Boas, a hundred years ago, wrote in his diary when exploring Baffin Land: "All that man can do for humanity is to further the truth whether it be sweet or bitter."

Evaluations of *Margaret Mead and Samoa*

Bradd Shore

Editor's Note
One of the ironies of the controversy was that two antagonists, Bradd Shore and Derek Freeman, could quote the privately expressed high opinion of the other against their publicly expressed criticisms of their respective Samoa books. Freeman maintained that his praise of Shore's doctoral thesis pertained to a manuscript but not to the book that eventually issued from that manuscript (*Sala'ilua: A Samoan Mystery*). It had undergone, he claimed, a fundamental alteration in the transition to publication. Shore referreed *Margaret Mead and Samoa* for the Princeton University Press in a communication dated January 21, 1982, portion of which is printed here. He subsequently claimed that Freeman exaggerated the praise of his referee's report by construing the conventional flattery of that medium literally, and by failing to balance the praise with the amendments he proposed. The dispute between these scholars continues.

Referee's Report

Professor Freeman has written . . . an extraordinary work, likely to attract considerable attention in a number of professional circles, with a possible significant non-professional audience as well. It is, in most ways, a closely reasoned, meticulously researched and eloquently constructed assault on what Freeman believes (and I largely concur) to have been a series of theoretical and ethnographic errors in Mead's Samoan writings, resulting from an important ideological bias that has come to have a strong influence on much modern cultural analysis . . . . While Mead's errors have long been recognized by anthropologists, and while her reliability on Samoa is not held in especially high regard by a current generation of Polynesianists, no one has until this work taken the trouble to document the relation between her theoretical biases and her ethnographic errors with the rigor and surgical scrupulousness of Professor Freeman. . . . I can make an unqualified recommendation that the work be published, with or without the suggested modifications.

. . . Professor Freeman's grasp of the intricacies and details of Samoan culture and society *and* behavior is unsurpassed. He knows intimately of what he writes, and has taken enormous care to document the historical antecedents to modern practices and institutions.

. . . I might reiterate how much I admire this work. As an account of Samoa it is, while a bit skewed by design, stunningly accurate. As a critique of Mead and the culturalist position it is smart and subtle and potentially helpful. It is masterfully written, unburdened by jargon or formalisms. It is, in fact, a singularly compelling tale which was hard to put down.

•*New York Times*
January 31, 1983

People who work on Samoa know Margaret Mead was wrong, and Freeman's book shows that beyond doubt. But if she suppressed the dark elements, Freeman painted all those dark elements in his book. She generated a myth out of opposition to eugenics, he generated a distorted picture out of opposition to Margaret Mead. But on the whole his book is brilliant.

•*The London Observer*
February 6, 1983

An expert who has read Freeman's manuscript, Professor Bradd Shore . . . found it to be "a brilliant work in certain ways" but was somewhat troubled by "its obsessive documentation of violence." He added: "Freeman knows as much about Samoa as any non-Samoan in the world, and he has had a 40-year vendetta against Margaret Mead. He is a brilliant man, but one wonders about the dark quality, the intensity and the passion behind the book. It seems to go beyond any reasonable expectation for scholarly debate."

"I read Margaret Mead's book [after my fieldwork] and it was correct in some detail but it did not remind me of Samoa. It was too idyllic, it left out all the aggression and was obviously written with a theoretical bias. She was attempting to prove the theory of her teacher Franz Boas. . . . Given that bias, she did not see Samoa for what it was, a society rife with conflicts. She simplified, and picked half of what she saw. Yet even today I am amazed at how insightful Margaret Mead was about the things she did observe in so short a time."

•*Time Magazine*
February 14, 1983

Anthropologist Bradd Shore of Emory University in Atlanta also found much more than Mead did below the surface of Samoan life. Shore spent five years in Samoa and in 1982 published a book on Samoan social structure. "Samoans punish their children in ways that encourage pent-up aggression," Shore says. "Many beat children and infants to make them stop crying, and you watch the kids hold it in."
    . . . Shore calls Freeman "brilliant" and "surgical" in his attack on Mead, but says Freeman makes too much of ferocity and the cult of virginity among the Samoans. Says Shore: "Why people would believe Samoans could be a wimpy as Margaret Mead says they are, or as violent as Derek Freeman says they are, I just don't understand."
    Like many U.S. sailors who stopped at Samoa after World War II, Shore thinks the cult of virginity on the islands is overestimated. Freeman derides Mead for saying that free sex and an insistence on virginity coexist in Samoan society. . . . But, Shore insists, that is exactly the way Samoans conduct their lives. "They are both sexually free and sexually restrained. Virginity is prized as an ideal and widely violated."
    Shore cites one case where Freeman and Mead contradict each other, but are both right: Freeman in saying that children are raised to be competitive; Mead in saying they are raised to be noncompetitive by parents who express shame if their youngsters outstrip other children. Says Shore: "Samoans know perfectly well how to deal with this apparent contradiction, though it often puzzles outsiders."

•*New York Times,* reporting a Barnard College symposium, Margaret Mead and Anthropology: An Evaluation
April 9, 1983

"The publicity surrounding Derek Freeman's unhappy book about Mead and Samoa has taken on something of a life of its own, strangely unconnnected with anything approaching fact," said Dr. Bradd Shore . . . who spent years studying Samoan society.
"Indeed," he said, "in some corners one senses that peculiarly American joy at deconstructing yet another American hero, and in the process Margaret Mead and the enterprise of anthropology she helped to found have been distorted and trivialized. We who followed her to the field, and at times have found it necessary to criticize her, also stand on her shoulders and have the minimal obligation to acknowledge our debt . . . ."

•*Barnard Bulletin*, reporting a symposium Margaret Mead and Anthropology: An Evaluation
April 13, 1987

Professor Bradd Shore of Emory University . . . described Freeman's book as having the "appearance of a refutation when what he has [d]one is brought out some of the contradictions and complexities of Samoan society." He cited the attention the book has received as an example of "the peculiar American joy in deconstructing another American hero. We who follow her stand on her shoulders; and while we may criticize them, we must acknowledge our betters. I find it remarkable that he [Freeman] finds nothing of value in her work."
Shore later commented, "This conference may in some way balance out the attack on her personal reputation, on her public reputation, and, by extraction, on cultural anthropology."

•*American Anthropologist*
December, 1987

. . . Let me clarify . . . why I initially recommended that [*Margaret mead and Samoa*] be published. Even though anthropologists have long recognized the inadequacies of Mead's earliest fieldwork, her portrait of Samoan ethos and life has remained fixed in the popular mythology of the South Seas, confirming our need to believe in a place free of the stresses that beset our own lives . . . .

It is in light of the power of this popular mythology associated with Mead's treatment of Samoa that I found Freeman's popularly aimed account a very strong and useful corrective. This is to say that Freeman is surely far from simply wrong in his ethnographic observations, and, whatever his methodological sloppiness, one must give credit to the depth of his knowledge of Samoa. The powerful aggressive undercurrents in Samoan life are vividly brought to the surface in Freeman's account, and his observations of the treatment of children (perhaps the weakest link in my own work on Samoa) and the implications of the often harsh punishments children endure are important, if unpleasant, ethnographic facts with the most far-reaching implications.

Freeman has claimed that he revised his original manuscript in light of *all* my suggestions. This is far from accurate . . . and makes me wonder if he ever read my Princeton review (which I sent him) beyond its initial flattering introduction. I had hoped that his sense of scholarly fairness and devotion to the complexity of ethnographic facts would lead him to soften his . . . descriptions of both Mead's work and of Samoa, and that a really valuable and scholarly work would come of it. This has not happened.

From the Freeman—Kohn Correspondence

Freeman to Kohn, March 19, 1987

. . . Yesterday I received from a colleague in the USA a set of photocopies of the dust-jacket, the table of contents, and of pp. 117-120 of your *False Prophets: Fraud and Error in Science.*

In his recently published book, *Varieties of Realism* (Oxford: Basil Blackwell Ltd., 1986), Rom Harré, the distinguished philosopher of science of the University of Oxford, has identified the scientific community as one that "enforces standards of honesty, trustworthiness and good work."

As a Professor of Virology in the University of Tel Aviv you are a member of the scientific community identified by Rom

Harré just as am I as an Emeritus Professor of Anthropology in the Research School of Pacific Studies of the Institute of Advanced Studies of the Australian National University.

I am then writing to you . . . seeking information. And I do this in the hope and expectation that as a member of the scientific community you will give me honest and trustworthy answers to the questions that I shall put to you in this letter.

Let me begin by recording my astonishment at the terms in which you have discussed my book . . . for your discussion contains numerous statements that, to the best of my knowledge, are in outright error.

I am, therefore, writing to you to request that you should provide me with the sources, if they do exist, on which you have, as a practising scientist, based various of the statements contained in [your synopsis of the controversy].

(1) On p. 118 . . . you state that . . . I claim that Margaret Mead misrepresented Samoan culture "because of 'self-delusion'." Here you will note, the term "self-delusion" is in quotation marks. Will you please refer me to the page of *Margaret Mead and Samoa* from which you are quoting the term "self-delusion"?

(2) On p. 118 you also state that I say that Margaret Mead "got things 'astronomically wrong'." Once again the phrase "astronomically wrong" is between quotation marks. Will you please refer me to source from which you have taken this phrase?

(3) On p. 119 you state: "Freeman's criticism of Mead is based on a cryptic assumption that standards of ethnography have not changed since 1920." Would you please inform me of the substantive evidence on which you base this statement? Can you point to anywhere in my writings in which I make this assumption or make statements on which such an assumption might logically be based? In fact, I have repeatedly emphasized that my refutation of Mead's main conclusion of 1928 primarily depends on evidence that Mead herself provides.

(4) Mead's main conclusion of 1928, which was in answer to the question "Are the disturbances which vex our adolescents due to the nature of adolescence itself or to the civilization?" (which Boas had sent her to Samoa to investigate) was that "we cannot make any explanations" of the "disturbances" of adolescence other than "in terms of" the "social environment." Further, it is specifically with this conclusion that the refutation . . . is concerned. Yet nowhere do you mention these crucially important scientific facts. How do you justify, in scientific terms, this omission?

(5) On p. 119, you state of me that although Freeman "actually assembled the materials for his book in the 1960s he waited until after Mead's death to publish it." Will you please provide me with the sources on which you base this statement? In fact, as I note in the Preface to *Margaret Mead and Samoa* (p. xiv), the researches on which my refutation of Mead's conclusion of 1928 is based "were not completed until 1981, when I finally gained access to the archives of the High Court of American Samoa for the 1920s." How then do you justify, in scientific terms, your failure to quote this crucially important evidence . . ., and your resort to the demonstrably erroneous statement that Freeman "actually assembled the materials for his book in the 1960s" and "waited until after Mead's death to publish it"? Further, is not your resort to this erroneous information a clear case of the kind of "fraud and error in science" that in your book you are intent on exposing?

(6) The fact that you have repeatedly failed to cite from *Margaret Mead and Samoa* the evidence relevant to the issues you discuss causes me to wonder if you have really read this book. Rather you seem to have relied on journalistic reports. May I then put to you the question: "Did you, before writing the section entitled Was Margaret Mead Misled by the Samoan Girls? in your [book] subject [my study] to a serious and detailed reading?

(7) On p. 120 you state that "subjecting" Mead "to criticism in a historical perspective would seem to be unfair." Would you please explain to me what is meant by this statement? Is it your view that criticism should not occur in science? Any criticism of a conclusion reached in the past as was Mead's conclusion of 1928, can only be in "historical perspective." Would you please then inform me of your reasons for judging "criticism in a historical perspective" to be unfair?

(8) Your discussion of my book . . . occurs in a book entitled: *False Prophets: Fraud and Error in Science* and in a Chapter entitled Criticism or Slander?

(a) Can you identify any statement in *Margaret Mead and Samoa* that is an example of "fraud"?

(b) Can you identify any statement in *Margaret Mead and Samoa* that is in "error"?

(c) Can you identify any statement in *Margaret Mead and Samoa* that is an example of "libel"?

If your answers to questions (a), (b) and (c) above are in the negative, how do you justify, in scientific terms, your inclusion of a discussion of *Margaret Mead and Samoa* in a book entitled

False Prophets: Fraud and Error in Science and Medicine, and in a Chapter entitled Criticism or Slander?

(9) On p. 119 you cite a passage from a letter "of Mead's daughter Mary Catherine Bateson." Yet this letter is not cited, in accordance with standard scholarly practice in your references. Am I correct in supposing that this was a personal letter from Mary Catherine Bateson to you? If not, would you please let me know to whom this letter was written, and also mention its date?

I am addressing this letter to you in the expectation that as a member of the scientific community you will provide me with honest and trustworthy answers.

Kohn to Freeman, May 1, 1987

. . . I am very sorry that my account of the Margaret Mead controversy has aroused your strong disapproval, I had meant to give an evenhanded picture, but on considering the section on Margaret Mead in my book in the light of your objections, I have to express my regret that perhaps the standards of scholarship which I maintain in my professional scientific publications were indeed not always applied here. But first let me clear up what appears to a misapprehension.

Your question No. 8 suggests that you are under the impression that the Margaret Mead controversy was included in my book . . . because your book . . . exemplifies one or other of these things. This is, of course, not the case. I was very interested in the case of Margaret Mead herself, as an example or "error in Science," what I refer to in my preface as "erroneous research . . . often unintentional and based on good faith," and the misgivings that have arisen about her work and its conclusions not only in your book, but of other anthropologists as well, that the story is included. In the final organization of my material I was undecided for some time in which chapter to place the Mead's story and I eventually placed it in a chapter on Criticism, owing to the strength and importance of the controversy which your book and statements by other anthropologists have engendered. In addition, in this chapter I included a number of varied cases which were very different in their nature, but which were pooled together because they all involved strong criticism and controversy. In the case of one of them the "controlled drinking" controversy the criticism verged on slander, whence the title of the chapter. In the light of your letter I see that this chapter heading might be interpreted as raising the question as to whether your criticism, too, was slanderous—a possibility which had not occurred to me at all. In any future editions I propose to rename the chapter Critics and Challengers and to reword the introductory paragraph.

With regard to your other questions:

(1), (2) and (6). It is true that I have taken certain expressions from reviews of your book and interviews. The word "self-delusion" was quoted from an article of John Dunn (*Time*, Feb 14, 1983). I used this word because it expressed briefly and succinctly what would have taken far longer to exemplify had I quoted directly from your book (for instance the passage starting p. 283, last paragraph and continuing through 2nd paragraph p. 284). I think the word self-delusion summed up fairly well the matter. The quotation marks should indeed be omitted. Also "astronomically wrong" (which is quoted from an interview with you) is similar in spirit to "mind boggling contradiction" (p. 289) though if you wish the latter will be substituted in future printings.

(3) This sentence was based on a statement of Ward Goodenough (*Science* 220 [1983]:906) and on E. Marshall (*Science* 219 [1983]:1044) quoting you: "What is needed . . . is more attention to human biology, cooperation between disciplines, and far more sophisticated methods for analyzing the data."

(4) I have written a book about fraud and error over the whole spectrum of the natural sciences and medicine, not a history of anthropology. The "crucially important scientific facts" you mention would indeed be important for the latter, but are not, in my view, of essential relevance for the former where considerable compression and condensation of material has been necessitated.

(5) Here indeed I take responsibility for an error of omission. I had not given your preface close attention to its end. Future printings or editions of my book will stress the fact that you finally gained access to the Samoan archives only in 1981. On this score I express my sincere apologies.

(6) I have indeed used your book (see (1), (2) and (6)).

(7) As I wrote at the beginning, I feel my desire to give an even-handed account has in fact resulted in too strong a defence of Margaret Mead. I propose to omit the last paragraph of the section on Mead, in future printings.

(9) The letter of Mary Catherine Bateson (9 July 1985) was indeed addressed to me. I sent her a draft of the story dealing with her mother and thought it proper to include some of her re-

marks in the book. The context of the sentence I quoted was as follows: ". . . Mead's Samoan work is valuable but flawed because of the methodological and theoretical ideas available in the period. Methodologically it was a pioneering work, but as you say times have changed. The tragedy is that Freeman's critique suffers, after 50 years of progress in the discipline, from many of the same theoretical and methodological weaknesses which more understandably characterized hers."

While I was in London, I learned that the second printing of my book has already gone to press and I was not given any opportunity for corrections. However, I shall make sure that any future printing (or edition) includes the changes indicated above.

Freeman to Kohn, June 25, 1987

. . . In your letter of 1st May, 1987 you state that in the section of *False Prophets* entitled Was Margaret Mead Misled by the Samoan Girls? you "meant to give an even-handed picture." I can only regard this self-exculpatory statement as disingenuous in the extreme, for an objective scrutiny of pp. 117-120 of *False Prophets* reveals bias of a most pronounced kind.

Thus, from the beginning to the end of this section Margaret Mead is portrayed in complimentary and favorable terms as a "pioneer" in "anthropological studies," and the author of a "famous book" . . . who "enjoyed tremendous authority among fellow anthropologists"; as the holder of a post at the American Museum of Natural History; as the founder and benefactor of the Institute of Inter-Cultural Studies; as one who "through the inspiring role she played" became "a national institution" in the USA, and whose "image" has *not* been "tarnished" by "criticism."

No reader of this assessment could possibly suppose that Dr. Margaret Mead was one of those engaging in the "misconduct in science" with which . . . your book *False Prophets* is concerned. In marked contrast, I am referred to merely as a "Professor Emeritus of Anthropology from Canberra."

. . . Charge No. 3. In your letter to me of 1st May, 1987 you state that Margaret Mead's daughter, Mary Catherine Bateson, in her letter to you of 9th July, 1985 wrote as follows: "The tragedy is that Freeman's critique suffers, after 50 years of progress in the discipline, from many of the same theoretical and methodological weaknesses which more understandably characterized hers" (i.e. Mead's).

On p. 119 of *False Prophets* you publish from, so you say, a letter of Mary Catherine Bateson's actual words: "The tragedy is that Freeman's critique is far more ideological and tendentious than the work he criticizes."

May I now draw your attention to the fact that whereas the first six words of the sentence you attribute to Mary Catherine Bateson on p. 119 of *False Prophets* are the same as those you report in the sentence I have already quoted from Bateson's letter to you of 9th July, 1985, the sentence you have published as being Bateson's is, from its seventh word onward, markedly different from the sentence in Bateson's letter to you of 9th July, 1985, as transcribed in your letter to me of 1st May, 1987. How do you account for this marked difference?

I have already noted your propensity for attributing to others, within quotation marks, words that are *not* their own. Can it be then that on p. 119 of *False Prophets* the words "far more ideological and tendentious than the work he criticizes" are, in fact, your own rendering of the more convoluted words actually used by Bateson in her letter to you of 9th July, 1985? If this is the case, how can you possibly justify, in a book devoted to the exposure of error in science, your action in attributing to Mary Catherine Bateson words that are not her own? And, if it is not the case that you have attributed to Mary Catherine Bateson words that are in fact yours, in what other way can you account for the discrepancy to which I have drawn your attention?

. . . Charge No. 5: In the final paragraph on p. 119 of *False Prophets* there occurs, in your continuing attack on me and my researches, another example of your unscholarly and unscientific methods. "Freeman's criticism of Mead," you state, "is based on a cryptic assumption that standards of ethnography have not changed since 1920."

Then, writing as a virologist, with no trustworthy knowledge of what it is you are discussing, you proceed, without adducing a whit of evidence to pontificate in a most unscholarly and unscientific way about the history of ethnographic method, asserting, quite erroneously, that it was not until a decade after Mead's Samoan researches (i.e , not until the mid 1930s) that "the concept of good ethnography" involved such things as "learning the local language," "participating in local events," and "studying the social system in its actual practice." Having thus completely misinformed your readers, while assuring them that you are conveying to them the facts, you then feelingly assert: "One surely cannot blame Mead for not having employed standards that developed after her study in Samoa."

Before documenting that what you claim to be facts, are, in reality, outright errors, let me comment briefly on your unwarranted innuendo that I have sought to "blame" Mead. As I have noted . . . the crucial question with which I am concerned in *Margaret Mead and Samoa* is "whether or not Margaret Mead drew an unscientific conclusion from her Samoan researches," and, as I have clearly stated, in investigating this question "I am quite uninterested in attributing blame in any way whatsoever."

I now turn to the erroneous account that you give in *False Prophets* of the development of ethnographic method.

In actual fact, as early as 1913, in a volume published in Washington, D.C., Dr. W. H. R. Rivers, who had participated in the Cambridge anthropological expedition to the Torres Straits in 1898-1899, described intensive ethnographic field research in the following terms (1913:6):

> A typical piece of intensive work is one in which the worker lives for a year or more among a community of perhaps four or five hundred people and studies every detail of their life and culture; in which he comes to know ever member of the community personally; in which he is not content with generalized information, but studies every feature of life and custom in concrete detail and by means of the vernacular language.

You will observe that all of the features of "the concept of good ethnography" which you claim were not realized until the mid 1930s are clearly identified in Dr. Rivers' account of 1913.

In actual fact, intensive ethnographic field research of the kind described by Rivers in 1913 was brilliantly and most effectively realized by Dr. Bronislaw Malinowski in the Trobriand Islands during the years 1915 to 1918. Thus, in his Preface to Malinowski's famous account of his researches in the Trobriand Islands, *Argonauts of the Western Pacific* (1922:vii) Sir James Fraser wrote:

> Dr. Malinowski lived as a native among natives for many months together, watching them daily at work and at play, conversing with them in their own tongue and deriving all his information from the surest of sources— personal observation and statements made to him directly by the natives in their own language without the intervention of an interpreter.

And this is followed in *Argonauts of the Western Pacific,* by detailed accounts by Malinowski himself of his methods of intensive ethnographic field research.

Argonauts of the Western Pacific was published in London and New York in 1922, and reviewed, early in 1923, in the *American Anthropologist* by E. W. Gifford.

Gifford began his review (1923:101) by describing *Argonauts of the Western Pacific* as "perhaps one of the most remarkable contributions to the science of anthropology." He then went on, however, to make the "stricture" that Malinowski's dwelling "frequently and at great length on ethnographic method" was likely to be regarded as "pedantry" by professional anthropologists, for the "matters of method" dealt with by Malinowski were "obvious to every properly trained ethnologist."

In other words, the ethnographic methods stated by you in *False Prophets* not to have been practised until the mid 1930s were, in fact, practised by Malinoswki in the Trobriand Islands during the years 1915-1918, and, as Gifford confirms, had become common knowledge among professional anthropologists in the USA by the beginning of 1923.

As we know from Ruth Benedict's diary . . . it was not until March, 1923 that Margaret Mead decided to become an anthropologist, and not until later that year that she began her graduate training at Columbia University under Franz Boas. During this training she certainly heard of the already celebrated field research of Malinowski. Indeed, in a letter dated 14th July, 1925, that Boas wrote to Mead on the eve of her departure for Samoa he commended to her a paper by Malinowski "on the behavior of individuals in the family in New Guinea."

Margaret Mead was thus, in historical terms, fully in a position to follow, during her investigations in Samoa, the methods of intensive ethnographic field research, the effectiveness of which had been fully demonstrated by Malinowski, and the importance of which was common knowledge among American anthropologists by the beginning of 1923 over two years before Mead left for Samoa.

In the event, as I document in my book (p. 66), Mead, out of considerations of personal comfort, chose not to live with a Samoan family, but instead with the family of a chief pharmacist's mate of the U.S. Navy, who was the local representative of the then U.S. Naval Government of American Samoa. Further, she conducted her researches into the behavior of Samoan adolescent girls with a very far from perfect command of the Samoan language, and completed these researches in about four months;

they began in mid-November, 1925, and as she noted in a letter, had been "almost completed" by 7th March, 1926.

Mead's researches in Samoa, during 1925-1926 were thus conducted by methods that fell far short of those of the intensive ethnographic field research that had been proved so effective by Malinowski in the Trobriand Islands about a decade previously.

While, as I have already noted, I have no interest whatsoever in this whole matter in attributing blame, it is certainly both rationally and scientifically justifiable to analyze the anthropological consequences of the methods that Mead actually employed. Furthermore, in this analysis, I have not dealt with Mead's Samoan researches, as you mistakenly claim, in terms of "standards that developed after her study in Samoa," for in fact, they have been developed some years before her researches in Samoa began. Once again, in making your false claim, you are revealed as both biased and unscientific.

Response to Derek Freeman

Jeannette Mageo

Editor's Note

Jeannette Mageo wrote Derek Freeman seeking his comments on the draft of "Mālosi: A Psychological Exploration of Mead's and Freeman's Work" (see Chapter 1). Freeman took strong exception to Mageo's construction of his use of ethological concepts for the interpretation of Samoan aggression. He maintained that Mageo's study, as it related to himself, was "unscholarly in the extreme," exhibited "extreme bias," and constituted an "intellectual defamation" because she had depicted him as an "extreme biological determinist." Mageo made some changes in her draft to satisfy Freeman's objections about his relation to Konrad Lorenz in particular, but maintained that her interpretation was warranted by what Freeman had written.

Freeman raised the question of professional ethics when he wrote that if Mageo did not make the changes he required, he would consider her article to be "disinformation" and "I would have no course but to complain to the Ethics committee of the American Anthropological Association and to record the situation in an open letter to *Anthropology Newsletter,* or some other anthropological journal." Mageo's reply maintains that his accusation of her scholarship was ill-considered. Freeman was satisfied with Mageo's corrections and did not pursue his threat to take the matter to the Ethics Committee of the American Anthropological Association. Freeman's letter is dated October 3, 1987. Mageo responded on October 22. The letter is abbreviated by about half.

Thank you for your letter of October 3 concerning my paper . . . I found some of your comments interesting and I am sure my paper will be better for having written you. I particularly appreciated your enclosing articles which you felt might be of assistance. I have considered all your comments at length and have decided to address them in my article, despite the fact that the article has already been type-set and the changes I have made will be expensive for my publisher. However, the fact that I have felt it necessary to address your remarks, does not mean that I concur with them.

As I disagree with you about some of the major points you raise in your letter, I have not been able to concede very much of what you ask. Therefore, as you consider this a matter that might concern the Ethics Committee of the American Anthropological Association, I have decided to send our correspondence, as well as the original and revised versions of my article, to them for further consideration. I am positive that we both will appreciate the scrutiny of the Ethics Committee in this matter. However, should you have any reasonable objection to my course of action please send me a written explanation prior to November 30.[1] I shall, however, take the present opportunity to outline precisely how our opinions diverge and to share with you my distress at the tack you take in the letter as a whole. Per your example, I regard this as an "open letter."

You protest that I unjustly portray you as a biological determinist. This is your term not mine, and it is far from the case as I clearly state that you also link Samoan aggression with the hierarchical nature of Samoan society. What I am saying is that your argument in *Margaret Mead and Samoa,* draws an equation between aggression and biology. First you charge Mead with neglecting biology for culture. To substantiate this charge you show that she failed to report sexual repression, evidence of social maladjustment such as suicide, and aggression. One can

---

[1]Mageo dispatched these materials to the Ethics Committee, whose Chair happened to be Mary Catherine Bateson. The matter lapsed because Freeman did not pursue it.

hardly argue that either sexual repression or social maladjustment are genetic problems or due to phylogenetically given impulses. Thus one is left to conclude that you see aggression as the biological element Mead ignored. If you do not see aggression as biological, then you can hardly accuse Mead of neglecting biology when she ignores aggression, nor of being a cultural determinist.

. . . You state that I falsely connect your position to that of Lorenz. You declare Lorenz to be a biological determinist and announce that, ipso facto, I am calling you a biological determinist. However, what I believe you have in common with Lorenz is an ethological orientation towards human aggression. Your actual characterization of aggression in *Margaret Mead and Samoa* is that culture imposes "conventional behavior" over "highly emotional and impulsive behavior that is animal-like in its ferocity" (p. 301). This depiction of aggression does not imply that the symbol systems in which culture consists are *a source* of aggressive behavior. On the contrary, it suggests that, inasmuch as we are aggressive we are animal-like.

You call yourself an interactionist. However, as far as I can decipher the interaction to which you refer is between biological factors and those social factors which are present at a pre-cultural level, such as dominance hierarchies. Thus you, like Lorenz, see a clear analogue between the genetic patterning of animals and the cultural patterning of human beings.

My concern in the article is your stance on aggression in your recent book, not in general. But as you have scolded me for not mentioning your 1971 article, let me do so here. In "Aggression: Instinct or Symptom" you give numerous examples of Samoan behavior which you believe directly parallels aggression in animals. You mention two experimental studies of human behavior, but in both cases they exemplify similar findings in work with animals. You state that aggression is affected by social factors, such as crowding and learning, but you base that conclusion on Southwick's work with the rhesus monkey and J. P. Scott's experiments with laboratory mice.

In the field of psychology this parallel with animal behavior has been overused for decades. What those who work with our animal brethren often fail to recognize is that new abilities emerge at the human level. . . . Human beings have language and construct symbol systems—such as cultures—and because of this fact our behavior does not necessarily resemble that of other species. Needless to say, we have something to learn from animal studies. I believe, however, that an interactionist model should take human culture into account, and culture is not reducible to those social behaviors we share with our evolutionary predecessors.

Because of my reading of *Margaret Mead and Samoa* you denounce my "polemical and political aims." Evidently you imagine that my polemics support my politics. What, pray tell, might these political aims be? One presumes you mean that I am guilty of the bias in favor of Mead, of which you accuse all your critics, and that I reject your views on Samoan culture and personality out of hand. Your accusation comes, however, in face of the very real criticism of Mead that underlies the first third of my article. I, like yourself, suggest that Mead presents us with a distorted view of Samoa. It is only as to the nature of her bias that we disagree.

In the mid-section of my paper I argue that you are indeed right to suggest that Mead underplays Samoan aggression in *Coming of Age*. In regards to this issue I consider the criticism of your work lodged by Eleanor Leacock who was . . . the American anthropologist most seriously taken up with proving the falsity of your claims about Samoan culture and personality. Leacock believed that Samoan violence towards children is new, and that the aggression you have found in Samoa is the product of modernization. I, however, disagree with Leacock and suggest that, although times have indeed changed in such a manner as to exacerbate parental violence, it is likely that the physical censure of children is a practice of long duration. I further support your claim that Samoan child-rearing practices produce aggression in adults, although my ideas about the psychological mechanism involved differ from yours.

Moreover, my final conclusion is that Mead did not find a society lacking aggression and in this sense failed to produce what you have called a "negative instance," although as to precisely why Mead was looking for a society which lacked aggression you and I disagree. How such arguments could support "political aims," which are somehow vindictively aimed against your "ineluctable truths," I cannot image.

Nonetheless, you insist that my interpretation of your work amounts to nothing less than "intellectual defamation" and hasten to add that I am an "ideologue," "unscholarly in the extreme," "misinformed," not to mention "puerile," and a veritable disgrace to my institution. In the same breath you most curiously convert my criticism of American anthropology's treatment of you into a criticism of you. You grumble that I identify you as a "bad guy" and then provide you with the trappings of a "bad guy" by depicting you as a biological determinist. Above I summarize my position on your relation to biology, but your indictment that I have attempted to prove that you are a "bad guy" astounds me. What I in fact say in the paragraph you cite is as follows:

> The tendency in American anthropology has been to divide the two sides of this controversy into the good guy (namely Mead) and the bad guy (namely Freeman) and to dismiss the bad guy. Goodness knows Freeman, in his manner of writing, gave us ample excuse. . . . However, now that the dust has settled, it is time to admit that this manœuver is too easy. In the analysis of culture the issue is how to combine a cacophony of information into a harmonious perspective, in which apparently contradictory elements make a common sense.

In short I am lodging a gentle reproach against those who, in the heat and dust of controversy, have dismissed your work. However, I must admit that I have a fresh empathy for their feelings—if not their stance on Samoa—in light of your tendency to call names. Surely the business of scholarship is the discussion of ideas, not mud-slinging. Even if, for the sake of argument, one was to ascribe to your belief that politesse is merely a "conventional behavior" which covers impulses that are "animal-like in their ferocity," surely one should resist such impulses and honor a scholarly decorum.

Not content with name calling, you go on to announce that you have sent your letter to my chairperson. You warn that you may drag me before the Ethics Committee of the American Anthropological Association. Surely you do not mean to intimidate scholarly criticism of your work. Your book itself is a testament to the importance of critical reviews within anthropology. Surely then you believe as I do, that scholarly debate must be encouraged rather than suppressed. I have no doubt that the Ethics Committee believes in such encouragement. But if in generosity I must assume that in your heart of hearts you mean to advocate debate, in all candor I must admit that your manner could easily lead one to believe that you brook no criticism.

I know sir that, in regards to your recent book, you have been treated by American anthropology more as a persecutor than as a scholar. Personally I value much of what you have to say about Samoa and intend to use your data in my future work on the subject, wishing only that there was more of it available. But my appreciation of your often apposite observations does not mean that

I always assent to your interpretations. Surely there is room for opposing views. But as far as I can determine you honor none.

You ask in your last paragraph how long I think it will take American anthropologists to recognize the "ineluctable truths" of which you write. As long as one regards one's own truths, whatever they are, as ineluctable and, therefore, not subject to criticism, one inspires suspicion. The very phrase sounds Messianic and not the words of a humble scholar. My answer to your query, sir, is that it depends upon no one but yourself. When you affect a manner which communicates to all your willingness to listen, not merely the desire to speak, others will also listen to you. With every good wish that the merit of your work on Samoa will someday be honored with the recognition that it deserves.

Truth Management in the Sciences[1]

Hiram Caton

Deprive the average man of his vital lie, and you've robbed him of happiness as well.
    Henrik Ibsen

By truth management I mean deception practiced by scientists who use authoritative institutions to perpetrate a distinct type of fraud upon some public. The fraud consists in representing a specific and contingent interpretation of evidence as if it were unalloyed truth enjoying the unanimous endorsement of the relevant cadre of scientists. Truth management, then, is wanton abuse of scientific authority.

Some may be tempted to read the truth management concept as a supposed conspiracy of experts. This presents a certain difficulty in communication since we all know that conspiracies, collusions, and machinations do not exist. These sordid activities are products of the febrile imaginations of literary persons such as C. P. Snow, who opened his Godkin Lectures at Harvard University by declaring that "one of the most bizarre

---

[1]Reprinted with permission from _Search_ 19 (1988), no. 5/6, 242-244.

features of any advanced industrial society in our time is that the cardinal choices have to be made by a handful of men: in secret."

As a historian I do not share Lord Snow's perception of this situation as bizarre; to me it seems ordinary. Indeed, because collusion is so ordinary—almost, one might say, a constant of organisational dynamics—it will open no window on the special phenomenon of truth management. It is more promising, I believe, to follow the lead of recent studies of self-deception, which suggest that this curious manœuvre lies deep in Homo sapiens' evolved psychology, and that it has several distinct adaptive functions. In this way we may think of truth management as the "vital lie," to borrow Ibsen's phrase, fostered in specific institutional circumstances.

Saintly Science

To indicate that scientists are subject to gross self-deception concerning matters with which they are thoroughly familiar, let us examine the standard response to the phenomenon of fraud in science. Fraud—the fabrication or manipulation of evidence—crosses the common self-image of scientists in the most severe manner. This image pictures the scientist as a sort of saint of truth. He or she is an impartial critic, scrupulously reports experimental findings, carefully weighs evidence, readily acknowledges error, and openly communicates with colleagues. Unlike lesser mortals, the scientist is not motivated by the ordinary forms of avidity, but is led to the secrets of nature by the gentle hand of curiosity. As for larger purposes of life, the scientist dedicates his or her labours to the amelioration of the human condition.

This image is promulgated through countless channels, including the heroic poetry of science idolatry. Let us sample it. The respected Oxford philosopher of science, Rom Harré, has written:

> In my view science is not just an epistemological but also a moral achievement . . . the scientific community exhibits a model or ideal of rational co-operation set within a strict moral order, the whole having no parallel in any other human activity. . . . [it] enforces standards of honesty, trustworthiness and good work against which the moral quality of say Christian civilisation stands condemned.

I call this poetry to draw attention to the edifying tone which transports the author's imagination to a vision of moral grandeur. He thrills to the discovery of an ethic so pure that it puts the ethical performance of a world religion to shame. The poet experiences his ecstasy illuminated by a vision of the world disenchanted by science, yet redeemed by science; for if we have lost religion, we have gained a new ethic superior to the old.

Returning to earth, I observe that this eulogy to honesty is a lie if we, unkindly, read it as the factual description it purports to be. Science, as sociologists know and philosophers of science should know, is just another profession whose organisation, social stratification, career expectations, and justifying mythology can be understood without the supposition of a moral order uniquely its own or the supposition that the pursuit of science builds character. Indeed, scientists, despite the ethic of truthfulness, may be more subject to self-deception than other professionals because reputation counts heavily toward success in status competition. Reputation lives in opinion; and often reputation for achievement substitutes for the thing. Reputation may be built up or diminished by bravado, gossip, and other dubious means. Reflecting on the capriciousness of academic status assignment, Donald Perry hit upon a thought in marked contrast to Harré's eulogy:

> Now I would like to challenge a simplistic value—that it is wrong to use unscrupulous means to advance one's career in biology. Before you steadfastly answer yes, look closely at some role models of the profession. . . . why should less distinguished scientists be honest when unscrupulous behaviour is rewarded with celebrated scientific recognition? Science advances by finding answers to questions about nature. Whether or not a scientist is scrupulous has no bearing at all on scientific discoveries.

Perry's thought may be enlarged by observing the institutional science is adaptable to many values. Research may be directed toward ends trivial or sublime. It may be made to serve profit, mass annihilation, entertainment, and social control. There is no discernable moral order implicit in applications of science.

Although these observations are commonplaces, the response of scientists to the fraud phenomenon invoked the image of saintly science in its most unreflective form. When the first damaging cases came to light about fifteen years ago, science leaders formulated a line that soon became orthodox. The line asserts that fraud is a rare phenomenon. It is said that cheating offends the scientist's credo of complete and veracious disclosure. Those skeptical of the restraining power of conscience in the era of Watergate are assured that the credo is enforced by two strong sanctions. One is that fraud is invariably detected; the other is that disgrace is sure to follow. With fraud thus verbally confined to a minute number, there remained only to find a suitable explanation of the atypical event. The explanation proposed is that fraud is the irrational act of a disturbed mind.

The utility of the psychiatric explanation in helping to extricate scientists from tight spots may be seen in the case of Eugene Braunwald, whose laboratory at the Harvard Medical School was the scene of the most extensive fraud uncovered to date. Braunwald declared:

> I believe that many instances of scientific fraud represent a form of unconscious self-destructive behaviour which may have aggressive components directed against the perpetrator's supervisors, colleagues and institutions; indeed, it mocks science as a whole.

Braunwald did not substantiate his belief by citing clinical evidence. As a medical scientist he presumably knows that psychiatric explanations made in the absence of clinical examination are of no value. Nevertheless, Braunwald's diagnosis reveals something about his own motives. Observe that he portrays himself, Harvard, and science itself as victims. In this way the scientist who presided over the worst fraud uncovered hitherto deflects culpability by attributing it to a chance, uncontrollable event—the subordinate John Darsee's neurosis. This explanation directs attention way from the point at issue, Braunwald's failure adequately to supervise his laboratory.

The psychiatric explanation was snatched from thin air in the early days of scandal. It continues to be advanced but now indirect evidence is offered. In his highly acclaimed study, *False Prophets: Fraud and Error in Science and Medicine,* virologist Alexander Kohn cited some opinions of L. S. Kubie, a psychiatrist who specialized in scientist clients. Kubie found that his patients often suffered from unresolved neurotic anxieties which in two cases involved tampering with evidence. This information, nearly three decades old when Kohn's book appeared, is his sole evidence for the neurosis hypothesis. It suggests that some scientists are driven by neurosis to cheat, but furnishes no information on whether persons till now detected in cheating were neurotic.

Kohn's other evidence indicates that this is not the case. He reports that "[i]n practically every conversation I have had on this subject with heads of laboratories, professors and teachers, they could report attempted cases of falsification or cheating which they had exposed early enough to get rid of the offending individual and bar his access to the halls of science." Winnowing is nevertheless not an effective safeguard according to the *New Scientist* survey Kohn cites. The 1976 survey found that 194 respondents (N=201) reported knowledge of cheating. One fifth of these cases were reported as having been detected, but only ten percent of offenders were punished by dismissal. He also reports a survey of 1309 scientists, of whom 25 percent complained of having their ideas stolen or inadequately acknowledged. One may conclude from Kohn's own data that cheating is the ordinary practice of ordinary people.

Such evidence concerning the prevalence of fraud, being largely anecdotal, is of limited value. More significant indicators perhaps are where fraud is occurring and how it occurs.

•Fraud is not being detected in institutions of low repute, but in the laboratories of eminent scientists holding appointments at prestige institutions.

•Evidence does not support the view that the detection of fraud is inevitable. Hundreds of papers reporting fabricated research have slipped through the main line of defense, peer review, despite tell-tale inconsistencies, some quite gross. Journal readers do not detect fraud either. Indeed, even the co-authors of articles reporting faked data did not detect it in the articles they sign. In the Harvard case, there were 100 publications involving 47 co-authors, yet none detected the cheating. Who did? A lab technician.

Despite all this, Daniel E. Koshland, Jr., editor of *Science*, recently stated that "we must recognize that 99.9999 percent of [scientific papers] are accurate and truthful."

This confident assertion exemplifies the ease with which scientists fabricate data in good conscience. The impressive certainty to four decimal places handily exceeds the precision possible in social measurement. Even if this figment were a real magnitude, it could not be obtained in the present case because the data requisite for a quantitative estimate of the incidence of fraud have not been collected. Koshland's intoxicated certainty registers the will to believe in the integrity of science regardless of evidence.

If the editor of *Science* furnished an example of deception in the course of denying that scientists deceive, Alexander Kohn has adduced a singular case of misconduct which strongly suggests that it is pandemic. It is the case of Alexander Kohn himself.

Kohn's Misconduct

In the Preface of the new edition of *False Prophets* Kohn states that he has withdrawn a chapter on the Samoa controversy published in the first edition because Derek Freeman presented evidence that certain facts and judgments contained in it are incorrect.

This brief acknowledgement scarcely hints at what actually transpired. In Kohn's 1500 word account of the controversy, Freeman detected about twenty errors, most of which tended to diminish Freeman's scholarship and reputation. So many errors bespeak culpable failure to observe scholarly standards. But in addition, Kohn groomed his evidence by altering a quotation to make it a substantially sharper jab at Freeman than the original had been.

Kohn stated in response to Freeman's first, exploratory letter that he had intended, and believed that he wrote, an "even-handed" account of the Samoa controversy. Freeman's second letter was a blistering indictment of Kohn's integrity, based on a detailed demonstration of the bias of Kohn's account and on an enumeration of errors. Kohn offered no defense in response to this letter. He simply agreed to withdraw the chapter.

Kohn's investigation of the Samoa controversy was superficial in the sense that undergraduate essays are superficial. He was unaware that his "balanced" account merely reproduced the line taken by Margaret Mead's defenders. The altered quotation seems damning, as Freeman showed with devastating effect. Yet when the evidence is closely considered, one is inclined to conclude that Kohn only practiced the usual improvement of data, free of malicious intent.

This case is singular in that it poses the question Kohn himself raises in the new concluding chapter of his book, Where does it end? If a respected virologist in a highly acclaimed book professing to expose the roots of cheating is caught cheating himself, who among the saints of truth is without sin?

The answer of course is "none" or "few." Either way, the Kohn case suggests that the prevailing approach to the cheating phenomenon may be fundamentally mistaken. The prevailing approach focuses on the worst case, fraud, with glances at other forms of cheating. It declares fraud to be rare, and analyses the problem as an ethical deficit to be remedied by the application of new safeguards and renewed exhortation.

The effect of this approach is to scapegoat a few hapless individuals. Their punishment creates the impression that science is putting its house in order. This effect has already become clear in the pattern of institutional response to fraud: the low ranking postdoc who faked the data is ruined, while the eminent supervisor is merely admonished ; or, as seems to be the latest fashion, the supervisor is actually praised by the review board for his part in bringing the postdoc to book. This adaptive strategy will come as no surprize to Sir Fred Hoyle, who states that "fraud, provided it is directed to what is considered a worthy cause, is never seriously punished."

These remarks have I hope furnished a critical framework for the self-image of scientists as heros of truth. Their feeling of moral excellence stems no doubt in part from the euphoria of success in the rigours of professional competition. Sportsmen and businessmen boost their self-esteem for similar reasons. The valorization of this delusion serves a multitude of public relations functions tending to support the public credibility of science. In this it is like the self-images of other professions, which function as professional conscience and define the profession's norms relative to its public. While professional norms are subjectively and sociologically significant, they must not be mistaken for actual behaviour.

. . . Another bias factor in peer review is the editor. The editor of the *American Anthropologist,* H. Russell Bernard, expressed what everyone knows when he declared: "It is really quite simple for me as editor to guarantee that an article will be killed by referees. All I need to do is to select referees I know can be trusted to clobber a particular manuscript." Bernard uses a randomized reviewer selection procedure to prevent this happening.

It might seem that a review process made porous by the chance effects of inattention, ignorance, bias, and favoritism, would be a poor tool for imposing orthodoxy. This is does not appear to be the case. Editors as well as students of peer review agree that whatever else they do, referees bring to bear a strongly stereotyped set of requirements. Among them are: proper grooming (the right mix of co-authors, the right mix of citations, the best way to present data); the right sort of conclusion (one that confirms average expectations); a show of originality strictly confined within current beliefs.

Many editors have independently observed that its effect is to level to the average. Their thought was voiced by medical journal editor David F. Horrobin when he said that "the referee system as it is currently constituted is a disaster. What is most disastrous is its built-in bias against highly innovative work." Editor estimates are confirmed by the testimony of many creative scientists. Among them are Thomas Gold, who in a recent reflection on his career had this to say:

> I have had to face a large amount of opposition in virtually every case in which I have produced anything of novelty. In 1948 when we proposed the steady state theory of cosmology, Bondi, Hoyle and I found all the official astronomers extremely hostile. My theory of hearing was totally ignored and now 40 years later, when it has been found to be correct, the original paper on the subject is mostly forgotten. In the meantime someone who espoused the opposing and incorrect theory received a Nobel Prize for it.

Astrophysicist R.A. Lyttleton diagnoses the problem as a mass of bad coin driving out the good. "Science journals today abound," he says, "with elaborate theories of alleged phenomena quite inadequately established other than by often intemperate asservation, and before the prime requirement of any theory has been found, namely an engine or cause of the phenomenon." He likens scientific information exchange to a club that aggressively excludes whose who do not adhere to the creed or please those whose egos require constant grooming. Of peer review he says:

> It is . . . short-sighted to leave the management of the production of the end-product, which is the publication of results for general dissemination, in entirely irresponsible hands answerable to no one beyond their immediate coterie for their conduct, or in some cases hands concerned only with commercial success. Unrestrained censorship goes on in all directions, but the system [of peer review] is widely regarded as one of freedom when it is really no better than anarchic suppression to keep in countenance manifest rubbish claimed to represent scientific research.

Unrestrained censorship? Retaliation? This is beginning to sound like a Mafia theory of science. Perhaps. Sir Fred Hoyle, who has been involved in many controversies, and who resigned as director of the Institute of Theoretical Astronomy after "certain academic manœuvering took place," had this to say about his fellows:

> Political rivalries are small passions compared to the hatred the average solid scientist has for the heterodox, hatred that has surely not been equalled in its fury since the days of the Spanish Inquisition. . . . Pressures are so great towards orthodoxy that it is unwise for a young scientist to report an observation or experiment should it happen to favour a declared heresy.

This assessment may be somewhat overdrawn. Halton Arp was allowed to continue in his heresy (that the red shift is not a measure of cosmological distance) for two decades before his colleagues excluded him from the Mt. Wilson telescope. Nevertheless, the evidence I have collected suggests that the value of knowledge for its own sake has been swamped by values attaching to power, reputation, and money. The Arp case illustrates where the priorities lie when these values come into competition: research of great theoretical significance was dismissed as valueless, and his standing was degraded. Not long ago such an incident would have occasioned an outcry. Today we prefer not to notice. We have learned that what counts is not ideas but institutional power. The growth of the sciences since 1945 has been accompanied by an enormous increase of the institutional power exercised by scientists. Truth management is a consequence . . .

Chapter VI

Documents

Freeman's Conception
of His Samoa Research, 1965-1967

Editor's Note

These documents describe Freeman's preparation for his field work in Samoa, 1966-1967. They also reveal something of the institutional opposition to his endeavors.

The first document is a memorandum from Freeman's department head, Professor W. E. H. Stanner, to the Director of the Research School of Pacific Studies, Sir John Crawford. The second is Freeman's rejoinder to Stanner. The memoranda are dated November 12 and November 18, 1965.

Stanner's objection to Freeman's proposed research is territorial: Freeman, he fears, is introducing "biopsychology" into a department dedicated to a sociological orientation. The approved domestic territory is validated by a participatory concept indicated by "shared conception," "coherence," and "communication." These values were threatened, Stanner thought, by Freeman's foraging in foreign territory.

Freeman's response describes his preparation for the Samoa fieldwork. His conceptions are marked by a determination to exhaust all available avenues of observational technique and analysis, and rejection of the "biopsychological" orientation that Stanner attributed to him.

The "problems of communication" to which Stanner alludes includes differences between Stanner and Freeman about the reliability of Mead's Samoa ethnography. In his study *The South Seas in Transition* (1953), Stanner presented an analytical digest of the findings of *Coming of Age in Samoa* in which Mead's ethnography was accepted without reservation. His over-all evaluation was: "[Mead's] percipient analysis sets off the synthesis of Samoan thought, behavior and values in a brilliant light against the crude comprehensions which have passed into the racialist politics of dependency."

Stanner to Crawford

In the statement of intentions which Dr Freeman has sent to you he gave an outline of five objectives. As I understand them, (1), (2) and at least part of (5) are in keeping with what I consider to be the disciplinary *raison d'être* of this Department. There is widespread professional interest in the completion of Dr Freeman's earlier work in Samoa, and I would think £2,000+ well spent for that purpose. I am not yet convinced that (3), (4) and possibly part of (5) will be as close to the Department's interests and policy, but must wait on the demonstration. My dubiety arises from emphases which Dr Freeman has introduced into his work, and on which he has addressed us several times. The matters at issue are not easy to state in a short memorandum but they may be summed up approximately in the following way.

Since 1951 this Department has worked within a widely shared conception of Social Anthropology. Three successive Heads of Department have not differed substantially about it. At an earlier stage Dr Freeman made some notable contribution within that conception. What we have sought to do, apart from our interest in Sociology, is to practise comparative field Ethnography and to interpret the behavioral facts thus collected through concepts depending on a particular universe of discourse. They relate on the one hand to co-adapted behavior and on the other to a general theory of social systems. The idea has been to try to connect Social Anthropology more cogently with cognate facts and theory used in Sociology, Political Science, Law, Economics, Social Geography and other such disciplines.

What I have understood Dr Freeman now to wish to do is to continue with this field Ethnography but to interpret the behavioral facts thus collected through concepts drawn from Ethology and Psychoanalysis. I hope that states the main difference compactly and fairly.

Here are two radically dissimilar orientations. They mix levels of organisation of data. They select different sets of variables. They use different notions of explanation and causality. They lie on different axes of development. They appear to me to lead to different universes of discourse. The common element— a dependence on Ethnography—does not of itself allow a clear disciplinary connection, because of the different modes of abstraction. For my own part I reject any notion that Ethnography + Ethology + Psychoanalysis = Social Anthropology. They add up to what may perhaps be called Biopsychological Anthropology. I do not see how the formulations of problems and the relevant strategies of research can be brought together.

A small Department must maintain coherence between its interests. I do not pronounce on the merits of Dr Freeman's new approach but I consider that it will make for incoherence in what the Department attempts. I think it advisable, therefore, to say that in endorsing his Samoa project I am not undertaking to support further developments along that line. There are already some problems of communication. I reserve the right as Head of the Department to withhold support if I consider that our work is being pushed in divergent directions.

Freeman to Crawford

. . . Professor Stanner's case rests on the premise that the Department of Anthropology and Sociology possesses a well-defined "policy," or "disciplinary *raison d'être*" from which I am departing in such a way as "to make for incoherence in what the Department attempts," and he states that as Head of the Department he reserves the right to "withhold support" from my researches.

I am not at all sure how seriously I should take this statement by Professor Stanner. As it stands it is a contingent statement, and I have decided that the wisest course for me to follow is to defer any specific comment on this particular issue until Professor Stanner, as Head of the Department of Anthropology and Sociology, actually takes action to curtail my researches by the withholding of support from them.

However, in the present situation, it does seem appropriate that I should present to the University some account of the development of my research activities in recent years and of my plans for Samoa.

First, however, I would like to comment briefly on Professor Stanner's views about a Departmental research policy.

As Reader in Anthropology at the Australian National University it is clearly my task to concern myself with the solution of anthropological problems. This I am doing with all my energies, and I would think that a Departmental research policy based on this principle would be acceptable to all reasonable men.

But the policy advocated by Professor Stanner . . . is based on a quite different principle, namely that the interpretation (or explanation) of behavioral facts ought to be made "through concepts depending on a particular universe of discourse." In other words, Professor Stanner is laying down procedural rules for the solution of anthropological problems, rules which he considers ought to be made binding on all Departmental members, including Readers and Professorial Fellows.

Binding procedural rules may well be compatible with certain forms of human activity, but experience has abundantly shown that such binding procedural rules are incompatible with fundamental scientific enquiry, this being for the reason that in scientific inquiry answers to problems are often found in quite unexpected directions. It is, therefore, stultifying of scientific endeavour to lay down in advance, and in a binding way, what the nature of explanation in a science must be.

Social anthropology, as is well known, is a young science and is still very much in its formative stages. A number of different conceptual schemes have been put forward as, for example, by Malinowski, Radcliffe-Brown, Nadel, Gluckman and others, but all of these have had serious short-comings of one kind and another. In other words, social anthropology is still in the course of working out the scientific bases in terms of which adequate explanations of customary and social behavior are to be attained. This is entirely to be expected in the formative stage of any science, and at this stage of development those interested in scientific progress tend to concern themselves with re-examination of the working assumptions of previous thinkers in the field.

. . . Some twenty-five years ago, Malinowski, in his essay "A Scientific Theory of Culture," sought to give anthropology such a biological basis. This attempt, because of the paucity of the evidence then existing on the biology of behavior, largely failed. Since that time, however, there have been most notable advances in the biological study of behavior, as in the allied behavioral sciences.

This means that we are now in the position effectively to integrate biological and anthropological understanding, and to work towards a science of human behavior which will have an adequate scientific basis.

. . . I would like to note that the preparations which I have made for my Samoan researches have been protracted, assiduous and systematic. Thus, in recent years (and especially in Europe during 1963-64) I have made an intensive study of the methods of ethology as these apply to the anthropological investigation of human behavior and I have discussed my methods and objectives with the world's leading ethologists.

It is encouraging to report their reactions to my research plans and aims. Professor Konrad Lorenz, F.R.S., the Director of the Max-Planck-Institut für Verhaltensphysiologie at Seewiesen in Germany, has written to me:

> As I am convinced that expression movements are the nearest approach to hereditary motor patterns in human beings, I think that their cross-cultural study and documentation in films is the best strategy for starting a science which merits the name of human ethology. On this point I emphatically share your opinion, and wish you the best success on your expedition to Samoa.

And Dr N. Tinbergen, F.R.S., Reader in Animal Behavior in the University of Oxford, has stated, with reference to my research plans:

"I am firmly convinced that you are tackling the field in exactly the right way."

. . . Professor Stanner has stated that he understands that my objective in Samoa is "to continue with field Ethnography but to interpret the behavioral facts thus collected through concepts drawn from Ethology and Psycho-Analysis." I would like to state categorically that this is *not* my intention. As I have many times stressed (cf. "Social Anthropology and the Scientific Study of Human Behavior," p. 21) I intend to include in my analysis of human social behavior (including such behavior as it exists in Samoa) *all* of the relevant sociological variables. Further, I would like to emphasize that I remain intently interested in the solution of the classical problems of social anthropology, with which I am well familiar.

Professor Stanner also writes: "For my part I reject any notion that Ethnography + Ethology + Psychoanalysis = Social Anthropology." This is a notion which I too would most certainly reject. It represents a grotesque caricature of my present approach to anthropological problems, and I am astonished that Professor Stanner should suppose that anyone might entertain such a notion. My object, let me reiterate, is to include in my analysis *all relevant sociological variables.*

Professor Stanner's characterization of my present approach to anthropological problems as being no more than "Biopsychological Anthropology" is thus baseless, and entirely an invention of his own devising. I wish, therefore, to state unequivocally that the phrase "Biopsychological Anthropology" is highly misleading as a description of my research objectives, as a scrutiny of the varied objectives outlined in my memorandum to Professor Stanner of 4 November 1965, will immediately confirm.

Again, I do not give the prominence to psychoanalysis in my general approach to anthropological problems that Professor Stanner's remarks suggest. For example, in my paper "Social Anthropology and the Scientific Study of Human Behavior," psychoanalysis is scarcely mentioned. In the scientific synthesis which I am seeking psychological factors are plainly of importance, and I have given some attention to psychoanalysis as a system of psychological understanding that gives due emphasis to man's biological nature. As Freud, himself an eminent neurophysiologist, once remarked: "In the psychical field the biological factor is really rock-bottom." However, I am highly critical of certain aspects of psycho-analytical theory, and I am interested only in those psycho-analytical discoveries which can be scientifically established and incorporated in a general theory of human behavior.

Further, although, at this stage in my researches, I am giving emphasis to the relevance of ethology to the solution of anthropological problems, this is in no sense to the exclusion of evidence from other sciences. Thus, in working towards the synthesis which has been my objective, I have paid much attention to the relevant findings of neuro-physiology, physiological psychology, endocrinology, genetics, evolutionary biology, ecology, palaeo-anthropology and primatology . . ., as well as to such behavioral disciplines as experimental and social psychology and psychiatry.

. . . A searching examination of the working assumptions of a discipline is unavoidably to some extent disturbing to long established and habitual ways of thought, but one might have hoped that work of this kind would be encouraged in an Institute of Advanced Studies that is devoted almost entirely to research.

It is, however, a commonplace that new knowledge and advances in scientific understanding are apt to meet with bigoted opposition of various kinds, including even attempts to curtail the freedom so essential to fundamental scientific enquiry.

In this situation I would hope that, for my part, I possess the capacity, while continuing with my researches, to cope with such opposition in a rational, understanding and effective way.

From the Holmes-Freeman Correspondence

Editor's Note

Contact between Holmes and Freeman began in 1960 when Holmes wrote asking Freeman's opinion of how the quality of Polynesian research might be improved. Subsequently Freeman came to believe that Holmes' restudy of Mead's Samoan ethnography, and the interpretations he placed upon them, were critical elements in the evidence that he was attempting to evaluate. In 1967 during his fieldwork in Samoa, Freeman initiated and pursued an exchange that was to leave each scholar with deep reservations about the other. Freeman's letter of October 10, 1967 revealed what he had ascertained about Mead's conduct in Ta'ū, and stated his determination to "get the record straight both for the sake of Samoa and for the science of anthropology." This letter persuaded Holmes that Freeman was on a vendetta (see p. 269). From the current perspective, the letter's critical importance is the linkage Freeman establishes between correcting Mead's ethnography, vindicating the Samoans, and refuting the doctrine of cultural determinism. Translations from Samoan have been supplied by Derek Freeman.

Holmes to Freeman, August 1, 1967

In your letter of May 25, 1967 you ask how I can criticize Mead on a number of points and then say (p. 232) that "the reliability of Mead's account is remarkably high." While I disagree on many points of interpretation as noted in my thesis I do believe that the majority of her facts were correct and considering she was about 23 years old and only spent six months in the area I think she did a reasonably good job in her descriptions of village organization, ceremonial life and family organization. I am surprised that she got as good material as she did. I am sure that she could have developed good rapport with young girls but I would have expected the chiefs to give her a complete line of bull. I believe that you are placing too much stress on the points where we disagree and not enough on the points where we agree. Remember, I was out to evaluate her account, not to discredit it. In a number of areas it was not possible to decide whether she was wrong or whether things had changed. Methodology was a difficult problem.

I must admit that I am not greatly competent in psychology and I did not attempt to evaluate her psychological interpretations but only her observations. I am not sure how sophisticated anyone's psychology was in 1925. I think it is quite true that Margaret finds pretty much what she wants to find. While I was quite critical of many of her ideas and observations I do not believe that a thesis is quite the place to expound them. I was forced by my faculty advisor to soften my criticisms.

I think it must be kept in mind that Margaret Mead was the first to study some of the things recorded in *Coming of Age* as earlier missionaries did not comment on a variety of areas. I think it was much easier for me to check out their reliability than for her to conceive of the ideas in the first place. Having her account to check out made things much easier for me. The only tragedy about Mead is that she still refuses to accept the idea that she might have been wrong on her first field trip.

Freeman to Holmes, October 10, 1967

I have not long returned from my *malaga* [journey, i.e., to Manu'a] which was most memorable.

I wonder if you know that there are strong traditional connections between Sa'anapu and Ta'ū.

This I was aware of before I set out, though I had not realized how very strong and emotionally tinged these connections were.

The title of Logona (which is the gift of Anapu), which I was given in 1942, as a young man of 26, and which I still hold, is recognized as having originated in Ta'ū (where it is the gift of Lefiti, of Si'ufaga); and this was formally recognized when a *malaga* from Ta'ū (including Lefiti, Sotoa and many others) formally came to Sa'anapu, at 'Anapu's invitation in 1959.

Thus, when I arrived a Si'faga (at the *'aiga* of Lefiti) I was lavishly welcomed, with a formal *usuga* [assembly] by all the *matai* [chiefs] of the *nu'u* [polity], and accepted as one of the Sa Lefiti, and recognized as a *matai* of Ta'ū, with the following *gafa* [genealogy]:

Usu Lepolofa'asoasoa (mai Amouli) ia Fulu'ula, fa'ae'e le gafa o Logona-i-fagugu;

Usu Logona-i-fagugu ia Samala'ulu (le taupou o le Tui Manu'a); fa' ae' e la gafa o Logona-i-taga (i Sa' anapu)—which is the title I hold.

And I was taken to Amouli (to the south of Si'ufaga) and shown the various traditional sites associated with the Logona title.

All this, as you will understand, assisted me greatly in my inquiries, and speaking Samoan fluently, as I do, I was able to make very rapid progress with my investigations.

In general the very many errors in Mead's writings, which I had detected in Western Samoa, also hold for Manu'a (although it emerges that there are a number of significant differences between Manu'a and the western islands—within what is unquestionably a common culture—that deserve further detailed investigation).

Did you know that Margaret Mead, as a young woman, was never permitted to sit in a *fono* [council of chiefs] in Manu'a (*e le solia se fono* ["she was never allowed to enter a *fono*"], *ua sā; sa le o'o i se 'ava, aua o le teine* ["she never participated in a *kava* ceremony because she was a girl"].

This adequately accounts for the inadequacy of her account of *fono* behavior, for she was never in a position to observe it—although she never had the honesty to admit this, and was not deterred from presenting a largely fabricated account.

She must also have been much annoyed at being so ignored by the matai [family heads] of Ta'ū, as is indicated by her complete failure to come to terms with the realities of male dominance in Samoa; cf her describing of Samoan society as "bilateral"—an error which has bedeviled Samoan studies ever since. (cf [Melvin] Ember's work).

Did you, yourself, I wonder ever inquire into Mead's behavior during the few months she spent in Ta'ū? I suppose not, for you have made no mention of it in any of your publications or in any of your letters to me.

Yet the facts are there to be discovered, as I soon established.

My principal informants were (a) Numela, now 67 years of age and the *tama sā* [lit. sacred son] of Sotoa Salofi. (Numela is now the leader of the *aumaga* [untitled men] in Ta'ū and in 1925-26 he was a *taule' ale' a* [untitled man] (of 25-26 years) who was *tautau* [serving] Sotoa Salofi and his wife Toaga); and (b) Fa'alaulā, of the Sa Lefiti, now a lady of 77 years who in 1925-26 acted as Margaret Mead's *tina fa' aSamoa* [lit. Samoan mother], and a most important witness.

Numela (and others) have recounted, in sworn testimony (tape recorded in the *falesā* [church] at Ta'ū), the full details of Margaret Mead's infatuated affair with Aviata (b. 1899) the profligate eldest son of Soata Salofi, and how she held *poula* [night dances] with him, she dancing *fa'asausau* [bare breasted] in the two story palagi-style house of Sotoa, which you will know was just to the north of the *falesā* [church], and of how she was in the habit of sleeping with him, etc, etc., etc.

Had news of any of these goings-on previously reached your ears?

Knowing about them is of importance, for they provide us with an explanation of Mead's fantastically erroneous account of Samoan sexual behavior—and especially that of young women.

In reality, her account (as I had long half-suspected) is a *projection* on to Samoan females of her *own* sexual experiences as a young woman, in the far-away, romantic South Seas.

I have, indeed, been long interested in the way in which anthropological fieldwork presents immature personalities with massive opportunities for what might be called cultural regression. And of which not a few anthropologists avail themselves.

The young woman from Pennsylvania seems to have imagined that she had arrived in a Polynesian Eden; in fact, she was in an aristocratic and rigorously Christian community which was shocked at her demeanor, which it still describes as *pei o le amio o se tufanua* [like the behavior of a common person], and says of her that she was *pei o se mea ola tafao vale, pei o se manu* [just like a vagrant, like an animal].

These discoveries came as a shock to me too, and I found that my feelings were very deeply stirred—both for the sake of Samoa and the science of anthropology, which both mean much to me.

So much then for what Boas called (in 1928) "painstaking investigations" which were accepted by him as by American anthropology in general as confirming (in the words of Boas) "the suspicion long held by anthropologists that much of what we ascribe to human nature is no more than a reaction to the restraints put upon us by our civilization"; so much for the main cornerstone of the hallowed doctrine of cultural determinism. Oh, anthropology! thy salad days.

You will also know, I take it, that Margaret Mead's name is execrated in Manu'a (as elsewhere in Samoa), for her writings, and especially *Coming of Age in Samoa,* are regarded as a *luma fai tele* (i.e., a defamatory libel). Indeed, the people of Ta'ū told me that if she ever dared to return they would tie her up and throw her to the sharks.[1]

I must now ask you to keep as *confidential pro tem* the information I have conveyed to you in this letter.

The sworn testimony which I collected in Ta'ū is now being transcribed and translated (with the approval of the Prime Minister) by the official interpreters of the Government of Western Samoa.

I hope to be able to make it available to other anthropologists in due course, but until proper advice has been taken, the contents of this testimony, as of this letter, must remain *confidential*.

Please feel completely free however to make any comment that you may wish in letters to me.

You say in your letter of [August 1, 1967] that you believe that I am not placing enough stress on the points on which we agree, and too much stress on the points on which we disagree.

I am sorry if this is the case. I would put it to you that this is not the expression of any intention on my part, but merely a part of the process of trying to establish the true facts about Samoa.

I have, naturally, very carefully checked (both here and in Manu'a) on the points on which I find myself (as the result of my own inquiries) in marked disagreement with you, and I would hope that one of these days there might be an opportunity for us to talk over Samoan ethnography together.

As I have noted in an earlier letter [May 25, 1967] I am quite unable to accept your opinion that "the reliability of Mead's account is remarkably high."

However, from your letter of [August 1, 1967] it is plain that this does not really reflect your private view of Mead's work. I refer to your words:

> While I was quite critical of many of her ideas and observations I do not believe that a thesis is quite the place to expound them. I was forced by my faculty advisor to soften my criticisms.

While I am sympathetic with the situation in which you were thus placed, it seems to me an extraordinary attitude for a faculty

---

[1]Mead's brief visit to Ta'ū in 1971, as the guest of Governor and Mrs. John M. Haydon, was without life-threatening incident. See *Pacific Islands Monthly*, December 1971, p. 27.—Ed.

advisor to take, for he, surely, should have valued the establishment of scientific truth above all else.

Who was he I wonder? I note that in *Ta'ū*[1] you express your indebtedness to Herskovits and Bascom. Can it have been Herskovits, who was an admirer of Boas and a leading proponent of the doctrine of cultural determinism?[2]

And how did your advisor, whoever he was, justify himself?

Finally let me note that it is also no part of my purpose to "discredit" Mead's writings on Samoa (cf. your letter of [August 1, 1967]). What I want to do is to get the record straight both for the sake of Samoa and the science of anthropology. And this I shall do.

With every good wish,

Freeman to Holmes November 22, 1967

. . . I hope you will have had my confidential letter of [October 10, 1967].

Inasmuch as the motivations of an investigator must be kept entirely distinct from the evidential value of any report that he might make, I have now decided to vigorously *exclude* from any reappraisal of Mead's publications on Samoa that I might write any mention of her personal behaviour as reported to me by witnesses in Manu'a.

I shall, meanwhile, merely store this evidence securely away reflecting that it has deepened my historical and psychological understanding of anthropology as a vocation.

Nonetheless, I should still be interested in having your confidential comments.

Holmes to Freeman October 9, 1968

I am sorry that you took personally the fact that I had not answered your last few letters. The fact is that I am a very poor correspondent. The administrative duties of department chairman

---

[1]The reference is to Holmes' book *Ta'ū: Stability and Change in a Samoan Village* (1958).—Ed.

[2]Holmes subsequently identified his supervisor as Herskovits. He states that Herskovits' instruction to him was that Holmes should be "icily objective," but that, having no love for Mead, he would have be delighted had Holmes contradicted her findings. *Quest for the Real Samoa*, pp. 144-145.—Ed.

plus the writing that I am doing sometimes puts me a bit behind in writing the letters that I should.

I must admit that I thought that your methods were a bit unusual in regard to Margaret Mead's activities back in 1925-26. I would prefer to deal with her published works rather than her personal life. I again would also like to state that my restudy satisfied me that the reliability of her Manu'a work was "remarkably high." The areas in which we differed were rather insignificant and I feel that her general discussion of the culture was good. I have a great deal of respect for Dr Mead and I believe that all anthropologists owe her a debt of gratitude for many of her pioneer activities. I do believe, however, that no one is perfect and I indicated in the thesis where my interpretations differed from hers. My field work was partly an experiment to see if a restudy could be made thirty years later. While it was my purpose at the time to point out every area of disagreement with Dr Mead my overall view of her study is that it was a good study for its time in the history of anthropological science. If you want to do a critique of my writing along with that of Mead's please feel free to do so. I believe that is what science is all about. I do support the majority of her findings on Samoa and differ only in some areas of interpretation and on some minor facts.

Mead Recognizes Her Error

Lola Romanucci-Ross

Editor's Note

In Reflections on Later Theoretical Work on the Samoans, in the second edition (1969) of the *Social Organization of Manu'a,* Mead discussed Samoan ethnography since her 1925-1926 fieldwork. There she records her recognition of marked discrepancies between her observations and those of Lowell D. Holmes, Gloria Cooper, Derek Freeman, and Melvin Ember. The discrepancies concern the absence of aggression, casualness in sexual relations, and permissive upbringing of children. She acknowledged that there was "a serious hiatus in my accounts of childrearing and social organization and a failure to explain the touchiness and vulnerability to insult which the Samoan displayed" (p. 226). Mead made several proposals toward the reconciliation of the discrepancies. One was to encourage further observation to multiply detail. Freeman's observations on upbringing are mentioned in this connection. Related to this point was her suggestion that the duration of observations may profoundly affect what one observes. She wrote: "Dr Schwartz and I have estimated that it might take continuous observation over thirty years to exhaust a repertoire of small, sporadically used customs, many items of which informants would completely disown for most of that period" (p. 225). This is a gloss on the immersion requirement. Mead did not apply it, in the Reflections, to her Samoan fieldwork, from which she derived not only the broad generalizations that made her *Jugendschrift* famous, but details on homosexuality, birth control, abortion, and other secretive practices. One possible application of the maxim was to declare that in view of the brevity of her field-work, her observations were only first impressions. Instead she proposed an "explanation" of the

> serious problem of reconciling these contradictions be-
> tween the mildness, the willingness to gloss over and
> compromise, which I found in Manu'a, and other
> records of historical and contemporary behavior. I see,
> at present, only two possibilities. Manu'a in 1925 might
> have represented a special variation on the Samoan pat-
> tern, a temporary felicitous relaxation of the quarrels and
> rivalries, the sensitivity to slight and insults, and the use
> of girls as pawns in male rivalries. . . . The other pos-
> sibility is that to the young girl . . . the preoccupations
> of the whole society may have seemed more remote than
> they would have appeared from any other vantage point.
> And this is the vantage point from which I saw it. [M]y
> primary task was to get to know and understand
> adolescent girls; the ethnography was a by-product . . .
> hopefully we will soon have some sophisticated micro-
> cultural studies: Gloria Cooper's on paralinguistics and
> her study of the use of social space; and Derek Free-
> man's proposed intensive attention to early experience
> (pp. 227-228).

Another possibility, not mentioned in the Reflections, was that she had been in error. According to Lola Romanucci-Ross, this was Mead's belief after her interview with Derek Freeman in November 1964. Her account of Mead's admission of error is taken from Derek Freeman, *et al.*, *Transcript of Interviews for the Documentary Film Margaret Mead and Samoa*, Tape 28, pp. 39-40, 43-44.

Question: Tell me what happened in 1964 when Margaret Mead confided in you.

Romanucci-Ross: Yes, well that was very dramatic, and of course I've never forgotten it. She had just come to Pere village in Manus [from her stop in Canberra]. I had to go to Rabaul for a medical visit and she wanted to come with me. I thought that rather odd but of course I was very happy to have her company. That evening in our room she told me that she had met with Derek Freeman and that he had told her about his research in Samoa, and what he thought of her work, and that he was going to publish. And I gave her a "so what?" look and she said: "You don't understand, he has proven me wrong." She looked very sad and puzzled and I thought it was very odd that I was feeling sorry for Margaret Mead and even stranger that I would have to tell her that it was not important. But I did. I said that what you have done for anthropology and for the world is not Samoa-dependent; it really doesn't matter whether you were right or wrong about Samoa. She asked what she ought to do about it, and I said "just nothing." Controversies die if one side doesn't make a fuss, so just forget about it.

But it bothered her a lot. Some years later when I invited her to La Jolla to give a talk, she asked me not to let a certain young researcher [Eleanor Gerber] get close to her because she had found some discrepancies and Margaret didn't want to talk to her about them. So I said, "you bet, she won't get within ten feet of you." So it did bother her.

. . . . Q: Did Margaret Mead invent cultures?

Romanucci-Ross: Well she invented yes, in a very interesting way she invented cultures. I'm not using that in an invidious sense. I don't mean she made them up. I don't mean that. But invention in the sense that you do see all the elements, and you put them together and maybe you put them together in a way that, well, you have a goal in mind. It's been said that she was a Boasian in anthropology. I don't think so at all. To me Margaret was more like the nineteenth century English intellectuals who invented the culture of ancient Greece. That doesn't mean that many of the elements of ancient Greece were not there, but the English had a goal. They knew what they wanted to do with the ancient Greeks. That's what Margaret did. She brought Apollo to Samoa and she and Ruth Benedict were very busy misinterpreting Nietzsche, for years.

Q: Fieldwork in Samoa?

Romanucci-Ross: Oh well, first of all she certainly—and Margaret said this herself—she wasn't there long enough, she didn't know the language well enough, she only spent several months talking to the girls, it was all done outside the clinic, it was not *in situ* so to speak. . . . Margaret expected people to come back and correct what she had done and see it differently. She always said to me that she would be very annoyed when I was looking for "the real thing," the real truth. She said it isn't there, you know, we just see what we see, we interpret it and in time we get better data. Margaret knew that in time, you could study the same situation and get more data and better data. . . . She knew all these things, and it seems to me that her self-appointed public defenders don't seem to know this. Or don't appear to know this. And I think that Margaret would be shocked at the controversy itself.

Referee's Report on *Margaret Mead and Samoa*[1]

I think it is quite a fascinating book (although marred by a certain polemical redundancy), and should be published—although it is bound to arouse considerable controversy. As far as the historical material is concerned, I'd say that on the whole Freeman avoids distortion, and is quite illuminating. He does tend to over-simplify things at points, for polemical and dramatic purposes. But not, I think, in such a way to do violence to the material, which, on the whole, he controls rather well. As a matter of fact, the dramatic structure and sense of immediacy which he creates by juxtaposing various documents and statements in time—so that we know that a paper by Boas come at the

---

[1] The report was submitted to the Harvard University Press about March, 1982. The author is described by the Press as a historian of anthropology. It is reprinted unabridged.

same time, or immediately after, an event in the eugenics movement, etc.—seems to me to work quite well. I am sure that it could be faulted on particular issues (though not, I think, on "fact"). For instance, he seems to me to take at face value (because it suits his own polemical purpose) the Boasian view of social evolutionism as applied biological evolutionism, which I think greatly oversimplifies things. Some historians might make a larger issue of this than I am inclined to, because by and large I think his argument "works."

All other things considered, I would regard his history (in the context of other polemically-motivated histories) as quite adequate to his purpose, and at points distinctly illuminating.

If I may offer some further remarks on the book as a whole: I am sure that you must be aware that this is likely to be quite controversial. He has attacked several sacred cows—most notably Margaret Mead, the "mother of us all," and cultural determinism (the two being, of course, necessarily interrelated in his argument). A few thoughts on each of these:

Mead is not, as it happens, all that popular a figure among anthropologists—for reasons that have something to do (among other things) with their unstated and probably unacknowledged feelings about strong women. She has long been regarded as a popularizer, not to be taken all that seriously. From this point of view, many will be pleased to see the fieldwork on which her reputation was originally founded so devastatingly undercut—although it will doubtless be noted that Freeman waited until after her death to publish. She has, I think also, had a somewhat ambiguous relationship to the modern feminist movement. But she is at the same time one of the very few popularly apotheosized anthropologists, and this critique will doubtless provoke response (although I must say in passing that on the whole Freeman seems to me to have kept the argument at a substantive and not *ad feminem* level).

The issue of cultural determinism and the relation of the cultural and biological is perhaps even more problematic and potentially controversial. Anthropologists may not like Margaret Mead, but they are almost unanimous (by votes at the A[merican] A[nthropological] A[ssociation]) in their extreme disapproval of E. O. Wilson and they tend to regard sociobiology as the next thing to racism. I'm sure that Freeman does not wish to be regarded as a racist (though I think you might make it a point to capitalize Negro in the *un*quoted passages on page 8). And I personally agree with him that some kind of (non-racist) rapprochement between culture and biology is (25 years after A. L. Kroeber predicted it in 1955) in some cases "in the cards." But it is being resisted, and not without some good reasons. The point of all this is that the biological alternative that Freeman wishes to advance (or, rather, the complement, since he does speak of biological determinism as a second "half-truth") is not very fully argued for in this book. It simply exists as part of an undeveloped paradigm. That may be O. K., intellectually, in terms of what he is trying to do in this book. But he is likely to lay himself open to a lot of attacks—guilt by associations which he himself quite casually makes. I refer for instance to E. O. Wilson in the last chapter—he's not necessary to the argument. And I can imagine writing this book without accepting Wilson. But Freeman apparently does, and it is going to raise a lot of hackles.

Clarification on Sociobiology

Derek Freeman

Editor's Note

This statement was among numerous other comments on various aspects of *The Reader* that I received from Freeman in February 1989. It is a criticism of that part of my essay, "Freeman's Quest for an Interactionist Anthropology" (Chapter I), in which I identify a regression to conventional anthropology provoked by the encounter with Mark I sociobiology. In response to my proposal to include this text, Freeman wrote that he would "greatly welcome" its publication because "in my estimation [it] accurately summarise my intellectual position." The tacit dimension of this debate—to which Freeman alludes—is the difference between us about the motor of cultural evolution. For him it is choice; for me it is polytechnic rationality, a thesis I developed in *The Politics of Progress*.

I have no difficulties with your account of the development of my anthropological ideas in your pages [98] to [108]. Indeed, the account you give in these pages reads extremely well, and I congratulate you on it.

At the beginning of p. [109] however, my ideas about human choice behavior have been seriously misunderstood and misrepresented, and your account, as far as I am concerned, goes right off the rails.

Thus, it has never been nor is it now my view (as you put it) that choice is "a free, biologically untethered creation of the mind." This is highly misleading. If you will consult my paper of September 1978, "A Precusory View of the Anthropology of Choice," you will find that I say the human capacity to make choices "is definitively characteristic of the 'ultimate nature' (to use Wilson's phrase) of the human animal."

In other words, I have (like J. Z. Young and J. T. Bonner) always given human choice behavior *a biological basis.* Further, I have always held that humanly made choices operate *within the determinism of nature.* Thus in 1980 I wrote: "I accept the same 'scientific materialism' as that in which E. O. Wilson places his trust, as also the theory of evolution by means of natural selection in its modern form. Indeed, I hold it to be of the utmost important *that anthropologists should recognize and incorporate in their theories* all those biological mechanisms *which have been shown,* on scientific grounds, *to be relevant to the understanding of human behavior"* (emphases added, 1989).

As an example let me take the metabolic disease, phenylketonuria which is (as Vogel and Motulsky in the 2nd ed., 1986 of their *Human Genetics* note) "now one of the best-known inborn errors of metabolism in humans." In other words, it is a genetic defect, with the gene in question being located on chromosome 12.

For many years phenylketonuria, which is a most serious life-threatening condition, was untreatable. However, since the biochemical mechanisms that produce the enzyme defect in phenylketonuria have become known, successful treatment by *choice* of the expedient of the introduction of a low-phenuylaline diet has become feasible, and effective.

Those who, because of their scientific acumen, have successfully resorted to this life-saving expedient, may be defined by this action of theirs. No animals, other than members of the species Homo sapiens have, to the best of my knowledge, so defined themselves. It is in this sense then, that "Homo sapiens can only be defined . . . as a self-defining animal." In short, it is our capacity for making choices, together with evolution by natural selection, which has given rise to this capacity, that makes us what we are, as our history continues.

In his letter to me of [September 6, 1983] Ed Wilson wrote: "The key is indeed, as you decided independently, the evolution of choice behavior."

I would only comment that I was arguing for this, some years *before Genes, Mind and Culture: The Co-Evolutionary Process* was published in 1981.

My paper of 1980, if it is to be construed correctly, must be viewed in this context.

On p. [109] you say that I "denied that any cultural phenomenon has been demonstrated to be tethered to the genetic leash."

This referred, of course, to Wilson's earlier formulation and not to the position he adopted in *Genes, Mind and Culture* (which I was at once able to accept), when the question of the exact extent to which a cultural behavior is tethered to a genetic program is a matter for empirical investigation and determination.

You also quote my declaration about "the autonomy of culture." Here, as surely must be evident to you from my whole evolutionary position, I am referring, of course, to a relative, and not an absolute autonomy.

In Samoa, one of the requirements of Samoan culture is that an umbrella be folded and lowered in the presence of a chief of rank.

This rule is a part of the Samoan culture, and as such has a relative autonomy. It cannot be fully understood however until put in the general context of dominance behavior the roots of which are certainly pre-cultural.

It is thus *not true*, as you assert on p. 83, that "the genetic menace" drove me back to "the conventional anthropological thesis of the autonomy of culture" which I had previously seen to be inconsistent with a unified science of man.

Indeed, I was intent on ensuring that cultural variables were recognized for what they are within an evolutionary interactionist framework, and were not swallowed up by Wilson's Mark I biological determinism.

I would also point out that this move by me has, in the event, proved successful, for it was Wilson who, for whatever reasons, changed his position in a radical way to take account of cultural variables and of choice.

May I also note once again that I do not suppose that when a human animal makes (i.e. enacts) a choice[1] he is in any way altering or departing from the determinisms (i.e. mechanisms) of nature. We know that certain neuropeptides are decisively involved in the etiology of human anger and aggressive behavior (cf. *New Scientist* of January 28, 1989).

Some Buddhists by dint of 'mindfulness' and the development of their powers of inhibition are able, to a marked extent, to control their anger. (In this way, I would note, in passing, they become self-defining). This does *not* mean, of course, that their natures have changed. They still have the *same* neuropeptides and will continue to have them for as long as they live. (Similarly, these and other phylogenetically-given elements are present and *continue to operate*[2] whatever be the cultural situation). What one can say, I think, is that while the natures of my Buddhists have not changed, their characters have, and by deliberate choice.

I now turn to your last three paragraphs on pp. [111] and [112].

These, it seems to me, stem from your mistaken depiction of my interactionist position, especially in regard to choice and culture, on p. [109]. These three paragraphs have virtually nothing to do with your announced subject, i.e. *my* "quest for an interactionist anthropology" but rather are a discussion of the concept of epigenetic rules, etc. If you really want to discuss *my* "quest for an interactionist anthropology" might I suggest that you should consider (a) the final chapter of *Margaret Mead and Samoa*; (b) my statement of [October 10, 1987] "on the emergence in the behavioral and human sciences of an interactionist paradigm" and (c) my concluding statement in Frank [Heimans'] film (I enclose a copy of my statement of [October 10, 1987], for ready reference).[3]

I think it is fair to say (especially when one considers the position from which I began in 1960), and it is certainly very much my opinion, that my quest for an interactionist anthropol-

---

[1]Nor do I suppose that all choice is deliberate; cf. K. Bailey, *Human Paleopsychology*.

[2]This means that the interaction of biological and cultural variables is incessant.

[3]This statement consists of numerous quotations from recent publications endorsing an interactionist approach. The film mentioned is the television documentary *Margaret Mead and Samoa*.—Ed.

ogy has been highly successful. This is evidenced in the documentation, provided in my statement of [October 10, 1987], of the emergence of an interactionist approach in many (if not all) of the behavioral sciences during the 1980s. One of the positions I quote is that of Professor Robert Paul of the Department of Anthropology at Emory University, where interactionist anthropology has been in place *for several years.*

The essentials of an interactionist anthropology have now, in my view, been established. The details most certainly still need to be worked out, but we have plenty of time ahead of us for that.

Finally, may I direct your attention to my words at the end of Frank's film:

> My passion in life is that we will develop a genuine science of the human species. Nothing is more important for humans than that we succeed in that task . . . . It is apparent to all knowledgeable behavioral scientists that we must operate within a framework in which we simultaneously take into account our evolutionary history, and our cultures. It is only when these two things are combined within an interactionist paradigm that you have the imperative pre-condition for a genuine science of our species.

Certainly, if I were given the choice, it is this statement (properly identified) that *I* would *choose* to end any account of my "quest for an interactionist anthropology." It adequately summarizes the position I have held since the early 1960s and still hold in 1989, with my sense of humor and the ridiculous alive and well.

I cannot ask that you *agree* with my interactionist anthropological position, especially as it involves the biologically-given human capacity for make choices. In this matter, you are fully entitled to make your own choices, as I am sure you will.

What *I* am entitled to ask of you, as a responsible scholar, is that my interactionist anthropological position be accurately described.

In this long excursus I have tried to convey to you what my position is. You are free to question me further, at any time, about it.

In my view, your account of my quest for an interactionist anthropology needs to be redrafted from the beginning of p. [109] onwards.

If you decide to do this redrafting I shall be glad, if you wish, to give you my further comments.

I thank you for letting me see the draft of which I have just been commenting. Prosit!

Bibliography

This bibliography is divided into two sections. The first lists writings relevant to the Samoa controversy, plus miscellaneous other titles; the second lists recent research on Samoa. The first section has drawn substantially on the bibliography of the Samoa controversy published in *Canberra Anthropology* 6 (1984):86-97. I have reproduced many of these titles because it seemed to me that readers would find a bibliographic conspectus of the controversy's first year an important means of forming an impression of its scope and temper. The bibliography does not list the titles of writings published in *The Reader*.

The complete bibliography of Margaret Mead's writings until 1975 will be found in Gordan 1976 (Section 1). Derek Freeman's bibliography will be found in Appell and Madan 1988 (Section 1). The latter list omits numerous publications after 1983, a deficiency remedied in this bibliography.

A bibliography of the diplomatic, colonial, commercial and missionary literature on Samoa is in Gilson 1970:435-445 (Section 2) and a bibliography of Samoan studies is in Holmes 1984 (Section 2). A bibliography of interactionist anthropology will be found in Caton and Salter 1988 (Section 1). A bibliography on contemporary Samoa, with emphasis on behavioral medicine and medical anthropology, will be found in Paul Baker, *et al.* 1986 (Section 2). In preparing Section 2, I have drawn substantially on Baker.

Section 1
Selected Writings Relevant to the Samoa Controversy

Ala'ailima, Fay. 1984. Review of *Margaret Mead and Samoa, Pacific Studies* 7:91-92.

American Anthropological Association. 1983. *Professional Ethics: Statements and Procedures of the American Anthropological Association.* Washington: American Anthropological Association.

Angier, Natalie. 1984. Coming of age in anthropology, *Discover* 4 (April):26-30.

Anonymous. 1989. Informant admits teasing Mead, *The Samoa Times* (January 6), pp.1, 12.

Anonymous. 1983. ANU scholar explodes myth of sexual freedom in Samoa, *Australian National University Reporter* (Canberra) 14(1), 25 February.

Anonymous. 1983.   Coming of age in anthropology, *The Economist*, 12 February.

Anonymous. 1983.   Coming of age with Dr Mead, *Christian Science Monitor*, 2 February.

Anonymous. 1983.   Coming to terms with Samoa? (editorial), *Nature* 301 (10 February):461.

Anonymous. 1983.   Coup de grâce pour Margaret Mead, *Le Monde* (Paris), 9 February.

Anonymous. 1983.   Margaret Mead's Samoa (editorial), *The Sun* (Baltimore), 6 February.

Anonymous. 1983.   Nature v. nuture (editorial), *The Sydney Morning Herald*, 12 February.

Anonymous. 1983.   Paradise lost (editorial), *San Francisco Chronicle*, 6 February.

Anonymous. 1983.   Review of *Margaret Mead and Samoa: The Making and Unmaking of an Anthropological Myth, Mankind Quarterly* 23:216-219.

Anonymous. 1983.   Samoans laud Freeman's book, *The Samoa Times* (Apia), 18 February.

Anonymous. 1983.   The anthropology of anthropology (editorial), *The New York Times*, 3 February.

Anonymous. 1983.   The Margaret Mead debate: was author of classic study wrong?, *Current Controversy* 2(8):4-5.

Anonymous. 1983.   Unmasking in Samoa (editorial), *The Boston Globe*, 9 February.

Anonymous. 1986.   Untrashing Margaret Mead, *Scientific American* 225(5):58-58B.

Anonymous. 1984.   Attendance surges at post-reorganization business meeting, *Anthropology Newsletter*, January:1, 4-5.

Anonymous.   Coming of age in anthropology: doubts on Samoa, *The New York Times*, 6 February:E7.

Anthropology on Trial. 1983.   Nova documentary television film on Melanesian anthropology, including Mead's study of the Manus.

Appell, George N. 1978.   *Ethical Dilemmas in Anthropological Inquiry: A Case Book.* Waltham, Ma.: Crossroads Press.

Appell, George N. 1984.   On the coming of age of American cultural anthropology (letter), *Anthropology Newsletter* 25(2):4.

Appell, George N. and Triloka N. Madan. 1988.   Derek Freeman: notes toward an intellectual biography, in *Choice and Morality in Anthropological Perspective: Essays in Honor of Derek Freeman.* (Albany: SUNY Press), pp. 3-25.

Appell, George N. and Triloka N. Madan. 1988.   Selected bibliography of Derek Freeman, in *Choice and Morality in Anthropological Perspective: Essays in Honor of Derek Freeman.* (Albany: SUNY Press), pp. 27-40.

Bateson, Mary Catherine. 1983.   Of Margaret Mead, her critics and unhelpful sensationalism (letter), *The New York Times*, 13 February.

Bateson, Mary Catherine. 1984.   *With a Daughter's Eye: A Memoir of Margaret Mead and Gregory Bateson.* New York: Morrow.

Begley, Sharon, John Carey, and Carl Robinson. 1983. In search of the real Samoa, *Newsweek*, 14 February.

Benedict, Ruth. 1945 *Patterns of Culture*. London: Routledge

Berndt, Ronald M. 1983. The unmaking of a myth, *The Weekend Australian* (Magazine), 16-17 April..

Bernstein, Richard. 1983. Samoa: a paradise lost?, *New York Times Magazine*, 24 April.

Buchholz, Todd G. 1984. Cultural determinism: review of *Margaret Mead and Samoa*, *Commentary*, January.

Carmody, Deirdre. 1983. Speakers at a symposium defend the work of Margaret Mead, *The New York Times*, 9 April.

Caton, Hiram and Frank K. Salter. 1988. *A Bibliography of Biosocial Science: 2500 Titles Across Fourteen Fields*. Brisbane: St Albans Press.

Caton, Hiram. 1984. Margaret Mead and Samoa: in support of Freeman's critique, *Quadrant*, March:28-32.

Clifford, James. 1983. The Other side of paradise, *London Times Literary Supplement*, May 15:474, 475, 476.

Cox, Paul Alan. 1983. Review of *Margaret Mead and Samoa*, *American Scientist* 71(4), July-August:407.

Cranberg, Lee. 1983. Coming of Mead in Samoa: harsh memories linger on Ta'ū, *Pacific Magazine* (Honolulu), January-February.

Cressman, Luther. 1983. Mead's first husband comes to her defense (letter), *The New York Times* (Science Times), 3 May.

Crombie, Lea. 1983. Margaret Mead under fire on new front, *The Bulletin* (Sydney), 20 September:114, 117-18.

Dakuvula, J. 1984. Mead and Western disillusionment (letter), *Pacific Islands Monthly* (Sydney), January:7.

Elshtain, Jean Bethke. 1983. Coming of age in America: why the attack on Margaret Mead, *The Progressive* 47(10), October:33-35.

Ember, Melvin. 1985. Evidence and science in ethonography: reflections on the Freeman-Mead controversy, *American Anthropologist* 87: 906-910.

Fa'apua'a Fa'amū. 1987. Transcript of interview by Frank Heimans; Interpreter: Galea'i Poumele, Secretary of Samoan Affairs, Government of American Samoa. Sydney: Cinetel Films.

Feinberg, Richard. 1988. Margaret Mead and Samoa: *Coming of Age* in fact and fiction, *American Anthropologist* 90: 656-663.

Fields, Cheryl M. 1983. Controversial book spurs scholars' defense of the legacy of Margaret Mead, *The Chronicle of Higher Education* 26(11), 11 May:27-8.

Firth, Rosemary. 1983. Review of *Margaret Mead and Samoa*, *Royal Anthropological Institute Newsletter* (London) 57, August:11-12.

Freeman, Derek, *et al.* 1987. *Transcript of Interviews for the Documentary Film Margaret Mead and Samoa*. Sydney: Cinetel Films.

Freeman, Derek. 1968. On Believing as many as six impossbile things before breakfast. Paper presented to the Australian Branch of the Association of Social Anthropologists of the British Commonwealth.

_____. 1971. Aggression: Instinct or symptom?, *Australian and New Zealand Journal of Psychiatry* 5:66-73.

_____. 1972. *Social Organization of Manu'a* (1930 and 1969) by Margaret Mead: Some errata, *Journal of the Polynesian Society* 81:70-78.

_____. 1977. On Sociobiology and anthropology, *Canberra Anthropology* 1:24-32.

_____. 1978. Towards an anthropology both scientific and humanistic, *Canberra Anthropology* 1:44-69.

_____. 1978. Sweet Analytics, 'tis thou hast ravished me: an appreciation of the sexual values and behaviour of the Samoans of Western Polynesia, lecture in the Research School of Pacific Studies, May 24.

_____. 1980. Sociobiology: The 'antidiscipline' of anthropology, in *Sociobiology Examined*, edited by Ashley Montagu (New York: Oxford University Press), 198-219.

_____. 1981. The Anthropology of choice, *Canberra Anthropology* 4:82-100.

_____. 1983 *Margaret Mead and Samoa: The Making and Unmaking of an Anthropological Myth*. Cambridge: Harvard University Press.

_____. 1983. A University for Samoa. Address to the University of Samoa given at Malua, Western Samoa on 24 August.

_____. 1983. Magna est veritas [Great is truth]. ASAO Newsletter (Association for Social Anthropology in Oceania) 47, Summer 1983.

_____. 1983. Inductivism and the test of truth, *Canberra Anthropology* 6: 101-192.

_____. 1983. "Everything's got a moral . . .," *Pacific Islands Monthly* (Sydney), July:7.

_____. 1983. Freeman criticizes Mead's research, not Mead (letter), *Barnard Bulletin* (New York), 18 October.

_____. 1983. Mead and Samoa: an exchange (letter), *Natural History* 92(12):4.

_____. 1983. Of denial and animadversion: A rejoinder to C. M. Turnbull, *Quadrant*, June:11-15.

_____. 1983. On Margaret Mead: Derek Freeman denies bias (letter), *The New York Times* (Science Times), 26 July 1983:C3.

_____. 1983. On the importance of Samoan studies, *The Samoa Observer* (Apia), 5 October.

_____. 1983. Samoa revisited (letter), *The New Republic*, 29 August 1983.

_____. 1984. 'O Rose Thou Art Sick!': Rejoinder to Weiner, Schwartz, Holmes, Shore, and Silverman, *American Anthropologist* 86: 400-404.

_____. 1984. Addendum, *Margaret Mead and Samoa: The Making and Unmaking of an Anthropological Myth*, xvii-xx. London: Pelican Books.

_____. 1984. Grasping the significance of Samoa (letter), *Pacific Islands Monthly* (Sydney), March:18.

_____. 1984. Response to reviews of *Margaret Mead and Samoa*, in Book Review Forum, *Pacific Studies* 7:140-196.

_____. 1984. Samoa and Margaret Mead, *Royal Anthropological Institute News* 60:6-8.

_____. 1984. Samoa and Margaret Mead: a rejoinder to Paula Brown Glick and Rosemary Firth, *Royal Anthropological Institute Newsletter* (London), February:60.

_____. 1984. The Burthen of a mystery, review article on Bradd Shore's *Sala'ilua: A Samoan Mystery, Oceania* 54:247-54.

_____. 1984. The Truth will out (letter), *Science 84* 15(2):18.

_____. 1984. There will be Samoa: a reply to Lowell D. Holmes and Marvin Harris, *The Sciences*, January/February:6, 8.

_____. 1985. A Reply to Ember's reflections on the Freeman-Mead controversy, *American Anthropologist* 87: 910-917.

_____. 1985. Response to Reyman and Hammond, *American Anthropologist* 87: 394-395.

_____. 1985/1987. Taped Interviews of Derek Freeman by Hiram Caton, July 1985 & January, 1987. Canberra: The Freeman Papers.

_____. 1986. Some notes on the development of my anthropological interests. Ms. Pp. 63.

_____. 1987. There will be Samoa, in *Anthropology: Contemporary Perspectives*, edited by Phillip Whitten and David E.K. Hunter, pp. 224-28 5th edition. Boston: Little, Brown. [Reply to Lowell D. Holmes and Marvin Harris].

_____. 1987. Letter, *Scientific American* 256(2):6. See Rappaport.

_____. 1987. On the emergence in the behavioural and human sciences of the interactionist paradigm. Ms. Pp. 4.

_____. 1987. Comment on Holmes's *Quest for the Real Samoa*, *American Anthropologist* 89:930-935.

_____. 1989. Comment on Heider's "The Rashomon Effect," *American Anthropologist* 91, September.

_____. 1989. Holmes, Mead and Samoa, *American Anthropologist* 91: 758-762.

_____. In press. Fa'apua'a Fa'amū and Margaret Mead, *American Anthropologist*.

Gellner, Ernest. 1988. The Stakes in anthropology, *American Scholar* 57: 17-30.

Glick, Paula Brown. 1983. Brouhaha among the breadfruit, *Nature* 302, 28 April:758-9.

Glick, Paula Brown. 1983. The attack on and defence of Margaret Mead, *Royal Anthropological Institute Newsletter* 58, October:12-14.

Gold, Jerrry. 1983. Anthropology and uncertainty, *Samoa News* (Pago Pago), 18 February.

Goodenough, Ward. 1983. Margaret Mead and cultural anthropology, *Science* 220:906-8.

Goodman, Richard A. 1983. Margaret Mead (letter), *Science 83*, June.

Goodman, Richard A. 1983. *Mead's Coming of Age in Samoa: A Dissenting View*. Oakland: The Pipperine Press.

Gordan, Joan. 1976. *Margaret Mead: The Complete Bibliography 1925-1975.* The Hague: Mouton.

Gray, J.A.C. 1960. *American Samoa.* Annapolis: US Naval Institute.

Haley, Ken. 1983. The man who unmade the myth of Margaret Mead, *The Age* (Melbourne), 8 February.

Harris, Marvin. 1983. The sleep-crawling question, *Psychology Today*, May:24, 26-7.

Heider, Karl G. 1988. The Rashomon effect: When ethnographers disagree, *American Anthropologist* 90: 73-81.

Herskovits, Melville J. 1950. *Man and His Works: The Science of Cultural Anthropology.* New York: Knopf.

Holmes, Lowell D. 1957 *The Restudy of Manu'an Culture: A Problem in Methodology.* Ph.D. Thesis, Northwestern University.

_____. 1957. Ta'ū: Stability and Change in a Samoan Village, *Journal of the Polynesian Society* 66: 301-338, 398-435.

_____. 1974. *Samoan Village: Stability and Change in a Samoan Village.* New york: Holt, Rinehart and Winston.

_____. 1983 A Tale of two studies, *American Anthropologist* 85:929-935.

_____. 1983. Margaret Mead's Samoa: view and reviews, *Quarterly Review of Biology* 58:539-544.

_____. 1983. On the questioning of as many as six imposible things about Freeman's Samoan study before breakfast, *Canberra Anthropology* 6:1-16.

_____. [Reply to Derek Freeman.], *The Sciences*, January/February 1984:8.

_____. South seas squall: Derek Freeman's long-nurtured, ill-natured attack on Margaret Mead, *The Sciences* 23(4), July/August 1983:14-18.

_____. 1987 Transcript of Interview with Frank Heimans. Sydney: Cinetel Films.

_____. 1987. *Quest for the Real Samoa: The Mead/Freeman Controversy and Beyond.* South Hadley, Mass.: Bergin and Garvey.

_____. 1989. Concerning Derek Freeman's comment on Holmes' *Quest for the Real Samoa, American Anthropologist* 91: 753-758.

Howard, Jane. 1983. Angry storm over the south seas of Margaret Mead, *Smithsonian* 14(1), April:67-74.

Howard, Jane. 1984. *Margaret Mead: A Life.* New York: Simon & Schuster.

Huxley, Francis. 1983. Story-telling in Samoa, *The Guardian* (London), 10 April:21.

Inder, Stuart. 1983. So much for Mead's special race!, *The Bulletin* (Sydney), 15 March:58, 63.

Jarvie, I. C. 1983. Freeman on Mead, *Canberra Anthropology* 6:80-5.

Katz, Alfred H. 1983. Another side of paradise (letter), *Los Angeles Times* (Book Section), 1 May. See also Nader.

Katz, Alfred H. 1983. Poisoned Mead (letter), *The New Republic* 4 July:2.

Kessler, Julia Braun. 1983. The war rages over Margaret Mead, *Daily News Magazine* (New York), 1 May.

Kroeber, A. L. 1955. On human nature, *Southwestern Journal of Anthropology* 11:195-204.

Kuper, Adam. 1983. Love under the palm trees, *London Times Higher Education Supplement* , 29 April.

Kuper, Adam. 1989. Coming of age in anthropology?, *Nature* 338: 453-455.

Laurie, N. O. 1984. Formal protest, *Science 84* (New York) 15(2):20.

Leach, Edmund. 1983. The Shangri-la that never was, *New Society* (London), 24 March:477-8.

Leacock, Eleanor. 1983. The recent debate on Margaret Mead's work, *International Women's Anthropology Conference Newsletter*, August:3-4.

Lelaulu, Lelei. 1983. Exposing the Samoan love myth, *The Weekend Australian* (Magazine), 12-13 March:4.

Leo, John, Joelle Attinger, and John Dunn. 1983. Bursting the South Sea Bubble: an anthropologist attacks Margaret Mead's research in Samoa, *Time Magazine*, 14 February:50-52.

Lesser, Alexander. 1985. *History, Evolution, and the Concept of Culture: Selected Papers of Alexander Lesser.* Edited with introduction by Sidney W. Mintz. Cambridge: Cambridge University Press.

Levy. Robert I. 1984. Mead, Freeman, and Samoa: The problem of seeing things as they are, *Ethos* 12: 85-92.

Lieber, Michael D. 1983. Margaret Mead is the victim of media hype, *Chicago Sun-Times*, 4 April.

Lutali, A. P. 1987. Transcript of Interview of Frank Heimans. Sydney: Cinetel Films.

Marcus, George E. 1983. One man's Mead, *The New York Times Book Review*, 27 March:3, 22.

Marshall, Eliot. 1983. A controversy on Samoa comes of age, *Science* 219, 4 March:1042-1045.

Martin, Claire. 1983. Panel raps critic of Mead's study, *The Denver Post*, 18 October.

Matane, Paulius N. 1983. Margaret Mead and PNG, *Pacific Islands Monthly* (Sydney), August:7.

McCall, Grant. 1983. Shock! Horror! Freeman proves Mead false!!!, *Australian Anthropological Association Newsletter* 18, April:13-19.

McCall, Grant. 1984. Flapper Margaret vs. Derek the punk? (letter), *Pacific Islands Monthly* (Sydney), January:9.

McCutchen, C.W. 1984. Trouble in paradise (letter), *The Sciences*, January/February:5-6.

McDowell, Nancy. 1984. Review of *Margaret Mead and Samoa, Pacific Studies* 7:99-140.

Mead, Margaret. 1928. The Role of the individual in Samoan culture, *Journal of the Royal Anthropological Institute* 58:481-495.

_____. 1928. *Coming of Age in Samoa: A Psychological Study of Primitive Youth for Western Civilization.* New York: Morrow.

_____. 1930. Adolescence in primitive and modern society, in *The New Generation* , edited by V. F. Calverton and S. D. Schmalhausen, pp. 169-188. London: Allen & Unwin.

_____. 1930. *The Social Organization of Manu'a.* Honolulu: Bishop Museum.

_____. 1931. Jealousy primitive and civilized, in *Woman's Coming of Age,* edited by V. F. Calverton and S. D. Schmalhausen. New York: Liveright.

_____. 1937. The Samoans, in *Cooperation and Competition among Primitive Peoples*, edited by Margaret Mead. New York: McGraw-Hill.

_____. 1959. Cultural contexts of puberty and adolescence, *Bulletin of the Philadelphia Association for Psychoanalysis* 9:59-79.

_____. 1961. Review of Lowell D. Holmes *Ta'ū:Stability and Change in a Samoan Village, American Anthropologist* 63:428-429.

_____. 1965. *Anthropologists and What They Do.* New York: Watts.

_____. 1969. *The Social Organization of Manu'a.* 2nd edition. Honolulu: Bishop Museum.

_____. 1972. *Blackberry Winter: My Earlier Years.* New York: Morrow.

_____. 1974. Margaret Mead, in *A History of Psychology in Autobiography,* vol. VI, ed. Gardner Lindzey. New York: Prentice-Hall.

_____. 1974. What I think I have learned about education 1923-1973, *Education* 94 (April-May):289-406.

_____. 1977 *Letters from the Field, 1925-1975.* New York: Harper & Row.

Milliken, Robert. 1983. Was Samoan sex idyll a myth?, *The Sunday Times* (London), 6 February:15.

Minton, Robert. 1983. Challenging Margaret Mead: When a scholar assaults a classic work, *Boston Globe Magazine* (July 17), 8-9, 14, 16, 2-22, 26.

Montagu, Ashley. 1983. Trouble in paradise (letter), *The Sciences* (New York), January/February:6.

Murray, Stephen O. 1988. The Reception of anthropological work in sociology jouranls, 1922-1951, *Journal of the History of the Behavioral Sciences* 24:135-151.

Nader, Laura. 1983. Reply to Katz, *Los Angeles Times* , 1 May 1983.

Nader, Laura. 1983. Review of *Margaret Mead and Samoa, Los Angeles Times* (Book Review), 10 April:2.

Owen, Elizabeth. 1983. Samoa—an uproar over sex and violence in Margaret Mead's idyllic isles, *Life Magazine* 6(7), May 1:32-40.

Perlman, David. 1983. The debunking of a myth of anthropology, *San Francisco Chronicle*, 3 April.

Peters, Falani A. 1983. Recollections of a Samoan student (letter), *Pacific Islands Monthly* (Sydney), January:9.

Rappaport, Roy A. 1987. Reply to Freeman, *Scientific American* 256(2):6-7.

Rensberger, Boyce. 1983. The nature-nurture debate: two portraits. (1) Margaret Mead; (2) On becoming human. *Science 83* (New York), April:28-37.

Reyman, Jonathan E. and Joyce D. Hammond. 1985. Some comments on the Freeman-Mead controversy, *American Anthropologist* 87:393.

Romanucci-Ross, Lola. 1976. With Margaret Mead in the Field: Observations on the Logics of Discovery, *Ethos* 4:439-454.

Romanucci-Ross, Lola. 1980. Anthropological field research: Margaret Mead, muse of the clinical experience, *American Anthropologist* 82:304-318.

Romanucci-Ross, Lola. 1985. *Mead's Other Manus: Phenomenology of an Encounter.* Boston: Bergin & Garvey.

Saler, Benson. 1984. Ethnographies and refutations, *Eastern Anthropologist* 37:215-225.

Schneider, David M. 1983. The Coming of a sage to Samoa, *Natural History* 92 (no. 6):4, 6, 10.

Schneider, David M. 1983. Reply to Derek Freeman, *Natural History* 92(12), December:4.

Schoeffel, Penelope, and Malama Meleissea. 1983. Margaret Mead, Derek Freeman and Samoa: the making, unmaking and remaking of an anthropological myth, *Canberra Anthropology* 6(1):58-69.

Schoeffel, Penelope. 1983. Review of *Margaret Mead and Samoa, Mankind* (Sydney) 13(6), April:535-6.

Schwartz, Theodore. 1983. Anthropology: a quaint science, *American Anthropologist* 85:919-28.

Shankman, Paul. 1983. The Samoan conundrum, *Canberra Anthropology* 6(1):38-57.

Shore, Bradd. 1983. Paradox regained: Freeman's *Margaret Mead and Samoa, Canberra Anthropology* 6: 17-37.

Silverman, Martin G. 1983. Our great deception, or, anthropology defiled!, *American Anthropologist* 85:944-7.

Spate, O. H. K. 1983. Exposure may rank with Piltdown Man, *Australian National University Reporter* 14(1), 25 February:2.

Sterba, James P. 1983. Tropical storm: new book debunking Margaret Mead dispels tranquillity in Samoa, *The Wall Street Journal* 14 April.

Stocking, George W. 1968. *Race, Culture, and Evolution.* New York: Macmillan.

Stocking, George W., ed. 1974. *A Franz Boas Reader: The Shaping of American Anthropology 1883-1911.* Chicago: University of Chicago Press, 1974.

Strathern, Marilyn. 1983. The Punishment of Margaret Mead, *Canberra Anthropology* 6:70-79.

Theroux, Joseph. 1987. Review of *Quest for the Real Samoa, Pacific Islands Monthly* 58 no. 6 (June):49.

Trinca, Helen, and Kathleen Alexander. Rebuttal of Mead's *Coming of Age* fuels cultural bias debate. *The Australian*, 16 March 1983:19.

Turnbull, Colin. 1983. Reply to Katz, *The New Republic* 4 July:2.

Turnbull, Colin. 1984. Trouble in paradise, *The New Republic*, 28 March:32-4. Reprinted in *Quadrant* June 1983:9-11. See also Freeman, Katz.

Vogt, Evon Z., Jr. 1983. The Samoans revisited: did Mead report myth?, *Boston Sunday Globe*, 10 April.

Wendt, Albert. 1983. Review of *Margaret Mead and Samoa, Auckland Star* (New Zealand), 26 March.

Wendt, Albert. 1983. Three faces of Samoa: Mead's, Freeman's and Wendt's, *Pacific Islands Monthly* (Sydney), April:10-14, 69.

Wendt, Felix. 1984. Review of *Margaret Mead and Samoa, Pacific Studies* 7:92-99.

Wilford, John Noble. 1983. Customs check: leave your ideological baggage behind, *The New York Times*, 6 February:8E.

Wilford, John Noble. 1983. Earlier criticisms surface in reactions to book on Dr Mead, *The New York Times*, 1 February.

Section 2
Recent Research on Samoa

Baker, Paul T. and Joel M. Hanna, Perspectivs on health and behavior in Samoans, in *The Changing Samoans: Behavior and Health in Transition*, ed. Paul T. Baker, Joel M. Hanna, and Thelma S. Baker, pp. 419-34. New York: Oxford University Press.

Baker, Paul T., Joel M. Hanna, and Thelma S. Baker, eds. *The Changing Samoans: Behavior and Health in Transition*. New York: Oxford University Press.

Bindon, J. R. 1981. *Genetic and Environmental Influences on the Morphology of Samoan Adults*. Ph.D. diss., The Pennsylvania State University: University Park, Pa.

Bowles, J. R. 1985. Suicide and attempted suicide in contemporary Western Samoa, in *Culture, Youth and Suicide in the Pacific: Papers from and East-West Center Comference*, ed. F. X. Hezel, D. H. Rubenstein, and G.M. White. Honolulu: East-West Center.

Chen, P. 1973. Samoans in California, *Social Work* 18:41-48

Clements, D. 1982. Samoan folk knowledge of mental disorders, in *Cultural Conceptions of Medical Health and Therapy*, ed. A. Marsella and G. White. Boston: Reidel.

Crews, D. E. 1985. *Mortality, Survivorship and Longevity in American Samoa 1950 to 1981*. Ph.D. diss. The Pennsylvania State University: University Park, Pa.

Fox, J. W. and K. B. Cumberland. 1962. *Western Samoa: Land, Life, and Agriculture in Tropical Polynesia*. Christchurch, New Zealand: Whitcombe & Tombs, Ltd.

Franco, R. 1985. *Samoan Perception of Work: Moving Up and Moving Around*. Ph.D. diss., University of Hawaii, Honolulu.

Freeman, Derek. 1964. Some observations on kinship and political authority in Samoa, *American Anthropologist* 66:553-565.

Gerber, E. R. 1975. *The Cultural Patterning of Emotions in Samoa*. Ph.D. diss., University. of California, San Diego.

Gerber, E. R. 1985. Rage and obligation: Samoans in conflict, in *Person, Self and Experience: Exploring Pacific Ethnopsychologies*, ed.G. White and J. Kirkpatrick. Berkeley: University. of California Press.

Gilson, R. P. 1970. *Samoa 1830-1900: The Politics of A Multi-Cultural Community*. With Introduction and Conclusion by J.W. Davidson. Melbourne: Oxford University Press.

Grattan, F. J. H. 1948. *An Introduction to Samoan Custom*. Apia, Western Samoa: Samoa Printing and Publishing Co.

Greksa, L. P. 1980. *Work Requirements and Work Capabilities in a Modernizing Samoan Population*. Ph.D. diss., The Pennsylvania State University: University Park, Pa.

Hanna, J. M. and P. T. Baker. 1979. Biocultural correlates to blood pressure of Samoan migrants to Hawaii, *Human Biology,* 51:481-497.

Holmes, Lowell D. 1961. The Samoan kava ceremony, *Science of Man,* June 46-57.

_____. 1972. The role and status of the old in a changing Samoa, in *Aging and Modernization*, ed. D. O. Cowgill and L. D. Holmes. New York: Appleton-Century-Crofts.

_____. 1978. Aging and modernization: The Samoan aged of San Francisco, in *New Neighbors: Islanders in Adaptation*, ed. C. Macpherson, B. Shore, and R. Franco. Santa Cruz: Center for South Pacific Studies, University. of California, Santa Cruz.

_____. 1980. Facts contributing to the cultural stability of Samoa, *Anthropological Quarterly* 53:188-197.

_____. 1984. *Samoan Islands Bibliography*. Witchita: Poly Concepts Publishing Co.

Holmes, Lowell D. and E. Rhoads. 1983. Aging and Change in Samoa, in *Growing Old in Different Societies*, ed. J. Sokolovsky, Belmont, Calif.: Wadsworth Press.

Holmes, Lowell D., G. Tallman, and V. Jantz. 1978. Samoan personality, *Journal of Psychological Anthropology* 1:453-72.

Howard, Alan. 1986. Questions and answers: Samoans talk about happiness, distress and other life experiences, in *The Changing Samoans: Behavior and Health in Transition*, ed. Paul T. Baker, Joel M. Hanna, and Thelma S. Baker, pp. 174-202. New York: Oxford University Press.

Howard, Alan. 1986. Samoan coping behavior, in *The Changing Samoans: Behavior and Health in Transition*, ed. Paul T. Baker, Joel M. Hanna, and Thelma S. Baker, pp. 394-418. New York: Oxford University Press.

James, G. D. 1984. *Stress Response, Blood Pressure and Lifestyle Differences among Western Samoan Men*. Ph.D. diss., The Pennsylvania State University: University Park, Pa.

James, G. N.d. A preliminary report on the relationship between body build, body composition and blood pressure and indices of the psychosocial environment in a traditional Western Samoan communtiy. Department of Anthropology, The Pennsylvania State University: University Park, Pa.

Janes, C. R. 1984. *Migration and Hypertension: An Ethnography of Disease Risk in an Urban Samoan Community.* Ph.D. diss., University of California, San Francisco and Berkeley.

Janes, C. R. and I. G. Pawson. 1985. Migration and Biocultural fitness: Samoans, *California. Soc. Sci. Med.*

Keene, D. T. P. 1978. *Houses Without Walls: Samoan Social Control.* Ph.D. diss., University of Hawaii, Honolulu.

Keesing, F. M. 1934. *Modern Samoa: Its Government and Changing Life.* Stanford: Stanford University Press.

Keesing, F. M. 1934. Samoa: Islands of conflict, *Foreign Policy Reports* 9:293-304.

Macpherson, C. and L. Macpherson. 1985. Suicide in Western Samoa: A sociological perspective, in *Culture, Youth and Suicide in the Pacific: Papers from an East-West Center Conference,* ed. F. X. Hezel, D. H. Rubenstein, and G. M. White. Honolulu:East-West Center.

Macpherson, C., B. Shore, and R. Franco. 1978. *New Neighbors: Islanders in Adaption.* Santa Cruz: Center for South Pacific Studies, University of California, Santa Cruz.

Mageo, Jeannette Marie. 1989. Aga, Amio and Loto: Perspectives on the structure of the self in Samoa, *Oceania* 59:181-199.

Markoff, R. A. and J. R. Bond. 1980. The Samoans, in *People and Cultures of Hawaii: A Psychocultural Profile,* ed. J. F. McDermott, Jr., T. Wen-Shing, and T. W. Maretzki. Honolulu: John A. Burns School of Medicine and the University Press of Hawaii.

Maxwell, J. R. 1969. *Samoan Temperament.* Ph.D. diss., Cornell University, Ithaca, N. Y.

O'Meara, J. Timothy. In press. *Samoan Farmers.* New York: Wiley.

Oliver, D. 1985. Reducing suicide in Western Samoa, in *Culture, Youth and Suicide in the Pacific: Papers from an East-West Center Conference,* ed. F. X. Hezel, D. H. Rubenstein, and G.M. White. Honolulu: East-West Center.

Orans, M. 1981. Hierarchy and happiness in a Western Samoan community, in *Social Inequality: Comparitive and Developmental Approaches,* ed. G. Berreman. New York: Academic Press.

Parson, C. J. 1982. *Samoan Migrants and Nonmigrants: A Morphological and Genetic Comparison.* Ph.D. diss., The Pennsylvania State University: University Park, Pa.

Pawson, Ivan G. 1986. The Morphological characteristics of Samoan adults, in *The Changing Samoans: Behavior and Health in Transition,* ed. Paul T. Baker, Joel M. Hanna, and Thelma S. Baker, pp. 254-74. New York: Oxford University Press.

Pelletier, D. L. 1984. *Diet, Activity and Cadiovascular Disease: Risk Factors in Western Samoan Men.* Ph.D. diss., The Pennsylvania State University: University Park, Pa.

Schoeffel, Penelope. 1977. The Origin and development of women's associations in Western Samoa, 1830-1977, *Journal of Pacific Studies* 3:1-21.

Schoeffel, Penelope. 1978. Gender, status, and power in Samoa, *Cambridge Anthropology* 1(2):69-81.

Shore, Bradd. 1977. *A Samoan Theory of Action: Social Control and Social Order in a Polynesian Paradox.* Ph. D. diss., University of Chicago.

Shore, Bradd. 1982. *Sala'ilua: A Samoan Mystery.* New York: Columbia University Press.

Watters, R. F. 1958. Culture and environment in old Samoa, in *Western Pacific: Studies of Man and the Environment in the Western Pacific*, ed. Dept. of Geography. Wellington: Victoria University of Wellington and the New Zealand Geographical Society.

Young, F. A. 1972. *Stability and Change in Samoa.* Ph. D. diss., University of Oregon, Eugene.

Young, N. F. 1974. *Searching for the Promised Land: Samoans and Filipinos in Hawaii.* Honolulu: University of Hawaii Press.

Index

American Anthropological Association, 57, 63, 205, 212, 228, 229, 267, 271, 274, 275, 276, 276n1
American Anthropologist, 220, 269, 276, 278
Animals, 94ff., 104, 297; human animal, 99
Anthropology, 2, 3, 7, 46, 53, 59f., 64, 99, 206, 219, 225, 250, 320; American, 57, 169, 235, 255, 263, 273, 275, 299; as science, 29f., 31, 264ff., 312, 315; error of, 30; evolutionary, 166, 177-181, 325f.; fragmentation of, 62f., 131; harm to, 208, 219, 221f., 229, 231, 268, 286; history of, 1, 165f., 191, 193ff., 200, 235f., 256; physical, 2, 236; not science, 69f., 261; theory in, 29f. *See also* Culture; Cultural anthropology; Cultural determinism
Anti-science; *See* Science
Appell, George N., 79, 275, 208n1
Arnold, Matthew, 64f.
Bargatzsky, Thomas, 255
Basham, Richard, 218, 272
Bateson, Gregory, 18
Bateson, Mary Catherine, 21, 160, 164, 203
Beaglehole, Ernest, 102, 201
Behavior, 28, 34, 49f., 55, 82, 100, 104f., 107, 200, 213, 231, 327ff.; mechanisms of, 30
Behaviorism, 65, 77, 92f., 103f., 176
Benedict, Ruth 18, 21, 123, 129, 131, 192, 200
Bennett, John, 79
Bernard, H. Russell, 306
Biological determinism, 25, 92, 111, 209, 213, 233ff.
Biology, 2, 3, 32, 33, 35, 37ff., 47, 65, 67, 81, 92, 94, 99, 105, 107, 109, 112, 148, 167, 175,

194, 210, 225, 231, 265, 312, 314, 326
Bloch, Marc, 49
Boas, Franz, 2, 32, 33, 65, 81ff., 86, 89, 92, 103, 106, 118, 165, 199, 209, 215, 220, 235, 240, 294, 318; affirmed the autonomy of culture, 178; attitudes to science, 186f.; contribution of, 177, 181, 184f.; doctrine of, 57, 221, 235; fieldwork of, 185f., 236; on history, 180f.; on racial conflict, 187f., 220; opposition to evolutionary anthropology, 166, 177-181, 190, 194f.; school of, 183ff.; skepticism about genetics, 189, 196f.; values of, 209, 220
Bowlby, John, 82, 101
Brady, Ivan, 41f., 68, 270, 276
Caton, Hiram, 98, 158, 205, 300
Causality, 49ff., 76f.
Chamberlain, Houston Stewart, 187
Choice, 77, 102, 107, 167, 176, 182, 251, 327ff.
Civilization, 22, 36-41, 37ff., 79, 87, 94, 123, 199
Clements, Colleen D., 33
Colonialism, 9ff.
Coming of Age in Samoa , 4, 5 15, 81, 87, 95, 104n1, 115n1, 117, 137, 141, 192, 201, 211, 250, 253; conclusion of, 150, 152, 156, 191, 199; criticism of, 122f.; Freud's influence on, 91, 93; historical place of, 165, 167; influence of, 12, 201f., 213, 225, 251, 264f., 309; opinion of, 205, 218, 221, 223, 318; unrevisable, 157, 215
Comte, Auguste, 65
Configurationalism, 79ff., 122ff.; *See also* Mead, Margaret
Conservatism, 32, 210f., 251
Cooper, Gloria, 115-117
Cornell, S. D., 253

Heredity, 24, 39, 56, 195-198,
212
Herrick, C. J., 108
Herskovits, Melville, 183, 185
193, 281*n*1, 320
History, 37; no laws of, 40
Hobhouse, L. T., 8
Holmes, Lowell D., 42, 81, 133,
154, 159, 193, 201, 203, 226,
232, 255-262, 281, 320, 321,
315
Homans, George, 30
Homo sapiens, 50, 58, 105, 111;
evolution of, 51, 52
Howard, Jane, 160, 222, 241
Human nature, 46, 53, 96, 236;
and custom, 47
Hume, David, 76, 145, 132, 154
; on induction, 145
Hunt, Robert C., 211, 216
Huxley, Sir Julian, 64, 195
Huxley, T. H., 151
Individual, 18ff., 25, 30, 33, 35,
68, 124, 129; as real unit of
analysis, 26, 28; relation to
group, 37, 53f., 65, 68
Induction, problem of 145f.,
Inductivism, 153, 154
Instinct, 87f.,92-94, 96, 104,
105, 107, 111
Instinctivists, 92
Interactionism, 1f., 16, 20, 50f.,
58, 99, 106ff., 210, 264, 328
Irons, William E., 110*n*1
Jarvie, Ian, 205
Kety, Seymour, 24
Kevles, Donald J., 55
Kluckhohn, Clyde, 48, 65, 197
Knowledge, 42, 58
Kohn, Alexander, 270, 286ff.
Koshland, Daniel E., 24, 304
Krishnamarti, Jiddu, 102
Kroeber, Alfred, 28, 29, 32, 36,
56, 64f., 105f., 152, 183, 188f.,
192, 199, 326
Kuhn, Thomas, 144
Lamarck, J.-B., 106, 196
Language, 56, 58, 67, 105
Leach, Sir Edmund, 69, 101,
217, 245

Leacock, Eleanor, 85
Learning, 53, 92; theory, 104
Lefkowitz, Mary, 241
Lesser, Alexander, 36, 165f.
Levy, Robert I., 205
Locke, John, 71
Lorenz, Konrad, 96, 101, 103,
105, 313
Lowie, Robert, 81, 199
Lumsden, Charles J., 111, 238
Lutali, A. P., 11*n*3
Mageo, Jennette Marie, 84, 135,
295
Malinowski, Bronislaw, 26,
293ff., 312
Man, 47, 54; a cultural animal,
51; modern, 50; unity of, 67
Marcus, George E., 223, 264ff.
Margaret Mead and Samoa, 1,
33, 93, 103, 110, 142, 208, 211,
218
Marx, Karl, 189
Matai system, 138
Mayr, Ernst, 195, 209, 213
McDowell, Edwin, 3, 208f.
McDowell, Nancy, 125
Mead, Margaret, 2, 20, 72f., 148,
215; as mythmaker, 9f., 60, 129,
132, 215, 250ff.; attack on, 209,
219, 268; configurationalism of,
15ff. , 80, 122ff., 133; contribution of, 205, 221, 323; ethnography of, 124, 126f., 128, 130,
133; humanism of, 32; impact
of, 3; inductivism of, 154; language competence of, 158ff., 214
; mentors of, 200, 323; on male
fantasy, 115f.; on adolescence,
169-177, 192; on nature and nurture, 16f., 123, 129; on sex differences, 20ff.; on Samoan aggression, 95, 114; on Samoan
sexual behavior, 173ff.; on
Samoans, 135, 169-176, 212;
psychological studies of, 86f.;
Samoan field trip, 203f., 315ff;
Samoan ethnography, 4, 82;
Samoan research problem of, 89,
170, 191, 199; rebuffs critics,
117; rejected behaviorism, 93;